District Gazetteers of India Series 156

MADRAS DISTRICT GAZETTEERS

VIZAGAPATAM

District Gazetteers of India Series 156

MADRAS DISTRICT GAZETTEERS

VIZAGAPATAM

W. FRANCIS

23 VOLUMES (IN 25 BINDINGS)

(VOL. 23rd)

GYAN

Published by

Gyan Publishing House
5, Ansari Road
Daryaganj, New Delhi-110002
Phone: 011-47034999, 9811692060
E-mail: books@gyanbooks.com

Distribution Network
gyanbooks.com
India, USA, Canada, UK, Australia, France

ISBN: 978-93-6208-562-7 (Set) 23 Volumes (In 25 Bindings)
978-81-212-4195-3 (PB)

First Published, 1907

2nd Impression 2024

Printed at: Gyan Press, Delhi.

MADRAS DISTRICT GAZETTEERS (Vol. 23rd)
Author: W. FRANCIS

LIST OF VOLUMES

S. NO.	ISBN NO.	VOLUME	TITLE	AUTHOR	PRICE	PAGES
			ASSAM DISTRICT GAZETTEERS			
1	9788121285926	1st	Cachar	B. C. Allen	600	300
2	9788121285919	2nd	Sylhet	B. C. Allen	750	378
3	9788121285902	3rd	Goalpara	B. C. Allen	400	203
4	9788121285896	4th	Kamrup	B. C. Allen	675	344
5	9788121285889	5th	Darrang	B. C. Allen	725	364
6	9788121285872	6th	Nowgong	B. C. Allen	560	280
7	9788121285865	7th	Sibsagar	B. C. Allen	675	343
8	9788121285858	8th	Lakhimpur	B. C. Allen	690	347
9	9788121285841	9th	Naga Hills and Manipur	B. C. Allen	580	294
10	9788121285834	10th	The Khasi And Jaintia Hills, The Garo Hills And The Lushai Hills	B. C. Allen	675	363
11	9788121285827	11th	The Sadiya and Balipara Frontier Tract	B. C. Allen	375	190
			BENGAL DISTRICT GAZETTEERS			
12	9788121218672	1st	Angul	L. S. S. O'Malley	340	168
13	9788121259637	2nd	Bakarganj	J. C. JACK	970	194
14	9788121218696	3rd	Balasore	L. S. S. O'Malley	450	228
15	9788121259590	4th	Bankura	L. S. S. O'Malley	1000	199
16	9788121218375	5th	Bhagalpur	J. Byrne	390	194
17	9788121218290	6th	Birbhum	L. S. S. O'Malley	300	150
18	9788121259651	7th	Eastern Bengal and Assam - Bogra	J. N. Gupta	940	188
19	9788121218351	8th	Burdwan	J. C. K. Peterson	450	227
20	9788121259538	9th	Calcutta District Gazetteer - Statistics, 1901 - 02		340	68
21	9788121218313	10th	Champaran	L. S. S. O'Malley	410	205
22	9788121259613	11th	Eastern Bengal District Gazetters - Chittagong	L. S. S. O'Malley	1080	216
23	9788121259552	12th	Chota Nagpur Tributary		130	26
24	9788121259415	13th	The Cooch Behar Gazette: Statistics		1460	292
25	9788121218412	14th	Cuttack	L. S. S. O'Malley	490	248
26	9788121261357	15th	Eastern Bengal District Gazetteers Dacca	B. C. Allen	400	207
27	9788121218436	16th	Darbhanga	L. S. S. O'Malley	360	180
28	9789362089335	17th	Darjeeling	L. S. S. O'Malley	500	248
29	9788121259453	18th	Eastern Bengal District Gazetteers - Dinajpur	F. W. Strong	890	178
30	9788121259392	19th	Faridpur	L. S. S. O'Malley	700	140
31	9788121218474	20th	Gaya	L. S. S. O'Malley	540	270
32	9788121214032	21st	Bihar and Orissa District Gazetteer: Hazaribagh	E. Lister	715	234
33	9788121218337	22nd	Hooghly	L. S. S. O'Malley	680	340
34	9788121218191	23rd	Bengal District Gazetteer Howrah	L. S. S. O'Malley	390	199
35	9788121259293	24th	Eastern Bengal and Assam - Jalpaiguri	John F. Gruning	890	178
36	9788121259279	25th	Jessore	L. S. S. O'Malley	960	192
37	9788121259231	26th	Khulna	L. S. S. O'Malley	1100	220
38	9788121259217	27th	Malda	G. E. Lambourn	670	134
39	9788121267854	28th	Manbhum	H. Coupland	600	313
40	9788121218498	29th	Midnapore	L. S. S. O'Malley	500	252
41	9788121218597	30th	Monghyr	L. S. S. O'Malley	560	280
42	9788121259156	31st	Murshidabad	L. S. S. O'Malley	1250	250
43	9788121259576	32nd	Bengal District Gazetteers - Muzaffarpur	L. S. S. O'Malley	940	188
44	9788121259132	33rd	Mymensingh	F. A. Sachse	960	192
45	9788121259118	34th	Nadia	J. H. E. Garrett	1070	214
46	9788121259095	35th	Eastern Bengal and Assam - Noakhali	J. E. Webster	580	115
47	9788121218450	36th	Feudatory States of Orissa	L. E. B. Cobdenramsay	790	395
48	9788121259071	37th	Pabna	L. S. S. O'Malley	710	142
49	9788121218511	38th	Palamau	L. S. S. O'Malley	380	190
50	9788121218634	39th	Patna	L. S. S. O'Malley	500	250
51	9788121218535	40th	Puri	L. S. S. O'Malley	650	328
52	9788121218757	41st	Purnea	L. S. S. O'Malley	440	220
53	9788121258937	42nd	Rajshahi	L. S. S. O'Malley	1080	216
54	9788121256681	43rd	Bihar and Orissa District Gazetteers: Ranchi	M. G. Hallett	1350	278
55	9788121258913	44th	Eastern Bengal and assam - Rangpur	J. A. Vas	890	178
56	9788121218559	45th	Sambalpur	L. S. S. O'Malley	480	242
57	9788121214056	46th	Santal Parganas	L. S. S. O'Malley	940	308
58	9788121218610	47th	Saran	L. S. S. O'Malley	380	190
59	9788121218658	48th	Shahabad	L. S. S. O'Malley	380	190
60	9788121256704	49th	The Gazetteer of Sikhim	H. H. Risley	960	481
61	9788121218573	50th	Singhbhum, Saraikela And Kharsawan	L. S. S. O'Malley	560	280
62	9788121259439	51st	Eastern Bengal District Gazetteers - Tippera	J. E. Webster	730	146
63	9788121259033	52nd	24 Parganas	L. S. S. O'Malley	1420	284

S. NO.	ISBN NO.	VOLUME	TITLE	AUTHOR	PRICE	PAGES
			CENTRAL PROVINCES DISTRICT GAZETTEERS			
64	9789362081728	1st, Vol. A	Akola (Descriptive)	A. E. Nelson, C. Brown	870	436
65	9789362085481	2nd, Vol. A	Amraoti (Descriptive)	S. V. Fitzgerald, A. E. Nelson	1050	524
66	9789362089267	3rd,Vol. A	Balaghat (Descriptive)	R. V. RUSSELL	430	216
67	9789362083494	4th, Vol. A	Betul (Descriptive)	R. V. RUSSELL	610	306
68	9789362085146	5th, Vol. A	Bhandara (Descriptive)	R. V. RUSSELL	580	292
69	9789362088390	6th, Vol. A	Bilaspur (Descriptive)	R. V. RUSSELL	870	434
70	9789362086044	7th, Vol. A	Buldana (Descriptive)	A. E. Nelson	1090	543
71	9789362089014	8th, Vol. B	Chanda (Descriptive)	R. V. RUSSELL	470	234
72	9789362086938	9th	Chhattisgarch Feudatory State	E. A. De Brett	880	440
73	9789362082961	10th	Chhindwara (Descriptive)	R. V. RUSSELL	550	274
74	9789362089342	11th, Vol. A & B	Damoh (Descriptive and Statistical Tables 1891-1901)	R. V. RUSSELL	830	414
75	9789362081230	12th, Vol. A	Durg (Descriptive)	A. E. Nelson	460	232
76	9789362086037	13th, Vol. A	Hoshangabad (Descriptive)	R. V. RUSSELL	860	430
77	9789362086792	14th, Vol. A	Jubbulpore (Descriptive)	A. E. Nelson	950	474
78	9789362089663	15th, Vol. A & B	Mandla (Descriptive and Statistical Tables 1891-1901)	R. V. RUSSELL	370	186
79	9789362086419	16th, Vol. A	Nagpur (Descriptive)	R. V. RUSSELL	790	394
80	9789362080646	17th, Vol. A	Narsinghpur (Descriptive)	R. V. RUSSELL	510	257
81	9789362084835	18th, Vol. A	Nimar (Descriptive)	R. V. RUSSELL	600	299
82	9789362087737	19th, Vol. A	Raipur (Descriptive)	A. E. Nelson	790	396
83	9789362080264	20th, Vol. A	Saugor (Descriptive)	R. V. RUSSELL	570	285
84	9789362081117	21st, Vol. A	Seoni (Descriptive)	R. V. RUSSELL	460	232
85	9789362084965	22nd, Vol. A	Wardha (Descriptive)	R. V. RUSSELL	600	302
86	9789362083401	23rd, Vol. A	Yeotmal (Descriptive)	R. V. RUSSELL	550	277
87	9789362080325	24th, Vol. I, Pt. I	Gwalior (Text and Tables)	R. V. RUSSELL	980	489
88	9789362087133	24th, Vol. I, Pt. II	Gwalior (Maps)	R. V. RUSSELL	400	198
89	9789362086341	24th, Vol. I, Pt. III	Gwalior (Village List)	R. V. RUSSELL	810	406
90	9789362085467	24th, Vol. I, Pt. IV	Gwalior (Photos)	R. V. RUSSELL	1400	698
91	9789362087393	25th, Vol. II	Indore (Text and Tables)	C. E. Luard	1050	524
92	9789362084422	26th, Vol. III	Bhopal (Text and Tables)	C. E. Luard	540	272
93	9789362086815	27th, Vol. IV	Rewah (Text and Tables)	C. E. Luard	500	250
94	9789362087584	28th, Vol. V, Pt. A	Western States - Malwa (Text)	C. E. Luard	1520	762
95	9789362087300	29th, Vol. VI, Pt. A	Eastern States - Bundelkhand (Text)	C. E. Luard	930	463
96	9789362082169	30th, Vol. VI, Pt. B	Eastern States - Bundelkhand (Tables)	C. E. Luard	830	417
			GAZETTEER OF THE BOMBAY PRESIDENCY:			
97	9788121283441	1st, Part I	History of Gujarat	Ed.: James M. Campbell	3220	644
98	9788121285582	1st, Part II	History of the Konkan Dakhan and Southern Maratha Country	Ed.: James M. Campbell	4200	840
99	9788121285568	2nd	Gujarat, Surat and Broach	Ed.: James M. Campbell	2990	598
100	9788121285544	3rd	Kaira and Panch Mahals	Ed.: James M. Campbell	1690	339
101	9788121285520	4th	Ahmedabad	Ed.: James M. Campbell	1860	372
102	9788121285506	5th	Cutch, Palanpur, and Mahi Kantha	Ed.: James M. Campbell	2390	478
103	9788121285483	6th	Rewa Kantha, Narukot, Cambay, and Surat States	Ed.: James M. Campbell	1450	290
104	9788121285469	7th	Baroda	Ed.: James M. Campbell	3260	652
105	9788121285445	8th	Kathiawar	Ed.: James M. Campbell	3790	758
106	9788121285421	9th, Part I	Gujarat Population - Hindus	Ed.: James M. Campbell	3170	636
107	9788121285407	9th, Part II	Gujarat Population - Musalmans and Parsis	Ed.: James M. Campbell	1520	304
108	9788121285384	10th	Ratnagiri and Savantvadi	Ed.: James M. Campbell	2500	501
109	9788121285360	11th	Kolaba and Janjira	Ed.: James M. Campbell	2550	513
110	9788121285346	12th	Khandesh	Ed.: James M. Campbell	3190	638
111	9788121285322	13th Part I	Thana	Ed.: James M. Campbell	2050	413
112	9788121285308	13th Part II	Thana	Ed.: James M. Campbell	1770	357
113	9788121285285	14th	Thana - Places of Interest	Ed.: James M. Campbell	3290	659
114	9788121285261	15th Part I	Kanara	Ed.: James M. Campbell	2340	348
115	9788121285247	15th Part II	Kanara	Ed.: James M. Campbell	1740	348
116	9788121285223	16th	Nasik	Ed.: James M. Campbell	3490	698
117	9788121285209	17th	Ahmadnagar	Ed.: James M. Campbell	3860	772
118	9788121285186	18th Part I	Poona	Ed.: James M. Campbell	2930	586
119	9788121285162	18th Part II	Poona	Ed.: James M. Campbell	2680	537
120	9788121285148	18th Part III	Poona	Ed.: James M. Campbell	2500	503
121	9788121285124	19th	Satara	Ed.: James M. Campbell	3450	692
122	9788121285100	20th	Sholapur	Ed.: James M. Campbell	2730	547
123	9788121285087	21st	Gazetteer of the Bomaby Presidency: Belgaum	Ed.: James M. Campbell	2570	514
124	9788121285063	22nd	Dharwar	Ed.: James M. Campbell	4200	841
125	9788121285049	23rd	Gazetteer of the Bombay Presidency:Bijapur	Ed.: James M. Campbell	3550	712
126	9788121285025	24th	Kolhapur	Ed.: James M. Campbell	2250	450

S. NO.	ISBN NO.	VOLUME	TITLE	AUTHOR	PRICE	PAGES
127	9788121285001	25th	Botany	Ed.: James M. Campbell	2040	408
128	9788121284981	26th, Part I	Materials Towards a Statistical Account of the Town and Island of Bombay - History	Ed.: James M. Campbell	2500	504
129	9788121284967	26th, Part II	Materials Towards a Statistical Account of the Town and Island of Bombay - Trade and Fortifications	Ed.: James M. Campbell	2690	538
130	9788121284943	26th, Part III	Materials Towards a Statistical Account of the Town And Island of Bombay - Administration	Ed.: James M. Campbell	2450	702
131	9788121284929	27th	General Index	Ed.:R. E. Enthoven	2190	428
			MADRAS DISTRICT GAZETTEERS			
132	9788121258814	1st	Anantapur	W. Francis	1140	227
133	9788121258555	2nd	Malabar	C. A Innes & F. B Evans	3010	602
134	9788121258791	3rd	Bellary	W. Francis	1890	377
135	9788121258777	4th	Statistical Appendix For Chingleput		280	56
136	9788121258753	5th	Coimbatore	K. N. Krishnaswami Ayyar	3420	628
137	9788121232814	6th	Madras District Gazetteers District Gazetteer Cuddapah	C. F. Brackenbury	1120	285
138	9788121258715	7th	Statistical Appendix For Ganjam		370	73
139	9788121256766	8th, Vol. 1st	Godavari District Gazetteer	F. R. Hemingway	650	320
140	9788121256803	8th, Vol. 2nd	Godavari District Gazetteer	F. R. Hemingway	160	83
141	9788121258678	9th	Statistical Appendix For Kistna		640	127
142	9788121258654	10th	Statistical Appendix For Kurnool		270	54
143	9788121258616	11th	Madura	W. Francis	1900	379
144	9788121258579	12th	Statistical Appendix For Madura		740	148
145	9788121258630	13th	The Nilgiris	W. Francis	2190	437
146	9788121234276	14th	Madras District Gazetteers Gazetteer Of The Nellore District Brought Upto 1938		1150	386
147	9788121258517	15th	North Arcot		590	118
148	9788121258494	16th, Vol. 1, Part I	Salem	F. J. Richards	1710	343
149	9788121258593	16th, Vol. 1, Part II	Salem	F. J. Richards	1800	360
150	9788121258456	17th	South Arcot	W. Francis	2400	480
151	9788121258470	18th	Statistical Appendix For South Canara		400	80
152	9788121258432	19th, Vol. 1st & 2nd	Tanjore: Main Volume and Statistical Appendix		2070	401
153	9788121258395	20th	Tinnevelly	H. R. Pate	2740	547
154	9788121258418	21st	Statistical Appendix For Tinnevelly		320	64
155	9788121258371	22nd, 1st & 2nd	Trichinopoly: Main Volume and Statistical Appendix	F. R. Hemingway	2440	487
156	9788121241953	23rd	Vizagapatam District Gazetteer	W. Francis	760	385
			PUNJAB DISTRICT GAZETTEERS			
157	9788121255943	1st	Ambala District 1883-84		620	124
158	9788121255967	2nd	Amritsar		1180	236
159	9788121255981	3rd	Delhi		1300	260
160	9788121256001	4th	Ferozepore		950	188
161	9788121256025	5th	Faridkot		350	70
162	9788121256049	6th	Gujranwala 1893-94		1270	254
163	9788121256063	7th	Gujrat	C. E. Luard	1140	228
164	9788121256087	8th	Gurdaspur 1891-92		1260	252
165	9788121256100	9th	Gurgaon 1883-4		1020	203
166	9788121256124	10th	Hazara	H. D. Watson	2290	458
167	9788121256148	11th	Hissar district and Lohar State		1840	367
168	9788121256162	12th	Hoshiarpur		1420	283
169	9788121256186	13th	Jhang		1070	213
170	9788121256209	14th	Jhelam		1010	202
171	9788121256223	15th	Jalandhar District 1883-84		540	108
172	9788121256247	16th, Vol. XIV-A	Jullundur District, with maps and Kapurthala		1990	398
173	9788121256261	17th, Pt. I	Kangra (Proper)		1450	290
174	9788121256285	17th, Pt. II	Kangra (Kulu, Lahual, Spiti)		1800	357
175	9788121256308	18th	Karnal		1930	386
176	9788121256322	19th	Kohat		1540	307
177	9788121256346	20th	The Lahore District 1883-84		1220	244
178	9788121256384	21st	Ludhiana and Maler Kotla		1680	335
179	9788121256407	22nd	Lyallpur		735	147
180	9788121256421	23rd	Mianwali		1170	234
181	9788121256445	24th	Montgomery	P. J. Fagan	1590	318
182	9788121258364	25th	Multan (1901-02)	E. D. Maclagan	2400	480
183	9788121258708	26th	The Rohtak District 1883-84		980	196
184	9788121258746	27th, Vol. III A	Dujana State 1904		500	16
185	9788121256483	28th	Shahpur District		1780	356
186	9788121256506	29th	Simla District		800	159

S. NO.	ISBN NO.	VOLUME	TITLE	AUTHOR	PRICE	PAGES
187	9788121256520	30th	The Chamba State		2040	408
188	9788121256544	31st	The Chenab Colony 1904		1550	310
189	9788121256568	32nd	Kalsia State		270	53
190	9788121256582	33rd	Suket and Mandi		770	154
191	9788121256605	34th	Phulkian States, Patiala Jind And Nabha 1904		2070	414
192	9788121256643	35th	Simla Hill States		2220	443
193	9788121256667	36th	Sirmur		920	183
			RAJPUTANA DISTRICT GAZETTEERS			
194	9789362088994	1st, Vol. I-A & B	Ajmer-merwara (Text and Statistics Tables)	C. C. Watson	1230	246
195	9789362080882	2nd. Vol. II-A & B	Mewar Residency (Text and Statistics Tables)	K.D. Erskine	1700	339
196	9789362088444	3rd, Vol. III-A & B	The Western Rajputana States Residency And The Bikaner Agency	K.D. Erskine	3590	718
			UNITED PROVINCES OF AGRA AND OUDH DISTRICT GAZETTEERS			
197	9789362087560	Vol. I	Agra	H. R. Nevill	2260	452
198	9789362082466	Vol. II	Aligarh	H. R. Nevill	1300	260
199	9789362089779	Vol. III	Allahabad	H. R. Nevill	2050	409
200	9789362081346	Vol. IV	Almora	H. G. Walton	1670	333
201	9789362085658	Vol. V	Azamgarh	D. L. Drake Brockman	1750	349
202	9789362080547	Vol. VI	Bahraich	H. R. Nevill	1410	281
203	9789362085214	Vol. VII	Ballia	H. R. Nevill	1750	350
204	9789362084668	Vol. VIII	Banda	D. L. Drake Brockman	1750	349
205	9789362086518	Vol. IX	Bara Banki	H. R. Nevill	1720	344
206	9789362084101	Vol. X	Bareilly	H. R. Nevill	1640	327
207	9789362086631	Vol. XI	Basti	H. R. Nevill	1610	321
208	9789362083814	Vol. XII	Benares	H. R. Nevill	2290	458
209	9789362086105	Vol. XIII	Bijnor	H. R. Nevill	1820	363
210	9789362081674	Vol. XIV	Budaun	H. R. Nevill	1890	378
211	9789362086891	Vol. XV	Bulandshahr	H. R. Nevill	2100	419
212	9789362081520	Vol. XVI	Cawnpore	H. R. Nevill	2210	442
213	9789362088031	Vol. XVII	Dehra Dun	H. G. Walton	1710	342
214	9789362088710	Vol. XVIII	Etah	E. R. Neave	1600	320
215	9789362082992	Vol. XIX	Etawah	D. L. Drake Brockman	1390	277
216	9789362082220	Vol. XX	Farrukhabad	E. R. Neave	1620	324
217	9789362083869	Vol. XXI	Fatehpur	H. R. Nevill	1890	377
218	9789362085962	Vol. XXII	Fyzabad	H. R. Nevill	1700	339
219	9789362087997	Vol. XXIII	Garhwal	H. G. Walton	1270	254
220	9789362089892	Vol. XXIV	Ghazipur	H. R. Nevill	1600	320
221	9789362085436	Vol. XXV	Gonda	H. R. Nevill	1650	330
222	9789362080271	Vol. XXVI	Gorakhpur	H. R. Nevill	1890	378
223	9789362086129	Vol. XXVII	Hamirpur	D. L. Drake Brockman	1390	277
224	9789362087638	Vol. XXVIII	Hardoi	H. R. Nevill	1680	336
225	9789362081636	Vol. XXIX	Jalaun	D. L. Drake Brockman	1180	236
226	9789362084309	Vol. XXX	Jaunpur	H. R. Nevill	1750	350
227	9789362084187	Vol. XXXI	Jhansi	D. L. Drake Brockman	1960	391
228	9789362089168	Vol. XXXII	Kheri	H. R. Nevill	1650	330
229	9789362086778	Vol. XXXIII	Lucknow	H. R. Nevill	1760	352
230	9789362088635	Vol. XXXIV	Mainpuri	H. R. Nevill	1740	348
231	9789362080424	Vol. XXXV	Meerut	H. R. Nevill	2170	434
232	9789362081087	Vol. XXXVI	Mirzapur	D. L. Drake Brockman	2430	486
233	9789362085443	Vol. XXXVII	Moradabad	H. R. Nevill	1900	380
234	9789362082763	Vol. XXXVIII	Muttra	D. L. Drake Brockman	2140	428
235	9789362089915	Vol. XXXIX	Muzaffarnagar	H. R. Nevill	2260	451
236	9789362086143	Vol. XL	Naini Tal	H. R. Nevill	1890	377
237	9789362086761	Vol. XLI	Partabgarh	H. R. Nevill	1560	312
238	9789362081124	Vol. XLII	Pilibhit	H. R. Nevill	1570	314
239	9789362084453	Vol. XLIII	Rai Bareli	H. R. Nevill	1610	322
240	9789362088284	Vol. XLIV	Rampur	H. R. Nevill	1170	234
241	9789362083654	Vol. XLV	Saharanpur	H. R. Nevill	2190	438
242	9789362083142	Vol. XLVI	Shahjahanpur	H. R. Nevill	1510	302
243	9789362083623	Vol. XLVII	Sitapur	H. R. Nevill	1590	317
244	9789362089939	Vol. XLVIII	Sultanpur	H. R. Nevill	1330	266
245	9789362080851	Vol. XLIX	Unnao	H. R. Nevill	1530	305

AGENTS FOR THE SALE OF MADRAS GOVERNMENT PUBLICATIONS.

IN THE EAST.

R. CAMBRAY & Co., Calcutta.
A. J. COMBRIDGE & Co., Bombay.
COMBRIDGE & Co., Madras.
M. GULAB SINGH & SONS, Mufid-I-Am Press, Lahore.
HIGGINBOTHAM & Co., Mount Road, Madras.
V. KALYANARAMA IYER & Co., Esplanade, Madras.
S. MURTHY & Co., Kapalee Press, Madras.
G. A. NATESAN & Co., Madras.
NEWMAN & Co., Calcutta.
P. R. RAMA IYAR & Co., 192, Esplanade, Madras.
* T. K. SITARAMA AIYAR, Kumbakónam.
SUPERINTENDENT, NAZAIR KANUN HIND PRESS, Allahabad.
D. B. TARAPOREVALA SONS & Co., Bombay.
TEMPLE & Co., Mylapore, Madras.
THACKER & Co. (Limited), Bombay.
THACKER, SPINK & Co., Calcutta.
THOMPSON & Co., Madras.

IN ENGLAND.

E. A. ARNOLD, 41 and 43, Maddox Street, Bond Street, W., London.
B. H. BLACKWELL, 50 and 51, Broad Street, Oxford.
CONSTABLE & Co., 16, James Street, Haymarket, W., London.
DEIGHTON, BELL & Co., Cambridge.
GRINDLAY & Co., 54, Parliament Street, S.W., London.
HENRY S. KING & Co., 65, Cornhill, E.C., London.
P. S. KING & SON, 2 and 4, Great Smith Street, Westminster, S.W., London.
KEGAN PAUL, TRENCH, TRÜBNER & Co., 43, Gerrard Street, Soho, W., London.
B. QUARITCH, 15, Piccadilly, W., London.

ON THE CONTINENT.

FRIEDLÄNDER & SOHN, 11, Carlstrasse, Berlin.
OTTO HARRASSOWITZ, Leipzig.
RUDOLF HAUPT, Halle-a-S, Germany.
KARL W. HIERSEMANN, Leipzig.
ERNEST LEROUX, 28, Rue Bonaparte, Paris.
MARTINUS NIJHOFF, The Hague, Holland.

* Agent for sale of the Legislative Department publications.

MADRAS DISTRICT GAZETTEERS.

VIZAGAPATAM.

VOLUME I.

MADRAS DISTRICT GAZETTEERS.

VIZAGAPATAM.

BY

W. FRANCIS,

INDIAN CIVIL SERVICE.

MADRAS:

PRINTED BY THE SUPERINTENDENT, GOVERNMENT PRESS.

1907.

PREFACE.

THIS book follows the plan prescribed by Government, and statistics have for the most part been given in a separate Appendix which is to be revised decennially, after each Census.

The original 'District Manual,' written by Mr. D. F. Carmichael, I.C.S., when Collector and Agent, was published so long ago as 1869. One of its chief features was the section devoted to the early history of the numerous zamindaris, and this has been freely utilized in Chapter XV of the present volume. Much interesting matter regarding the 'Agency tracts' of the district has also been extracted from the annual administration reports of the Agents to the Governor, the earlier of which give vivid accounts of the difficulties of the pioneers of law and order in that wild country.

Thanks to the many gentlemen, official and non-official, who have helped with this book have been tendered where possible in the body of the volume, but special obligations have been incurred to Mr. R. H. Campbell, the present Collector and Agent, who has been kind enough to read the whole of the proofs and make a large number of important corrections and improvements in them.

W. F.

PLAN OF CONTENTS.

TABLE OF CONTENTS.

CHAPTER I.

PHYSICAL DESCRIPTION.

CHAPTER II.

POLITICAL HISTORY.

CHAPTER III.

THE PEOPLE.

PAGE

CHAPTER IV.

AGRICULTURE AND IRRIGATION.

CHAPTER V.

FORESTS.

CHAPTER VI.

OCCUPATIONS AND TRADE.

CHAPTER VII.

MEANS OF COMMUNICATION.

CHAPTER VIII.

RAINFALL AND SEASONS.

CHAPTER IX.

PUBLIC HEALTH.

CHAPTER X.

EDUCATION.

CHAPTER XI.

LAND REVENUE ADMINISTRATION.

CHAPTER XII.

SALT, ABKÁRI AND MISCELLANEOUS REVENUE.

CHAPTER XIII.

ADMINISTRATION OF JUSTICE.

CHAPTER XIV.

LOCAL SELF-GOVERNMENT.

CHAPTER XV.

GAZETTEER.

PAGE

GAZETTEER

OF THE

VIZAGAPATAM DISTRICT.

CHAPTER I.

PHYSICAL DESCRIPTION.

General Description—Position and boundaries—Taluks and chief towns—Etymology of name—Natural divisions. Hills—In the Párvatípur division—The 3,000 feet plateau—Gálikonda as a sanitarium—The 2,000 feet plateau—The Malkanagiri taluk. Rivers—The Varáha—The Sárada—The Chittivalasa river—The Góstani—The Lángulya—The Vamsadhára—The Tél—The Indrávati—The Koláb and Saveri—The Siléru. Soils. Climate—Rainfall—Temperature. Geology. Minerals—Manganese—Iron—Graphite—Limestone—Steatite—Sapphirine—A meteorite. Flora. Fauna—Domestic animals; cattle—Sheep—Goats—Game.

CHAP. I. General Description. Position and boundaries.

Vizagapatam lies on the east coast of the Presidency and, except Ganjám, is the northernmost of all the Madras districts. Its head-quarters, after which it is named, is 487 miles by rail from Madras. It is the largest district in India and the most populous in the Province, having an area of no less than 17,222 square miles and containing, in 1901, 2,933,650 inhabitants. On the east (see the map in the pocket at the end of this volume) it is bounded by the Bay of Bengal and Ganjám; on the north by the Native State of Kálahandi in Bengal, which runs down into it like a wedge, and by the Raipur zamindari of the Central Provinces; on the west by the Native State of Bastar belonging to the same Provinces; and south by the Gódávari district of this Presidency. Here and there the boundaries follow for some distance the courses of various rivers, but usually, excepting the line of the coast, they are not defined by any well-marked natural features.

Taluks and chief towns.

As the map shows, Vizagapatam consists of an open strip of land facing the shore, and of two large areas of hilly country rising north and west of this. These hills are for the most part

CHAP. I. GENERAL DESCRIPTION.

covered with jungle and inhabited by backward people to whom it is considered inexpedient to apply the whole of the ordinary law of the land. They are accordingly administered, under a special enactment passed in 1839 (see p. 196), by the Collector in his special capacity of 'Agent to the Governor' for these tracts, and are known as 'the Agency.' The ordinary courts of justice have no jurisdiction within them (the Agent being the chief civil and criminal tribunal) and the Agent is moreover endowed with unusual powers there, such as authority to deport on warrant, without formal trial, persons whose presence is harmful to the cause of law and order.

The district is arranged for administrative purposes into the five divisions and twenty-three taluks shown in the margin. Those of the latter which are marked with one asterisk are partly in the Agency above referred to, while those with two asterisks are included wholly within that area. Only three of the taluks (Golgonda, Pálkonda and Sarvasiddhi) are ryotwari land, the others (which make up nine-tenths of the whole district) being zamindari. The head-quarters of the various taluks are at the places after which each is named except in the cases of Golgonda, Sarvasiddhi and Víravilli, the chief stations in which are Narasapatam, Yellamanchili and Chódavaram respectively. The chief towns in the district are the municipalities of Vizagapatam (with its European suburb of Waltair), Vizianagram, Anakápalle and Bimlipatam, and the unions of Bobbili, Párvatípur, Sálúr, Pálkonda and Narasapatam. Excepting these, there is no town of as many as 10,000 inhabitants. Some account of them, and also of other places of interest in the district, will be found in Chapter XV below.

Vizagapatam division.
- Vizagapatam.
- * Srungavarapukóta.

Vizianagram division.
- Vizianagram.
- Bimlipatam.
- Chípurupalle.
- Gajapatinagaram.
- * Pálkonda.

Narasapatam division.
- * Golgonda.
- Anakápalle.
- Sarvasiddhi.
- * Víravilli.

Párvatípur division.
- * Párvatípur.
- * * Bissamkatak.
- Bobbili.
- * * Gunupur.
- * * Ráyagada.
- * Sálúr.

Koraput division.
- * * Koraput.
- * * Jeypore.
- * * Pádwa.
- * * Pottangi.
- * * Malkanagiri.
- * * Naurangpur.

Etymology of name.

The name Vizagapatam is properly Vaisákhapattanam, 'the town of Vaisákha' or Kártikeya, the Hindu Mars. Tradition has it that some centuries ago a king of the Ándhra dynasty encamped on the site of the present town on his way to Benares, and, being pleased with the place, built a shrine to Vaisákha, his favourite deity, just south of Lawson's Bay there. Encroachments of the sea are supposed to have long since swept away this building, but it is said to have given its name to the town and its traditional site is still supposed to be an auspicious spot for religious bathings. The name is popularly shortened to 'Vizag,' and the form 'Vizac' was in use from almost the earliest days of the English occupation of the district in the latter half of the eighteenth century. Similar abbreviations for Gajapatinagaram and Srungavarapukóta are badly needed.

Vizagapatam and the four other northernmost districts of the Presidency are known as 'the Northern Circars.' This name dates from the time of the Musalman occupation (see p. 30), when the five 'Sarkárs' (divisions of territory) in the north (the chief town of which was Masulipatam) were Guntúr, Kondapalli, Ellore, Rajahmundry and Chicacole. The Chicacole Circar included the present Ganjám and Vizagapatam districts.

Natural divisions.

Vizagapatam consists, broadly speaking, of the two great natural divisions already mentioned; namely, the strip of land along the coast and the hills which flank it on the north and west. The hills, however, as will be seen immediately, comprise several widely differing areas.

The strip of land along the coast drains eastward to the Bay of Bengal by the series of rivers referred to below. In the north of it, the Pálkonda taluk consists for the most part of rather monotonous wet land. Further south, Chípurupalle and Bobbili are also somewhat treeless and unlovely. But the rest of it (though barren, scrub-covered intervals occur) is chiefly made up of an undulating expanse of fertile soil (mostly red, but changing to black in the basins of the rivers and other alluvial spots) which is picturesquely diversified by numerous groves and hundreds of low, bare, red and black hills.

In Sarvasiddhi and Anakápalle these hills are wonderfully alike in appearance, being whale-backed in outline and seamed with black rocks showing through the sparse scrub like ribs. They are generally scattered at hap-hazard, but sometimes they are arranged in long lines, and then they have an almost comic resemblance to a solemn procession of some vast monsters silently following one another in Indian file.

The inland parts of this strip of land differ in aspect from those next the shore. Inland, the basins of the streams are occupied by almost continuous stretches of rice-fields, and much

CHAP. I.
GENERAL DESCRIPTION.

of the same grain is grown under the numerous tanks fed by torrents from the hills; so that in the cultivation season the country has an air of exceeding prosperity. The higher, red land there is occupied by dry fields, each usually separated from its neighbour by rows of palmyra palms; and these same palms stand in groups in every hollow and, though on the west their supremacy is challenged by the date, they are the prevailing tree in this part of the district.

Along the shore lies a series of salt or sandy swamps; but the coast line itself is broken, in refreshing contrast to the monotonous dead levels further south, by a number of bold headlands and beacons which act as groins to protect the land against the constant encroachments of the waves and currents. The best known of these are the Pólavaram rock, the Dolphin's Nose at Vizagapatam, Rishikonda ('the Sugar-loaf hill') just north of Lawson's Bay at Waltair, and the big Narasimha hill at Bimlipatam.

HILLS.

The only hills in this open plain are the low red and black ones already referred to. These, as has been said, are generally scattered but sometimes stand in rows; and the latter run from north-east to south-west parallel to the coast. In the Anakápalle and Sarvasiddhi taluks are two prominent parallel lines of this kind, and between Sarvasiddhi and Golgonda is quite a considerable and continuous range. West of Vizagapatam and Bimlipatam stands a great confused group of the same kind of hills, the best known of which is called after the Simháchalam temple (see p. 323) near its summit.

North and west of the open plain rise the hills of the Agency already mentioned. They are a section of the great line of the Eastern Gháts.

In the Párvatípur division.

In the north, in the Ráyagada, Gunupur and Bissamkatak taluks of the Jeypore zamindari and Párvatípur division, they are lower than elsewhere and consist of steep and rugged lines, devoid of plateaus, hedging in the two broad, almost parallel, valleys of the Vamsadhára and Nágávali rivers, which drain them southwards down an easy gradient into the Bay of Bengal. A line of heights runs north and south through the middle of this tract and separates these two valleys. It is called the Kailásakóta hills and the highest point on it is 3,895 feet above the sea. In the north-west corner of Bissamkatak taluk is a curious group of larger hills, called the Nímgiris, which rise abruptly from the upper valley of the Vamsadhára (here 1,100 feet above the sea) to close on 5,000 feet.

CHAP. I. HILLS.

As a rule (the appearance of the various taluks is referred to in more detail in Chapter XV) the hills in this part of the district are covered with stunted forests ruined by constant felling and burning, while the valleys are open expanses of park-like land cultivated with a little paddy and much dry crop. The forests here and elsewhere are briefly described in Chapter V and the roads and passes in Chapter VII.

The 3,000 feet plateau.

The hills on the west of the coastal plain consist of three main plateaus. The highest and largest of these, which is made up of the main line of the Eastern Ghâts and runs parallel to the shore of the Bay, is usually known as 'the 3,000 feet plateau.' It sweeps down from the southernmost limit of the wedge-shaped bit of Kálahandi State already mentioned on the north, right through the middle of the district, to the Gódávari boundary on the south; and is about 110 miles long with an average width of 40 miles. The whole of it is tilted slightly to the west and its eastern edge is boldly marked by a line of the biggest hills in the district and drops sharply to the plains. Between this escarpment and the low country proper, however, often intervene range behind range of lower foot-hills, hidden among which are secluded valleys of all sizes and shapes, cut off from the outer world except for rough tracks across the passes, but inhabited and cultivated. Viewed from the plains, these outer hills lend the main plateau a charm which is lacking in ranges not thus attended. It does not stand boldly forth to be appraised at a single glance; only its higher peaks can be seen, peering over the shoulders of their lesser vanguard and across the mysterious-looking valleys which divide the ranks of this latter.

Except a narrow strip on its high eastern side which falls away to the plains, the whole of this 3,000 feet plateau drains westwards into the basin of the Gódávari through the Indrávati, Koláb, Machéru and other tributaries of that great river. Some description of the plateau will be found in the accounts in Chapter XV of the various taluks of which it is made up, and it is sufficient to say here that it consists of a table-land of red soil profusely scattered with hundreds of little red hills of remarkable similarity of appearance. In the north, the hills and valleys have long since been denuded of almost all their forest and cultivated, but in the south, especially in the Golgonda taluk, all but the tops of the hills are still covered with heavy forest.

According to the maps, the highest point on this plateau (and therefore in the district) is Deomali hill, seven miles due north of Pottangi and on the edge of the eastern scarp, which is 5,470 feet

CHAP. I.
HILLS.

above the sea. Other well-known heights are Sinkaram (5,300) and Yendrika (5,188), which rise head and shoulders above their fellows in the interior of the Pádwa taluk, and Gálikonda ('windy hill,' 5,300 feet) which stands on the edge of the plateau south-west of the former, amid a group of several other notable peaks.

Gálikonda as a sanitarium.

In 1859 this last was examined under orders from Sir Patrick Grant, the Commander-in-Chief of Madras, to see whether it would make a good sanitarium for the troops serving in the old 'Northern Division' of the Presidency. A committee of five members presided over by Dr. Duncan McPherson, Inspector-General of Hospitals, went up the hill in February of that year to prospect, the country being marked in the maps of that day as unexplored territory. They named the saddle which joins the two crescentic ridges of Gálikonda 'Grant's range,' and selected a site for a sanitarium on an elevated spot 600 feet lower than this and lying 'a little to the west of north (of Gálikonda) and about a mile from the foot of the hill,' which they called (after Lord Harris, then Governor of Madras) 'the Harris valley.' It is in reality less a valley than a shoulder of Gálikonda, and is a little over 4,000 feet above the sea. Government ordered that a party of European soldiers should go up and reside there for a few months to test the climate. A company of 60 Sappers went up in December 1859 to clear the ground and make approaches, and in the March following twenty-one men of the European Veteran Company at Vizagapatam, with two officers, followed them and lived there for three months. But of this party 'only one escaped fever. The men returned subject to frequent relapses and greatly enfeebled in constitution. Three of them died; two on the hill, one in the way back to Waltair.' It was thought that this melancholy result was partly attributable to the fact that the men were old and worn-out veterans, so a party of the 2nd European L.I. was sent up in their place at the end of May. But only one of these escaped fever. The Sappers, who had remained on the hill at a spot called 'Taylor's knoll,' on the eastern side of the saddle and about 380 feet above the Harris valley, also suffered severely from malaria.

Mr. Fane, the Collector, who had built himself a bungalow on a hillock about 100 feet above Taylor's knoll, said that his servants had escaped; and he thought this was due to their being higher up the hill and having better water. Doubtless, also, the fact that the unfortunate soldiers went through part of the south-west monsoon (the most malarious time of the year) with no better shelter than leaky grass huts had much to do with their sickness.

CHAP. I.
HILLS.

It was next suggested that Kapkonda, a higher hill south-west of Gálikonda 'having a considerable extent of table-land on the summit, sufficient to encamp an army upon,' might make a better site for the sanitarium, but this was examined and also condemned; and in 1861 it was decided to proceed no further with this unlucky venture. Mr. Fane gave his bungalow to his head sheristadar, Mr. McMurray, in 1865. The remains of his garden and the graves of the two veterans may still be seen on the hill. The Rája of Vizianagram has a coffee estate at Anantagiri, on the way up to Gálikonda from the plains, and close by stands the bungalow which Mr. H. G. Turner, Collector from 1881 to 1889, built when he was constructing the Anantagiri ghát (see p. 137) up to this part of the plateau.

The 2,000 feet plateau.

West of, and parallel to, this 3,000 feet plateau, and about 1,000 feet below it, lies a table-land which consists of the Jeypore and Naurangpur taluks and is known as 'the 2,000 feet plateau' or 'the Jeypore plateau.' Like its more elevated neighbour, it drains westwards into the Gódávari basin through the Koláb, Indrávati and other rivers, but at the northern corner it drops down into the valley of the Tél, a tributary of the Mahánadi.

This tract differs altogether from the 3,000 feet plateau in other matters besides altitude. It receives a heavier rainfall, so that the basin of the Indrávati and much of Jeypore taluk are covered with broad sheets of rain-fed paddy instead of dry crops; it is almost level instead of being one mass of hills; and in the north of Naurangpur and the west of Jeypore it contains miles and miles of thick forest, chiefly sál.

The Malkanagiri taluk.

At its southern extremity it drops abruptly down to the third plateau—the Malkanagiri taluk—which is another thousand feet lower on an average, and a good deal more than this in its south-western corner. Malkanagiri village is only 641 feet above the sea. This part of the hills is the most sparsely populated tract in the Presidency, and is one great jungle containing thick forest in places but being largely covered with coarse grass ten feet high dotted with scattered saplings. It drains into the Saveri and Siléru, two more tributaries of the Gódávari.

All this hilly country, though malarious in the extreme and held in abject dread by the natives of the plains, wins the best affections of almost every European officer whom fate leads to serve within it. The beauty of its scenery, its cooler and more invigorating air, the chances of sport, the absence of the mass of detail and routine which binds an official in the plains hand and foot to his office-table, the infrequency of petty squabbles, intrigue

CHAP. I. HILLS.

and litigation, the freshness of its cheery highlanders with their curious customs and their unsophisticated ways, the scope for action on broad and original lines afforded by an unopened country, and the survival of personal and paternal rule and responsibility, more than compensate for the remoteness, discomforts and unhealthiness of the Vizagapatam hills.

RIVERS.

The rivers of the district group themselves into two sets; namely, those which flow eastwards through the coastal plain into the Bay of Bengal and those which drain the Ghâts and the country west of them westwards into the basin of the Gódávari.

The Varáha.

Of the former, the first, beginning in the south of the district, is the Varáha-nadi, or 'boar river,' which is so called because it is supposed to have been made by Vishnu during his incarnation as a boar. It rises in the Golgonda hills to the north of Narasapatam and flows south-eastwards, past the sacred fane of Balighattam to the west of Narasapatam, under holy Sanjívikonda, through a deep and narrow gorge in the red range of which that hill is the highest point, across the Sarvasiddhi taluk, and so into the Bay of Bengal at Vátáda. Its only noteworthy tributary is the Sarpa-nadi, or Kottakóta stream, which fills the natural lake near Kottakóta called the Komaravólu áva. Like the other rivers of the Vizagapatam plains, its shallow, sandy bed is dry during the hot weather and no part of it is ever navigable. The irrigation from it (which is referred to on p. 105 below) is of considerable importance.

The Sárada.

North of it flows the Sárada-nadi. This rises in the Mádgole hills, runs south to Anakápalle, where it is crossed by the trunk road and Madras railway bridges, turns south-west past Kasimkóta, and flows into the Bay at Vátáda through the same mouth as the Varáha. A channel from it fills the pretty natural lake six miles south of Anakápalle called the Kondakarla áva, which swarms with lotuses, fish and wildfowl. This and the Komaravólu áva are two of the very few real freshwater lakes in the Presidency. The irrigation under it and under the other channels from the Sárada is referred to on p. 105 below. The river is liable to sudden and terrific floods, and the damage it has more than once caused to Anakápalle town is referred to in Chapter VIII below.

The Chittivalasa river.

The Chittivalasa (or Bimlipatam) river rises in the slopes of the great Gálikonda hill mentioned above and runs nearly south, past historic Padmanábham and busy Chittivalasa (where the trunk road crosses it on a bridge which has twice been swept away) into the Bay at Bimlipatam.

CHAP. I. RIVERS.

The Góstani.

The Góstani (also called the Champávati) rises just north of this last and flows in an almost parallel course past Gajapatinagaram into the sea near the Kónáda salt-factory.

The Lángulya.

The Lángulya, called the Nágávali in the upper part of its course, is a perennial stream which has its source among the steep hills of the Ráyagada taluk and the Kálahandi State. It flows nearly due south, past Ráyagada, to within six miles east of Párvatípur; and then turns slightly eastwards and enters the Bay at Mahfuz Bandar, near Chicacole in Ganjám district. For the last twenty miles of its course it forms the boundary between Ganjám and Vizagapatam. The trunk road crosses it at Chicacole on a fine bridge. At Ráyagada it rushes through a narrow passage close under the lee of a wooded hill, and over a most picturesque double fall. The upper part of this is about 20 feet high and 50 yards wide, and the river dashes over a sort of natural anicut, formed by an almost level ridge of rock, into a deep pool below. Issuing from this, it leaps the lower fall, about 30 feet, and swirls through a deep channel strewn and flanked with enormous boulders (about several of which local legends are told) until at length it arrives at a placid reach below. In the storm in the autumn of 1905, when the river was in very high flood, a woman with a baby in her arms, supported by a sort of life-belt of bamboos, was being conveyed across the stream some distance above the falls when she was swept away by the current and, incredible as it may appear to those who see the place when the river is low, was carried right over both these falls and through the maze of boulders below them without injury to herself or the child.

Just below the falls the Nágávali is joined by its first important tributary, the Kumbikóta-gedda, a stream which runs from the west in a deep and narrow gorge and is crossed at Ráyagada by a girder road bridge (see p. 142) standing nearly 100 feet above its bed. Some ten miles higher up the whole body of this stream is forced through a narrow cleft in the rocks across which a man can jump.

Twenty miles below this confluence, at Gumpa, the river receives the Janjhávati, which drains the tangle of little valleys round Náráyanapatnam, and still lower down it is joined by the united streams of the Suvarnamukhi and Végavati, which run from the 3,000 feet plateau in almost parallel courses across Bobbili taluk.

The irrigation from the Nágávali and the Suvarnamukhi, and the dam which it is proposed to throw across the former, are referred to on p. 106 below.

CHAP. I.
RIVERS.

The names Nágávali and Lángulya are derived from words meaning 'plough,' and the local legends say that the river was made by Balaráma with that implement. Five shrines have been built upon its banks; namely, those to Pátálésvara at Páyakapád in the Ráyagada taluk; to Sómésvara at Gumpa, where the Janjhávati joins it; to Sangamésvara ('the Siva of the confluence') at Sangam, where the Suvarnamukhi flows into it; to Kótésvara at Chicacole; and to Maninágésvara where it enters the sea. At all of these, largely-attended festivals are held at Sivarátri. The Gumpa temple was in great danger in the flood caused by the storm at the end of 1905. The pújári offered incessant and unwearying oblations, and at last the river fell.

The Vamsadhára.

The Vamsadhára, so called from the bamboo (vamsa) which fringes its banks, rises in the extreme north of the Bissamkatak taluk and passes southwards, through the centre of Gunupur, into Ganjám. It belongs rather to the latter district than to Vizagapatam.

The Tél.

Of the second group of the rivers of the district, namely those which drain the Gháts and the country west of them, the northernmost of all, the Tél, similarly belongs rather to Bengal than to Madras. It merely receives the drainage of the northern corner of Naurangpur taluk and forms for some distance its northern boundary. The river dries up in the hot weather, but in the rains it would probably serve for timber-floating if the falls at the point where it drops down from the 2,000 feet plateau could be somewhat improved.

The Indrávati.

The next river to the south, the Indrávati, rises in the jungles of Kálahandi, winds in a very zig-zag course from east to west across the Naurangpur taluk a couple of miles south of Naurangpur village, and thence runs into Bastar State (receiving at the boundary the Bhaskél, which drains part of north Naurangpur), passes to the north of Jagdalpur, the capital of Bastar, over the beautiful Chittrakóta falls 25 miles further west, and so eventually into the Gódávari. In the Naurangpur taluk it flows in a deep silent stream which, at the point where it is crossed by the main road northwards from Jeypore, is in flood time 465 feet wide and 24 feet deep. Though a ferry is maintained here, the river (which is never dry) is at present a most formidable obstacle to all traffic passing north and south. In Bastar the current is also quiet up to the Chittrakóta falls, but thereafter the bed is full of rocks and a succession of rapids, and navigation and timber-floating are alike almost impossible.

CHAP. I. RIVERS.

The Koláb and Saveri.

Passing further southwards down the 2,000 feet plateau, the next river of importance is the Koláb. This rises near Sinkaram hill on the 3,000 feet plateau, flows north-west in a very winding bed, drops rapidly down to the 2,000 feet plateau not far south of Jeypore, holds on the same course for another 20 or 30 miles and then suddenly doubles back and runs nearly south. For a time it forms the frontier between Jeypore and Bastar, and then it turns south into the former, through a gorge in the wild hills west of Rámagiri which are called the Tulsi Dangari range. As it issues from this, it falls about 40 feet into a large pool, 12 or 14 feet deep, into which, in days gone by, witches used to be thrown with a stone round their necks. Turning west again, and passing Salimi, the Koláb flows into Bastar, past Súnkam, and at last again divides this State from Jeypore, forming the western boundary of Malkanagiri taluk for many miles. In this last part of its course it is called the Saveri or Sabari, and is joined by the Potéru, which drains the centre of Malkanagiri taluk. At Mótu, at the extreme south-western corner of that taluk it meets the Siléru referred to below, and the two pass out of Vizagapatam into Gódávari and fall into the Gódávari river 25 miles further down.

This stream and the Indrávati, draining as they do a country which receives a heavy rainfall and is often covered with forest, are two of the most important of all the tributaries of the Gódávari. They are perennial, and contribute almost the whole of the water which is used for second-crop cultivation in the delta of that river.

In 1856 Mr. Tuke went 132 miles up the Saveri from its confluence with the Gódávari and his detailed account of it will be found in Lieutenant Haig's *Report on the navigability of the Gódávari* (Madras, 1856). He pronounced it navigable during parts of the monsoon, by small boats and with difficulty, for the first 25 miles, that is, to just below Mótu. But he considered that above that point up to Súnkam (near which a huge barrier of rock 600 yards long with a drop of 50 or 60 feet causes a mighty rapid) the river was certainly not navigable by boats at any time of the year, being a maze of rocks, shoals, islands and strong currents. Even wood could only be floated down during certain short seasons and with great difficulty. From Súnkam to Salimi, however, the stream is quieter and timber could come down it.

The Siléru.

The Machéru or Machkand ('fish river') rises in the Mádgole hills on the 3,000 feet plateau and at first runs nearly north along a very meandering course, passing close under Yendrika

CHAP. I. RIVERS.

hill (the curious fish-pool near here is described on p. 285 below) and through the wide Pádwa valley. When about 35 miles south of Jeypore it winds westwards along the edge of the plateau, as if looking for a way down through the low hills which fringe this there, and then suddenly turns at a sharp angle to the south-west down a steep descent. The drop changes a somewhat sluggish river flowing between banks of red earth into a series of rapids foaming between enormous masses of boulders. Three miles from the bend, about the same distance south of Bádigada, and 26 miles from the nearest road, the descent is barred by a huge barrier of rock shut in on either side by walls of rock two or three hundred feet high. Below this is a sheer abyss of 480 feet, over which the river flings itself into a boiling pool half hidden by dense clouds of spray on which the sunlight throws the brightest of rainbows. In the dry season it is possible to scramble to the edge of the abyss and look straight down through the spray into the great pool beneath, while from beneath the scene is the most impressive in all the district. Below these falls, which are the highest in the Presidency, the river flows south-westwards in a deep and gloomy gorge, hemmed in on both sides by rock walls hundreds of feet high, into which it is impossible to descend and which is said to continue for many miles.[1]

This slowly widens until at Kondakambéru, 32 miles as the crow flies from the falls, it has become a narrow valley shut in by high hills. A few miles further on the river, which is now called the Siléru ('rocky stream') and still runs at the bottom of a deep hollow in the mountains, forms the boundary between Malkanagiri taluk and the Gódávari district and flows on, abounding in mahseer and crocodiles, until at Mótu it joins the Savori. 'Nothing can exceed the extreme beauty of this lonely river, with its bamboo-covered banks, its deep, long reaches of water, its falls, its grass-covered islets and its rushing clear water. From the grand fall at Bádigada to the gorge where it emerges from the Kondakambéru level, it would not be difficult to pole a boat; but this gorge altogether prevents boats from coming up from Mótu, and indeed it is equally destructive of all timber-floating operations.'

SOILS.

The soils of the district have been scientifically classified only in the three Government taluks, in which alone regular settlement operations have been conducted. There they divide themselves into the two main groups of red ferruginous and black, which are

[1] From a description kindly supplied by Mr. H. A. B. Vernon, I.C.S. The height of the falls was taken by Mr. H. G. Turner with an aneroid.

CHAP. I. SOILS.

again subdivided into clays, loams and sands. The figures subjoined show the percentage of the assessed area of each of the three taluks which is covered with these different kinds of earths :—

Description of soil.		Pálkonda taluk.	Golgonda taluk.	Sarvasiddhi taluk.	Total of the three taluks.
Red	Loam	41·7	51·5	53·1	49·0
	Sand	16·3	38·5	15·1	25·5
	Total ...	58·0	90·0	68·2	74·5
Black	Clay	13·9	2·7	14·8	9·3
	Loam	24·9	7·3	17·0	15·2
	Sand	3·2	...	...	1·0
	Total ...	42·0	10·0	31·8	25·5
	Total ...	100·0	100·0	100·0	100·0

It will be noticed that three-fourths of them consist of red soils and only one-fourth of the richer black earths; that the loams (the most fertile of the subdivisions for wet crops) are not uncommon; that a third of the red land is of the sandy, the least fertile, variety; and that Pálkonda and Sarvasiddhi are far more favoured than Golgonda, in which last nine-tenths of the soil is of the red kinds. This final point is clearly brought out by the figures of assessment given on p. 100 below, which show that only one-eighth of the assessed dry land in Golgonda is rated at more than Re. 1 per acre and less than one-fourth of the wet land at more than Rs. 4–8–0. The black soil occurs chiefly in the alluvial valleys of the streams and rivers, the higher land being usually red.

Though no accurate figures can be quoted, it may be stated in general terms that (except in these valleys) the prevailing soil of the whole of the plains, of the Párvatípur division, and of the 3,000 feet plateau is red, while on the 2,000 feet plateau beyond it the black soils become commoner. The red earth is often of the most vivid colour and adds not a little, by its contrast with the green trees and crops, to the picturesqueness of the district.

CLIMATE. Rainfall.

The rainfall in Vizagapatam is referred to in some detail in Chapter VIII (p. 146) below. The average fall in the plains is 41 inches and in the Agency, which receives more of the south-west monsoon, 57 inches. Jeypore gets as much as 75 inches, while some stations on the coast receive less than 35.

CHAP. I.
CLIMATE.

Temperature.

The temperature is officially recorded only at Waltair, though meteorological observations of much value are made at the G. V. Jagga Rao observatory at Vizagapatam referred to on p. 332 below. The average maxima and minima and the mean for each month and for the whole year registered at the former station are shown in degrees Fahrenheit in the margin. The annual mean (82°) is rather higher than that of Gopalpur in the next district to the north (79°·6), and rather lower than that of Cocanada, the next recording-station to the south (82°·1); but the average maxima in the three hottest months (April, May and June), though five degrees in excess of those at Gopalpur, are from two to six degrees below those of Cocanada. Waltair is damp, but less so than Cocanada and much less than Gopalpur, the annual mean humidity at the three places being respectively 72·6, 74·6 and 81·0. The moistest part of the year is the middle of September and the driest the middle of December. From November to February Waltair is pleasant enough, though like many seaside places in the tropics it is relaxing. The station has one great advantage which figures do not exhibit; namely, that it stands 200 feet above the sea, and so gets all the air there is, and that the Dolphin's Nose headland to the south of it deflects the debilitating long-shore wind and turns it into a sea-breeze. Waltair is cooler than Vizianagram, and far cooler than either Párvatípur or Narasapatam, both of which are shut off from the sea-breeze by low hills; but in the more relaxing months it is a less healthy place of residence than the drier stations further inland, such as Vizianagram or Bobbili.

Month.	Average maximum.	Average minimum.	Mean.
	°	°	°
January	82·5	63·6	73·1
February ...	86·2	68·9	77·6
March	90·9	73·4	82·2
April	92·7	78·8	85·8
May	95·0	81·9	88·5
June	93·7	82·0	87·8
July	92·1	80·5	86·3
August	91·6	79·2	85·4
September ...	89·3	78·5	83·9
October	89·0	76·3	82·7
November ...	84·5	69·9	77·2
December ..	82·3	64·7	73·5
The year ...	89·2	74·8	82·0

The climate and temperature of the hilly parts of the district naturally differ altogether from those of the plains. Statistics are not available, but in the cold months on the 3,000 feet plateau fires and two blankets are required at night and the days are never really hot. The malaria which infests most of this country and others of the more virulent diseases of the district are referred to in Chapter IX below.

CHAP. I.
GEOLOGY.

No detailed account of the geology of the district has yet been published.[1] The fundamental rocks are all gneisses and plutonic igneous rocks of the archæan group. They outcrop in lines running mainly from north-east to south-west, which direction determines that of the chief plateaus and minor hill ranges. The district may be divided geologically into four parallel zones; namely, (i) the 2,000 feet plateau in the north-west, composed of the older sub-group of archæan gneisses, namely biotite and hornblende mixed gneiss with layers of steatite, some younger diabase dykes (almost the only dykes in all the district) and a few outliers of Cuddapah quartzites with some crystalline limestone,

(ii) the north-west portion of the 3,000 feet plateau, made up of bands of the younger archæan sub-group of khondalite and intrusive bands of charnockite,

(iii) the south-east part of the same plateau, consisting of more khondalite (with local beds of iron and manganese ore and crystalline limestone) and bands of charnockite again and coarse porphyritic biotite gneissose granite, and

(iv) a coastward low-level zone containing minor ridges composed almost exclusively of yet more khondalite with a few bands of charnockite and gneissose granite.

In these last rocks occur the manganese deposits mentioned below. The most obvious characteristic of the gneisses is the number of brown or purple-brown iron garnets which are scattered through them. White quartzose gneiss streaks the surface of parts of the country, especially between Vizagapatam and Vizianagram, with conspicuous reefs and ridges, but it does not occur in true veins and is not auriferous.

The surface rocks include horizontal plateaus of high-level pisolitic laterite some 80 feet thick at an elevation of from 3,500 to 4,000 feet above the sea, chiefly to the north of Koraput and spreading out in the direction of the Kálahandi State. This laterite, which has been thought to be a sedimentary deposit laid down in water, is limited to a fairly constant level, and surrounds the hills like a belt of shore through which the bare rocks, which were perhaps islands in the lateritic age, raise themselves. It contains much hydrated alumina and may possibly prove of value as an ore of aluminium. Other recent deposits include the younger alluvium of the plains, an older red lateritic loam and the blown sands of the coast, both of which latter are very noticeable at Waltair.

[1] The following publications of the Geological Survey of India refer to the subject:—*Records*, xix, pt. 3; xxxi, pt. 1; xxxii, pt. 2; xxxiii, pt. 2; and the General Reports for 1899–1900 and 1902–03.

CHAP. I.
MINERALS.

Manganese.

The most important, industrially, of the minerals of the district is manganese ore. The mining of this is referred to on p. 125 below.

Iron.

In many villages in the Umarkót, Kótapád, Rámagiri and Koraput tánas of the Jeypore estate iron ore is rudely smelted by the natives in the usual way for the manufacture of implements and tools, but apparently no large or continuous out-crop of ore exists.

Graphite

Graphite is commonly used for giving a finish to the ordinary earthen pots of the district. It is said to be found in the Mérangi, Kásipuram and Sálúr zamindaris and at a spot seven miles to the north-east of Narasapatam, but no clear account of its distribution or qualities has yet been published and all that can be said is that it has never yet been exploited with commercial success.

Limestone.

The crystalline limestone at Guptésvara and the Borra Cave is referred to in the accounts of those places on pp. 260 and 285. At the former the Koláb cuts its way through beds of grey, argillaceous limestone which in some spots has been dissolved away by the running water and formed into fantastic pillars, *blocs perchés*, circular caverns and wide arches.

Steatite.

Coarse grey steatite (potstone) outcrops at numerous points west and south-west of Jeypore, and at Ontagaon, three miles from that town; is quarried for buildings and for the manufacture of images of the Hindu gods. It also occurs on the road between Boipariguda and Rámagiri, and on the Malkanagiri road, four or five miles south of the Kollar bungalow.

Sapphirine.

Sapphirine, which hitherto has been found only at Fiskernäs on the west coast of Greenland, was discovered by Mr. Middlemiss 1½ miles south-south-west of Pádéru on the bridle-path to Gangaráz Mádgole.

A meteorite.

On the 23rd January 1870 a meteorite fell in the village of Nedagolla, five miles south of Párvatípur. It was rescued from the villagers, who had put it in their temple and were doing worship to it, by Colonel Saxton of the Topographical Survey, and was found to be a meteoric iron of 10 lb. weight.[1] Stony meteorites are very common, but this was the first iron one known in peninsular India. A second, weighing 35 lb., was discovered (near Kodaikanal) in 1899.

[1] Progs. of R.A.S.B., 1870, 64.

CHAP. I.
FLORA.[1]

The flora of the Vizagapatam district may be taken as typical of the Northern Circars generally. It is not possible to separate it in its character from that of Ganjám on the north and Gódávari on the south. Only in the possession of a great river and its irrigated delta is the latter district peculiar. In this region there is however a gradual transition from north to south, a gradual dying out of the northern forms as we proceed along the Eastern Gháts to their southern termination in the Gódávari gorges.

Comparatively little collecting has been done in the district. There are no records of its having been visited by any botanist of note in the past and we are dependent for exact details on a short collecting tour made through several taluks in the year 1900. Sufficient information was then got together for a brief statement on the flora and the following notes have been put together.

As in most parts of the Coromandel coast, in passing inland from the sea we meet with a series of well-defined geographical areas, and each of these has a different set of plants distinguishing it, while others are evenly distributed from the sea-side to the hills. The plains flora possesses little of interest, as it is practically the same for the greater part of the Madras coast. In it we can separate the sea-side flora, the salt-marsh plants and the dry scrub-jungle. Wherever cultivation exists, on the other hand, we have an assemblage of weeds, shrubs and climbers which may be met with from Tuticorin to Bengal, including a number of exotic plants introduced from various parts of the tropics.

On the sea coast we meet with the sandbinders such as *Spinifex squarrosus*, a thorny grass of great size, widely spreading over the beach, and whose ball-like flowering heads break off and roll before the wind, dropping their seeds in favourable spots; *Ipomæa biloba*, a 'convolvulus' with brightly-coloured, large, pink flowers, which sends out long streamers over the low sand hills; *Launæa pinnatifida*, a small plant with dandelion-like flowers, also a sandbinder with a complex network of branches, *Spermacoce hispida*, *Lippia nodiflora*, *Hydrophylax maritima*, *Ipomæa tridentata* and *Phaseolus trilobus*. The salt marshes may be searched for *Suæda nudiflora*, *Salicornia brachiata*, *Sesuvium Portulacastrum* and other succulents. It is a curious fact that the plants growing in situations with abundant salt so frequently share this fleshy character with those of very dry regions. The

[1] This section has been kindly contributed by Mr. C. A. Barber, Government Botanist.

CHAP. I. FLORA.

great cultivated plain of the district teems with the usual plants of the Coromandel coast, finding place on the bunds separating the fields, in the hedges and waste places. Small herbs such as *Sphæranthus indicus*, *Oldenlandias*, *Bonnayas*, *Coldenia pocumbens*, various species of *Heliotropium*, *Aristolochia indica*, *Cleomes*; hedge plants and climbers such as various species of *Vitis*, *Dregea volubilis*, *Tragia involucrata*, *Modecca Wightiana*, and such shrubby plants as have been able to resist the cultivator's efforts at clearing the original scrub forests. This flora of cultivation presents a great mass of diverse species, of great use to the amateur but of little interest to the explorer. Here may be met representatives of all the chief orders of Indian plants, a veritable botanical garden laid out for the study of the beginner.

The scrub jungle is, as usual, more interesting. We have a great collection of drought-resisting or xerophytic forms which have no end of contrivances by which they have adapted themselves to the severity of the climate and the scarcity of water. Broadly speaking, we may divide these into the dry and thorny plants with little leaf surface and much hard stem frequently covered with thorns, and the succulents where the whole plant surface has been reduced to a minimum and is filled with fleshy tissue with nauseous contents. A double purpose is fulfilled by these characters, diminution of the evaporation of water and resistance to the onslaughts of the predatory goat. It is well to take note of these facts in botanical rambles, and special clothing is needed for collectors in these parts. The following plants may be looked for in the scrub jungle: low-growing specimens of *Cassia Fistula* with brilliant tresses of yellow flowers, thorny *Acacias* and dwarf *Albizzias*, and the closely allied *Dichrostachys cinerea* with its bright spikes of half-yellow, half-pink flowers, stunted trees of *Chloroxylon Swietenia* (satinwood) with rough bark and delicate foliage, the sweet-scented *Glycosmis pentaphylla*, *Maba buxifolia*, *Capparis sepiaria*, *Pterolobium indicum* with beautiful white racemes and gaily painted fruits guarded, however, by wait-a-bit thorns, *Asparagus racemosus*, a typical 'bridal' plant with its finely divided 'leaves' and sprays of minute white flowers, *Barleria Prionitis*, *Dodonæa viscosa*, *Hibiscus micranthus*, *Waltheria indica*, *Erythroxylon monogynum*, *Cassia auriculata*, *Randia dumetorum*. Less abundant are *Gmelina arborea*, *Dalbergia rubiginosa*, *Elæodendron glaucum*, *Ochna squarrosa*, *Polyalthia cerasoides*, *Elytraria crenata*, *Olax scandens* (parasitic on the roots of other trees), *Diospyros montana*, *Aristolochia bracteata*, and *Streblus asper*. Here and there may be discovered the bushy *Phyllanthus pinnata*, a gregarious plant which covers the ground with delicate green almost to the exclusion of all other vegetation and is especially interesting as having evaded the careful compilers of Hooker's Flora. And, generally scattered over the ground, may be found *Asclepiad* succulents such as *Boucerosia* and *Caralluma*, and 'lilies' such as *Urginea* and *Pancratium*, while that strange child of the tropics, *Gloriosa superba*, a sprawling climber, raises its gorgeous, spotted red and yellow flowers from the midst of the most unpromising thorns. The struggle for existence in such a jungle is of the fiercest and there appears to be less foothold for the parasitic plants of the mistletoe order. Here and there various species of *Loranthus* may be met with, but the dodder-like *Cassytha filiformis* is everywhere at home on the parched vegetation.

The rocky gullies are of greater interest, and may be explored by the adventurous for *Calycopteris floribunda*, *Gardenia latifolia* with great white-scented flowers which would grace any English green-house, *Combretum ovalifolium* and *Symphorema involucratum* with pretty parachute-like papery bracts.

It is only when the hills are approached that the flora becomes interesting to the scientific botanist, and it is just here that we are confronted with an unexplored country. The Eastern Ghâts are typically developed in this district and the survey of their untracked fastnesses will certainly repay a careful examination. Here we meet with the outliers of the flora of the great central plateau of India and the tops of the highest peaks show small collections of plants which have strayed, no one knows how, from the plains of Bengal or even the far-off Himalayas.

Among the lower hills are found such plants as the following :—*Holarrhena antidysenterica*, *Toddalia aculeata*, various *Randias*, *Acalypha alnifolia*, *Grewia hirsuta*, *G. orbiculata*, *G. salvifolia*, *G. tiliæfolia*, *G. asiatica*, *Alangium Lamarckii*, *Zizyphus xylopyrus*, *Diospyros montana*, *Terminalia belerica*, *T. Chebula*, *Celastrus paniculata*, *Zehneria umbellata*, *Dendrocalamus strictus*, *Carissa macrophylla*, *Phyllanthus Emblica*, *Strychnos potatorum*, *Vitis Linnæi*, *Stemona tuberosa*, *Glossocardia linearifolia*, *Anogeissus acuminata*, and, higher up, *Mimusops Elengi*, *Hemicyclea sepiaria*, *Bassia latifolia* whose thick, white, fleshy flowers produce both sugar when dried and spirit when distilled, *Albizzia odoratissima*, *Ægle Marmelos* and *Xylia dolabriformis*. Here too we approach the edge of the sál forest, *Shorea robusta*. This tree in the north of Ganjám has monopolised large areas of forest land in the hills and approaches to within thirty miles of the coast, but the sál

CHAP. I. FLORA.

recedes further and further inland as we pass to the south. The value of sál timber is well known as producing the most indestructible railway sleepers. Other interesting plants which may be sought for in the Eastern Gháts are the following :—

Woodfordia floribunda, *Indigofera pulchella*, *Anogeissus latifolia*, *Pterocarpus Marsupium*, *Martynia diandra* (an introduced American weed with handsome flowers and clawlike fruits), *Atylosia crassa*, *Oroxylum indicum*, *Bauhinia variegata*, *B. purpurea*, *B. Vahlii*, *Butea superba*, *Ventilago calyculata*, *Terminalia tomentosa*, *Rhinacanthus communis*, *Pimpinella Heyneana*, *Desmodium Cephalotes*, *D. gyrans*, *D. pulchellum*, *Ougeinia dalbergioides*, *Sterculia urens*, *Cochlospermum Gossypium*, *Hymenodictyon excelsum*, *Coffea bengalensis* (found in the Ganjám Maliahs), *Adhatoda Vasica*, *Micromelum pubescens*, *Pogostemon plectranthoides*, *Hypericum japonicum*, *Acacia concinna*, *Clematis smilacifolia*, *Embelia robusta*, *Justicia Betonica*, *Thespesia Lampas*, *Cansjera Rheedii* (parasitic on the roots of other trees), *Androsace saxifragæfolia* (a small herb of the Gangetic plain but recently found in the Ganjám hills), *Dillenia pentagyna*, *Baliospermum axillare*, *Flemingia Chappar*, *Holoptelea integrifolia*, *Albizzia stipulata*, &c., &c.

In conclusion a note may be added as to the assemblages of plants to be found on the more isolated peaks. In Ganjám, close to the Vizagapatam border, the great mass of Mahéndragiri raises its 5,000 feet, and, thanks to the presence of rest houses, has been explored at various times with interesting results. Almost every peak of the Eastern Gháts would repay a visit. Even lesser heights are of interest, as will be seen from the following small collection taken on the summit of Karakakonda, a 2,000 feet hill in the Golgonda taluk of Vizagapatam: *Glossocardia linearifolia*, *Sauropus quadrangularis*, *Chlorophytum attenuatum*, *Olax nana*, *Buettneria herbacea*, *Tylophora macrantha*, *T. rotundifolia*, *Ischæmum angustifolium*, *Grewia* dwarf near *tiliæfolia*, *Grewia* dwarf near *salvifolia*. Of these, *Glossocardia linearifolia* is a Central Indian plant, *Sauropus quadrangularis* is not found south of the Gódávari and may be considered a rare plant, *Chlorophytum attenuatum* belongs to the Western Gháts, *Olax nana* is only recorded in Hooker's Flora as occurring in the 'hot valleys of the Western Himalayas.' *Buettneria herbacea*, although not uncommon on out of the way hills, is a most interesting and peculiar little plant. *Tylophora macrantha* is a Nilgiri plant, *T. rotundifolia* is a North and Central Indian plant but is also recorded from the Ánaimalais, *Ischæmum angustifolium* is not reported further south than Central India. The dwarf *Grewias* are more interesting still. According to current opinion they must be regarded as species new to science. They seem rather to be derivatives from species of the neighbourhood, *i.e.*, *tilæfolia* and *salvifolia*, rendered permanently dwarf by the recurrence of annual forest fires. Arising from forms with well defined tree-like stems, they have lost this character but acquired an underground rootstock from which flowering shoots are sent up after each rainy season, but which fruit and wither before the period of grass burning. It is possible that *Olax nana* has been derived in the same way from *Olax scandens*.

FAUNA. Domestic animals; cattle.

The cattle of the district belong to no special local variety and no particular care is taken to improve them by judicious breeding. At the two shows which the District Agricultural Association has held up to date, the class of the exhibits was exceedingly high, but the majority of the prize-winners appear to have possessed a strain of the Nellore blood. The ordinary plough and milch cattle are bred locally or in some cases in the southern taluks are imported from Gódávari. The thousands of pack-cattle used by the Brinjáris in their trade with the interior are of the most ordinary variety. Two of the most important cattle-fairs on the plains are those at Kottavalasa and Álamanda in the Srungavarapukóta taluk and at Tummapála just north of Anakápalle.

The Vizagapatam buffaloes, however, are remarkable animals of great size, bone and power. There are two varieties of them, namely, a light-coloured animal with very long, straight horns, which is indigenous, and a darker and more hairy breed, the horns of which are short and curve upwards. The latter, which are locally known as Kási (Benares) buffaloes, come from the Ganjám district and are largely bought at the fairs at Santakaviti and Sítarámpuram in Pálkonda taluk. Both these varieties are exceedingly useful, doing much of the cultivation in the heavier soils and dragging almost all the grain-carts which pour down in thousands from the Jeypore country to the plains whenever the price of food-stuffs is high in the latter. They are not used for pack-work, as they are such slow walkers.

Sheep.

The sheep of the plains are of the usual hairy brown and white breed, but in parts of the Agency is found another variety called *ráchamanda*, which often produces two lambs at a birth and has a short coarse fleece. Though thousands of blankets are required annually by the hill people, the woolly sheep of the Deccan is unknown and no blankets are manufactured locally.

Goats.

On the plains the ordinary long-legged brown goats are numerous. In some parts of the hill taluks a breed exists which, if kept sheltered from cold and wet, brings forth three kids at a time.

CHAP. I.
FAUNA.
Game.

Big game is varied and on the whole plentiful, but it is practically confined to the wilder portions of the Agency, where no one but the local officers can command transport, supplies or beaters and where malaria is ever present. Along the southern part of the coast, and also inland, black-buck are fairly plentiful and there are some pig, barking deer and spotted deer, but no other game worth mention exists. The hills contain wild buffalo (found nowhere else in this Presidency), bison (gaur), spotted, swamp, ravine, and barking deer, sambhur, nílghai and four-horned antelope, as well as pig, bears, leopards and tigers. The flesh of the pig is highly esteemed by many of the hill people as an aphrodisiac, and fetches high prices. The bears, as elsewhere, are very fond of the mohwa flower, and often get extremely drunk upon it. Tigers used to be a perfect pest. The reports of even twenty years ago are full of accounts of the panics caused by man-eaters (especially in the Golgonda Agency), which the natives picturesquely called the tiger fitúris, or 'tiger rebellions.' Some of these brutes became extraordinarily bold. People were frequently carried off in broad daylight in the villages; on one occasion a woman was taken out of her walled backyard; on another a constable forming one of a guard escorting about a hundred people back from market was killed; and one tiger used even to claw down the doors of the houses to get at the inmates. Between June 1881 and March 1883, 133 persons were killed in the Nandapuram and Pádwa taluks alone. In their terror, the people fled from their villages, avoided the gháts and left whole tracts depopulated. In Golgonda the evil was increased by the current superstition that any one who killed a tiger would come out all over stripes. One officer tried to persuade the people that an infallible safeguard against the latter disaster was to stroke one's nose slowly with the dead tiger's tail, and in 1884 a number of old police carbines were distributed among the hill men to enable them to meet the foe on more equal terms.

The most famous tiger of recent times was the Tentulakunti man-eater in the south of Naurangpur, which was credited with having killed 200 persons before it was at length slain by Mr. H. D. Taylor, I.C.S., then in charge of Jeypore estate during the Mahárája's minority.

The Government reward for tigers is Rs. 100, or more than in any other district, and these animals are now almost scarce. In the Golgonda hills the professional shikáris and skin-hunters turned the carbines supplied to them against the deer-tribe and the bison, regardless of sex and age; and they shot the latter (over the salt-licks) in such numbers that it was reported that 'the whole country was dotted over with bison bones' and it became necessary to extend the game rules to the chief reserves to stop the wholesale slaughter which was proceeding. These rules have also been extended to some of the Pálkonda reserves. In Jeypore the game is much harried by the annual beats in the month of Chaitra (see p. 72), when the whole able-bodied male population turns out and remains out, sometimes for days together, until it has succeeded in killing some animal and so in avoiding the rough reception accorded by the womenfolk to the unsuccessful. One haunch of venison goes to the man who first hits the animal and the other to the headman of the village in which it dies.

The best small-game shooting on the plains is afforded by the duck and teal. Of the former, the red-headed pochard and the gadwall are the commonest kinds. Snipe and quail are comparatively scarce. Peafowl are common all over the hills and the Savaras sometimes catch them by chasing them from side to side of a steep, narrow valley until they are exhausted. Of the rarer game-birds, woodcock have been seen round Páderu, and in the hills the Imperial pigeon is not uncommon and a brown pigeon with a white head is seen now and again.

CHAPTER II.

POLITICAL HISTORY.

EARLY HISTORY—Formed part of the kingdom of Kalinga—Antiquity of this—Its conquest by Asóka, 260 B.C.—A long gap in its history—The Ganga kings—Attacked by their neighbours, tenth century—The later Gangas of Trikalinga—Anantavarman-Chóda-Ganga, 1078—Invaded by the Chólas, eleventh century—The Matsyas—Decline of the Gangas, 1434—The Gajapatis of Orissa—Defeated by Krishna Déva of Vijayanagar, 1515—End of the dynasty, 1541. MUHAMMADAN PERIOD, 1568—Aurangzeb overthrows Golconda, 1687—The Subadar of the Deccan becomes independent, 1724—Cedes the Northern Circars to the French, 1753—Difficulties of the French thereafter—Bussy at length obtains possession, 1757—Forde's expedition against the French, 1758—The French expelled from the Circars—The Circars ceded to the English, 1765. ENGLISH PERIOD—Foundation of Vizagapatam settlement, 1682—Its early progress—The cowle granted in 1685—The factory sacked by the Musalmans, 1689—Mr. Holcombe becomes Chief, 1692—Hidden treasure in Bobbili—Local disturbances, 1694—Extravagance at Vizagapatam—More local disturbances, 1697—Brighter prospects, 1698—Vizagapatam besieged, 1711—The defences strengthened—Waltair first occupied, 1727—Further strengthening of the defences, 1741-45—The place surrenders to Bussy, 1757—Is recovered and becomes the capital of the district, 1769—Growth of the power of the Vizianagram Rája—And of his díwán Sítaráma Rázu—Sepoy mutiny at Vizagapatam, 1780—Proposed cession of the Circars, 1781—Maladministration by the Vizianagram Rája—Dangerous growth of his power—Ordered to reduce his troops, 1788—Falls into heavy arrears with his peshkash, 1793—His estate is sequestrated—And he is ordered to leave the district, 1794—He resists this order—And is killed at Padmanábham—His son is given the estate—Which is greatly curtailed—The Permanent Settlement, 1802—Its unfortunate effects—Mr. Russell's Commission, 1833—Subsequent outbreaks.

CHAP. II. EARLY HISTORY.[1]

So far, no traces have been discovered in Vizagapatam of the prehistoric peoples whose burial places are so common in other districts.

Formed part of the kingdom of Kalinga

The earliest extant accounts of the country speak of it as part of the famous kingdom of Kalinga, which (though its exact boundaries were vague and constantly changing) stretched perhaps from the Mahánadi river on the north to the Gódávari on the south.

Antiquity of this.

The antiquity of this principality is amply established. It is referred to in Bráhmanical and Buddhist literature assigned by Professors Macdonell and Rhys Davids to the fifth and sixth

[1] For assistance with this section I am very greatly indebted to Rai Bahádur V. Venkayya, M.A., Government Epigraphist.

centuries, respectively, before Christ; by the Sanskrit grammarians Kátyáyana and Pánini, who flourished in the fourth century B.C.; and in the Rámáyana and Mahábhárata. The Buddhist chronicles refer to its forests and the settlement on its coast to which the left canine tooth of Buddha was brought in state immediately after his death; but the Bráhmanical writings speak scornfully of it, saying that 'he commits sin through his feet, who travels to the country of the Kalingas' and prescribing the purification necessary to expiate such an act. Megasthenes (302 B.C.) however writes of the Kalingas as a civilized people divided into classes which followed widely different occupations (among them the study of philosophy and the taming of wild elephants) and mentions their capital, where 60,000 foot-soldiers, 1,000 horsemen and 700 elephants kept watch and ward over their king.

Its conquest by Asóka, 260 B.C.

In 260 B.C. Asóka, the great emperor of the Buddhist Mauryan realms (the capital of which was at Pátaliputra, the modern Patna), attacked and conquered Kalinga. One of his famous rock-edicts shows clearly that it was the remorse he felt for the horrors of this campaign which led him in the same year to espouse the Buddhist religion which he afterwards spread throughout India and Ceylon. Says the edict[1]:—

'One hundred and fifty thousand persons were carried away captive (from Kalinga), one hundred thousand were there slain, and many times that number perished. . . . . His Majesty feels remorse on account of the conquest of the Kalingas, because, during the subjugation of a previously unconquered country, slaughter, death, and taking away captive of the people necessarily occur, whereat His Majesty feels profound sorrow and regret. There is, however, another reason for His Majesty feeling still more regret, inasmuch as in such a country dwell Bráhmans and ascetics, men of different sects, and householders, who all practise obedience to elders, obedience to father and mother, obedience to teachers, proper treatment of friends, acquaintances, comrades, relatives, slaves and servants, with fidelity of devotion. To such people dwelling in that country happen violence, slaughter, and separation from those they love.'

The terms of this inscription further show that Kalinga at that time was capable of offering considerable resistance even to so powerful an emperor as Asóka, and that its people were a civilized race. The Buddhist remains near Anakápalle referred to on p. 223 below probably belong to this period.

A long gap in its history.

For several centuries thereafter the history of Kalinga is almost a blank. Pliny (first century A.D.) mentions the country and

[1] Mr. Vincent Smith's *Asóka* (Clarendon Press, 1901), 130.

CHAP. II. EARLY HISTORY.

describes it as consisting of three divisions, which may have given rise to the name Trikalinga under which it is referred to later. Isolated references to scattered kings of the territory occur elsewhere, but they cannot be combined into any connected account.

Inscriptions show that in the sixth century A.D., Kalinga was conquered by the Chalukyas of Bádámi in Bombay and in the seventh by their offshoot the Eastern Chálukyas. A result of this latter campaign was the establishment of the Vengi kingdom (the ruins of the capital of which still stand at Pedda Végi, six miles north of Ellore) under the Eastern Chálukya king Vishnuvardhana I (615–33 A.D.). Copper grants of this monarch found at Chípurupalle in this district show that he once ruled as far north as that village.

The Ganga kings.

The chronicles are continued by the grants of a series of kings who describe themselves as of the Ganga family, lords of Kalinga, and worshippers of the Gókarnasvámi (Siva) on the Mahéndragiri hill in Ganjám (where the ruins of cyclopean shrines still stand), and as ruling from Kalinganagara, which has been identified with Mukhalingam on the bank of the Vamsadhára in Ganjám, where notable temples and inscriptions yet survive.

The period when this dynasty flourished is doubtful, as their grants are all dated in an era the initial point of which has yet to be determined. The names of eleven of them are known. and their inscriptions have been found in several places in Ganjám and at Álamanda and Vizagapatam in this district, but the material at present available supplies no connected account of the doings of any of them.

Attacked by their neighbours, tenth century.

The Eastern Chálukyas of Vengi appear to have constantly interfered in the affairs of Kalinga, and Vimaláditya of that line seems to have conquered much of it, since an inscription on Mahéndragiri states that the Chóla king Rájarája I of Tanjore overthrew him in 999–1000 and set up a pillar of victory on that hill.

Kalinga was apparently further attacked from the north, for the kings of Kósala in that direction, who have been tentatively assigned to this same eleventh century, claim to have made themselves 'lords of Trikalinga.'

The later Gangas of Trikalinga.

The Gangas were followed by a later line of the same name who, as they also worshipped the Gókarnasvámi on Mahéndragiri and ruled from Kalinganagara, were apparently of the same family. Calculations from dates in copper grants show that they were in power from the end of the ninth century. One of them, Rájarája, ascended the throne in 1070–71 and reigned eight years, during which time he says he helped the Vengi kings against the Chólas, and afterwards defeated both of them and also the ruler of Utkala (Orissa) and other monarchs.

Anantavarman-Chóda-Ganga, 1078.

Under his son, Anantavarman-Chóda-Ganga, who ruled from 1078 for no less than 72 years, this family reached the zenith of its power. Many copper grants and inscriptions of this monarch have been found in Ganjám and Vizagapatam, and these state that he replaced on their thrones the fallen kings of Vengi and Orissa, engaged in wars extending from the Ganges in the north to the Gódávari in the south, and built the famous temple of Jagannátha at Puri. An inscription on copper belonging to his reign shows that, after the manner of many who have suddenly got up in the world, he desired a lofty ancestry. This record traces the origin of his family back to Brahma, and says that the name Ganga was derived from the fact that the fourth in descent from Brahma begot a son by propitiating the Ganges.

Invaded by the Chólas, eleventh century.

The Chólas of Tanjore seem twice to have invaded the south of Trikalinga during his reign. Inscriptions of Kulóttunga I of that dynasty refer to his subjugation of the kingdom at a date previous to 1095, and again in 1114. The existence of a Tamil record of his, dated 1089, in the Simháchalam temple goes to confirm the success of the former of these incursions, and various circumstances seem to indicate that Anantavarman-Chóda-Ganga took less interest in the Vizagapatam district than in the north of his kingdom.

He married at least five queens and had by them four sons who ruled after him. Of them and their immediate successors little but their names is known. Inscriptions of theirs occur in the district, but the country eventually fell again to the Eastern Chálukyas of Vengi and their feudatories, the queen of one of the latter of whom is recorded to have covered with gold the image of Vishnu at Simháchalam. The Yádavas of Dévagiri (the modern Daulatábád) and the Kákatíyas of Warangal claim, moreover, to have humbled Kalinga at this period.

The Matsyas.

At Simháchalam occur several inscriptions of a line of chiefs called the Matsyas of Oddavádi. Copper grants found at Dibbida agrahåram in this district say that the founder of the family was descended from a fish (Matsya means fish), married a daughter of the king of Orissa, and was appointed to rule over 'the Oddavádi country.' The Matsyas seem to have become independent there in the thirteenth century. It is perhaps worth noting in

CHAP. II.
EARLY HISTORY.

this connection that (see p. 320) the Mádgole zamindars venerate fish, being installed on a fish-shaped throne and using as their signature a symbol representing a fish ; that they claim to be descended from 'the rulers of Matsya Désa' and bear the title of 'chiefs of Vaddádi'; that Vaddádi (just south of Mádgole) is locally derived from Odda-Vádi, meaning 'the beginning of the Uriya land'; and that in the country round Mádgole legends are still recounted of a line of local Golla chieftains who gave their name to Golgonda and built the forts of which traces still survive in those parts.

Decline of the Gangas, 1434.

The Simháchalam temple contains inscriptions of several of the later Ganga kings, but few details regarding them survive. In 1267–68 one of them, Narasimha I, built the central shrine, mukhamandapam, nátyamandapam and enclosing arcade of that temple (see p. 324) in black stone. Their power, however, was on the wane. Narasimha I and two of his successors are mentioned as having had to resist attacks from the Muhammadans of Bengal and Delhi. Firoz Shah of Delhi (1351–88) invaded Orissa; other Musalman raids into that country took place ; the Reddi kings of Kondavídu in Guntúr district penetrated to Simháchalam (where stands an inscription of one of them dated 1385–86) ; and on the death of the Ganga king Bánudéva IV, his minister usurped the throne and in 1434–35 founded the Gajapati ('lords of elephants') dynasty of Orissa under the title of Pratápa Kapilésvara.

The Gajapatis of Orissa.

His capital was at Cuttack, and he expanded his dominions until they stretched from the Ganges to the Kistna. His whole reign was spent in warring with the Hindu kings of Vijayanagar in the Bellary district, who by now were extremely powerful in the south, or with the Musalman Báhmani dynasty of the Deccan.

His son Purushóttama reigned from 1469–70 to 1496–97. He is declared to have conquered Vijayanagar, to have brought thence a jewelled throne which he presented to the Puri temple and to have led an expedition against Conjeeveram.

In the time of his successor, Pratápa Rudra (1496–97 to about 1539–40), Orissa was raided by the Bengal Musalmans, who sacked Puri and destroyed many temples.

Defeated by Krishna Déva of Vijayanagar, 1515.

Pratápa Rudra also suffered reverses at the hands of the Vijayanagar king Krishna Déva, the greatest of his line. In 1515 that monarch seized Udayagiri in Nellore, Kondavídu (taking prisoner Pratápa Rudra's son), Kondapalli in Kistna, Rajahmundry and other fortresses, halted at Simhádri (Simháchalam) and set up the pillar of victory at Potnúru referred to in the account of that place on p. 230 below. The Simháchalam

CHAP. II. EARLY HISTORY.

temple still contains inscriptions recounting his successes and relating how he and his queens presented the god with a necklace of 991 pearls and other costly gifts. A picturesque account of this expedition by the Portuguese chronicler Nuniz will be found in Mr. R. Sewell's *A Forgotten Empire (Vijayanagar)* [1] and this states that, furious with the hesitating tactics of Pratápa Rudra, Krishna Déva Ráya caused an inscription to be cut in the temple [2] saying : 'Perhaps when these letters are decayed, the king of Orya (Orissa) will give battle to the king of Bisnaga (Vijayanagar). If the king of Orya erases them, his wife shall be given to the smiths who shoe the horses of the king of Bisnaga.' If this insulting threat was really ever inscribed, it is not likely to have been allowed to remain on record a moment after it could be safely deleted, and it is not now to be found at Simháchalam. The war ended in the humiliation of Pratápa Rudra, who was forced to make a treaty with the conqueror and give him his daughter in marriage, but Krishna Déva (perhaps in a fear of a flank attack from the Musalmans of the Deccan) forebore to hold the country permanently and retired to the south.

End of the dynasty, 1541.

Of Pratápa Rudra's sons, two reigned one after the other for a short period but were murdered by a minister named Góvinda Déva, who became king about 1541 and ruled for seven years. Three of this man's sons held the kingdom until 1559–60, when Mukunda Harichandana, a Telugu by birth, raised a revolt, had two of them assassinated, and seized the throne. He reigned till about 1568, when his territories were seized by the Musalman king of Golconda.[3] This ruler was one of the confederacy of Musalman kings of the Deccan who had overthrown Vijayanagar at the great battle of Talikóta three years before, and he had risen to great power in consequence.

MUHAMMADAN PERIOD, 1568.

The kings of Golconda were nominally subject to the Mughal emperors at Delhi, but they paid them little real allegiance at any time and eventually became virtually independent. Few details of their rule survive. Their chief local officer was the

[1] Swan Sonnenschein, 1900.

[2] Nuniz says the temple was at 'Symamdary' and Mr. Sewell identifies this with Rajahmundry, supposing that the first syllable has been accidentally dropped, perhaps by the copyist. But Nuniz says that Symamdary was a 'hundred leagues' from Kondapalli, which suits Simháchalam better, and 'Simhádri' is still in use as a form of 'Simháchalam'. Nuniz says the place was a very large city, and he seems to refer thereby to Potnúru, which according to current tradition once extended as far as Bhógapuram, nine miles to the east, which was the quarter where its dancing girls (*bhógam*) resided.

[3] Babu Man Mohan Chakravarti's paper in J. A. S. B., lxix, pt. 1, No. 2. This is the authority for several other statements in this section.

CHAP. II. MUHAMMADAN PERIOD.

Faujdar of Chicacole, who was in charge of Ganjám and Vizagapatam. He seems to have governed through local chiefs or zamindars, to whom the collection of the revenue of the various divisions of the country was delegated on a commission of ten per cent. (see p. 165) and who were expected to keep their charges quiet. Two of these chiefs were the ancestors of the present Mahárája of Bobbili and Rája of Vizianagram, who entered the district in the train of Shér Muhammad Khán (name-father of Shérmuhammadpuram near Chicacole), who was Faujdar in 1652. The Muhammadan sway seems to have been weak, and revolts of the zamindars were common.

Aurangzeb overthrows Golconda, 1687.

In 1686 Aurangzeb, the emperor of Delhi, marched down to reduce the south to obedience; and by the next year he had wiped the kingdom of Golconda out of existence and brought the whole country under his direct rule. He appointed to the charge of it an officer called the Subadar of the Deccan and afterwards commonly known as the Nizam of Hyderabad under whom were a number of local subordinates in immediate control of the various smaller divisions of territory. The five 'Northern Circars' of Guntúr, Kondapalli, Ellore, Rajahmundry and Chicacole had Masulipatam for their chief town, and the northernmost of them, Chicacole, which included the present districts of Ganjám and Vizagapatam, continued to be ruled in the same manner as before by a Faujdar residing at the town after which it was named. Revolts by the local Rájas went on as merrily as ever under his government.[1]

Meanwhile, in circumstances which will be related immediately, the English had effected a settlement at Vizagapatam town. The Dutch had likewise established a factory at Bimlipatam. The latter however (see p. 226) had no influence on the political destinies of the district and the former was of small importance until 1767; neither need therefore be further referred to for the present.

The Subadar of the Deccan becomes independent, 1724.

Aurangzeb died in 1707 and his death was followed by great disorder in his southern possessions. In 1724 the Subadar of the Deccan, though still continuing nominally subject to the authority of Delhi, made himself virtually independent and began appointing his own officers. His first Faujdar of Chicacole was the Anwar-ud-dín who afterwards became so famous in the wars of the Carnatic and is the ancestor of the present Prince of Arcot. His firm but kindly rule was gratefully remembered for many years afterwards.

[1] See the numerous instances given below in the account of the early fortunes of the English settlement at Vizagapatam.

CHAP. II. MUHAMMADAN PERIOD.

Cedes the Northern Circars to the French, 1753.

This Subadar of the Deccan died in 1748 and the French and English took opposite sides in the disputed succession which followed. The events of this struggle belong rather to the history of the southern districts of the Presidency than to that of Vizagapatam, and it is enough to mention here that eventually a French protégé, Salábat Jang, secured the post of Subadar, and that Bussy, the French general, obtained from him in 1753 the cession of four of the Northern Circars (not Guntúr) for the support of his troops. Masulipatam and the country adjacent had been already ceded to the French in 1750; and Bussy sent M. Moracin, the French officer in charge there, instructions to take possession of the new acquisitions.

Difficulties of the French thereafter.

The Faujdar of Chicacole, Jafar Ali, was extremely disinclined to give up his charge to the French, and he persuaded Gajapati Viziaráma Rázu, head of the Vizianagram family and the most powerful of the local renter-chieftains who had come into being during the Musalman rule, to join him in opposing M. Moracin's entry. The latter, however, seduced Viziaráma Rázu from this compact by promising to lease him the Rajahmundry and Chicacole Circars at a rate much below their value. Finding himself deserted, Jafar Ali called in the help of the Maráthas of Nagpur, who crossed the hills by the ghát at Páchipenta (under the guidance of the zamindar of that place); devastated the two Circars from end to end; plundered and burnt the Dutch factory at Bimlipatam (but spared the Vizagapatam settlement of the English, whose friendship Jafar Ali courted and who had encouraged him in his revolt); defeated Viziaráma Rázu near Vizianagram; fought an irregular action against the combined forces of that chief and M. Moracin at Tummapála near Anakápalle; and then suddenly decamped south, crossed the Gódávari by a ford they had discovered, and regained their own country with an immense booty. Having secured the loot, they troubled no further about Jafar Ali's aspirations, and that gentleman was obliged to submit.

In July 1754 Bussy went in person to Masulipatam and Rajahmundry, settled affairs in the Circars, and appointed one Ibráhím Khán as Faujdar of Chicacole. Soon afterwards, however, relations between him and the Subadar of the Deccan became strained, at last an open rupture occurred, and for several weeks in the summer of 1756 he was obliged to entrench himself against attack in the gardens of Charmál near Hyderabad. The authorities at Madras were only prevented from joining the Subadar against him by the necessity of sending every available

CHAP. II. MUHAMMADAN PERIOD.

man to Bengal to recover Calcutta and avenge the massacre of the Black Hole.

His officers in the Circars, Ibráhím Khán included, now disavowed his authority and refused to pay their tribute. Viziaráma Rázu was the only man there who had the foresight to stand by him.

'He ordered his agents at Hyderabad to assure M. Bussy of his fidelity and the regular payment of his tributes; and one night, when little expected and most wanted, a man came to Charmál, and, being permitted to speak in private with M. Bussy, delivered with the message of Viziaráma Rázu a sum of gold, as much as he could carry under his garments. It was sufficient for the present want, and the same man afterwards furnished more as necessary.' [1]

Bussy at length obtains possession, 1757.

Bussy was eventually relieved by reinforcements from Masulipatam and received back into the Subadar's favour; and at the end of 1756 he marched into the Circars to restore his fallen authority there.

Ibráhím Khán fled in terror at his approach; but Viziaráma Rázu, confident in the proofs of attachment he had given, went to meet him with a body of troops, belonging to himself and others of the local chiefs, which numbered 10,000 men. He was graciously received and employed the favour in which he stood to gratify a long-standing animosity against his bitterest enemy, the chief of Bobbili. He persuaded Bussy that Bobbili was contumacious and must be repressed; and Bussy at length agreed to attack that chief's fort. The details of the horrible tragedy which followed are given on pp.237-241 below. Bobbili defended himself to the utmost, and then, when he saw that further resistance was hopeless, had all the women and children in his fort put to death and, with the remnant of his garrison, died fighting to the last. Three nights afterwards, Viziaráma Rázu was killed in his tent by some of Bobbili's adherents. He was succeeded by Ananda Rázu, the son of a first cousin.

From Bobbili, Bussy marched on into Ganjám, receiving the submission of the various local chiefs and zamindars as he went; sent a body of troops from Masulipatam to capture the English factories at Injaram, Madapollam and Bandamúrlanka in Gódávari (all of which surrendered at once); and then turned back to attack the Vizagapatam settlement in person. This (see p. 44 below) was in a wretched state of defence and also surrendered immediately. Bussy proceeded southwards again and returned eventually to Hyderabad. In July of the next year (1758) he

[1] Orme (Madras, 1861), ii, 103.

CHAP. II. MUHAMMADAN PERIOD.

received an unwise summons from Lally, the new Governor of the French at Pondicherry, to join him, with all the troops he could spare, to help in the war in the Carnatic and the siege of Madras.

Forde's expedition against the French, 1758.

Ananda Rázu, the new head of the Vizianagram family, 'dissatisfied with the arrangements made by M. Bussy on the death of his predecessor, had waited,' says Orme, 'an opportunity to take his revenge.' As soon as Bussy was summoned south, he captured Vizagapatam from the French garrison which was holding it, sent news of the event to Madras, and invited the English there to join him in expelling the French from the Northern Circars. The Madras authorities, however, had their hands too full with affairs in the south, so Ananda Rázu repeated his offer to the English in Bengal. 'The project seemed delusive or chimerical to all but Clive,' but eventually, in spite of the protests of the other Members of the Calcutta Council, Colonel Forde was despatched by Clive to Vizagapatam by sea with a force of 500 Europeans (including artillery), 2,000 sepoys and 100 lascars, and arrived on the 20th October 1758. Mr. John Johnstone had been sent in advance to arrange matters with Ananda Rázu and had been put in possession of the Vizagapatam factory on the 12th September. The Madras authorities sent up Mr. Andrews and several assistants to help him in re-establishing the settlement and also despatched an officer to act under Colonel Forde.

The force moved out of Vizagapatam on the 1st November, and on the third joined Ananda Rázu at Kasimkóta. Progress southwards was at first very slow. Orme says—

'Various excuses were employed by the Rajah to extenuate this delay; but the real cause was his repugnance to furnish the money which Colonel Forde demanded, who was not a little offended at his evasions. Mr. Andrews, who, having been chief of Madapollam, had long been personally known to the Rajah, adjusted their differences by a treaty, which stipulated that all plunder should be equally divided; that all the countries which might be conquered should be delivered to the Rajah, who was to collect the revenues; but that the seaports and towns at the mouths of the rivers should belong to the company, with the revenues of the districts annexed to them; that no treaty for the disposal or restitution, whether of the Rajah's or the English possessions, should be made without the consent of both parties; that the Rajah should supply 50,000 rupees a month for the expences of the army, and 6,000, to commence from their arrival at Vizagapatam, for the particular expences of the officers. He held out likewise other proposals of future alliance, which he had not yet authority to ratify.'

CHAP. II. MUHAMMADAN PERIOD.

The united forces now moved south in earnest. The Rája's levies, however, were of the wretchedest, consisting of '500 paltry horse and 5,000 foot, some with awkward fire-arms, the rest with pikes and bows: but he had collected 40 Europeans, who managed four field-pieces under the command of Mr. Bristol; besides which his own troops had some useless cannon.'

The French expelled from the Circars.

On the 9th December, near Condore, about 35 miles east-north-east of Rajahmundry, an action was fought with the French which ranks as one of the decisive battles of India and in which the French were utterly routed. The day was won by the European part of Colonel Forde's force. His sepoys broke and ran at an early stage, and even when the enemy was in full retreat the Rája's horse 'could not be prevailed upon to quit the shelter of a large tank, at this time dry, in which they, his foot, and himself in the midst of them, had remained cowering from the beginning of the action.'[1] Forde pushed on to Rajahmundry next day without the Rája's rabble, and shortly afterwards took Masulipatam by a most brilliant assault. Salábat Jang, the Subadar of the Deccan, who had advanced within fifteen miles of the place to assist his protégés the French, changed sides at once and on the 14th May 1759 made a treaty[2] with the English, granting them the country round Masulipatam, renouncing all friendship with the French, and prohibiting the latter from ever again settling in the Northern Circars.

Except the tract then ceded to the Company, the rest of the Northern Circars thus fell once more with dramatic suddenness under the sway of the Subadar of the Deccan. His rule, however, extended to it in little but name. 'For seven succeeding years, the completest anarchy recorded in the history of Hindustan prevailed over all the Northern Circars. The forms, nay even the remembrance, of civil government seemed to be wholly lost.'[3]

The Circars ceded to the English, 1765.

In 1765 Clive obtained from the Mughal emperor at Delhi a firman granting the Company the five Northern Circars. This recites the cession of the country to the French by the Subadar Salábat Jang without authority from Delhi, and the expulsion of the French therefrom by the emperor's faithful sepoy sirdars, the English Company, and then states that in consideration of the fidelity and good wishes of the said Company 'we have, from our

[1] Orme, ii, 381.

[2] The text of it is given in Aitchison's *Treaties, etc.* (1892), viii, 278.

[3] Grant's *Political Survey of the Northern Circars*, forming Appendix B to the *Fifth Report on the Affairs of the East India Company, 1812* (Madras, 1883), p. 146.

[4] Aitchison's *Treaties, etc.*, viii, 278.

CHAP. II. MUHAMMADAN PERIOD.

throne, the basis of the world, given them the aforementioned Circars, by way of enam or free gift without the least participation of any person whatever in the same.'

The Subadar, however, was in no way pleased at this cession of territory which he regarded as his own, and threatened to retaliate by an irruption into the Carnatic. In November 1766 a treaty [1] was accordingly hastily and weakly concluded with him by which the English agreed to pay nine lakhs annually for the territory that had already been granted them as a free gift. Soon afterwards the Subadar was defeated by the English in one or two actions, became more accommodating in consequence, and in February 1768 agreed to a new treaty by which the tribute was reduced. [2] The new acquisitions were at first governed from Masulipatam, but in 1769 Mr. John Andrews, then Chief at that place, was sent to Vizagapatam and made the first Chief in Council of that district.

ENGLISH PERIOD.

We may now go back and shortly trace the fortunes of the English settlement at Vizagapatam from its inception until it thus became the capital of the district.

Foundation of Vizagapatam settlement, 1682.

The settlement was founded in 1682. [3] In February of that year the Directors wrote to Fort St. George that an 'interloper (unauthorized trader) was designed for Metchlepatam or Gyngerlee' (*i.e.*, Masulipatam or Vizagapatam [4]) and left it to the Madras authorities to decide whether a factory should not be established at the latter place. The Madras Consultations of the 1st August 1682 say that 'The Comp^a having resolved to make some Investments this year at Gingerly & given order to ye Agent &c^a to send down some p̄sons to further the same, as likewise to hinder and defeat any Interlopers that shall come there, 'tis

[1] Aitchison's *Treaties, etc.*, viii, 280.

[2] This reduced amount continued to be paid until 1823, when the claim was extinguished by the disbursement of a large lump sum.

[3] Sir George Birdwood's *Report on the old records of the India Office* (W. H. Allen, 1891) twice (pp. 89 and 222) states that the date was 1668, but does not quote the records on which the statement is based. A personal search by the present writer (under expert guidance) among the India Office records failed to discover any papers about Vizagapatam of an earlier date than 1684. The 'interloper' Thomas Bowrey, who traded in these parts between 1669 and 1679, makes no mention of the settlement in his *Countries round the Bay of Bengal* (Hakluyt Society, Second Series, Vol. XII, 1905); nor is it referred to in the Fort St. George records of 1670-1681; indeed a list of factories in the latter year specifically says that Masulipatam and Madapollam were the only subordinate stations on this coast. If, therefore, a settlement was in fact made in 1668, it must have been almost immediately abolished again.

[4] Mr. Pringle's *Diary and Consultation book of the Agent Governor and Council of Fort St. George, 1684* (Madras Government Press, 1895), 170.

CHAP. II. ENGLISH PERIOD.

resolved that Mr. George Ramsden doe proceed for this year as Chiefe [1] there,' his Second in Council being one Clément du Jardin. Thus it is clear that it was largely fear of the rivalry of the ubiquitous interloper which led the Company to first settle in Vizagapatam. Thirteen days later the first official letter was sent from Fort St. George to 'Vizagapatam' and thereafter correspondence with the factory appears regularly in the records.

Its early progress.

Messrs. Ramsden and du Jardin did not let the grass grow under their feet. In October of the same year they wrote that in spite of the bitter hostility of the Dutch at Bimlipatam they had made a respectable investment; had obtained a cowle from the 'Seir Lascar' (apparently the same as the Faujdar) of Chicacole giving them liberties 'throughout the Carlingae (Kalinga) country farr greater than ever was granted to the Dutch, notwithstanding they have bin settled in these p̄ts for these 20 years, which is a very great heartburning'; had arranged to bribe the Kasimkóta chief ('a very powerful p̄son') not to molest their customers; had patched up for their quarters an old house standing on the piece of ground given them by the Seer Lascar; had engaged six 'Rashboots' (Rájputs) as a guard; and had searched in vain for interlopers but in accordance with orders had hung the King's proclamation and the printed rules and orders concerning those gentry round their dyeing room, 'wch God knows is scarce bigg enough to hould them.' They earnestly beg a reconsideration of orders which had been passed directing them to go to Masulipatam at the end of the year, pointing out how disappointed the Seer Lascar would be, and how triumphant the Dutch; and this request was evidently granted.

The next year, however, these two pioneers fell out; and Ramsden was temporarily suspended and du Jardin recalled. The latter was eventually dismissed, in spite of the protests of Fort St. George, by the Directors, who pronounced him 'a huffing, swaggering, ignorant, avaritious, prodigall person'; but his subsequent doings in Sumatra [2] showed that he was of the stuff of which successful merchant adventurers are made, being endowed with restless energy, a clear head, and a way with natives that carried them with him. As the Madras Council sorrowfully put it when he died in Sumatra in 1687, he was 'a fitting active man among those people.'

The cowle granted in 1685.

The records of 1684 show that the settlement was still very small then, the monthly expenses being only 100 pagodas (Rs. 350),

[1] A list of the Chiefs in Council and Collectors is appended to Chapter XI below.

[2] See Mr. Pringle's *Diary and Consultation book, etc., 1685*, Introd., xvi.

CHAP. II. ENGLISH PERIOD.

but that it possessed the right to collect dues in the town. The annual rent paid to the Seer Lascar was Rs. 4,500. At the end of that year the Madras Council, desirous of obtaining less limited privileges, resolved to send the new Chief (Mr. Browne) to the Seer Lascar with a big retinue hired for the purpose.

The mission was crowned with success. After having presented 'His Excellency' with many gifts, including a silver trunk, a case of spirits, fifteen maunds of sandalwood, a chest of rosewater, and some scarlet cloth and gunpowder, the Chief obtained a new cowle which exempted the Company's goods from land customs, granted privileges over Vizagapatam and permission to build a factory there, and brought the settlement into a position 'as good as we injoy in any part of India.'[1] In 1685 the friendship with the Seer Lascar was further cemented by a present of saltpetre, powder and lead, which he earnestly desired owing to the imminence of a war with his northern neighbours, but which the Dutch at Bimlipatam had steadfastly refused to supply. In July 1688 Mr. Browne was charged with private trading, resigned in consequence, and was succeeded by Mr. John Stables.

The factory sacked by the Musalmans, 1689.

In 1689 the footing in the country which had been won with such determination was suddenly lost. The Company fell out with Aurangzeb, the Mughal emperor at Delhi, and the latter issued orders that the English should be driven from his dominions and all their property seized. On the 13th September, therefore, the Seer Lascar sent his 'Rashwar' (Telugu, Rájáváru, the honorific form of 'Rája') to the Vizagapatam factory—

'In order to seize and bring away the English and all their concerns. The said Rashwar with his forces coming nigh the town in the night, where he had pitched his Tent, etc., about nine did surround the Factory with his men, and acquainted the English with the Seer Lascar's orders. To which was replied, they could not go up without their Master's orders. Then, as the first Rashwar was taking the Chief by the hand to pluck him out of the house, Mr. Hall fires his blunderbuss and kills three of their men; upon which they murdered Mr. Stables, Mr. Hall and Mr. Croke, taking the rest prisoners, and seizing upon all the Right Honourable Company's Concerns.'[2]

Mr. Holcombe becomes Chief, 1692.

In 1690, however, peace was made with Aurangzeb[3] and the Seer Lascar released his prisoners and restored the Company's

[1] *Vizagapatam Consultations* in the India Office, November 10, 1684.

[2] Talboys Wheeler's *Madras in the Olden Time* (Madras, 1861), i, 214.

[3] See the cowles granted by his general Zulfikar Khán which are quoted by Talboys Wheeler, i, 245–7.

CHAP. II. ENGLISH PERIOD.

property. Mr. Dubois was sent to set the factory on its legs again. During his time the place was attacked and looted by 'thieves and poligars,' and the Company accordingly asked leave to fortify it. The new Chief was afterwards found guilty of frauds and errors and 'severall considerable wrongs done to the Hon. Company,' and in 1692 was dismissed and replaced by Mr. Simon Holcombe with Mr. Charles Barwell as Second in Council.

They had rather a stormy entry. They arrived by sea and were met at the landing-place by Mr. Dubois and others and conducted to the factory. On their entering this, one of the peons spat in the new Chief's face and abused him in language 'not fit to be mentioned;' whereon swords were drawn and some blood was spilt. Mr. Dubois and the others, being asked for their books and registers, brought Mr. Holcombe only 'a few torne old dirty papers, saying ye rest were lost and consumed by ye Mogull's people in the late unhappy times.'[1] Mutual recriminations and other unpleasantnesses continue subsequently to fill many pages of the records. The head of the weavers also became contumacious, declining to sign his contracts when given the usual 'tasheriffs' (presents) and demanding in addition a coat with gold buttons and a gold bracelet. These latter were at length promised, as were also 'all further ceremonies of Hon^r, as fireing off Guns &ca. and being carried to his house in ye Comp^a Pallankeen with ye Musick &ca. attendance.'

Hidden treasure in Bobbili.

The records of 1693 [2] mention a curious incident :—

'Rangarow, a neighbouring Raja [clearly the Rája of Bobbili], upon clearing a Tank in his Country found a vast Treasure buried in earthen pots with a small p^s of Copper in each pot mentioning w^t contained therein and by whom buried, by wch it appeared to belong to ye ffamily of ye Sumberdues [the Rájas of Jeypore] and to be buried by ye great grandfather of y present Raja, wch has made a great contest between ye neighbouring Rajas and impeeded all commerce in those parts, Rangarow claiming itt because took up in his Governm^t and Sumberdue asserting a right to it by ye Copper plates wch specifie it to be buried by his ancestors who formerly had ye Governm^t of those parts. Y^e event we must leave to time, but 'tis conjectured and not without reason y^t upon ye Sier Lascar's return from Metchlepatam he will soon decide ye matter to ye dissatisfaction of both Parties by condemning itt all to ye king's and his own ꝑticular Treasure.'

[1] *Vizagapatam Consultations* at the India Office, 15th July 1692.
[2] *Ibid.*, December 6th, 1693.

Local disturbances, 1694.

In 1694 the Seer Lascar had his hands full with revolts by the local Rájas, among whom the Rája of 'Potnore' (Potnúru) and 'Sumba Deo' (the Rája of Jeypore) were prominent, and at length had to 'condescend to dishonourable terms.' The malcontents had made two attempts to plunder the factory at Vizagapatam (and also the Dutch settlement at Bimlipatam) and Mr. Holcombe accordingly seized the opportunity to begin fortifications there at the expense of the inhabitants. The Seer Lascar approved at the time, but afterwards demanded the destruction of the new walls. The Chief, however, stood firm and they were not touched.

Extravagance at Vizagapatam.

This Chief, who was a man of good birth, had a 'lavish way of living and fond affectation of appearing great in the eyes of the Country Government,' to which the Directors strongly objected. They said, 'The extravigantcy of Vizagapatam under the managm:t of Mr. Holcombe by theire last books, is insufferable, for 3 or 4 ffactors at most to spend 3902 Pagodas in one yeare whereof 1034 is for their servants. Wee know no necessity for their two horses and them of so great a vallue as 250 Pagodas; they must be better Husbands, and keep within bounds, and not give 40 Pagodas for a Saddle, etc.' The Directors strictly limited the Chief in future to 600 pagodas (Rs. 2,100) per annum to defray the charges of dyers, factors, provisions, servants' wages, stores and garden, exclusive of 100 pagodas for presents.

More local disturbances, 1697.

In October 1697 Jeypore ('Somberdu') and other Rájas again revolted 'and took and slew the Seer Lascar and the greatest part of his army.' His successor ('Rustundill Khan') was severe to all the friends of his predecessor, and the Madras authorities warned the Vizagapatam Council not to proceed, without his express approval, with certain additional fortifications which had been begun, but to level their foundations with the ground and cover them up until a more favourable opportunity. They also ordered the Chief to hold himself in readiness to abandon the factory immediately if the Seer Lascar should attack it, instructing him to embark everything he could and to leave a notice on the factory gate setting out the cost of the buildings, the reason for quitting them, and the items of property still remaining in them. These timid orders were partly due to the fear that resistance in Vizagapatam might light a general conflagration in the south, partly to the decline in the trade at Vizagapatam which had followed the numerous internal commotions there, and partly to the impossibility of carrying on the factory within the limit of expenditure which the Directors had prescribed and to which, in spite of protests from Madras, they for long vehemently adhered.

CHAP. II. ENGLISH PERIOD.

Brighter prospects, 1698.

In May 1698, however, another and friendlier Seer Lascar ('Fakera' or 'Fakerla Khan,' apparently Fakír-ulláh Khán) was appointed, and the prospect looked brighter. In February 1700 this potentate 'did our Chief great Honour, Setting him on his own Pallakeen, comeing to his house to Vissit him, and giveing him a rich suite of cloths, an Elephant, and two Horses, and making all demonstrations of love possible.' In the next month he was succeeded by a new Seer Lascar who tried to impose new taxes and thus kindled yet another revolt by the local Rájas. The latter defeated his troops on every occasion, burnt and plundered most of the country, shut the Seer Lascar up in Chicacole and threatened to attack that place, captured Kasimkóta and plundered the Dutch at Bimlipatam. Peace at length ensued and the people returned from the woods in which they had taken refuge; but in 1702 the flames broke out again and the Faujdar had to pay the Rájas a lakh of rupees to keep quiet.

'Rustundill Khan' was soon afterwards reappointed as Seer Lascar and showed symptoms of again giving the factory trouble. The Madras authorities said nothing about withdrawal this time, but sent to Vizagapatam twelve Portuguese and six English soldiers and fifteen candies of powder. The Seer Lascar came and camped in the Company's garden at Vizagapatam with 40,000 men and the factory had an anxious time. But at length judicious presents softened his heart and he granted a cowle for the place. Mr. Holcombe died in May 1705, after having been Chief for thirteen exciting years, and lies buried in the old cemetery at Vizagapatam which is usually erroneously called 'the Dutch cemetery.' He was succeeded by Mr. Stephen Trewen, who died within a year and was followed by Mr. Francis Hastings, afterwards provisional Governor of Madras.

Vizagapatam besieged, 1711.

In this Chief's time serious trouble occurred with Fakír-ulláh Khán, who had been reappointed Seer Lascar. About 1698 Mr. Holcombe had rashly borrowed 44,000 pagodas of Fakír-ulláh, then Seer Lascar, and lent it to Ananda Rázu, chief of Vizianagram, and Páyaka Rao of Páyakaraopéta (p. 312). At the time of his death (notwithstanding several threatening letters from Fakír-ulláh, who warned him that his money was 'like bread as hard as iron, and so not easily digested' and would be recovered by fair means or foul), Mr. Holcombe still owed 6,500 pagodas of the principal, while with interest the debt amounted to over 20,000 pagodas. Mr. Holcombe had still more rashly affixed the Company's seal to his bond, and Fakír-ulláh accordingly called upon the Chief and Council to pay up the amount.

They naturally hesitated about doing so, and unwisely further exasperated Fakír-ulláh by acknowledging the claims of a rival candidate for the post of Seer Lascar. At length, on the 8th December 1710, Fakír-ulláh came to enforce his demand and encamped on the sand-hill north of the town with 7,000 foot and 800 horse (other accounts say 3,500 and 500, respectively) and the next night fired into the factory's outposts. The garrison, however, returned the fire and obliged the enemy to turn the siege into a blockade.

Captain Hamilton, who was there at the time, gives a description [1] of the defence. The garrison at first numbered only nineteen Europeans, 20 topasses (Portuguese) and 280 natives, most of the last of whom were fishermen. They fortified the low rocks between the sand-hills and the factory, drew Captain Hamilton's ship within pistol-shot of the shore, placed eight minion guns to scour the sands in case the enemy tried to come that way, and held out for six weeks until reinforcements from Madras, which included twelve guns and some soldiers under Lieutenant Dixon (afterwards killed during the operations), at length arrived. Captain Hamilton then left, but the blockade went on for three months more until the end of April. Fakír-ulláh erected new batteries on the sand-hill and the Dolphin's Nose headland (which even then went by that name) and the factory sent urgent appeals to Madras for lead and stores to maintain the defence and for 'more shells for our mortar, and if possible another mortar and shells, and also shells for the cohorns and great and small granados, with shot, iron and stone of all sorts and sizes, and for God's sake fresh provisions.' At last the Company paid the 20,000 pagodas demanded and the siege was raised.

Captain Hamilton says, however, that the Seer Lascar tried soon afterwards to take the place by surprise :—

'He came into the Town one Day with 100 Horse, and some Foot, without advertising of his coming, as was usual, at the Town-gate, and before the Chief could have Notice, he was got into the Factory, with twenty or thirty of his Attendants. The Alarm being given, a resolute bold young Gentleman, a Factor in the Company's Service, called Mr. Richard Horden, came running down Stairs, with his Fuzee in his Hand, and his Bayonet screwed on its Muzzle and, presenting it to the Nabob's Breast, told him in the Gentow Language, (which he was Master of) that the Nabob was welcome, but if any of his Attendants offered the least Incivility, his Life should answer for it.

[1] *New account of the East Indies* (1744), i, 375–81.

CHAP. II. ENGLISH PERIOD.

The Nabob was surprisingly astonished at the Resolution and Bravery of the young Gentleman, and sat down to consider a little, Mr. Horden keeping the Muzzle of his Piece still at his Breast, and one of the Nabob's Servants standing all the while behind Mr. Horden with a Dagger's Point close to his Back. So they had a Conference of half an Hour long, in those above mentioned Postures, and then the Nabob thought fit to be gone again, full of wonder and Admiration of so daring a Courage.'

The defences strengthened.

At this time the Company were paying the Musalman government Rs. 4,862 annually for the town and the other villages rented from them and received in return the privileges of making and selling salt, arrack, betel-leaf, tobacco and other commodities, and the right to collect land and sea customs. The small factory at Injaram, on the Gódávari coast, was subordinate to Vizagapatam, and the Second in Council at one time resided there.

The records of the next few years are full of accounts of the fighting between the Faujdar (now Habid Khán, Fakír-ulláh's rival) and the local Rájas here and in Ganjám. In 1712 Ananda Rázu of Vizianagram with 10,000 men was actually plundering and destroying without hindrance within sight of Chicacole. These constant alarms not only prevented the reduction of the garrison collected to repulse Fakír-ulláh, but on the contrary led to its increase and to the construction of more defences. No plan of these survives, but the records speak of the flagstaff, southern and western bastions, northern point, and curtain facing the river (all of which were built of stone), the eastern curtain facing the sea, the fort gate and mainguard, and the back gate. By 1726 the garrison numbered 85 men, and outworks (see the map facing p. 44) had been built to protect the native town. In 1729 further disturbances resulted in the despatch from Madras of a sergeant and some more guns.

Waltair first occupied, 1727.

In 1727 the first move was made towards Waltair, which had long been included in the cowles, the cloth-washers and their families being established there in consequence of the discovery of 'a vein of very good water which cured and whitened cloth much better than the washermen's tanks formerly made use of.' In 1731 (and again in 1753) the question of the desirability of coining copper dubs at Vizagapatam was raised, but the Seer Lascar refused the necessary permission and no mint appears to have been established. In 1739 a building to the west of the fort was bought as a 'Garden House' for the reception of guests. It was irretrievably damaged by the great flood of 1752. Frequent references also occur throughout the early records to the Company's mango garden somewhere near by, which was a favourite place for strangers to camp in. It was apparently near the present Dábá Gardens.

Further strengthening of the defences, 1741–45.

In 1741 the Chief (Mr. John Stratton) earnestly invited the attention of the Madras authorities to the necessity of strengthening the Vizagapatam defences. He said—

> 'The Buildings and Fortifications at this Place are in so ruinous a Condition that in case any Disturbances should happen here we are but ill provided to resist only a small Body of Men. It's true we have 61 pieces of Ordnance mounted in this Garrison, but the carriages are so farr fallen to decay that they will not bear 2ce firing before they must fall to pieces. We are also in great want of fire Arms for the Military, for those now in use have been here so long that they are not to be depended on.'

The next year a threatened inroad of Maráthas led him to entertain 100 extra peons and a like number of lascars and to ask for 75 barrels of powder and more men and arms. The whole coast was in a panic, the Dutch at Masulipatam, Cocanada and Bimlipatam and the French at Yanam having embarked all their property ready for instant flight, the small factories at Injaram and Uppáda making similar preparations, and the people of the country 'retiring to the hills with all expedition possible.' Madras sent up 21 Europeans, fifteen barrels of powder and five candies of lead, and the Chief set to work to make 'a Palisado of Timbers from Flag Staff Hill to the sea-side, which is 216 yards.' This flagstaff hill, on which there was then a battery, is apparently the low outcrop of dark rock which stands in the quarter of Vizagapatam still known as Buruzupéta, or 'Bastion hamlet,' and which was afterwards called 'the Black Rock.' It was then (see the map facing p. 44) quite outside the town. Mr. Stratton, who was clearly a Chief of determination, was confident of being able to beat off the enemy, and the local Rájas all sent their families to Vizagapatam for protection.

The trouble, however, blew over temporarily and the only real work done on the defences seems to have been the construction of 'Benyon's battery and Middle Point, with a very small addition to Martin's Point.' The disappearance of all the plans of this period from the Madras records renders it impossible to identify these posts with certainty, but the map seems to show that Benyon's battery was the work on the Black Rock already referred to, the Mettah gate the opening on the low ground west of it, Middle Point the small bastion next west again and Martin's Point the outwork adjoining on the edge of the backwater just north of the town. They were shortly afterwards declared to be

CHAP. II. ENGLISH PERIOD.

of little service. It was observed that 'instead thereof if only a wall had been run from Martin's Point to the Mettah gate, another across the rock upon which Benyon's battery is built, and the platforms on each side the Mettah gate raised a proper heighth, the town would have been equally as secure.'

In 1744 the Marátha panic revived and estimates were submitted for 'building and repairing sundry fortifications,' namely, 'the great battery by the seaside' (apparently the work the ruins of which still stand on the Dolphin's Nose and which is usually wrongly called 'the Dutch battery'), 'the small battery fronting the fort, the powder magazine and the guardhouse.' It was urged that the houses between the fort and the sea should be pulled down and a battery put there to command the roadstead; that a battery which had already been begun with guns sent the year before from Madras on the Black Rock should be completed so as to secure 'that part of the Mangoe Garden which lies behind a rising ground called the Sand Hill, which overlooks the town, and what the country government constantly possess themselves of upon the least Dispute with Us;' and that the magazine should be removed from the side of the backwater (or 'river,' as it was then called), which was too damp a site and too far from the fort.

The declaration of war with the French in this same year lent additional weight to these requests, and in 1745 it was ordered that a battery should be put up in front of the fort and that the 'small one near the bar' (? the 'Dutch' battery) should be repaired. Further work was stopped in 1750 on the ground that the well-known Engineer Mr. Benjamin Robins was being sent out by the Directors to examine all fortifications, and that it would be best to await his advice.

The place surrenders to Bussy, 1757.

In 1753, as already narrated, the Circars were ceded to the French; and at the end of 1756 Bussy, free at last from other embarrassments, marched into them to restore his shaken authority, seized Bobbili, quieted Ganjám, captured Injaram and the other English factories in Gódávari and then marched in person against Vizagapatam. He reached that place on 24th June 1757, with the large force of 600 Europeans, 6,000 sepoys and 30 pieces of cannon.[1]

Orme gives the following disparaging account of the then fortifications of the place, illustrated by the interesting map here

[1] Cambridge's *War in India* (London, 1761), 103.

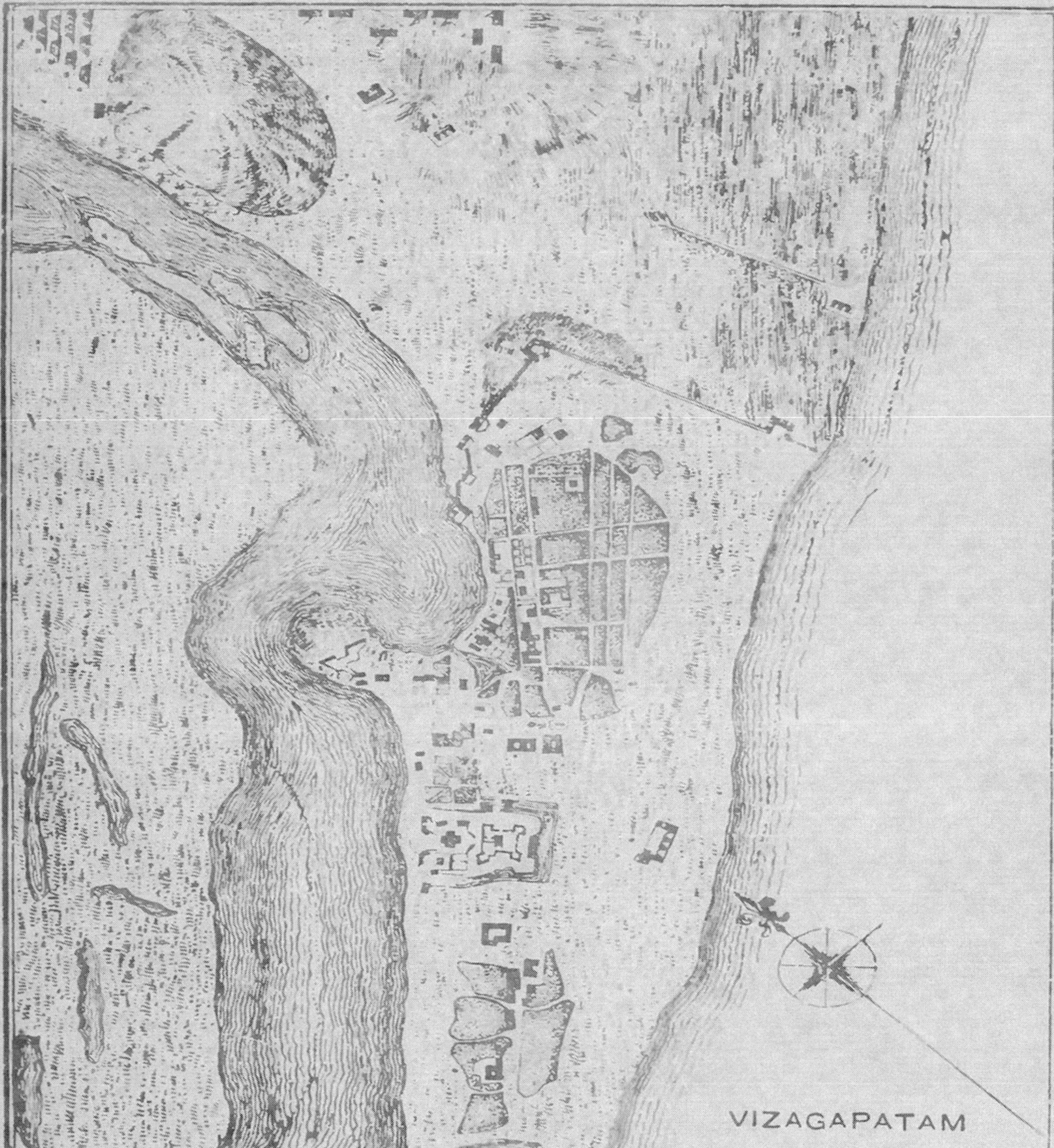

VIZAGAPATAM
IN 1758
(From Orme's History)

Reg. No. 123
Copies 500

reproduced which shows what immense changes have taken place in the town and backwater in the last century and a half:—

'A river coming from the north and turning short eastward to the sea, forms an arm of land, a mile and a half in length and 600 yards in breadth. Nearly in the middle of this ground stands the fort, of which the construction by repeated mistakes was become so absurd, that it was much less defensible than many of the ancient barons' castles of Europe. The face towards the river was choked by houses. A whole town lay within 300 yards to the north, a village at the same distance to the south, and several buildings on each of these sides stood much nearer the walls; towards the sea, the esplanade was clear, excepting a saluting battery, where a lodgment might be easily made; after many injudicious additions of works round the fort, which only made it worse, it was found necessary to throw up an entrenchment to the north, beyond the town, in the shoulder of the peninsula, quite across from the river to the sea, with a battery at each extremity, and another on a hillock near the center, but this was commanded by a sand-hill directly opposite, and within point-blank. The access across the river from the south was sufficiently secured by batteries, which commanded not only the passage, but the entrance of the river itself, through which all embarkations from the sea must gain the shore, as the surf prevents even a boat from landing on the beach: indeed the whole scheme of the defences seemed to have been calculated only to oppose the attempts of pirates and polygars. The garrison consisted of 150 excellent Europeans, and 300 Sepoys; the English families in the town were 50 persons.

On the same day that the van of Mr. Bussy's army appeared in sight, the Company's ship Marlborough anchored in the road, on board of which was the chief engineer of Madrass proceeding to Bengal. He landed, and having the next morning reviewed the works with Captain Charles Campbell, who commanded the troops, both gave their opinion that the extent could not be defended, even with a much greater force; and advised that all the Europeans should be immediately embarked, and the Sepoys, with two or three officers, left to make the best capitulation they could; but all the boat and fishermen had deserted in the night, and the wind blew so strong from the sea, that none but those accustomed could manage the boats over the bar, which that of the Marlborough carrying back the engineer experienced, being twice overset and a man drowned before she got out. At noon, cannon appeared on the sand hill; soon after, the main body of the enemy, and a summons to surrender; after two or three messages, the capitulation was signed at 11 at night. All the Europeans, whether troops or inhabitants, were to be prisoners of war; the sepoys and natives free to go where they liked; the Company's effects, capture; individuals, Mr. Bussy said, should have no reason to complain: he kept his word with the utmost liberality, resigning without discussion whatsoever property any one claimed as

CHAP. II. ENGLISH PERIOD.

his own. The Marlborough having anchored at the Dutch factory of Bimlipatam, 12 miles to the northward, he permitted the chief, Mr. Percival, Captain Campbell, and several others, to proceed in her to Bengal.'

Is recovered and becomes the capital of the district, 1769.

The subsequent history of the Vizagapatam settlement—its seizure from the French by the Rája of Vizianagram in 1758, the expulsion of that nation from the Circars by Colonel Forde's expedition in the next year, the eventual cession of the country to the English in 1765, and the elevation of Vizagapatam from the position of an isolated factory to that of the capital of a district in 1769—all these events have already been shortly sketched above.

Growth of the power of the Vizianagram Rája.

The twelve years of anarchy which followed Bussy's departure had enabled the Rája of Vizianagram to make himself more powerful than ever, and he was by far the most prominent person in the new territory. The Rája, Ananda Rázu, who had accompanied Forde's expedition died of small-pox at Rajahmundry shortly afterwards. He had no son, and the widow of his predecessor Viziaráma Rázu adopted Venkatapati Rázu, a boy of twelve and the second son of her husband's cousin Rámabhadra Rázu, and caused him to assume the name of Viziaráma Rázu by which he was afterwards so well known. This lad had a half brother, considerably older than himself, named Sítaráma Rázu, who (though the adoption of an eldest son is discouraged by Hindu law) cherished considerable resentment because of his apparent supersession. Owing to the new Rája's minority, all authority and state fell naturally into Sítaráma's hands and for very many years he succeeded in maintaining the position of superiority over his younger brother thus accorded him.

The two brothers were very powerful. They controlled almost all the district except the havíli land round about Vizagapatam, Kasimkóta and Chicacole (*i.e.*, the old demesne or household land of the sovereign, and tracts resumed by the Musalmans and appropriated to the support of their garrisons and establishments); in 1761 they also seized by force much of the estate of Parlákimedi in Ganjám; while later, it is said, they even possessed themselves temporarily of the Rajahmundry Circar. When the English came into possession of the country they persuaded the brothers to relinquish Parlákimedi and settled a peshkash of three lakhs annually on the rest of their estate. This latter included the indefinite rights in Jeypore referred to on p. 266 below.

Soon afterwards the various zamindars formed a strong confederacy to throw off the Vizianagram yoke. Sítaráma Rázu, however, was equal to the occasion. 'He persuaded the Chief and Council,' says Mr. Carmichael in his *District Manual* of Vizagapatam, 'to regard this as a challenge to their newly-constituted authority, and with the aid of the Company's troops he readily defeated the insurgents one after the other. At the close of the campaign, all the zamindars in the district but Ándra and Pálkonda, who had both kept aloof from the malcontents, were dispossessed, and their patrimony went to swell the rental of Vizianagram. The more considerable chiefs were admitted to 'towjees' or stipends; while men of less note, or who were objects of special resentment, were kept in fetters in the dungeons of the fort at Vizianagram.' The manner in which the Jeypore fort was captured about this time by the combined forces of the Company and Sítaráma is recounted on p. 267 below.

And of his díwán Sítaráma Rázu.

'In the year 1775,' continues Mr. Carmichael, 'a strong faction of the leading Rásavárs (Rájputs), who had their own advantage in view, coerced Sítaráma Rázu to retire from the prominent part he had heretofore taken in his brother's affairs. He agreed to resign the office of díwán and to retire to a private possession, on Viziaráma's covenanting to acknowledge his (Sítaráma's) son, Narasimha Gajapati Rázu, as his successor. To this, Viziaráma (who was then childless) readily acceded, it being a proviso that the title of the son of Sítaráma should not be preferred to that of any male issue that might afterwards be born to Viziaráma himself.'

In 1778, in the circumstances referred to on p. 167 below, the zamindars of the Northern Circars were summoned to Madras to have their peshkash settled, and the intriguing and ambitious Sítaráma succeeded by lavish bribery in obtaining, from the authorities there, orders reinstating him as díwán, instructing his brother the Rája to be reconciled to him, confirming the conditional succession of his son to the zamindari, and directing that all future leases of land in the estate should be made in this son's name.[1]

Sepoy mutiny at Vizagapatam, 1780.

On the 3rd October 1780 a serious mutiny occurred among the sepoys at Vizagapatam. To meet the invasion of the Carnatic by Haidar Ali of Mysore, the Government had ordered four companies of these troops to embark for Madras. The result is described as follows by the newswriter in Hickey's *Gazette*[2]:—

'We are informed that the Sepoy troops lately draughted at Vizacapatam, having all their arms, accoutraments, baggage, etc., ready to

[1] Second and Third Reports, Committee of Secrecy, 1781.

[2] Quoted in Mr. J. J. Cotton's *Inscriptions on Madras Tombs*. See also Wilson's *Hist. of Madras Army*, ii, 18, 19 and Mill's History, iv, 200.

CHAP. II. ENGLISH PERIOD.

embark on board the *Sartine* Frigue, and some other vessels then in that harbour in order to carry them to Madras, the day of their intended departure the Governor of Vizac invited all the military officers to dine with him and the Council. The troops were to embark that afternoon. The gentlemen made a cheerful repast, drank success to the British arms, and sat in company with all the tranquility of mind imaginable, but were soon alarmed by an uncommon noise. They sent some of their servants out to learn the cause, and was soon informed that the troops draughted for Madras had mutinied, and was endeavouring to force those Sepoys who were to remain behind in the barracks to join them, which they refused. This account soon brought their officers out, who instantly resumed their commands, and ordered them immediately to march down to the beach and go on board. This they refused one and all. The Grenadiers levelled their pieces, took aim, discharged a volley, and killed every officer on the spot. They took the Governor prisoner and all the civil servants, set free a French spy who had been confined there for some time, and placed him at their head, at the same time put the Governor and all the civil servants in the prison from whence they took the Frenchman. They plundered the Governor's house and factory of the treasure, plate and every other valuable that night, took the civillins out the next morning, tied them, and marched them off with them, with an intent to carry their prisoners to Hyder Ally, whom themselves intended to join. After they had marched several miles from Vizac, they unty'd the Governor Mr. Casmajor and the rest of the gentlemen, and told them they might return to Vizac if they pleased. Ensign Butler, the only surviving officer on that establishment, and who very fortunately had been on a visit to a friend at some distance from the settlement, finding what had happened, drew up a detachment of the remaining troops the next morning with a few field pieces, marched at the head of them in quest of the deserters, came up with them, and discharged a few rounds of grape shot amongst them, which brought several of them to the ground. Some ran off, leaving the most part of their arms behind, and the remainder he took prisoners, marching them in the front with the field pieces in the rear.'

The zamindar of Parlákimedi, then under surveillance at Vizagapatam, was strongly suspected of having engineered this outbreak, but he boldly claimed to have saved the lives of the other Europeans in the station and was eventually given back his estate as a reward for his doubtful services.

Proposed cession of the Circars, 1781.

In 1781 the Circars were within an ace of being ceded back again to Hyderabad in return for a body of horse to be placed at the disposal of the Governor-General. Lord Macartney, who had just arrived as Governor of Madras, protested, however, with such force against the proposal that it was abandoned.

CHAP. II. ENGLISH PERIOD.

Maladministration by the Vizianagram Rája.

Meanwhile the weak and corrupt administration of the Chiefs in Council, and the oppression of the ryots and the smaller zamindars by Sítaráma Rázu (who was not only *de facto* ruler of practically the whole of the zamindari area in the district, but also renter of the havíli land) had brought the district into a very unsatisfactory state. A Committee of Circuit consisting of five Members of Council (see p. 167) was sent to investigate matters, and reported in 1784 in the strongest terms of condemnation. It said that the havíli land was most oppressively administered by Sítaráma and was in the last stage of desolation; and as for the rest of the district, that constantly increasing taxes had resulted in a decrease of population and the ruin of several of the handicrafts; that the ryots were allowed to retain barely one-fifth of their crops; that the excessive customs duties had strangled trade; that there were no courts of justice; that the villages were 'composed of wretched hovels, the people meanly clothed and meagre through the extremes of labour and hard fare'; that 'the zamindar, converting all his gains to private purposes, and the native, destitute of all property and aiming at nothing more than a subsistence and the discharge of his assessment,' were alike indifferent to the needs of the future; that in spite of orders to reduce the number of his forces, the Rája of Vizianagram still maintained 7,760 troops of his own (including 1,620 sepoys dressed and armed after the European manner) at an annual cost of nearly 5½ lakhs of rupees and had a call on even more belonging to Pálkonda, Jeypore, Golgonda, and Ándra (his 'subjected tributaries') and to Kimedi and Tekkali; and that of the zamindars he had dispossessed, some had fled to Jeypore and were living on the bounty of the Rája there, others (like Kurupám) were in receipt of a pension, and yet others (including Bobbili, Páchipenta, Kásipuram, Sálúr, and the Tát Rája of Bissamkatak) were in imprisonment at Vizianagram.

Dangerous growth of his power.

The Committee considered it necessary in the interests of the people at large that the power of Vizianagram should be curbed; and recommended that all his troops except some 2,000 sibbandis for service in the malarious hills and a body-guard of 767 peons and 50 horse should be ordered to be disbanded, the cost of their upkeep (four lakhs) being added to the peshkash (five lakhs) which the Rája now paid; suggested that the Jeypore, Pálkonda and Golgonda chiefs should be given separate cowles and rendered independent of Vizianagram, and that the imprisoned zamindars should be set at liberty; and made numerous proposals for the improvement of the revenue and other branches of the administration.

CHAP. II. ENGLISH PERIOD.

Ordered to reduce his troops, 1788.

The **Rája** agreed at the time to disband his troops except certain Rájputs who belonged to his own clan, and in 1788 he was formally ordered to reduce his forces and was granted a new lease at the enhanced peshkash of nine lakhs recommended by the Committee, his zamindari being however increased by the addition of the estates of Anakápalle, Uratla and Satyavaram. He evidently disobeyed the instructions regarding the reduction of his troops, and in consequence had difficulty in meeting the enhanced peshkash.

His brother Sítaráma Rázu was removed from the office of díwán about 1784 and retired, it is stated, to Simháchalam, where he made the rose-garden which still stands (see p. 323) at the foot of the steps leading to the temple on the hill there. In 1790, however, he regained his post; was dismissed by his brother in November 1791; taken back again in February 1792; removed by order of Government; and required in August 1793 to reside in Madras, whither he proceeded accordingly and lived on a pension from Government of Rs. 5,000 a month.

Falls into heavy arrears with his peshkash, 1793.

By this time[1] the Rája's incompetent management of the estate had led to the accrual of arrears of peshkash amounting to no less than 6¼ lakhs, and the Chief and Council reported that the security of the revenue and the general welfare of the country could be ensured by no method short of the sequestration of the zamindari. The oppressions of Sítaráma had raised revolt among the lesser zamindars and very serious disturbances were apprehended unless 'a decided and immediate check and an entire change of system' could be introduced. The Government threatened that unless all the arrears were paid the estate would be attached and the Rája removed and pensioned, and they sent to Vizagapatam a detachment of Europeans, artillery and sepoys, under Lieutenant-Colonel Prendergast, to enable them to enforce these measures.

His estate is sequestrated.

The Rája, in this extremity, offered to pay 5½ lakhs of the arrears (which by now had grown to 8½ lakhs) in three equal instalments in a reasonable time, but the proposal was rejected by the Board of Revenue and the Government, and on 2nd August 1793 the sequestration was effected by Colonel Prendergast taking possession of the Vizianagram fort. The Rája was still, however, so powerful that no one would come forward to rent any part of the estate, and, while making every outward sign of submission, he intrigued to render impossible any management

[1] The account which follows, down to the surrender of the Rája's son, is taken from Mr. Carmichael's *District Manual*.

but his own. The sequestration therefore continued. The question of the arrears, indeed, was only one of several which were at stake. As the Board of Revenue put it in June 1794—

'The objects we had in view and which we trusted would result from the sequestration of the Zamindary, were, to reduce the military force which this Zamindar (notwithstanding the repeated orders, to the contrary, of the Honorable Court of Directors, within the last twenty years, and of successive Governments) had not only retained, but even increased; to meliorate the condition of the inhabitants and families of those Zamindars, who had been dispossessed by the most unjust and ambitious projects of the Vizianagram Zamindar; to afford relief to those who retained their countries, but who have been exposed to great oppressions; to heal the distractions, which had so long prevailed under a weak, fluctuating and improvident administration; to ascertain the real value of the different purgunnahs and the extent of the improper alienations of land, whether for military services, or to Braminies and favorites; to clear off all debts (particularly to the Rajah's troops); to introduce some fixed principle of management, in order to secure tranquillity, and the realization of an adequate revenue; and, by affording the Zamindar a more intimate knowledge of the resources of his country, we hoped to provide for the punctual discharge of the Company's future demands.'

And he is ordered to leave the district, 1794.

It seemed clear that as long as the Rája remained in the district the arrears would continue uncollected and the estate be unmanageable; and he was accordingly directed to proceed to Masulipatam within a stated time. He was given an allowance of Rs. 1,200 a month and the Chief made him an advance of Rs. 30,000 for the expenses of the journey. He marched out ten or twelve miles and then (11th May 1794) wrote to the Chief stating his inability to proceed further owing to the turbulence of his peons, who clamoured for their arrears of pay. These people were pacified by an assurance from the Chief that the Company would discharge their claims and the Rája was left without excuse for further non-compliance with the orders of Government. His reluctance to leave his country was however extreme. He considered the orders not only harsh and disparaging to his position, but a sure precursor of the entire extinction of his power. He seems to have hoped that a determined attitude would stave off extreme measures, and so retired with his camp to Padmanábham, a village between Vizianagram and Bimlipatam and in quite the opposite direction to the main road to Masulipatam.

He resists this order.

By this open movement he was now declared by the Chief and Council 'to have broken with the Company;' and intelligence was shortly received which left very little doubt of his intentions.

CHAP. II. ENGLISH PERIOD.

It was found that he was moving his family and effects; that some sepoys and cavalry who were in course of being paid off by the Chief at Vizagapatam had been re-called by the Rája and had actually joined him at Padmanábham; that the country peons were collecting; that promises had been made to the other zamindars for the purpose of conciliating them; and that it was imagined to be the Rája's intention to proceed to Jeypore or, further still, to the Bastar country of Nagpur. Once in the hills, a very large force of paiks would of course be at his disposal.

On the 14th May a company of the Rája's sepoys stationed at Vizianagram marched off, without informing the commanding officers of their intentions, to join the Rája at Padmanábham, and three companies which were at Srungavarapukóta acted in the same way. Spies were sent out by the Chief and Council and returned with the news that it was the Rája's intention to resist the Company's forces to the last, and, if finally overpowered, 'then to do as the Bobbili family did formerly' when their fort was captured by Bussy. Messengers, it was added, had arrived from Sítaráma Rázu, who was then under surveillance at Madras, stating that owing to war between the English and French all the Company's troops would be required in the south, in which event the Company would only be too glad to adjust matters in a conciliating spirit with the Rája. 'Since this report was published, Viziaráma Rázu seems to appear in good spirits.'

On the 29th May, Lieutenant-Colonel Prendergast arrived at Bimlipatam from Chicacole with five companies of sepoys, and was joined by Captain Cox from Vizianagram with two and a half companies. He reported that some European gunners were coming up from Madras by sea, and indented on the arsenal at Vizagapatam for two brigades of six-pounders and one brigade of three pounders, with their full complement of ammunition.

By this time the number of fighting men who had joined the Rája amounted to four thousand men. He appeared to be aware that he was engaged in a desperate enterprize, and to shrink from the actual hostilities that were imminent. He sent for a Doctor Martin, who was with the troops at Bimlipatam and to whom he was known, on the plea that he required his professional advice. The Chief gave the doctor permission to go. He found the Rája prostrated, both in body and mind, and after prescribing for his bodily ailments, he was asked by his patient whether he could administer to a diseased mind. The doctor replied that his skill did not extend so far, but that he hoped and believed the Rája was not afflicted in that way beyond all cure. The Rája

CHAP. II. ENGLISH PERIOD.

replied by a long narrative of his grievances and difficulties, and ended by entrusting the doctor with a letter for the Chief, in which he attributed his disobedience to the Company's orders to the restraint laid upon him by the rabble of sibbandis and others that had gathered around him. Mr. Chamier, in reply, offered to employ force against these obstructions, but to this no answer appears to have been received.

On the tidings of these events reaching Madras, the Governor, Sir Charles Oakeley, himself addressed a letter to Viziaráma Rázu, informing him that the Company would settle every just demand of his troops, and requiring him to repair forthwith to Vizagapatam accompanied by his common attendants only. In the event of his declining compliance with this summons, he was warned that he must be considered in a state of armed and wilful disobedience to the Government; that the Commanding Officer would proceed against him so soon as he might be prepared for that purpose, and use the most effectual means in his power for dispersing his people and securing his person and the persons of his principal adherents. No reply was received from Viziaráma Rázu, and on the 5th July Colonel Prendergast was directed to enforce the orders of Government, after giving the Rája twenty-four hours for the necessary preparations for his departure.

And is killed at Padmanábham.

On the 8th and 9th idem scouts brought the intelligence that the Rája and all his men had sworn to die, sword in hand; *mahápraśádam*, or food that had been offered in the temple at Padmanábham, having been distributed by the Rája with due solemnity to his chiefs. Early on the morning of the 10th all was over. The following brief report from Colonel Prendergast was received at Vizagapatam the same evening:—'I arrived at Padmanábham at half past five o'clock this morning, and finding the Rája's troops all arrived and prepared, attacked them, and after a severe conflict for about three-quarters of an hour, dispersed them. The Rája was killed, with many of his followers. Further returns to-morrow.'

The loss on the Company's side was thirteen killed and sixty-one wounded. The casualties amongst their opponents were far more numerous. No correct list of the wounded was ever procured, but no less than three hundred and nine were killed. Of these, two hundred and eight were Rájputs, and the bodies of forty Rájputs, of the first rank in the country, formed a rampart round the corpse of Viziaráma Rázu. The Dátlas, the Dantalúris, the Ságis, the Chintalapátis, the Gótimukkalas, the Vajarlas, the Pennumetsas, all left their dead on the

CHAP. II. ENGLISH PERIOD.

field. Padmanábham will long be remembered as the Flodden of the Rájputs of Vizianagram. The Chief and Council might well deem the fight decisive, as they proceeded to the principal objects they now had in view, viz., 'that the settlements of revenue be made, and the business of cultivation be forwarded as expeditiously as possible.'

His son is given the estate.

Matters however were very far from being at once adjusted. The late Rája had placed the ladies of his family, with his young son, Náráyana Rázu, a boy of eight years of age, at Annamarázupéta, a village about two kos from Padmanábham; and on the eve of the battle he sent the lad instructions to surrender, in the event of his own death, to the Chief and Council. It had become necessary for him to yield up his life to save his honour; but the 'Company were very just people' and would not visit their quarrel with the father on his young son. He at the same time induced his wife and mother to swear to him that they would not kill themselves on receiving the news of his death.

No sooner however was the fate of Viziaráma Rázu and his army known, than the guardians of the women and child fled precipitately with their charge to Kásipuram, at the foot of the hills. This place was at that time in the possession of one Mukki Rájabhúpála Rázu, who, claiming descent from the ancient zamindars of that portion of the district, had seized upon Kásipuram by force on the sequestration of the Vizianagram zamindari by the Government, and had continued ever since to defy the power of the Company and to resist their troops. This man received the fugitives with every attention, and shortly afterwards escorted them to Makkuva, still further to the north. From this place negotiations were opened with the other zamindars, especially with Rámachandra Deo of Jeypore, who then resided at Náráyanapatnam. The young Rája was soon surrounded with several thousand armed peons; the leaders collected the kists from the ryots, and seemed resolved to set the Company's government at defiance. Detachments of sepoys were rapidly pushed forward to the more important positions, but the Commanding Officer at the same time reported that if matters continued as they were it would not be practicable for him to hold the country without an additional force of three battalions at his disposal.

In these circumstances a temporizing policy was adopted by the Chief and Council. Letters were despatched to the chief surviving members of the late Rája's family inviting them to come in and bring Náráyana Rázu with them, since it was not

CHAP. II. ENGLISH PERIOD.

intended to take any further notice of past proceedings. This assurance however was regarded by the parties concerned as too vague to be satisfactory.

The Governor, Sir Charles Oakeley, accordingly sent an engagement under his own hand, dated 20th August 1794, promising that Náráyana Rázu and all the late Rája's family, dependents and adherents should be taken under the Company's protection provided that they returned within thirty days, but warning them that if they still held aloof they would be 'considered to be contumacious and disobedient' and 'to have forfeited all claim to the Company's future favour or countenance.'

To this, the boy's friends replied that they would return at an early date. The more ambitious zamindars by whom he was surrounded were however by no means pleased at this decision. It was their object to protract the disturbances until they could make advantageous terms for themselves with the Company, and they consequently loudly protested against the surrender and redoubled their hostilities against the Company's detachments. Colonel Prendergast applied for a reinforcement of three battalions, but the Chief replied that it was better to negotiate than to depend upon force against people who could not be followed into their hill fastnesses; and at length the Jeypore Rája was induced to hold aloof from the insurgents and Náráyana Rázu, escaping from the other zamindars, came to Ándra on the 21st September. A proclamation calling on the other chiefs to return to their estates, and guaranteeing them possession, resulted in their also coming in; and a most difficult and dangerous situation ended happily.

Which is greatly curtailed.

The Jeypore Rája was rewarded for his behaviour with a sanad for his estate, and in 1796 cowles were granted to the other zamindars reinstating them during their good behaviour in the properties of which they had been dispossessed by Vizianagram. Náráyana Rázu was given a cowle for three years for his estate on a peshkash of six lakhs, but the property was curtailed not only by the severance from it of the zamindaris which had been restored to their original proprietors, but by the absorption into the havíli land of the Anakápalle taluk and some adjacent areas.

The Permanent Settlement, 1802.

By the Permanent Settlement of 1802 (see p. 169) all these ancient zamindaris were handed over to their owners in perpetuity on a fixed peshkash and a number of other proprietary estates were also called into being by parcelling out the havíli land into a series of properties and selling these by auction subject to the payment of a permanent peshkash.

CHAP. II.
ENGLISH PERIOD.

Its unfortunate effects.

Politically, this settlement was a failure. It took no account of the personal equation among the zamindars. These men had for years been treated as feudatories rather than as mere farmers of the revenue, 'rather as captains of the borders, lords of the marches, chiefs of the hills, than as private landholders'; and the Government had been in part conducted through them, some of them having been entrusted with the responsibility of keeping the hill tribes in order. But under the new arrangement they were unceremoniously set aside; authority over the hill men was taken from them; their estates were declared liable to immediate attachment and sale for default in paying a single instalment of the peshkash; they were irritated by the working of the new revenue and judicial regulations; and the new police force, no longer under their control, took every opportunity, under cover of a pretence of enforcing law and order, of harassing and annoying them. Mr. Thackeray, the well-known Member of the Board of Revenue, wrote in 1819 that—

'The (police) darogahs were generally low men, such as kotwáls, turned-off writers, dubashes and butlers, the dregs of the courts and cutcherry: their peons good for nothing, batta peons, such as hang about every cutcherry and follow every dubash. Sending such men into the zamindaris was as if the Government, an hundred years ago, had sent a dozen London attorneys' clerks, with some Bow Street runners, to the highlands of Scotland, to control those proud chiefs, and establish a good police in that country.'

Owing to all these causes, the zamindars, for many years after the introduction of the permanent settlement, were in a chronic state of discontent and disaffection. Too often internal and domestic troubles accentuated their restlessness. Those of them who had been restored to their ancient patrimonies on the death of the Rája of Vizianagram in 1794 returned to them, of course, without capital or credit; and in several instances an illegitimate brother or a cousin disputed their title, got together a band of paiks, and seizing upon a portion of the estate contrived to hold it by force.

At first, troops were called out and an attempt was made to chastise these disturbers of the public peace and drive them from their fastnesses. But these expeditions were by no means uniformly successful and cost much in blood and treasure. Recourse was then had to negotiation, the only result of which was to increase the insolence of the malcontents. Fresh leaders of banditti started up in every direction, and the zamindars, believing that we were afraid to put the law in operation against them, began neglecting to pay their peshkash.

CHAP. II. ENGLISH PERIOD.

Sir Thomas Munro, Governor of Madras, in a minute of 7th January 1823 written at the close of a tour through the country,[1] summed up the then position as under :—

'The weakness of the authority of Government in the Circars is owing to our restoring the districts of the petty zamindars, who had been subdued, contrary to the opinion of the Committee of Circuit; to our erecting by the permanent settlement a new set of proprietary zamindars; to our not reserving a single village in which we could exercise direct control over the ryots; and to our transferring to these proprietors the karnams, who are the source of all information. In open countries long under the immediate authority of Government, the permanent settlement, though it tends to conceal the real state of the country, does not seriously affect the public authority by encouraging resistance or rebellion; but in mountainous unhealthy districts like the Northern Circars, the greater part of which has long been in the hands of a number of petty Rájas, some claiming independence, and all constantly ready to withhold their tribute and to raise disturbances whenever they see a favourable opportunity, the permanent settlement has the effect of weakening the authority of Government over the whole province, and of rendering the establishment of security and of good order more difficult than before . . . . Our system in the Circars is one of forbearance, and we are obliged to connive at irregularities which would not be tolerated in other provinces, lest we should be compelled to use force and involve ourselves in a petty warfare against banditti in a pestilential climate among hills and jungles.

The affairs of the Circars can never be well administered, nor the great body of the people protected against oppression, nor the country be secured from disturbance and the incursion of plunderers, until our Government becomes more respected in those provinces than it is at present . . . . No zamindari once forfeited for rebellion should ever be restored, whatever temporary evil the retention of it might occasion. All estates falling in should invariably be kept and annexed to the sirkar lands . . . . The gradual extension of the sirkar lands should be our main object, because it is by having the direct possession and management of landed property that we can best protect the ryots, grant them remissions of rent, assist them in agricultural improvements and attach them to our Government.'

Mr. Russell's Commission, 1833.

Ten years later, at the close of 1832, the disturbances in this district and in the Parlákimedi zamindari of Ganjám became so serious that Mr. George Russell, First Member of the Board of Revenue, was sent as Special Commissioner to investigate their causes and concert measures for their suppression. He was invested with extraordinary powers, including that of proclaiming martial law if necessary, and was supported by a strong force

[1] Arbuthnot's *Munro* (London, 1881), i, 208.

CHAP. II. ENGLISH PERIOD.

of troops. In this district his attentions were chiefly devoted to Mukki Vírabhadra Rázu of Kásipuram, Páyaka Rao of Páyakaraopéta and the zamindar of Pálkonda, and the action he took against them is referred to in the account of those three places in Chapter XV below.[1] The two former were captured and the estate of the third was forfeited and became the present Pálkonda taluk.

To check further disturbances of the same kind Act XXIV of 1839 was passed and (see p. 196) seven-eighths of the district was removed from the operation of much of the ordinary law and administered directly by the Collector with extraordinary powers conferred upon him in the capacity of 'Agent to the Governor.' Several of the zamindaris in the south were from time to time bought in by Government at sales for arrears of revenue, and these were formed into the taluks of Golgonda and Sarvasiddhi, but the owners of the others were quieted permanently.

Subsequent outbreaks.

Since then there have been troubles or outbreaks of the hill people ('fitúris', as they are locally called) in the Golgonda hills in 1845–48, 1857–58, 1879–80, 1886 and 1891; in the Jeypore zamindari in 1849–50 and 1855–56; among the Savaras of Gunupur taluk in 1864 and 1865; and at Korravanivalasa in Sálúr taluk in 1900. These are all referred to in the accounts of those places in Chapter XV. In 1882 the Khonds of Kálahandi State rose against the Uriyas and murdered some hundreds of them. Luckily the invitation to join them, conveyed by the circulation of the head, fingers, hair, etc., of an early victim, was not accepted by the Khonds of this district, but the Párvatípur police reserve under Mr. Prendergast[2] took a prominent part in restoring order across the frontier. The zamindars in the plains have given no trouble since Pálkonda was forfeited for rebellion.

[1] See also Mr. Russell's full report on his commission printed in No. XXIV of the *Selections from the Madras Records* (Madras, 1856).

[2] See his graphic narrative of events, printed in G.O., No. 952, Judicial, dated 14th August 1882.

CHAPTER III.

THE PEOPLE.

GENERAL CHARACTERISTICS—Density of the population—Its growth—Emigration—Parent-tongue—Education—Occupations—Religions. THE JAINS. THE CHRISTIANS—The London Mission—Roman Catholic Mission—Schleswig-Holstein Lutheran Mission—Canadian Baptist Missions. THE MUSALMANS. THE HINDUS—Villages and houses—Dress—Food—Amusements—Dancing—Chaitra feast—Superstitions. RELIGIOUS LIFE—In the plains—The village deities—In the Agency. PRINCIPAL CASTES—In the plains—Kápu—Velama—Telaga—Nagarálu—Aiyarakulu—Bagata—Gavara—Konda Dora—Golla—Kamsala—Sále—Sálápu—Sílávantulu—Yáta—Mangala—Jálári—Míla—Nágavásulu—Relli—Godagula—Beggar castes—Principal castes in the Agency—Poroja—Dombu—Paidi—Bottada—Rona—Bhúmiya—Sondi—Korono—Máli—Omanaito—Mattiya—Pentiya—Dhakkade—Khond—Játapu—Múka Dora—Savara—Gadaba—Kóya—Gónd.

CHAP. III. GENERAL CHARACTERISTICS.

Density of the population.

THE density of the population in the Agency of Vizagapatam is less than in any other area in the Presidency except the Gódávari Agency. The country as a whole contained in 1901 only 67 persons to the square mile, and Malkanagiri only 14—a smaller number than any other taluk in Madras.

The density of the people in the ordinary tracts is shown in the statistics of the 1901 census as 453 to the square mile, a number only exceeded in the rich districts of Tanjore and Malabar; but there is little doubt that this figure is higher than the facts warrant, owing to the incorrectness of the official statistics of area from which it is calculated. The zamindaris, which make up over nine-tenths of the district, have never been surveyed by Government; the figures of their area are only approximations; and recent surveys in the Vizianagram zamindari have shown that there, at any rate, they have always been grossly understated. Taking the census figures as they stand, it appears that Pálkonda (645 persons to the square mile) is the most densely peopled taluk; that it is closely followed by Vizagapatam, Vizianagram, Bimlipatam and Anakápalle; and that the most sparsely populated taluk is Golgonda, which has only 235 persons to the square mile. A marked movement of the people into the larger towns is in progress. In the decade 1891–1901 the inhabitants of Párvatípur increased by as much as 72 per cent., and other notable advances occurred in Sálúr (25 per cent.), Vizianagram (21), Bobbili (20) and Vizagapatam (19).

CHAP. III. GENERAL CHARACTERISTICS.

Its growth.

In the Agency the population in 1901 was actually less than that in 1891. Nine of the taluks showed a decrease, and the loss was especially heavy in Naurangpur. The decline has never been satisfactorily explained, and was probably due to careless enumeration. In Malkanagiri, Pádwa and Golgonda, however, considerable advances occurred.

The low country escaped the great famine of 1876, and therefore the growth of its population in the thirty years between 1871 and 1901 (though below that of its neighbour Gódávari) was in excess of the mean for the Presidency during that period. But in the decade 1881–91 the increase was much less than this mean, and in 1891–1901 it only just equalled it.

Emigration.

This result is largely due to the unusual amount of emigration which goes on. The census figures showed that in 1901 the Gódávari district contained no fewer than 120,940 persons who had been born in Vizagapatam, that Kistna included 17,524 more, and Ganjám another 8,795. On the whole, the net result in Vizagapatam of the movement of the people to and from other districts of the Presidency amounted to a loss of as many as 146,894 persons. From no other district in the Presidency did emigration occur on anything even approaching this large scale, and the inference arises that the people of Vizagapatam are not particularly contented with their lot.

Emigration to Burma is common, but the statistics do not distinguish genuine emigrants from ordinary travellers, so figures cannot be quoted; and apparently the emigration is usually only temporary (people going across for the paddy-harvest) and is almost balanced by corresponding immigration. Emigration to the Assam tea-gardens, which is so common in Ganjám, occurs in Vizagapatam on only a small scale. It is controlled under the Assam Labour and Emigration Act VI of 1901 [1] and recruitment in the Agency is strictly prohibited. Two recruiter's dépôts have been established at Párvatípur.

Parent-tongue.

The languages of the district form a veritable Babel. In the plains, 960 in every 1,000 people speak Telugu in their homes, 14 talk Uriya (Odiya), 9 Khond, 7 Gadaba and 5 Hindostáni; but among the same number in the Agency 481 speak Uriya, 206 Khond, 180 Telugu, 56 Savara, 30 'Poroja,' 23 Gadaba, 11 Kóya,. 3 Hindostáni, 3 Góndi and 5 other vernaculars, such as Lambádi, Bastari, Hindi, Chattisgarhi, etc. The 'Konda' language returned in the census reports appears to be merely

[1] A history of the control of this kind of emigration will be found in G.O., No. 618, Public, dated 23rd August 1905.

Khond under another name. 'Poroja' is a term which has occasioned much confusion, as there are some seven kinds of Poroja people who speak several different dialects (see p. 86 below) which are apparently forms of Khond, Uriya, Gadaba and Kóya respectively. Bastari, Hindi and Chattisgarhi are rare and occur only in the north of Naurangpur taluk; in the Golgonda and Víravilli Agencies Telugu is spoken to the exclusion of all other languages; Savara is only used by the people of that tribe in the hills east of Gunupur and in the Pálkonda Agency; and Kóya only by the Kóyas of south Malkanagiri. The other tongues are not definitely localized. Lambádi is the vernacular of the pack-bullock traders called Lambádis, Banjáris, Brinjáris or Boipáris. Uriya has a strong resemblance to Hindostáni and Bengali, and any one acquainted with either of those vernaculars can readily pick it up. The written language differs even more than usual from that in everyday use. These numerous vernaculars belong to as many as three different linguistic families; for Bastari, Chattisgarhi, Hindi, Hindostáni and Lambádi are Áryan tongues; Khond, Kóya and Telugu are Dravidian; and Gadaba and Savara are classed as belonging to the Munda (Kolarian) family.

The great diversity of tongues in the Agency constitutes an immense hindrance to administration; the more so that (except Uriya, Telugu, Hindostáni and Hindi) the vernaculars in use have no written character and have been but little studied, and that, thanks to the isolation enforced by difficult country, a language often possesses several local dialects. The Khonds of the north of Bissamkatak, for example, can scarcely make themselves understood by the Khonds of the 3,000 feet plateau, while neither of them can converse without difficulty with the lowland Khonds along the eastern fringe of the hills or with the Khonds of Kálahandi. The Gadabas of the Jeypore country, again, speak a patois which is unintelligible to the members of the same caste living on the eastern slopes of the 3,000 feet plateau.

No trained philologist has ever worked at these less-known tongues or their dialects, and a wide field is awaiting exploration. It would probably be found that Kóya and the dialect of the Bhúmiyas of Naurangpur and Jeypore taluks, which are usually classified as forms of Góndi, are in reality nothing of the kind; that 'Poroja,' which has long been classed as a separate language, resolves itself into a series of dialects of recognized vernaculars; and that Gadaba is not a Kolarian tongue. An interesting point in several of these languages is

CHAP. III. GENERAL CHARACTERISTICS.

their deficiency in words for numerals. After 'five' or 'seven' they have often to borrow the Uriya or Telugu words for the higher numerals. Mr. H. G. Turner sent a note on this subject to the *Indian Antiquary* (ii, 97).

Education.

The education of the people is referred to in Chapter X below, which shows that the district (and particularly the Agency) has long been a byword for illiteracy.

Occupations.

The means of subsistence of the inhabitants are discussed in Chapter VI, from which it will be seen that arts, industries and trade support but few of them, and that an overwhelming proportion depend upon the land for a livelihood.

Religions.

The religion of the district before the beginning of the Christian era was probably (see p. 25) Buddhism. Nowadays practically the whole of the population of the Agency are Hindus or Animists, Christians numbering only 37 in 10,000 in 1901, and Musalmans only 18 in the same number. The census figures attempt to differentiate Hindus (that is, those who worship the orthodox gods of the Hindu pantheon) from Animists (that is, those who reverence only animistic deities); but the accuracy of the result is vitiated by the fact that many members of the hill tribes, though Animists at heart, offer none the less a perfunctory and spasmodic worship to the Hindu gods of the plains and thus come within the four corners of the definition of a Hindu.

In the low country, nearly 99 per cent. of the people are Hindus and Animists, and Musalmans (108 in every 10,000) and Christians (20 in the same number) are proportionately fewer than in any district in the Presidency except Ganjám.

THE JAINS.

The Jains number only 49. Jain remains appear to occur in only one place in the plains (Rámatírtham, see p. 335) and the faith was presumably never powerful. In the Canarese country and the Deccan the Jains were ousted by the Lingáyats, and perhaps the same fate overtook them in Vizagapatam, for the district contains a proportion of Lingáyats which is curiously high for a tract so remote from the birthplace of that faith. Many of the Dévángas, Sáles and Kómatis belong to the sect, there are Lingáyat gurus at Anakápalle and Pálkonda, and Pondúru is a great centre of the creed.

THE CHRISTIANS.

The Christians, as has been said, form a smaller proportion of the total population than in any other district except Ganjám. They are relatively least scarce in the Vizagapatam and Koraput taluks, where they number about 2 per cent. of the population, and in the Sálúr Agency. In these latter two areas they consist almost entirely of Dombus converted by the Schleswig-Holstein

Lutheran Mission. Nearly all of them are natives. Of those in the plains, more than half are Roman Catholics; in the Agency Lutherans are the most numerous sect. CHAP. III. THE CHRISTIANS.

The London Mission.

The oldest Christian mission in the district is the London Mission.[1] Its pioneers, the Revs. G. Cran and A. des Granges, came from Tranquebar as far back as 1805 and were the first Protestants to preach in the Telugu country. Government invited them to hold services in the Court House in the fort at Vizagapatam, for the benefit of the soldiers and other British residents, and made them an allowance for so doing. They were assisted by a converted Bráhman from Tranquebar who had originally been a Roman Catholic. Educational work and translations of the Scriptures appear to have occupied more of the attention of the earlier missionaries than direct evangelization, and twenty-seven years elapsed before a single convert was made.

In 1840 a printing press was set up in Vizagapatam from which have issued, besides numerous tracts, two editions of a translation into Telugu of the New Testament and one of a version, in the same language, of the Old Testament. In 1845 the smaller vernacular schools belonging to the mission were closed and one central anglo-vernacular institution was started which eventually developed into the existing high school at Vizagapatam. Two missionaries, one stationed at Vizagapatam and one at Anakápalle, and two lady workers make up the present European staff; and there is a meeting-house in the fort at the former town and three other smaller ones elsewhere. After a century of effort, the number of native adherents of the mission is still less than 250.

Roman Catholic Mission.

It was not until 1845 that the Roman Catholic Church established any regular mission in the district.[2] In that year five missionaries of St. Francis of Sales were sent thither. Their leader was the Very Rev. L. Gailhot, and in 1847 he was succeeded by the Very Rev. S. S. Neyret, who was consecrated Bishop of the diocese about two years afterwards and remained in charge of it until his death in 1862. Father Neyret was followed by the Right Rev. Dr. J. M. Tissot, one of the five original missionaries above mentioned, who held the post for 28 years and is buried at Súrada. During his time, in 1886, the existing diocese of Vizagapatam (which consists of the districts

[1] Further particulars will be found on pp. 285–96 of the second volume of the *Report of the Missionary Conference of South India and Ceylon*, 1879.

[2] For assistance with this section, I am indebted to the courtesy of the Rev. J. Contat of Vizagapatam.

CHAP. III. THE CHRISTIANS.

of Cuttack, Ganjám, Vizagapatam and Gódávari) was formed. The present Bishop, the Right Rev. Dr. J. M. Clerc, was consecrated in 1891.

Besides the cathedral, a building of brick and chunam in the Gothic style dating from 1854, the mission possesses three churches in Vizagapatam town; namely, one in the fort, erected in 1887, one near the Waltair station, put up in 1903, and a third, the chapel of Our Lady of the Sacred Heart, picturesquely placed on Ross Hill overlooking the mouth of the Upputéru and visible from almost every part of the town. This last was finished in 1877 and is a well-known place of pilgrimage. Other Roman Catholic churches in the district are those in the Vizianagram cantonment (built in 1882–83) and at Kottavalasa (1899), and the half-finished erection at Pálkonda; while in nine other villages chapels have been put up.

The European staff of the mission in the district consists of eighteen Priests and four Brothers. Sixteen of these twenty-two are stationed in Vizagapatam town, seven of them being employed in the mission's schools, which are referred to in more detail in Chapter X below. Some forty members of the Sisterhood of St. Joseph are also working in the various girls' schools. A small theological seminary is maintained at Vizagapatam and also an orphanage containing about fifty European boys. An orphanage for European girls was formerly kept up, but has now been moved—partly to Cuttack and partly to Cocanada.

Schleswig-Holstein Lutheran Mission.

The Schleswig-Holstein Lutheran Mission is a much more recent arrival than either of the foregoing, having begun work only in 1882.[1] In that year its pioneers, the Revs. H. Bothmann and E. Pohl, began the foundations of a mission house at Koraput, but suffered so severely from fever that they abandoned the place in favour of Sálúr. Work at the latter town was begun in 1883. Koraput was re-occupied in 1885 and in the next five years beginnings were successively made at Jeypore, Kótapád, Naurangpur, Párvatípur and Gunupur. Seventeen European missionaries and five lady workers are now posted to these seven stations; there are churches at Sálúr, Párvatípur, Kótapád and Naurangpur; numerous out-stations have been established; the number of adherents is returned at over 7,000 already; theological seminaries have been opened at Kótapád and Párvatípur, a lower secondary school at Sálúr, leper asylums at that place (financed by the Edinburgh Mission to Lepers in India and the

[1] The notes which follow have been kindly furnished by the Revs. P. Schulze and J. Th. Timmcke.

East) and Jeypore, three industrial classes, an orphanage at Sálúr and a boarding-school at Kótapád in which there are 130 girls.

Canadian Baptist Missions.

The Canadian Baptists (Ontario and Quebec board) of the Gódávari district sent over one of their body in 1890 to Yellamanchili, where he erected a mission house and took up his residence.[1] Medical work being a part of the policy of the mission, a hospital with accommodation for ten in-patients was built there in 1897. Yellamanchili is now the only place in the district where the mission has any European worker left. A church was founded at Anakápalle in 1898, but that town is now included in the Yellamanchili field; and a station was opened in 1893 at Narasapatam, but is now under the missionary at Tuni in the Gódávari district.

The Baptists of the Maritime Provinces of Canada are also working in the district.[2] Stations are in existence at Bimlipatam (started in 1875), Bobbili (1876), Vizianagram (1889) and Pálkonda (1891); the European staff consists of three missionaries and six lady workers; and, besides primary schools, the mission keeps up a lower secondary school for boys at Bimlipatam and another for girls at Bobbili.

THE MUSALMANS.

As has been stated, Musalmans are proportionately fewer in Vizagapatam than in any other district except Ganjám. Seeing how long the country was under Muhammadan dominion, this is curious. They are relatively most numerous in the taluks of Vizagapatam, Sarvasiddhi (Kasimkóta was once an important fort) and Vizianagram. Those in the Vizagapatam fort are known as Jamáyats. In Túba and one or two other villages round Nandapuram in the Pottangi taluk are quite isolated settlements of Musalmans who say they are the descendants of soldiers who came on a military expedition from Hyderabad against the Jeypore country, and settled down there and married Poroja women. They still wear the Musalman costume and observe the Mohurrum.

The Muhammadans of the plains speak excellent Telugu, seldom keep their womenkind gósha, and are on friendly terms with the Hindus, who make vows to the famous Musalman darga in Vizagapatam town and join in the Mohurrum. The feeling that the Mohurrum should be kept rather as a fast

[1] The account which follows has been kindly contributed by the Rev. E. G. Smith, M.D.

[2] The Rev. W. V. Higgins has been good enough to supply information regarding them.

CHAP. III. THE MUSALMANS.

than a feast is, however, spreading among the better classes of Musalmans.

The Dúdékulas, the cotton-cleaning section, are scarcely to be distinguished, in outward appearance, from Hindus, and have adopted many Hindu ways—tying a táli (called *pusti* in Telugu) at weddings, worshipping the village deities, marrying according to the rule of *ménarikam* (see p. 76) and following the Hindu laws of inheritance.

THE HINDUS.

There remain for consideration the Hindus (among whom will be included the Animists), who make up the mass of the population. These divide themselves into two widely differing sections; namely, the Telugus of the low country, who in caste customs resemble generally the rest of the Telugu-speaking population of the Northern Circars and in religious ritual follow semi-Bráhmanical ceremonies; and the backward peoples of the Agency, whose ways have been protected from outside influences by their isolation and whose religious beliefs are even yet but little imbued with Hinduism. It will be convenient first to refer shortly to a few of the more distinctive points in the social and religious ways of these two classes of the people and then to attempt briefly to describe the castes and tribes among them which are especially characteristic of this district or occur in it in greater strength than in any other.

In the case of the Agency, both these tasks are of extreme difficulty. The people there may be said to be more diverse, more out of the common and less known than any others in the Presidency. Their origins, their ways and their religious beliefs are the most interesting things in the district; but all three are almost untrodden ground. Except Lieutenant Smith, who contributed a few pages of somewhat general statements to Mr. Carmichael's *Manual* of the district, Messrs. H. G. Turner and H. D. Taylor, who supplied the Census reports of 1871 and 1891 with brief notes on some of the castes of the Jeypore country, and Mr. F. Fawcett, who has written to the magazine *Man* an account of the Dombus—none of the many officers who have served in the Agency have placed on record the information they acquired concerning the people of their charges. The time at my own disposal has been too limited to admit of any pretence of supplying this unfortunate gap by systematic personal enquiry, and the notes which follow are chiefly based on second-hand information or material collected by my Assistant, M.R.Ry. C. Hayavadana Rao, B.A., who has had a long training in matters ethnographical and was able to spend a considerable time in the hill country.

Enquiries are much hampered by the absence of any really complete statistical lists of the castes. The original census returns are made in Uriya by people who often do not understand the other vernaculars spoken in the Agency, and these have hitherto had to be compiled into caste tables by officers without any knowledge either of Uriya or of the intricate caste system in the hills. At the census of 1911 a list of all castes returned in each taluk, with the languages returned as spoken by each, should be preserved as a basis for further detailed and local enquiry. Another great difficulty in the path of the enquirer in the Agency is the extraordinary diversity which occurs in different localities in the customs of the same caste. Geographical isolation has prevented free intercourse between the various sections of a community, and the ways of each have developed upon independent lines. This fact often greatly limits the applicability of the statements made in the accounts of the hill tribes below.

Villages and houses.

In the plains, the villages usually straggle along the two sides of one long street, off which lead narrow alleys. The weavers' quarter often boasts wider lanes, since space is required there for preparing the warp. Remains of fortifications are rare, and never embrace the whole village site, as in the Deccan. Hamlets (*valasas*) are exceptionally common. The Málas live in a separate Málapilli, and the Mádigas and Yátas also dwell apart. In the middle of the village tank usually stand two wooden posts side by side, one rather taller than the other. These represent Náráyana the Preserver and Lakshmi his wife, the goddess of prosperity, and were placed there at the solemn dedication (*pratishta*) of the tank when it was first completed. They are usually made of *sómida* (*Soymida febrifuga*) wood, which is almost rot-proof. Similar posts are planted in topes when they first come into bearing. On the banks of the tanks often stand numbers of little masonry erections resembling *tulasi* altars, which have been erected by sorrowing relations over a portion of the remains of their dead, and on which flowers and lights are placed in affectionate remembrance every now and again.

In the south of the plain country the usual house of the lower classes is a circular, one-roomed, windowless, palmyra-thatched erection of mud plastered on to a rough framework of branches, the walls of which are smeared with the local red mud and decorated with neat devices in dots done in white chunam with the forefinger, or, sometimes, more elaborate patterns and drawings of the deities. These decorations are renewed annually at

CHAP. III. THE HINDUS.

Sankránti. The eaves of these huts nearly reach the ground and make a shelter for cattle; the household cooking is usually done beneath them also, and the fires thus started often burn down a whole hamlet. Inside the one room is a broad shelf, five feet from the ground, where lumber is stored and valuables are hidden

Further north, the circular house gives place to a continuous line of connected huts, their roofs thatched with cholam-straw or grass and all of the same height aud pitch, so made that the whole side of a street looks like one house. These have a loft under the rafters which serves the same purposes as the shelf in the circular huts. The granaries are everywhere a distinctive feature, being circular wattle-and-daub constructions quite separate from the houses. The bottoms of the front door-posts are universally and regularly marked on Fridays with saffron and kunkumam in honour of Lakshmi.

In the Agency, the villages are often tiny temporary affairs, the population moving on as the needs of kondapódu (p. 111) dictate. Many of them contain only a couple of huts and a cattle-byre. Where more permanent, they generally consist of one main street flanked on either side by a continuous row of connected huts similar to those just described, behind which are the dwellings of the Dombus and other inferior castes. Uriya Bráhmans and Sondis (if any) live in superior quarters apart. Round many houses runs a neat bamboo wattle fence, some six feet high, which is probably a relic of the days when tigers were common and aggressive. The Savaras and Kuttiya Khonds are fond of putting their habitations on hill-tops. The village boundary (*sandhi*) is held in some honour and is often marked by a post at which, when cholera threatens to intrude, sacrifices are made, or a string of leaves and crows' or peacocks' feathers is hung across the path, or a broom is suspended to sweep away all harm.

Dress.

In the plains, the standard of dress is far lower than in the southern districts. Both the men and women of all but the richer classes wear the coarsest cloths, made usually of home-spun cotton woven by the local weavers. These are narrower than in the Tamil country (so narrow, in fact, that the ladies of some castes wear a langúti underneath them) and when at work in the fields the women tuck them between their legs and pull them up in front to a height which would shock their southern sisters. The men's langútis, on the other hand, are not the inadequate rags in use in the Tamil country, but broad and flowing affairs which often reach to their knees both before and behind, and the ends of which flap about so much that they are often tucked into the waist-string. The men are less particular about wearing a turban than in the south and the women follow the Tamil fashion of dispensing with the tight-fitting bodice.

The prevailing colour of the women's cloths is white, with a very narrow red or blue border. Round about Rázám, however, where coloured cloths are woven, white is less universal. These white garments are hardly ever clean and are unpleasantly discoloured with the turmeric which is so commonly and lavishly used. This powder is not only used as an aid to beauty, as in the south, but is supposed to prevent skin diseases ; and even tiny children and grown men rub it on their bodies. In Pálkonda and Párvatípur the Kalinga Kómati women mix it with kunkumam powder when they employ it as a cosmetic, and their faces are consequently often of a comical scarlet hue.

The men do not usually shave their heads, as in the Tamil country, but leave their hair to grow quite long (in which case it requires a metal *tíga* to keep it out of the eyes and is often coquettishly ornamented with a flower or two) or cut it fairly short all round—somewhat after the European fashion.

All the lower castes—men, women and children—wear necklaces of beads made of real or sham coral or of bits of coral stuck together with lac. They are imported from Bombay and Nellore and are on sale in every bazaar. Both men and women are very fond of ear-rings made of a bit of brass (sometimes gold) wire, curled round and round to symbolize a snake and with one end flattened out and pointed to represent its head. Next to these and the ever-present coral necklets, the most noticeable forms of jewellery are the bangles of yellow lac studded with bits of looking-glass ; the circular brass ring suspended from the central cartilage of the nose ; the silver anklets, made either in the form of chains or curved so as not to chafe the ankle-bone ; the waist-belts of the men, formed of little chased plaques hinged together ; the gold bangle, a wedding-present from their fathers-in-law, worn by men of the upper classes on their left wrists ; and the very elaborate gold jewellery displayed by the Gavara and Kalinga Kómati women, especially on the Párvatípur side. This last comprises beautifully wrought necklaces formed of strings of golden paddy-grains cunningly linked, rows of gold coins old and rare enough to make a numismatist's mouth water, and most elaborate jewelled nose-studs, often an inch wide and almost meeting across the point of the nose.

In the Agency, the dress of the masses is even commoner and coarser than on the plains. The usual wear is the coarse *dupati*

CHAP. III. THE HINDUS.

made by the Dombus, with a black blanket in case of rain or cold. The distinctive dress of the Gadabas, Khonds, Porojas and Savaras is mentioned in the accounts of those communities below. Everyone carries a *tangi*, a light kind of axe. The jewellery of the hill people chiefly consists of glass beads and of massive and clumsily-worked brass and copper ornaments. German silver is the latest cry, and the correct thing in rings in some places is a cast of an eight-anna bit in this metal worn *à la marquise*. Much of this finery is made on the plains and sent up to the hills by Kómatis, but some of it is locally manufactured by the Chitra Ghásis. Many of the hill folk wear the palm-leaf umbrella-hat which is so popular on the west coast.

Food.

In the plain taluks, the staple food of the masses is either cambu or ragi. In general terms it may be stated that south and west of Vizagapatam the former is more eaten than the latter, while north of that town the reverse is the case. Rice, as elsewhere, is the food of the Bráhmans and the rich.

On the 3,000 feet plateau and in the Ráyagada country sámai is the staple food; round Gunupur, Naurangpur, Jeypore and Malkanagiri much rice is eaten; and in the Savara country, hill cholam. The hill people eke out their grain with unusual substitutes, such as the pith of the sago-palm, pounded mango-kernels and dried mohwa flower. The Uriya-speaking Bráhmans, unlike others of that caste, eat fish and flesh and also smoke. The numerous strong drinks of the hill folk are referred to in Chapter XII.

The average Telugu eats more chutneys and vegetables and less meat than the Tamil, and flavours his food more with mustard and less with pepper and chillies. Betel-chewing is little practised, but, except in the higher castes, all the men, most of the women (who usually put the lighted end of the cheroot in their mouths) and many of the children smoke much tobacco.

Amusements.

The people have no lack of amusements. On the plains, wandering acrobats and ballad-mongers are commoner than usual. At the village deities' festivals, boys amuse themselves by dressing up in character and pretending to be girls, elephants, tahsildars, constables and so on. This practice has developed into the acting of regular plays, one of the most popular of which is the old story (Mr. Carmichael describes it as flourishing forty years ago) of the extortionate tahsildar who at first in his might bullies everyone around him; afterwards falls a victim to the blandishments of the dancing-girls and spends all his substance upon them; and at last gets a tákíd from the Nawáb cancelling his appointment and is then hustled and kicked to the satisfaction of everyone until the curtain falls. Puránic stories are also acted, and marionette shows representing episodes in the Rámáyana are given by Bommalátas and others and at least one company of Bondili Rájputs. In Vizianagram, the present Rája's grandfather introduced at the Dasara the elaborate representations of scenes from the Rámáyana which are so popular in Northern India, and the three miniature forts which he built to represent Ayódhya, Janakapatnam and Lanka are still to be seen in the town. Dasara, Sankránti (the Tamil Pongal) and Sivarátri are the three most popular festivals in the country. Some account of the ceremonies performed at the first of these at Jeypore is given on p. 262. On the plains it is followed by the Gauri feast, celebrated by the women in memory of Párvati, who in the form of the beautiful Gauri, saved the corn from the rákshasas. Gauri, represented by a bundle of paddy ears, is carried in procession while the women chant songs setting forth her life and doings.

Cock- and ram-fighting are very popular. The latter is rather an aristocratic pastime, but few are too humble to have a likely cock or two. The best-known breeds are called Dinki and Punzu, and are sold for astonishing prices. Sharp knives are tied to the combatants' spurs and the fights are short and gory. Gambling with cowries is a favourite pastime, especially among Dévángas and Kómatis. It is a kind of glorified pitch and toss, the players betting on how many out of sixteen cowries tossed into the air will come down wrong side uppermost.

In the Agency, cock-fighting is again popular, shikár is often available, drinking-parties are frequent and hilarious, and the periodical ceremonies at the shrines of the indigenous and imported gods provide excuses for festivities. Many of the men are fond of music; and while away the lonely hours in the fields by warbling to themselves plaintive melodies on bamboo flutes, or twanging at a two-stringed mandoline provided with a dried gourd for a sounding-board.

Dancing.

But dancing is the most popular diversion. The men and women dance in separate sets and a party begins at nightfall and usually lasts till daylight doth appear. There are several different tribal dances. The Khonds and Savaras pride themselves on their skill, but their best efforts are little more than clumsy stamping in time; the Brinjári women's idea of dancing is to stand in a bunch and clap their hands while their menfolk hop round them jingling their anklets; the Gadabas usually display more energy than science—though those round Boipariguda

CHAP. III. THE HINDUS.

are more expert; the Kóya girls of Málkanagiri dance prettily in a ring with their hands on each others' shoulders; and perhaps the best exponents of the art are the Jódia Poroja girls of the Koraput and Nandapuram country.

Picturesque in the extreme is a dancing party of these cheery maidens, dressed all exactly alike in clean white cloths with cerise borders or checks, reaching barely half way to the knee; great rings on their fingers; brass bells on their toes; their substantial but shapely arms and legs tattooed from wrist to shoulder and from ankle to knee; their left forearms hidden under a score of heavy brass bangles; and their feet loaded with chased brass anklets weighing perhaps a dozen pounds. The orchestra, which consists solely of drums of assorted shapes and sizes, dashes into an overture, and the girls quickly group themselves into a couple of *corps de ballet*, each under the leadership of a *première danseuse* who marks the time with a long baton of peacock's feathers. Suddenly, the drums drop to a muffled beat and each group strings out into a long line, headed by the leader with the feathers, each maiden passing her right hand behind the next girl's back and grasping the left elbow of the next but one. Thus linked, and in time with the drums (which now break into *allegro crescendo*) the long chains of girls—dancing in perfect step, following the leader with her swaying baton, marking the time by clinking their anklets (right, left, right, clink; left, clink; right, left, right, clink; and so *da capo*), chanting the while (quite tunefully) in unison a refrain in a minor key ending on a sustained falling note—weave themselves into sinuous lines, curves, spirals, figures-of-eight and back into lines again; wind in and out like some brightly-coloured snake; never halting for a moment, now backwards, now forwards, first slowly and decorously, then, as the drums quicken, faster and faster, with more and more abandon and longer and longer steps, until suddenly some one gets out of step and the chain snaps amid peals of breathless laughter.

Chaitra feast.

The most jovial occasion in the Agency is the feast in the month of Chaitra (March-April), which is usually known as the *Chaitra parvam* but in the Golgonda and Víravilli Agencies is called the *Ittika panduga*. Everything makes for jollity in that month. There is nothing to be done in the fields, the sap is rising in the trees, the jungles have been burnt and are clear for shikár, and, above all, the sago-palms are giving toddy and the mohwa flower, from which strong waters are brewed, is falling. The month is spent in feasting, deep potations, night-long dancing and singing parties (in which the young men and maidens take opposite sides and wind up with extempore verses of a personal flavour designed to provoke equally personal repartees) and in expeditions into the jungles to gather the mohwa-blossom during which, it is said, free love is the rule among the unmarried. But the great event of the month is the beat for game. In this all the able-bodied men take part, and they stay out, often for days together, until some male animal has been shot. Should they dare to return empty-handed, the women collect and pelt them with most unsavoury missiles.

This Chaitra Saturnalia is still observed with all its ancient enthusiasm throughout the wilder part of the Agency, but in the more civilized hill-tracts, such as the Ráyagada taluk, it is falling into desuetude.

Superstitions.

The hill people are extraordinarily superstitious, and their beliefs and fears would fill a volume. Every ill that befalls them is attributed to witchcraft; suspected witches (see p. 205) get short shrift; charms of all sorts are widely worn; and a crowd of exorcists, medicine-men and magicians live by pretending to counteract the effects of the black art. These impostors are known in different parts and among different castes as jannis and díssaris (ordinary pújáris also bear these titles, however) and as bezzus (who are eunuchs), siras and guniyas. The powers attributed to witches are almost unlimited. They are supposed, for example, to be able to transform themselves into tigers (though one foot always still retains its human shape), to be able to wither up any limb they touch, and even to draw the life-blood from their victim by sucking at one end of a string the other end of which is laid upon his breast.

Devil-drivers, who profess to cure 'possessed' women, are common and employ much the same methods as elsewhere. They seat the woman in a fog of resin-smoke and work upon or beat her until she declares the supposed desire of the devil in the way of sacrifices; and when these have been complied with one of her hairs is put in a bottle, formally shown to the village goddess, and buried in the jungle, while iron nails are driven into the threshold of the woman's house to prevent the devil's return.

Rain-making spells are numerous, from the common plan of covering a frog with green leaves and water until he croaks, to the mysterious *barmarákshasi panduga* of the Kalyána Singapur Khonds, which consists in making life-size mud images of women seated on the ground and holding grinding-stones between their knees, and in offering sacrifices to them.

CHAP. III. RELIGIOUS LIFE.

In the plains.

In the plains, the general religious attitude of the people has been considerably affected by the numerous Bráhmans, whose forefathers were attracted to this district by the liberal grants of land made them by former zamindars. The Bráhmanical festivals (especially Sivarátri) are popular; Bráhman holy days, such as Amávásya, are widely observed; the larger Bráhmanical temples (such as those at Puri in Orissa, Simháchalam and Appikonda) attract a great following; and small shrines to the orthodox gods are numerous. These latter, it may here be mentioned, are usually mean erections, architecturally considered, and are surmounted by a squat pyramidal tower thickly covered with coarse plaster work, still more coarsely decorated, and topped (if they are dedicated to Vaishnava deities) with the chakram in open iron-work. Stone pillars (where they occur) have usually a capital formed of an inverted lotus blossom and the lower third of them often consists of some grotesque squatting animal.

But Bráhmanical influence has not sunk very deeply. The better class Súdras display more energy in celebrating Rámabhajanas (Saturday evening meetings round a picture or image of Ráma at which songs in honour of that hero are chanted) than in worship at the ordinary temples; the grámadévatas abound; and hardly a village is without its shrine to some pérantálamma, or woman who committed sati.

The village deities.

These grámadévatas, ammas, or village deities are numerous and all of the female sex. They include Núkálamma, Ellamma, Paidamma, Bangáramma, Maridamma, Ammátalli, Paiditalli, Muthyálamma, Pólamma, Gangamma, Asiramma, Pádálamma, Gavariamma, Pattábhiamma and others; but, unlike the village gods of the south, none of them appear to have any clear history, definite attributes, or (except that some like buffalo sacrifices and some do not) any special ritual. They are all equally feared, and are worshipped as averters of sickness and possible granters of boons to those who make vows before them. Their shrines are the poorest constructions, seldom consisting of more than one small cell and often being merely a spot under a tree marked by a few sacred emblems. The history of the pérantálammas is often better known (see, for instance, p. 315), but, except that they seem to have no powers over epidemics, the reverence paid to them differs little from that accorded to the grámadévatas.

In the Agency, Bráhman influence is naturally even slighter than on the plains. The Uriya conquerors brought their own gods with them and established these in shrines in some of the larger towns, but the mass of the people in the wilder parts worship exclusively their aboriginal forefathers' animistic deities, which differ altogether from those of the low country. Villages nearer civilization, however, exhibit curiously the transition which is occurring. In Chollapadam in Párvatípur taluk (to give only one instance) are simultaneously worshipped the Khonds' ancient Kondadévata, nameless mountain spirits who dwell in a cave on the hills ; Jákara, the aboriginal Khond deity, to whom a Khond janni is priest ; Pólamma, a village deity imported from the Telugu country whose priest is a Játapu, or civilized Khond ; and Kásivisvésvara, an orthodox god of the Hindu pantheon, at whose shrine a Jangam (Lingáyat) officiates and who has a festival at Sivarátri.

In the Agency.

The aboriginal deities of the Agency include the Jákara (or Jankari) above mentioned, Tákuráni, Pindráni, Mauli, Báripennu, Dharivipennu ('pennu' means 'god'), and a host of others. These again have apparently no separate attributes or personalities, and in some places the people worship the whole crowd of them together under the name Bododévata, 'the great gods.' Jákara and Tákuráni are more often met with than any others and Hindus are at pains to explain that the latter is merely another form of Durga or Káli. None of these deities have any proper shrines; a stone under a big tree, a sacred grove (from which no twig is ever cut), a mountain peak or a deep pool are their habitations. They are usually worshipped (always by priests belonging to the hill tribes themselves) with offerings of buffaloes, goats, pigs and pigeons, and much burning of resin ; and if sufficiently propitiated grant good seasons and good hunting, and avert disease. When cholera or small-pox are virulent a ceremony is observed which is curiously parallel to that practised in the Deccan.[1] A little car is made on which is placed a grain of saffron-stained rice for every soul in the village and also numerous offerings such as little swings, pots, knives, ploughs and the like and the blood of certain sacrificial victims, and this is then dragged with due ceremony to the boundary of the village. By this means the malignant essence of the deity who brings small-pox or cholera is transferred across the boundary. The neighbouring villagers naturally hasten to move the car on with similar ceremony, and it is thus dragged through a whole series of villages and eventually left by the roadside in some lonely spot.

[1] See *Bellary Gazetteer*, 60.

CHAP. III. PRINCIPAL CASTES. In the plains.

We may now go on to refer shortly to the castes which are found in especial strength in Vizagapatam or are in other ways characteristic of the district. A beginning will be made with the castes of the low country, who, with a few exceptions expressly noted, all speak Telugu. It will save space if a few points common to most of the non-polluting non-Bráhman castes are first mentioned.

Caste organization is scarcely as systematic as in the southern districts, and the headman (*kula-pedda*) has more limited powers. Castes are generally split into the usual endogamous sections, but, what is less common, these are generally again divided into exogamous septs called *inti pérulu* or 'house names' (apparently ordinarily derived from traditional birthplaces or supposed ancestors), the members of which may not marry among themselves. Here and there, between these two, occur instances of the totemistic exogamous sections which are so common among the agency castes and are referred to below. Besides the restrictions on the choice of a bride effected by these subdivisions, there are others imposed by caste rules. Ordinarily a man must follow the Dravidian custom known as *ménarikam*, and marry his maternal uncle's daughter; and if no such daughter exists he may follow what (though it is the ordinary rule among many Tamil castes) is here called *éduru ménarikam* or 'reversed *ménarikam*,' and wed his paternal aunt's daughter, if such there be.

The ceremonies at marriages, though differing widely in different castes, are of one general type. The preliminary understanding (or betrothal) is ratified either by a dinner at which the bride's dower in the way of jewellery is announced, or, among castes which have a *vóli*, or bride-price, by the acceptance of half the sum fixed by custom therefor. A propitious day having subsequently been chosen, the wedding takes place—in the bridegroom's house if *vóli* is paid and otherwise in the bride's. A pandal of *Eugenia jambolana* poles decorated with *Erythrina indica* twigs is set up; beneath this the couple are seated and sprinkled with rice, saffron and kunkumam; the bridegroom is shaved and has his nails trimmed; the pair are bathed and dressed in new cloths; and a caste dinner follows. The priest having arrived, the couple stand one on each side of a curtain hung between them and touch feet below it, their right wrists are tied together with a saffron-coloured string called the *kankanam*, rice is thrown over them again, the marriage-badge (*táli* in Tamil or *pusti* in Telugu) is tied round the bride's neck, the pair hook their little fingers and the priest knots their cloths together, they walk round the pandal three times, are shown the star Arundhati, the emblem of constancy, and then the priest unties the knot in their cloths and the ceremony is over.

Except among the more Bráhmanized castes, divorce and widow remarriage are allowed, but a widow's marriage is a much simpler affair. The party whose conduct occasions the divorce has to repay the other the expenses originally incurred at their wedding.

Funeral ceremonies, like those at weddings, follow one general type but differ in details. Vaishnavites usually burn their dead, while Saivites bury. The latter generally have Jangam Lingáyats as priests, and so follow the Lingáyat custom of burying the dead in a sitting posture. Among some castes only the two days following the death are kept as the days of pollution during which no work should be done. On the third day, called the *chinna rózu*, the relations meet at the deceased's house, cook food, carry it to the cremation ground, offer some of it to an image made out of the dead man's ashes, and eat the rest. Among other castes, pollution lasts till the twelfth day, or *pedda rózu*, when the relations, accompanied by a Sátáni, take food to the nearest tank, throw some of it into this, and bathe and return to a dinner. Some castes keep both days.

Kápu.

By far the most numerous caste in Vizagapatam are the Kápus. In 1901 they numbered nearly 525,000 persons (more than in any other district) while with their branches and offshoots (the Velamas, Telagas, Nagarálu, Aiyarakulu and Bagatas mentioned below, three out of which five are also more numerous in this district than in any other) they amounted to no less than 971,000 souls, or one-third of the whole population of the district. They are the great cultivating caste of the community and the word Kápu is often used in the sense of 'ryot,' so that the more civilized sections of the Gadabas and Savaras are called Kápu Gadabas and Kápu Savaras although they have no connection with the Kápu caste proper.

The Kápus are split into numerous endogamous sub-divisions, of which the most prominent in this district are Panta and Gázula. The former are commonest in the coast taluks, and the latter inland, especially round Párvatípur. The word Gázula means 'bangle,' but nowadays Gázula Kápus have nothing to do with bangle-making. They differ from the Panta Kápus in showing signs of totemism. The tiger and cobra are totems of certain septs and are reverenced by these accordingly; but the primal function of the totemism has been dropped and the septs are no longer

CHAP. III. PRINCIPAL CASTES.

exogamous. The same relaxation of this essential characteristic of totemism is observable in several other castes in the plains and is an interesting example of the decay of the old ideas. Both the Panta and Gázula subdivisions comprise several exogamous *inti pérulu*; marriage follows the *mēnarikam* rule, the *vóli* is Rs. 3 and a Bráhman officiates; divorce and widow remarriage are allowed; the dead are burnt and *chinna rózu* ceremonies observed.

Velama.

Velamas are a branch of the great Kápu clan and their name is sometimes supposed to mean 'seceder' therefrom. They number 274,000 in this district, or more than in any other. Their most prominent endogamous subdivisions are (i) Pedda ('big') *alias* Padma ('lotus') Velamas, who are said to be immigrants from Venkatagiri, are largely followers and dependents of the Bobbili family, forbid widow remarriage and keep their womenkind gósha; (ii) Kamma Velamas, who are found chiefly in Vizianagram town, are said to be descended from people who immigrated from Kistna in the train of the early Rájas of that place, keep their women gósha but allow widow remarriage; and (iii) Koppala Velamas (so called because they do not shave their heads but wear their hair in a tuft) who are the commonest of the three and who resemble the Kápus in their internal constitution, totemistic practices and marriage and funeral customs.

Telaga.

Another branch of the Kápus are the Telagas, who, including the Vantari subdivision, number 114,000 in this district. They have the same names as the Kápus for their *inti pérulu* and occasionally intermarry with that caste, but are more Bráhmanized—having Bráhman gurus, marrying their girls before puberty, and refusing to recognize divorces and the remarriage of widows—are fonder of service under the zamindars and Government than of cultivation, and keep their women gósha.

Nagarálu.

The Nagarálu, another branch of the Kápus, are said to get their name, which means 'dwellers in towns,' from the fact that in the eighteenth century their ancestors went to Vizianagram and rose into prominence as physicians. They are now physicians and cultivators by occupation and number some 11,000, or more than in any other district. The caste is divided into the three genuinely totemistic groups of the cobra, tortoise and mouse, which are again subdivided into *inti pērulu*. Marriage follows *mēnarikam*, usually takes place before puberty and is performed by a Bráhman. Except that there is no *vóli*, the ceremony is of the usual type. Divorce and widow remarriage are forbidden. The dead are burnt, both *chinna* and *pedda rózu* ceremonies are performed and a Bráhman officiates.

Aiyarakulu.

The ancestors of the Aiyarakulu, yet another offshoot of the Kápus, are said to have been soldiers under Vizianagram, and stories of their military prowess are still recounted. In a campaign against Golconda, says one of these, they gave the Musalmans so much trouble that, when they were at last with difficulty exterminated, a Musalman general marched against their native villages to try and root out the whole brood once for all. But the Aiyarakulu women dressed and armed themselves like men and fell upon the invaders with such fury that the latter beat a hasty retreat. The people of the caste are now cultivators and cart-owners and number 17,000, or more than in any other district. They are commonest in the Srungavarapukóta taluk. They have the cobra and tortoise totems, and their marriage customs are similar to those of the Nagarálu.

Bagata.

The Bagatas (Bhaktas), who number 30,000 (more than in any other district), are a branch of the Kápus who chiefly reside in the Mádgole and Golgonda hills and form the aristocracy there. The Golgonda muttadars were usually of this caste. The Bagata *inti pérulu* are in several cases the same as those in the Kápu and Telaga castes and their marriage customs resemble generally those of the Nagarálu. They are both Vaishnavites and Saivites, but members of the two sects intermarry and dine together. The former own allegiance to, and are often branded with the Vaishnavite chank and chakram emblems by, a guru who lives in Gódávari; and the latter bury their dead in the usual sitting posture instead of burning them.

Gavara.

Another cultivating caste are the Gavaras, who live chiefly in the Anakápalle taluk and number some 47,000, or more than in any other district. They say that they fled from Végi near Ellore (p. 26) because the Eastern Chálukya kings molested their women, and came by sea to Púdimadaka, the port to the south of Anakápalle, and founded one or two villages between these two places. Páyaka Rao (p. 312) afterwards invited them to Anakápalle itself, where they founded the existing Gavarapálaiyam. They say they were originally traders (and some of their *inti pérulu* bear this out) but they are known nowadays as perhaps the most careful cultivators in all the district. They follow *ménarikam* and marriage is of the usual type and either infant or adult; widow remarriage is encouraged and divorce permitted; some are Vaishnavas and burn their dead, a Sátáni officiating as priest; and others are Saivas who have Jangam priests and bury in the sitting position. They pay especial reverence to the god Jagannátha of Puri, making frequent

CHAP. III. PRINCIPAL CASTES.

pilgrimages to his shrine and holding car-festivals in their villages on the same date as the Puri car-festival.

Konda Dora.

The last of the cultivating castes requiring mention are the Konda Doras ('lords of the hills') or Konda Kápus, who number 81,000 people, or more than in any other district. They mostly reside along the south-eastern edge of the 3,000 feet plateau and in the country below it, and they provide an interesting example (several others occur in this district) of the manner in which a section of a hill tribe which comes in contact with the people of the plains will gradually drop its original customs and adopt those of its more civilized neighbours, and thus in time become almost a distinct caste. They are split into two well-marked subdivisions, known as Pedda Kondalu and Chinna Kondalu, which still dine together and intermarry; but the former of these live on the plateau and are highlanders with highland customs while the latter reside in the low country and have taken to almost all the ways of the lowlanders. Thus the Chinna Kondalu have adopted *inti pérulu*, while the Pedda Kondalu still regulate their table of affinity by their ancient totemistic septs (tiger, cobra and tortoise); the former follow the lowland custom of *ménarikam*, but the latter adhere to *éduru ménarikam*; the marriage rites of the one resemble those of the plains, and those of the other the highland ceremonial; the women of the one class wear the jewels of the plains and those of the other the barbaric ornaments of the hill folk; and one subdivision names its children in the lowland fashion while the other continues to call them after the days of the week on which they were born. Both sections allow widow remarriage and divorce and both burn their dead.

Golla.

The Gollas are the shepherds of the community, and say that their name is a contraction of the Sanskrit Gópála, 'protector of cows.' They also call themselves Kónárlu, the Telugu form of the corresponding Tamil title Kónán. They are 148,000 strong (more than in any other district), are most numerous in the southern taluks, and say that they are descended from the Golla kings of that country above alluded to (p. 28), the last of whom (five brothers) were overthrown and slain by kings from Nellore. Each Telugu New Year's Day, it is stated, Gollas come across from Gódávari and go round the Golla villages reciting the names of the progenitors of the fallen line and exhibiting paintings illustrative of their overthrow. The caste is now split into five endogamous subdivisions: the Erra Gollas, descended from a Bráhman father and so superior; the Gangeddu Gollas who take round performing bulls; the Gauda Gollas, a set of wandering cowherds; the Puni Gollas, who tend only buffaloes and cows; and the Mékala Gollas, who keep sheep and goats only. The last are the most numerous, have *inti pérulu*, follow *ménarikam*, generally marry before puberty (a Bráhman officiating), allow widows and divorcées to remarry not more than thrice, bury their dead, observe *chinna* and *pedda rózu* (a Sátáni officiating) and are Vaishnavites who pay especial reverence to Krishna because he sported with the girls of their caste.

Kamsala.

The Kamsalas are the artisans of the district and are commoner than in any other Collectorate, numbering 78,000 souls. As elsewhere, they are split into the five occupational subdivisions of Kamsáli or goldsmiths, Kanchari or brass-smiths, Kammara or blacksmiths, Vadrangi or carpenters, and Silpi (or Kási) stonemasons, who dine together and intermarry. These have again the usual *inti pérulu*. As in other districts (see p. 159 of the Report on the Madras census of 1901), the Kamsális claim to be superior to the Bráhmans owing to their alleged descent from Visvakarma, the architect of the gods, wear the sacred thread, have their own caste puróhits and in marriage and other matters follow closely the Bráhman ritual. But in Vizagapatam they assert this claim with less vehemence than in some places, and do not affect to possess gótras, or prohibit animal food and strong drink. Marriage follows the usual Dravidian rule of *ménarikam*.

Sále.

The Sále weavers number 65,000 souls, again more than in any other district. They are split into the two endogamous subdivisions of Padma ('lotus') and Pattu ('silk'), the main differences between which are that the latter wear the sacred thread, will take food and water only from Bráhmans, and weave specially fine cloths, sometimes containing an admixture of silk. The peculiarly fine thread spun by the Pattu Sáles and their skill in tobacco-curing are referred to on pp. 123–4. Both subdivisions have exogamous *inti pérulu* septs and each has a headman called the Sénápati. The traditional origin of the caste is as follows: The celestials applied to Márkandéya rishi to provide them clothing, and he accordingly made a great sacrifice to Indra out of the flames of which issued Bhávana rishi bearing a ball of thread manufactured from the lotus which sprang from Vishnu's navel, from which he wove the garments sought for. He subsequently married Bhadravati, daughter of the sun, and begat 101 sons of whom one hundred became the ancestors of the Padma Sáles and the remaining one the progenitor of the Pattu Sáles. Reverence is still periodically paid to Bhávana rishi, who is represented by

CHAP. III. PRINCIPAL CASTES.

a ball of thread. Marriage is of the usual type, follows *ménarikam* and occurs before puberty; neither widow remarriage nor divorce is recognized. The Vaishnavites of the caste burn their dead and the Saivites bury them sitting.

Sálápu.

The Sálápus are a small weaving caste and are practically confined to this district. They only make very coarse fabrics. They neither marry nor dine with the Sáles, but resemble them in claiming descent from Márkandéya rishi and in calling their headman Sénápati. Bráhmans officiate at their weddings, but they allow widow remarriage and divorce.

Sílávantulu.

The Sílávantulu are another small weaving community. They make fabrics of superior kinds. They seem (though they do not admit it) to be an offshoot of the Pattu Sáles, and to have become a distinct caste owing to their embracing the Lingáyat faith and adopting the unusual custom (*síla* means a religious custom) of investing children with the lingam as soon as they are quick in their mothers' wombs. This lingam is tied to the string which carries the mother's, and is eventually hung round the child's neck when he or she has been weaned. Before the child can be married it has to be replaced by another lingam affixed with much ceremony by the family guru. The other social practices of the Sílávantulu are not peculiar; they have the usual *inti pérulu*, follow *ménarikam*, copy Bráhman wedding ceremonies, disallow divorce and widow remarriage, are vegetarians and abstainers and, of course, bury their dead in a sitting posture. The deceased's lingam is buried with him and to different parts of his body are affixed six little copper tablets on each of which is engraved one of the syllables of the holy invocation 'Om! Namasiváya!'

Yáta.

The Yátas, the toddy-drawer caste, number nearly 49,000, or more than in any other district. Their name is supposed to be a corruption of *íta*, the date-palm. They do not carry the same pollution as toddy-drawers in the south. Marriage is of the usual type, occurs after puberty and follows *ménarikam*. Divorce and widow remarriage are allowed. The dead are usually burnt and a Sátáni officiates at the *chinna rózu*.

Mangala.

The Mangalas, the barbers of the Telugu country, are more numerous here than in any other district and muster 33,000 souls. They have two endogamous subdivisions, called Kápu and Telaga, who are supposed to be descended from two half-brothers and therefore do not intermarry but will dine together. Unlike the barbers of the south, they carry no pollution when not actually engaged in their profession. They teach their boys to shave by making them practice for some months on an old chatti smeared with wet mud. They will not shave the polluting castes, but will lend them razors for a consideration. They are musicians as well as barbers, are often (like the Uriya barber caste of Bhondáris) store-keepers to rich households, and their women are sometimes midwives. Marriage occurs before puberty and is of the usual kind. A Bráhman officiates. Remarriage is generally permitted only in the case of childless widows, but divorce is allowed. The dead are burnt and *chinna rózu* rites observed.

Jálári. Jáláris, fishermen in the sea, number some 15,000 and are more common than elsewhere. The name is derived from the Sanskrit *jála*, a net. The caste seems to have originally been an inland community, fishing only in fresh water, and to have afterwards gravitated to the sea-shore. Its marriage ceremonies are not peculiar, except that no pandal is used; widow remarriage and divorce are allowed; the dead are burnt and a Sátáni performs the *pedda rózu* ceremonies.

Míla. The Mílavándlu (*míla* means fish) or Ódavándlu ('boatmen') are another caste of sea-fishermen. Their ways resemble generally those of the Jáláris, but they have different *inti pérulu* and are apparently a distinct caste. The caste goddess is Pólamma, in whose honour an annual festival is held.

Nágavásulu. The Nágavásulu, who are in greater strength (nearly 20,000 persons) here than elsewhere, were originally a dancing-girl caste (*nágavásamu* means a company of dancing-women) but are now chiefly well-to-do agriculturists. Some of the women are still *dásis*, and they gather recruits from other castes. Both *ménarikam* and *éduru ménarikam* are followed; marriage is either before or after puberty; a *vóli* is paid; widow remarriage and divorce are allowed; and the dead are burnt. The caste is commonest in the Pálkonda country.

Relli. The Rellis, also known as Sachcharis and called Sapiris among themselves, are a caste who speak Uriya (though they are not found in the Agency) and are partly gardeners and partly scavengers. The latter are said to have only taken to their present occupation during the 1877 famine, when they were starving, but they are now held to carry pollution and seldom marry with the other section.

Godagula. Another Uriya-speaking caste found on the plains are the Godagula basket-makers who live all along the foot of the hills. They should not be confused with the Gúdalas, and are a polluting caste, which the Gúdalas are not. They make special kinds of winnowing-fans and other articles which the Médaras, Gúdalas and other basket-making castes do not manufacture.

CHAP. III. PRINCIPAL CASTES.

Beggar castes.

The Sátánis frequently referred to above are the most prominent of a number of castes in this district who are half priests and half beggars. They are family priests to non-Bráhman Vaishnavas, gurus to several of the cultivating castes, and also go round singing and begging with a huge *námam* on their foreheads, strings of tulasi beads round their necks, a fan, and a copper vessel shaped like a melon. The word Sátáni is said to be a form of Sáttádavan, 'the uncovered one,' because these people wear no tuft of hair nor sacred thread. Its supposed connection with Chaitanya has no foundation. The Vizagapatam Sátánis are initiated and branded with the usual Vaishnavite emblems by gurus of Goomsur in Ganjám.

The Dásaris are also beggars who are branded with Vaishnava emblems. In the Tamil country they are essentially religious mendicants, but here they are generally wandering ballad-mongers who go about singing the popular rhymes of the countryside, such as those about the fall of Bobbili (pp. 237-41); the evil deeds and tragic end of Ammi Náyudu, a village headman in Pálkonda taluk; the fate of Lakshmamma, a Velama woman who was murdered by her husband for marrying her daughter according to *éduru ménarikam*; and the sati (p. 318) of Yerakamma of Srungavarapukóta.

There are also several beggar communities who are supported by certain particular castes, because they are supposed either to be illegitimate descendants of those bodies or to have done them some notable service in days gone by. Thus the Víramushtis, who are Lingáyat acrobats, beg only of Dévángas and Gavara Kómatis; the Mailáris and Nettikótalas only of the Gavara Kómatis, whom they say they assisted in their legendary struggle with king Vishnuvardhana; the Gósangis of Mádigas; the Mástigas of Málas; the Sádhuasúrulu of the Padma Sáles; the Samayamuváru of both Padma and Pattu Sáles; the Singamuváru of the Dévángas; and the juggler Vipravinódis of the Bráhmans.

Principal castes in the Agency.

The people of the Agency belong to two broad classes; namely, the original people of the soil and the foreigner Uriyas who in some remote past swept down and imposed their rule upon them. Uriya ousted (and is still ousting) the tribal dialects, and castes now speak it who are not Uriyas by descent; but which of the hill people are the original inhabitants and which are invaders and emigrants from elsewhere is an interesting question which the information at present on record is insufficient to solve.

Among the agency castes the exogamous septs are generally totemistic, a rare character in this Presidency. The commonest totems are the tiger, cobra and tortoise, but the bear, iguana, dog, monkey, goat, bull, cow, lizard, parrot, peacock, and vulture also occur, and in addition certain plants such as the pumpkin and the *Bauhinia purpurea*, and a few inanimate objects like stone and the sun. The usual Uriya name for a totem is *boms*, which seems to be the same word as *vamsa*, a family. Members of the same totem may not intermarry, and children take their father's totem. Every totem is revered. Animal totems may on no account be killed or eaten. The very idea of such a possibility makes the totemist shudder, and he declares that so unspeakable an act would result in the entire destruction of his whole tribe. Totems must, indeed, be befriended where possible—a tortoise, for example, being put in the nearest water. If the totem attacks a man he may kill it in self-defence; but its dead body is then often given funeral rites almost as if it was the corpse of a man. When a man sees his totem he folds his hands across his breast and does reverence. Plant totems are not eaten, injured, or even touched. The sun is venerated by the people of its totem fasting when it does not appear; and stone by being excluded from all buildings and all service—stone mortars, for example, being taboo. The idea that members of a totemistic division are all one family is strong. If one of them dies, all the others are under pollution for three days and have to get their food from their wives' relations.

The recognized forms of marriage in the Agency include several of those expressly forbidden by Manu. There is marriage by purchase, by service for three years in the house of the girls' parents, by mutual consent and clandestine elopement (the man having then to pay a fine called *dos tonka*), by forcible compulsion on the part of the bridegroom and his friends, and by selection at the *dhangadi basa* or girls' sleeping-hut. One form of this last is described in the account of the Banda Porojas below.

But the usual procedure is for the man's parents to go to the girl's house, leave presents (usually pots of strong drink) there, and judge of the likelihood of their suit being successful by seeing whether the liquor is thrown away or drunk. If it is drunk, they renew the suit with other presents until at length an understanding is arrived at. Subsequent ceremonies are simple and consist mainly in the provision of caste dinners and more liquor.

Divorce and widow remarriage are universally permitted. The younger brother may marry his elder brother's widow, but not conversely, for the elder brother is as the father of the family. If a widow has children and marries outside the family her new husband has to pay a fine called *ránd tonka* or 'widow-money.' The right to divorce is mutual and is exercised on slight grounds. The husband generally makes the woman a small present first. She often forestalls him by running off to the man she fancies, who then has to pay the expenses of her original wedding and return her jewellery.

The dead are nearly always burnt, but among some castes the ashes are afterwards buried and the spot marked in some way. Children who have not cut their teeth, pregnant women, and people who have died of small-pox are usually buried. Pollution lasts for from three to ten days.

In referring to the various castes we may first take those which talk Uriya and then those which have languages of their own; and within each of these groups we may usually arrange them in the order of their numerical strength.

Poroja.

The Porojas (91,000), the most numerous of the Uriya-speaking castes, form an appropriately difficult beginning to this difficult subject. The name is a generic term (some say it means merely 'ryot') which is loosely applied to a series of castes which differ in appearance, customs and even language. Apparently there are seven kinds of Porojas; namely, (i) Bárang Jódia Porojas, who speak a dialect of Uriya and eat beef; (ii) Pengu Porojas, who comprise two groups one of which will eat buffalo and the other will not, but both speak a tongue of their own which is said[1] to be akin to Khond; (iii) Khondi-Porojas, who eat beef, are a section of the Khonds and speak the Khond language; (iv) Parengi Porojas, who are a section of the Gadabas and speak their language; (v) Banda, Nanda or Langla Porojas (all of which words mean 'naked'), also called Banda Gadabas, who are again a section of the Gadabas and apparently speak a dialect of Gadaba; (vi) Tagara Porojas, who are a division of the Kóyas and talk Kóya; and (vii) Dúr Porojas, also called Didáyi Porojas, who speak Uriya.

Only the first and fifth of these are readily distinguishable. The Bárang Jódias, sometimes called merely Jódias, are prominent round Koraput and Jeypore, where their short cerise and white cloths and their left arms covered with a dozen or more brass bracelets render them very conspicuous.[2]

[1] Report on Madras census of 1891, para. 272.

[2] No sooner, however, has the enquirer congratulated himself on differentiating these people than he is pulled up short by the fact that round Náráyanapatnam are persons calling themselves Jódias who differ altogether in appearance (their characteristic ornament being a pile of necklets of coral and blue beads a foot deep) and say they have no connection with any Porojas.

Round about Koraput, their marriage ceremonies are of the typical kind. The parents of the boy deposit two pots of liquor and some rice at the house of the girl they want their son to marry and, if these are not thrown into the street, follow up their move by taking more liquor and rice, a new cloth and money as the price of the girl. A dinner follows in token that the match is arranged and next day the bride goes to the groom's village in state. Outside the latter's house two poles are planted, between which a pumpkin is suspended from a string. As the bride's party approach, this is cut down with a tangi (axe), the party enter the house, the bride is given a new cloth, and liquor is liberally distributed. Cheered by this, the wedding party dance most of the night through, and next day, after a caste dinner, the bride is formally handed over to her husband in the presence of the janni (priest) and headman of the village.

Round Jeypore, however, the ceremonies differ considerably and as they doubtless change again every few miles, it would be profitless to point out the variations.

The Banda Porojas are the best recognized of the seven Poroja sections, because they have special ways of their own and live in a definite and prescribed locality in what is known as the Juangar mutta of Malkanagiri taluk, south-west of the falls of the Machéru referred to on p. 12. They are called 'naked' because the women (the men are not distinctive in appearance) shave their heads completely, wear nothing above the waist except brass ornaments and strings of beads, and have for their only garment a strip of coloured cloth woven from jungle fibre (*Asclepias gigantea*, apparently) eight inches wide and two feet long which they tie round their middles in such a way as to leave the left thigh bare both in front and behind. They explain this scanty costume by saying that some of their ancestresses once came upon Síta when she was bathing in the Machéru with very little on, and laughed at her; and that she pronounced a curse upon them if they ever wore more clothes than she was wearing then Mr. H. G. Turner, it is said, once induced one of them to wear a cloth, but she died soon after and none of the others has since dared to follow her example. Mr. H. C. Daniel, Assistant Superintendent of Police at Koraput, who provided some of the foregoing particulars, also gives the following account of the extraordinary manner in which matches are made among these people, the method being a rude variant of the custom prevalent among many of the hill tribes whereby a boy desirous of marriage goes at night to the *dhangadi basa*, or hut set aside for

CHAP. III. PRINCIPAL CASTES.

the unmarried girls to sleep in, and proffers his suit to the maiden of his affections. About two months before Dasara each village naik (headman) has a hole about eight feet square and nine feet deep dug in his village and roofed with logs and mud so arranged as to leave one small opening. In this all the unmarried girls of the village have to sleep. Any youth desirous of matrimony joins them there at night and next morning leaves his brass bracelet with the girl of his choice. The pair afterwards go together to the girl's people and explain matters and then, with the relatives on both sides, repair to the jungle, where a fire is lit and the girl takes a hot brand and applies it to the boy's posteriors. If he cries out 'Yam! Yam!' in pain, the girl refuses him, but if he makes no sound the couple are considered to be man and wife. The girl of course takes care not to hold the brand too close to a youth she likes, and this system has the advantage of giving both parties a choice in the matter.

Dombu.

The Dombus, Dombos or Dombs number 51,000 and are the beggars, weavers, musicians and Pariahs of the Agency. They speak Uriya, but differ altogether in appearance both from other Uriyas and from the hill folk, and whence they originally came is not obvious. They seem to be closely akin to the Pános of Ganjám. Though almost the lowest caste in the country (the Ghási horsekeepers and Chitra Ghási brass-smiths are even deeper down in the social scale) they have succeeded by dubious means in acquiring much influence. Their superior intelligence enables them to lead the Khonds by the nose, their talent for cattle-theft (see p. 204) makes them not only hated but feared, their supposed powers over devils and witches result in their being consulted when troubles appear, and their skill in weaving and petty trading is rendering them well-to-do. Some of them are cultivators. All the native Christians of the Agency are recruited from this caste.

The Dombus seem to consist of six subdivisions; namely, Mirigáni and Kobbiriya, who live round Kótapád and with whom the others will neither dine nor intermarry; Odiya (Uriya), who are commonest round Pottangi, Koraput and Jeypore; Sódabisiya, from the Lakshmipuram side; Andiniya, who are also found near Kótapád; and Mándiri, who live chiefly round Rámagiri and Malkanagiri The last four dine together and intermarry. These subdivisions are again split into totemistic septs, of which the Odiyas possess as many as ten.

When a girl attains puberty she is held to be polluted for five days, and at the end of that time drink is distributed among her relations. Marriage usually occurs after puberty and preferentially follows *éduru ménarikam*. Overtures are first made by offering presents to the bride's parents in the usual way and the actual ceremony takes place in the bride's house. The rites are much as usual, the couple hooking their little fingers together, having their cloths knotted, and being bathed in saffron water. The relations feast on pork and strong drink. The untying of the knotted cloths is the final ceremony. The dead are usually buried, but the richer Dombus cremate them. Near relations shave on the tenth day.

When selecting a site for a house, the Dombus place, at the four corners, one grain of rice upon two others and shield them with stones and earth. If after several days the top grain still remains balanced on the other two, the site is considered lucky. Children are supposed to be born without souls and to be afterwards chosen as an abode by the soul of an ancestor. The coming of the ancestor is signalized by the child dropping a chicken bone which has been thrust into its hand and much rejoicing follows among the assembled relations.

Paidi.

Some of the Dombus of the Párvatípur Agency follow many of the customs of the low country castes (including *ménarikam*), and say they are the same as the Paidis (or Paidi Málas) of the plains adjoining, with whom they intermarry. These Paidis, who speak Telugu, are 40,000 strong and are also (p. 203) a low and criminal caste. Paidi Mála means 'hill Mála,' but the Paidis repudiate with indignation all connection with the ordinary Málas (and in most places with the Dombus also) and in the south and west of the district claim descent from Válmíki, the compiler of the Rámáyana. At their weddings they follow the ceremonies of the plains. Some of the Paidis cultivate land, but most are traders. They are nearly all Vaishnavites.

Bottada.

The Bottadas are 50,000 strong and their traditions say they came from Bastar. They speak a kind of Uriya (or perhaps Bastari) and are principally found near Naurangpur, Kótapád and Umarkót. They are perhaps the best cultivators in Jeypore, stand high in the social scale and wear the sacred thread, permission to use which was bought by their ancestors from the Rája of Jeypore. They are split into the three endogamous divisions of Bodo ('big'), or pure Bottadas; Madhya ('middle'), descendants of Bottada men by women of other castes; and Sanno ('little'), children of Madhya men and other women.

CHAP. III. PRINCIPAL CASTES.

Bodo Bottadas have several totemistic septs. Marriage occurs either before or after puberty and follows *éduru ménarikam*. The usual preliminary overtures to the girl's parents are made, but the actual ceremony is far more elaborate than an ordinary hill wedding. In front of the bridegroom's house a pandal of nine sál poles is erected, the caste díssari officiates as priest, the couple's little fingers are hooked together and their cloths knotted, they walk seven times round the pandal, hómam is lit, the pair are marked on the forehead with saffron and bathed in saffron water, and a caste banquet concludes the affair. The dead (with the usual exceptions) are burnt, and pollution lasts ten days during which the deceased's relations cannot cook any food; ceremonies are performed at the cremation ground on the second and eighth days.

Rona.

The Ronas, or Rona Paikos (29,000), are another immigrant tribe. They say that seven brothers, their ancestors, came long ago to Nandapuram, then the capital of the Jeypore country, and took military service under the Rája there. They are still most numerous round Nandapuram (where their caste headman resides), Pádwa and Koraput; *rona* means 'battle' and *paiko* 'sepoy'; and some of them are still personal retainers of the Mahárája. They speak Uriya, wear the sacred thread (leave to do so having been purchased from the Rája in days gone by) and hold their heads high, declining to accept food from any but Bráhmans. They are split into three endogamous divisions resembling those of the Bottadas; namely, Rona Paiko proper; Kottiya Paiko, children of Rona men by women of other castes; and Puttiya Paiko, descendants of Kottiya Paiko men and other women. The last two rank below the pure Ronas in social matters. The Kottiyas (who numbered 12,000 in 1901) have usually, but apparently wrongly, been classed as a distinct caste. The people called Odiya Paikos, on the other hand, have generally been treated as Ronas, but they seem to be separate and to follow the customs of the upper Uriya castes, notably their very elaborate seven-days' wedding with its tiresome ceremonial.

The Rona Paikos have several totemistic exogamous septs. When a girl attains maturity she is kept in an enclosure within the house made of thread wound round seven arrows placed on end. Marriage occurs either before or after puberty, follows *éduru ménarikam*, and is somewhat similar in form to the Bottada ceremony.

Bhúmiya.

The Bhúmiyas, 'soil-folk,' number 19,000 and reside chiefly on the western fringe of Jeypore between Kótapád and Salimi.

Tradition says that they were the first to cultivate land on the hills. They speak Uriya; have totems; follow *éduru ménarikam*; and resemble the Bottadas in their marriage and funeral customs.

Sondi. The Sondis (18,000) are Uriya-speaking distillers, liquor-sellers and usurers who are scattered all about the hills. By pandering to the hill man's taste for strong drink they have in many places got him and his property entirely in their hands, and they are the best-hated class in all the Agency. Their own traditions say that they are descended from a Bráhman. This man, a great magician, was ordered by the king to exhibit his powers by setting a tank on fire. A distiller promised to show him how to do so on condition of being given his daughter to wife, and then covered the surface of the tank with liquor, which of course burnt readily enough. His descendants by the Bráhman magician's daughter are the present Sondis.

Like the Bottadas, the Sondis are split into the three endogamous divisions of Bodo, Madhya and Sanno, the first of which is again sub-divided into exogamous septs corresponding to the *inti pérulu* of the plains. The caste headman is called Bissóyi. Marriage occurs before puberty and, as among the upper Uriyas generally, a man marries outside his family if he can. The actual ceremony, as with all these Uriyas, lasts seven whole days, and is a wearisome round of rites of which the meaning has been lost. On each day the couple play with cowries, part of the game consisting in the bride trying with both her hands to capture the shells her husband holds in one of his, and in his trying to force from her, with one finger, the cowries she is holding in both hands clasped. A Bráhman presides and *hómam* is lit, a *pusti* is tied, and offerings are made to ancestors. The dead are burnt and pollution lasts ten days. On the tenth night the heir performs an odd ceremony. He gets a pot, makes holes in its sides, puts food and a light in it, and carries it to the burning-ground. There he puts it down, calls thrice to the dead, saying that food is ready and asking him to come, and then returns home.

Korono. The Koronos, who speak Uriya, have usually been classed with Karnam in the statistics, and under this head have also been included the Telugu-speaking Shristi Karnams, who are apparently an entirely different body, though following the same occupation of clerk, village accountant, etc. The Koronos are split into several divisions, two of which are Mahanti and Patnaik. They marry outside their family if they can, and have the usual seven-days wedding ceremony above referred to, at which a Bráhman officiates.

CHAP. III. PRINCIPAL CASTES.

Máli.

The Mális (14,000) say they were originally growers of flowers for temples and came from Benares. They are now among the most careful of all the hill cultivators, being especially skilful at raising garden crops. They speak Uriya and drink very little liquor. The caste is said to be split into six endogamous subdivisions which chiefly reside in six different parts of the Agency; namely, Bodo in Pottangi and Koraput, Pondra (which has often been wrongly treated as a separate caste) in Naurangpur and Kótapád, Kosalya in Parlákimedi in Ganjám, Pannara in Jeypore, Sonkuva in Gunupur, and Dongrudiya round Nandapuram. Marriage must take place, under penalty of being outcasted, before puberty, and among the Pondra Mális, if no suitable husband has been found as that time draws near, a mock wedding, without any bridegroom, is held. At ordinary weddings a Bráhman or caste elder officiates and the rites are not peculiar, but at marriages among the Pondra Mális the auspicious moment is awaited by the couple seated on either side of a curtain with their cloths knotted, the *makkutas* (fillets) on their heads, their hands touching and on them a myrabolam wound in cotton. As the auspicious moment passes the cotton is unwound, the knotted cloths are untied and the curtain is pulled down. These Pondra Mális also practise an unusual ceremony on the ninth day after funerals, the heir digging a hole in the deceased's house and burying in it a light and the remains of his supper.

Omanaito.

The Omanaitos (Amanaito, Omaito) are cultivators who reside chiefly about Naurangpur. They have two endogamous divisions called Bodo and Sanno, of whom the latter are the illegitimate children of the former. The Bodos are split into totemistic septs. Their marriage and funeral ceremonies are much the same as usual except that one item in the former is a free-fight with mud for missiles.

Mattiya.

The Mattiyas (the name means 'of the soil') are careful cultivators who live chiefly in the north-eastern corner of the Malkanagiri taluk and seem to belong to the original population of the country. They talk Uriya but follow the primitive fashion of naming their children after the day of the week on which they were born. The Mattiyas have totemistic septs, marry after puberty with much the same ceremonies as usual, and burn the dead. The spot where the body was burnt is first marked with a bamboo to which is tied some portion of the deceased's cloth and round which are broken the pots he last used. On the ninth day the ashes are collected and buried in a square pit roughly floored, and over this is erected a kind of small hut.

Pentiya.

The Pentiyas say their real name is Holuva or Halba and that they are called Pentiya because they emigrated from Bastar to Pentikonna near Sembliguda in Pottangi taluk. They speak Bastari mixed with Uriya. They are split into Bodo and Sanno divisions, like the Omanaitos, and have totemistic septs. The caste headman is called the Bhatto naik, is assisted in his duties by a pradháni (minister) and two others, and has a servant called the choláno who bears a silver wand of office when he summons pancháyats. This sort of pomp is unknown among the agency people proper. The pancháyats take themselves very seriously, also, and any one outcasted by them can only be readmitted after elaborate ceremonial which includes the branding of his tongue with silver wire. Marriages and funerals are of much the usual type.

Dhakkado.

Dhakkados (1,760 in number) are the illegitimate children of women of non-polluting castes by Uriya Bráhmans, who are less particular than their castemen elsewhere about forming *liaisons* outside their own community. Dhakkados wear the sacred thread and take Bráhmanical names; but at weddings and funerals they observe the customs of their mother's caste and they adopt these people's occupation.

Khond.

We now come to the tribes of the Agency who speak their own tribal dialects. Of these by far the most numerous are the Khonds, who are 150,000 strong. An overwhelming majority of this number, however, are not the wild barbarous Khonds regarding whom there is such a considerable literature[1] and who are so prominent in Ganjám, but a series of communities descended from them which exhibit infinite degrees of difference from their more interesting progenitors according to the grade of civilisation to which they have attained. The only really primitive Khonds in Vizagapatam are the Dongria ('jungle') Khonds of the north of Bissamkatak taluk, the Désya Khonds who live just south-west of them in and around the Nímgiris, and the Kuttiya ('hill') Khonds of the hills in the north-east of the Gunupur taluk. Time did not permit of any expedition to these out-of-the-way corners and any enquiry into the customs of the people there would have necessitated double interpretation from Khond

[1] *E.g.*, Macpherson's *Report on the Khonds of Ganjám and Cuttack* (1841); Maj.-Gen. Campbell's *Service among the Wild Tribes of Khondistan* (1864); Dalton's *Ethnology of Bengal* (1872); Hunter's *Orissa* (1872); Risley's *Tribes and Castes of Bengal* (1891); the papers in J.R.A.S., vii, 172 (Macpherson), xiii, 216 (Macpherson) and xvii, 1 (Lieut. Frye); in M.J.L.S., vi, 17 and vii, 89; in *Calcutta Review*, viii, 1 and x, 278; and in J.A.S.B., xxv, 39 and lxxiii, 39.

CHAP. III. PRINCIPAL CASTES.

into Uriya and from Uriya into Telugu or English, for a knowledge of both Khond and Telugu or Khond and English is rare. No fresh information has thus been obtained about these people. They were the classes who were most addicted to the meriah sacrifices referred to on p. 199. Their headmen are called majjis. The Kuttiya Khond men wear ample necklets of white beads and prominent brass earrings, but otherwise they dress like any other hill people. Their women, however, have a distinctive garb, putting on a kind of turban on state occasions, wearing nothing above the waist except masses of white bead necklaces which almost cover their breasts, and carrying a series of heavy brass bracelets half way up their forearms. The *dhangadi basa* system already referred to prevails among them in its simplest form and the youths and girls have opportunities for the most intimate acquaintance before they need inform their parents that they wish to marry. Special ceremonies are practised to prevent the spirits of the dead (especially of those killed by tigers) from returning to molest the living. Except totemistic septs, they have apparently no subdivisions.

The dress of the civilized Khonds of both sexes is ordinary and uninteresting. These people are called by themselves (sometimes) Kuvinga; in Telugu, generically, Kódulu; and by their neighbours by a whole series of terms, which differ according to the locality and the degree of civilization attained, among them being Poroja Kódulu, Konda Doralu, Doralu, Játapu Doralu, Játapu, Janapa Doralu and Múka Doralu. Whether these, or any of them, should be held to be distinct castes, and, if so, at what point a man ceases to be a Khond and becomes (say) a Játapu, are matters which need much careful enquiry to clear up.

The interesting aspect of the case is the manner in which fresh castes can be seen actually in the making. These civilized Khonds worship all degrees of deities from their own tribal Jákara down to the orthodox Hindu gods; follow every gradation of marriage and funeral customs from those of their primitive forefathers to those of the low-country Telugus; speak dialects which range from good Khond through bastard patois down to corrupt Telugu; and allow their totemistic septs to be degraded down to, or divided into, the *inti pérulu* of the plains.

Játapu.

The Játapus or Játapu Doras are usually classed as a separate caste and were returned as 66,000 strong at the 1901 census. The Khonds in the Pálkonda hills call themselves by this name and it is supposed to be short for Khonda Játapu Doralu, or 'lords of the Khond caste.' They speak a kind of Khond among themselves, worship Jákara, call their priests jannis and their soothsayers díssaris, have exogamous septs which are a mixture of totems and *inti pérulu*, marry after the low-country fashion but tie no *pusti*, observe only three days pollution at funerals and make periodical sacrifices to propitiate their ancestors.

Múka Dora.

The Múka Doras may perhaps be classed as a separate caste. The Páchipenta zamindar is one of them. They speak Telugu, have totems as well as *inti pérulu*, follow *ménarikam*, observe at weddings ceremonies which are an odd mixture of hill rites and low-country practice, seclude girls within an enclosure of arrows when they attain puberty but observe no pollution at subsequent periods, practise a variant of the *chinna rózu* or *pedda rózu* ceremonies but also have a feast in honour of their ancestors in general, have taken to pack-bullock trading and give their children Telugu names.

Savara.

The Savaras, like the Khonds, consist of two differing classes—the primitive race which lives on the hills east and north-east of Gunupur, and the more civilized sections which inhabit the Pálkonda hills and the low country in that corner of the district and are called Pallapu or Kápu Savaras. The two together number 50,000 persons. The former have a distinctive dress, the men using long langútis which hang down in front and behind like tails, wearing a plume of white crane's feathers in their cone-shaped red turbans and carrying a bow and arrows adorned with peacocks' feathers; and the women dressing in one short cloth with a broad red border round their waists and nothing above this except masses of brass wire and bead necklets a foot deep which almost prevent them from turning their heads and into which they stick their cheroots. Among these people are certain occupational subdivisions such as the Arisis, who weave the tribal cloths; the Kundáls, who make baskets; and the Loharas or Múlis, who are iron-workers; but there is no theoretical bar to marriage between these, and there are no totemistic septs among them. The Savaras' careful methods of cultivation are referred to on p. 257 below and the outbreaks amongst them on p. 258. Their remoteness and language hindered the collection of information regarding them, but Mr. F. Fawcett has described elaborately[1] the ways of the tribe just across the border in Ganjám (to which district it really belongs) and it will be sufficient to include here a few notes about the more numerous Savaras of the plains.

[1] *Journ. Anthrop. Soc. of Bombay*, i, 218.

CHAP. III. PRINCIPAL CASTES.

These people worship either Jákara or Loddalu,[1] who have no regular temple but are symbolized by a stone under a big tree. Sacrifices of goats are made to them when the various crops are ripening and the victim must first eat food offered to it. The hill Savaras, on the other hand, chiefly fear the deity Jalia, who in many villages is provided with a small habitation with a circular thatched roof in which are placed wooden images of household implements and requisites and figures of men, animals, birds, etc. The Kápu Savaras, like the primitive section, have no real marriage divisions, but are taking to *ménarikam* although the hill custom requires a man to marry outside his village. Their wedding ceremonies bear a distant resemblance to those among the hill Savaras. When a youth among the latter wishes to marry a girl, his parents take an arrow, a white crane's feather and some liquor to the house of her parents, and if these latter at first throw the presents into the street and attack the bringers, they try again until they are peacefully welcomed and matters are put in train, or until the youth, tired of refusals, carries off the girl by stealth or force. Among the Kápu Savaras the preliminary arrow and liquor are similarly presented, but the bridegroom goes at length on an auspicious day with a large party to the bride's house, and the marriage is marked by his eating out of the same platter with her and by much drinking, feasting and dancing.

A death is announced by the firing of guns, the body is burnt, the bones are collected and buried along with the deceased's tangi and other possessions, the spot is marked with a sál post to which a bit of the departed's garment is attached, and a drink and dance conclude the ceremony. This again is a copy of the hill Savaras' rite, but the latter eventually mark the place with a stone. Both sections perform a great annual sacrifice to their departed ancestors on a full moon day in the spring at which a buffalo or goat is slain for every death during the year and the spirits of the dead are entreated not to return and molest the living. Savara headmen are called Gómangos.

Gadabas.

The Gadabas are palanquin-bearers and cultivators by profession, number 40,000 persons, and are split into six subdivisions; namely, Bodo Gadabas and Ollár Gadabas, who dine together and intermarry; Parengi Gadabas, whose women do not wear the bustles and chaplets referred to below; Kalloyi Gadabas, who are the only section which will touch a horse (professional palki-bearers naturally have no love for the rival animal) and are contemned by the others accordingly; and Kápu and Kattiri

[1] This seems to be sometimes used as a generic term for the gods as a body.

Gadabas, who are the more civilized sections living on or near the plains. Each of these subdivisions is again split into totemistic septs, but some of the low-country Gadabas have abandoned these.

Gadaba men dress like other hill people, but the women of the tribe have perhaps the most extraordinary garb of any in this Presidency. Round their waists they tie a fringed, narrow cloth, woven by themselves on the most primitive loom imaginable, of which the warp is the hand-spun fibre of different jungle shrubs and the woof is cotton, dyed at home with indigo and *Morinda citrifolia*, and arranged in stripes of red, blue and white; either over or under this they wear a bustle made of some forty strands of stout black cord woven from other shrubs and tied together at the ends; round the upper part of their bodies is another cloth, similar to but smaller than the waist-cloth; on their right forearms, from wrist to elbow, are a number of brass bracelets; over their foreheads is fixed a chaplet of cowrie shells, the white seeds of the *kúsa* grass, or the red and black berries of the *Abrus precatorius*; and in their ears are enormous coils of thick brass wire (one specimen was eight inches across and contained twenty strands) which hang down on their shoulders and in extreme cases prevent them from turning their heads except slowly and with care. The above are the essentials of the costume; the details differ in different places. The bustle is accounted for by the following tradition: A goddess visited a Gadaba village incognita and asked leave of one of the women to rest on a cot. She was brusquely told that the proper seat for beggars was the floor; and she consequently decreed that thenceforth all Gadaba women should wear a bustle to remind them to avoid churlishness.

Marriage usually occurs after puberty and, as among the Khonds and Savaras, a man generally weds a girl from outside his family. The usual preliminary presents of toddy etc. are sent to the bride's people by the parents of the suitor, and eventually, if there is no just impediment, the latter and his relatives go to the girl's house with more presents and bring her to their village. The wedding is celebrated in a pandal there and is followed by the usual drinking and dancing. If the girl's parents dislike the match she often elopes with the youth, who eventually is punished for his transgression by having to provide a caste dinner. Gadaba children, like those of other primitive tribes here, are usually named after the day of the week on which they were born. Stone slabs are erected to the memory of the dead and sacrifices offered to them now and again.

CHAP. III. PRINCIPAL CASTES.

Kóya.

The Kóyas, who number 11,000 in this district, live in the corner of Malkanagiri taluk south-west of Malkanagiri town and are immigrants from Gódávari, to which district, rather than to Vizagapatam, they belong. Their customs in that country have been closely studied by the Rev. Mr. Cain, who spent years among them as a missionary and has published accounts of them in the *Indian Antiquary* for 1876 and 1879 and the *Christian College Magazine* for 1887 and 1888. In this district they have several exogamous, but not totemistic, septs, marry after puberty, follow *éduru ménarikam* and pay a bride-price or *vóli*. The wedding ceremony is conducted in a pandal, and one of the essential rites consists in the bridegroom bending his head over the bride's while the relations pour water over both. Drinking and riotous dancing all night conclude the marriage.

Apparently there is no pollution at deaths. The ashes of the dead are made into little balls and buried with some of his belongings and marked with a perpendicular stone slab. To this a buffalo is sacrificed. The tail is tied to the slab and left there, and the rest of the animal is eaten by the relations. They explain [1] that as long as the tail is there the deceased thinks he has got the whole of the buffalo and is contented. A mile east of Malkanagiri, on the Kondakambéru road, is a great collection of these slabs. The Kóyas reverence the Pándava brothers and are often named after them. They are keen shikáris and often place their trophies on poles outside their habitations.

Gónd.

The Gónds (19,000) are another race who belong less to Vizagapatam than to adjoining areas. They are numerous in Naurangpur taluk, but their real home is in the Central Provinces, where their customs have been frequently studied.[2] In Naurangpur they are split into the three divisions of Ráj, Dúr and Muria, each of which is subdivided into totemistic septs. *Éduru ménarikam* is followed and weddings take place in the bride's village.

[1] *Teste* Mr. G. F. Paddison, I.C.S., who has kindly contributed other particulars embodied in these notes.

[2] See *Aboriginal Tribes of the Central Provinces*, edited by Sir R. Temple, and also the works of Messrs. Dalton, Risley and Crooke.

CHAPTER IV.

AGRICULTURE AND IRRIGATION.

AGRICULTURAL STATISTICS—The crops most grown—Indigo—Sugar-cane—Jute—Others. CULTIVATION METHODS—On the hills—The Agricultural Association. IRRIGATION—The protected area—Wells—Tanks—Channels—From the Varáha—From the Sárada—From the Nágávali—The Nágávali project. ECONOMIC CONDITION OF AGRICULTURISTS.

CHAP. IV. AGRICULTURAL STATISTICS.

MORE than nine-tenths of Vizagapatam consists of zamindari land, and of the remaining tenth a fifth is whole inam. Consequently agricultural statistics are available for only about eight per cent. of the area of the district, namely for the ryotwari and minor inam land in the three Government taluks of Golgonda, Pálkonda and Sarvasiddhi. Figures for these are appended, but the three areas differ widely in their soils, rainfall and facilities for irrigation, and cannot be considered representative of the district as a whole :—

Taluk.	Percentage of area by survey which is				Percentage of area in village accounts of				
	Ryotwari.	Minor inam.	Whole inam.	Zamindari.	Forest and other area not available for cultivation.	Cultivable waste other than fallow.	Current fallows.	Net area cropped.	Irrigated by all sources.
Golgonda ...	70·7	2·2	7·9	19·2	67·8	2·5	5·6	24·1	7·2
Pálkonda ...	58·2	5·3	13·6	22·9	38·1	5·4	6·5	50·0	25·7
Sarvasiddhi ...	36·0	6·6	4·3	53·1	32·8	4·2	11·2	51·8	27·1

The divergencies in the circumstances of the three taluks are further exhibited in the following statistics of the percentage of the assessed wet and dry land, respectively, in each which is assessed at the various rates :—

CHAP. IV. AGRICULTURAL STATISTICS.

Taluk.	Percentage of assessed wet land which is assessed at—						
	Rs. 8-0-0.	Rs. 7-0-0.	Rs. 5-8-0.	Rs. 4-8-0.	Rs. 3-8-0.	Rs. 2-8-0.	Rs. 2-0-0.
Golgonda	...	12·0	12·3	27·6	25·6	12·3	10·2
Pálkonda	5·5	12·7	17·5	23·7	21·4	11·7	7·5
Sarvasiddhi	4·8	14·2	19·9	19·2	16·8	17·5	7·6

Taluk.	Percentage of assessed dry land which is assessed at—								
	Rs. 3-0-0.	Rs. 2-8-0.	Rs. 2-0-0.	Re. 1-8-0.	Re. 1-4-0.	Re. 1.	As. 12.	As. 8.	As. 6.
Golgonda .	...	0·1	0·6	3·4	8·3	19·2	25·3	26·2	16·9
Pálkonda ...	1·0	3·7	16·9	22·0	17·4	14 6	13·7	10·7	...
Sarvasiddhi ...	2·5	2·9	20·0	13·0	10·7	21·0	11·9	9·0	...

The crops most grown.

The percentage of the total area cropped in each of these taluks and also in certain zamindari areas (including the Vizianagram estate) which was cultivated with the more important crops in fasli 1313 is given below :—

Items.	Golgonda taluk.	Pálk onda taluk.	Sarvasiddhi taluk.	Estates under management.	Total.
Rice	18·7	46·5	34·3	34·2	33·5
Cambu	16·8	2·3	19·5	12·8	12·5
Ragi	8·3	14·8	12·6	12·4	12·1
Gingelly	18·3	9·7	11·4	10·5	11·8
Horse-gram ...	7·6	5·5	5·7	8·3	7·5
Green gram ...	9·4	6·3	4·2	4·1	5·4
Cholam	5·5	1·2	1·1	1·7	2·2
Others	15·4	13·6	11·1	16·0	15·0

CHAP. IV. AGRICULTURAL STATISTICS.

It will be noticed from all these figures that in Pálkonda, which has plentiful channels from the perennial Nágávali and its tributary the Suvarnamukhi, rice occupies nearly one half of the total cultivated area, and ragi a notable proportion; that in Sarvasiddhi, which depends upon the less excellent irrigation from the Sárada and Varáha rivers and contains much very fertile dry land, rice gives place to cambu and gingelly; and that in Golgonda, where the water-supply is defective and much poor land exists which is taken up for a year or two and then abandoned again, gingelly occupies nearly as great an area as rice, while cambu is but little behind. Ragi and cambu are the staple food-grains. Gingelly (see p. 229) is one of the principal exports from Bimlipatam.

Indigo.

Indigo was extensively cultivated in Pálkonda during Messrs. Arbuthnot's lease of that taluk (see p. 289), but in consequence of competition from the German synthetic dye it is now no longer grown and the indigo factories are all in ruins.

Sugar-cane

Sugar-cane is chiefly raised in Pálkonda taluk (*cf.* p. 290) and in the valley of the Sárada round Anakápalle (see p. 124). In the former place the commonest cane is a small, hard, white variety which seems to be the same as the *dêsavâli* cane of Gódávari.[1] Round Anakápalle, at least eight kinds are recognized, of which the Ráyagada and *dubbukêli* are the most popular, and all of them are heavy varieties which require wrapping and propping to save them from damage by storms. Mauritius canes were tried as long ago as 1839 by M.R.Ry. Godé Súrya Prakása Rao of Anakápalle (see p. 219) and also by Messrs. Arbuthnot & Co. in Pálkonda, but did not do well. A new striped Mauritius variety, called after Mr. H. F. W. Gillman, I.C.S., who imported it in 1899 when in charge of the Vizianagram zamindari, now bids fair, however, to oust all the indigenous kinds. In Anakápalle cuttings are often obtained[2] from the stunted canes grown on alkaline land, which, though they produce only the poorest jaggery, make excellent seed-cane.

Jute.

The 'jute' of the district (which is really *Hibiscus cannabinus* 'the Deccan hemp,' and is locally known as *erra gógu*) has risen into much prominence recently owing to the increase in the price of the fibre from Rs. 26 per candy of 500 lb. to Rs. 45. It is chiefly grown on red soils in the centre of the district round Bobbili, Sálúr, Gajapatinagaram, etc. This being all zamindari

[1] Bulletin No. 43 of the Madras department of Land Records and Agriculture, p. 189.

[2] *Ibid.*, 210.

CHAP. IV. AGRICULTURAL STATISTICS.

land, the acreage sown is not ascertainable with exactness but has been computed at 49,000 acres. Deep ploughing and plentiful manuring improve the product. Two crops are grown, of which the first is sown in May and June and reaped in August or September, and the second is put down in June and July. The former is much the less important of the two; its fibre is shorter than that of the latter, but, as water is plentiful when it is harvested, is better cleaned. The cleaning is always done by soaking the whole plant in water for a fortnight or three weeks and then beating it on a stone to loosen the outer bark. The fibre thus obtained is again washed and then dried and taken either to Kalingapatam or (more generally) to Bimlipatam. Some of it is pressed into bales by machinery and exported, and the rest is spun and woven into gunny at Messrs. Arbuthnot's steam mill (see p. 228) at Chittivalasa. The hemp is well known in the markets in Europe, where it is considered as good as the Calcutta jute. The rise in price is already, however, leading to extreme carelessness among the ryots in cleaning the fibre.

Others.

Wheat is raised on the hills as a dry crop, but is poor stuff. Niger, mustard and turmeric are other characteristic crops in the Agency. The Rája of Vizianagram has a coffee plantation under European supervision at Anantagiri, about 3,000 feet up the hill below Gálikonda.

CULTIVATION METHODS.

The ryots of the district divide the agricultural year into three seasons; namely, *punása*, the period of the south-west monsoon, when the staple dry grains are sown; *pedda panta*, the regular wet-crop season from August to December; and *payira*, the period from November to April when the second dry crop is raised with the aid of the north-east monsoon. The year is also divided into the 27 *kártes* or asterisms of the lunar zodiac, and the ryots commonly hold that each of these asterisms is the proper season for certain agricultural operations and believe that if, owing to want of rain or other preventing cause, that season is allowed to pass, the particular operation cannot afterwards be carried out with equal chances of success. The joint result is that (see p. 151) cultivation operations of some sort are proceeding for ten months out of the twelve. Tables of the dates of seed-time and harvest appear in G.O. No. 784, Revenue, dated 15th September 1897. The *punása* crops are by far the most important, as they comprise cambu and ragi, the staple food of the mass of the people, and a failure of the south-west monsoon is a serious calamity.

CULTIVATION METHODS.

In several directions methods of cultivation in Vizagapatam differ from those in the south. Rice-fields (especially in Pálkonda, where the Nágávali silt is very rich) are often left unmanured for years together, but the seedlings are given a good start by plentiful supplies of fertilizers to the seed-beds. Where manures are used, the wild indigo and sunn hemp plants are frequently ploughed in when green. Dry land, on the other hand, which in the south is often neglected, is here usually plentifully manured, especially with tank silt, and ragi and cambu (and sometimes cholam) instead of being sown are transplanted in dry fields from seed-beds after rain, the seedlings being put out by hand in a furrow and their roots covered over by ploughing another furrow alongside. Instead, again, of being threshed directly they are harvested, as in the south, the crops are often stacked on the fields for months until the ryot has nothing more emergent to do. Except in Pálkonda, double crops of paddy are rare, the wet-fields being either utilized, after the paddy has been removed, for growing gingelly, green gram, or a multiplicity of garden crops and vegetables, usually with tho help of wells; or being sown with ragi during the south-west monsoon and then with paddy with the north-east rains later on. The paddy is of very numerous varieties, differing from taluk to taluk, and it is not possible to point to any one kind as being universally the most popular. Vizagapatam rice has a high character, and it is said that at one time rice used regularly to be sent from Gódávari to Anakápalle to be exported again as Vizagapatam rice

On the hills.

On the hills the paddy is practically all of it rain-fed, but on the 3,000 feet plateau some is raised in the beds of nullahs and irrigated with their water. Gunupur, Jeypore and Naurangpur taluks (see the accounts of these in Chapter XV) are the three tracts where most is raised. Gunupur rice is favourably known as far afield as Calcutta. The crops grown in *pódu* cultivation (see p. 111) are usually dry grains like sámai, hill cholam and the like. The greater part of the seed is thrown on the higher part of the patch and left to be washed down to the lower portions by the rains. The careful terracing of the hills carried out by the Savaras in Gunupur is alluded to on p. 257.

The Agricultural Association.

In 1904 an Agricultural Association was formed at Vizagapatam. It has held two most successful cattle shows and has opened an experimental farm on 21 acres of land near Vizianagram granted by the Rája's adoptive sister. The District Board will very shortly open a veterinary hospital at Vizagapatam.

CHAP. IV. IRRIGATION.

The protected area.

The chief irrigation sources in the three Government taluks are the Varáha in Golgonda; this river and the Sárada in Sarvasiddhi; and, in Pálkonda, the Nágávali and its tributary the Suvarnamukhi. The area protected by these (and by minor tanks and channels) in each of the taluks is shown below:—

Source of irrigation.	Area protected in all seasons (in hundreds of acres).			Area protected in ordinary seasons (in hundreds of acres).		
	Golgonda.	Pálkonda.	Sarvasiddhi.	Golgonda.	Pálkonda.	Sarvasiddhi.
The Varáha system.	34	...	22	41	...	101
The Sárada system.	...	..	48	...	..	132
Nágávali river and Suvarnamukhi river channels ...	...	92	...	...	94	.
Minor tanks and channels ...	76	203	16	163	223	26
Total ...	110	295	86	204	317	259
Percentage of area occupied ..	12	46	15	21	50	44
Percentage of area cultivated ...	15	53	18	28	57	53

It will be seen that it is considerable only in Pálkonda. The great difference in the area safeguarded in ordinary and in all seasons in Sarvasiddhi is due to the fact that the taluk lies at the tail of the Varáha and Sárada channels and so suffers considerably if the seasons are adverse, as the upper anicuts (sometimes private property) take all the water. This evil promises to increase rather than diminish, as the present tendency is to replace inferior and temporary anicuts by permanent and substantial works.

Wells.

In this district wells are of comparatively small importance. The returns show only 7,293 * of them, of which 2,840 are supplementary wells dug in wet land and used chiefly for growing the second crops thereon already referred to. Less than a score of the whole number are pucka constructions with revetments, the average well being a big irregular pit with crumbling sides. The picottah is the universal water-lift, motes being unknown. The buckets are made of riveted sheet iron or of the hollowed-out root end of a palmyra, bound round the top with hoop iron. For small lifts of three or four feet from channels to fields, the swinging basket, operated by two ropes on each side held by two

* Golgonda	...	2,498
Pálkonda	...	1,764
Sarvasiddhi	...	3,031
Total	...	7,293

CHAP. IV. IRRIGATION.

men facing one another, is very common. It generally spills half its contents each swing. In places an ingenious tool, resembling a long-handled shovel with a string attached to the lower end of the shaft, is used for sprinkling water from the well-channels over garden crops such as ragi and chillies. The shovel is dipped into the water and brought out with a jerk by means of the string.

Tanks.

The tanks are mostly small. Only two of them, namely, the Rámaságaram tank in Vákapádu and the Pedda tank of Uppalam, both in Sarvasiddhi taluk, have an ayacut of over 1,000 acres. In the Pálkonda taluk they often have no proper sluices, and the ryots get the water out by cutting the embankments.

A Tank Restoration Party has investigated 142 of these works irrigating 20,000 acres assessed at Rs. 55,000, and spent nearly $1\frac{1}{3}$ lakhs upon them. This is expected to raise the area irrigable by them to 22,500 acres and the revenue to Rs. 90,000

Channels.

The most important sources of irrigation are the channels from the four rivers already mentioned.

From the Varáha.

On the Varáha there are eight Government anicuts,* of which the uppermost, the Gabbáda dam, lies three miles north-north-west of Narasapatam, and was built in 1862–63 at a cost of Rs. 17,630. It supplies the tanks at Narasapatam and its neighbour Balighattam. An affluent of the Varáha, known as the Sarpanadi or Kottakóta stream, is crossed by five smaller anicuts, a channel from one of which fills the natural lake at Kottakóta called the Komaravólu áva, which irrigates some 430 acres.

Name.	Ayacut in acres.
* Gabbáda	1,592
Duggáda	1,178
Koppáka	3,011
Móllapólam	545
Penugollu	972
Lakshiráju	2,053
Lingarájupálem	945
Pedda Uppalam	1,601

Both the Varáha and Sárada channels are thought to be less constant in supply than in former years and the blame has been laid upon the clearance of the forests on the Golgonda and Mádgole hills.

From the Sárada.

On the Sárada there are eight anicuts † belonging to Government, the most important of them being the Godári dam, which is the uppermost of the series and supplies the big natural lake called the Kondakarla áva, about six miles south of Anakápalle. This reservoir, which has been artificially enlarged and never

Name.	Ayacut in acres.
† Godári	2,146
Kázimadam	393
Mámidiváda	472
Dimila	2,100
Kattubólu	1,280
Kummarapalli	2,411
Marripálem	642
Boddéti kattu	200

CHAP. IV. IRRIGATION.

quite dries up, holds an available supply for eight or nine months in the year and irrigates 2,500 acres in twelve villages, some of them zamindari land. Proposals have been made to extend the cultivation under it by still further increasing its capacity, but the difficulty and cost of the scheme have led to its abandonment. This lake and the channels under the Godári anicut were the only irrigation sources which were placed, at the last settlement of Golgonda and Sarvasiddhi, in the first class and in the same category as the Nágávali channels and the tanks fed directly from them in Pálkonda taluk. On the Gókiváda gedda, a spill channel, are six lesser anicuts; and, on the Málagedda, a seventh. A combined regulator and surplus weir across the former is under construction.

From the Nágávali.

The Nágávali and Suvarnamukhi channels are 41 in number, but only four—the Nílánagaram, Venkamma and Honzarám channels from the Nágávali and the Sékharapalli from the Suvarnamukhi—irrigate more than 1,000 acres, only five have head-sluices (all put up in the last fifteen years) and not one of the whole number has a masonry dam. They are all native works, and their heads are in many cases badly placed, their alignments too winding, their sections indifferent, and the provision for cross-drainage insufficient. None the less they do their work fairly well and irrigate, in this district, 8,200 acres of Government land besides 16,100 acres belonging to the Bobbili and Siripuram zamindaris. They chiefly water the lower part of the taluk, in the basin of the river, while the higher ground nearer the hills is supplied only by small tanks or from precarious hill streams.

The Nágávali project.

To improve the conditions in the portion of this latter area lying to the west of Pálkonda town, a scheme called the Nágávali project has recently been sanctioned and is now in course of execution. This consists in constructing a bridge, fitted with nine rising iron shutters each 40 feet long, across the Nágávali at Tótapalli, about six miles east of Párvatípur, where the river bed is 420 feet wide and the maximum flood discharge 17 feet deep, and taking a main channel thence along the left bank of the river to near Pálkonda, a distance of 21 miles. As the bridge will be used to carry the Párvatípur-Pálkonda traffic, which is now frequently interrupted for long periods by freshes, and perhaps also the Párvatípur-Gunupur road later on, the District Board have contributed Rs. 30,000 towards the cost of the scheme. The project will command 78 square miles of country, of which it is proposed to irrigate 25,000 acres of ryotwari and minor inam land and 6,200 acres of zamindari and whole inam. The scheme is estimated to cost Rs. 10,82,000 and to give a return of 8 per cent. on the total capital outlay.

ECONOMIC CONDITION OF AGRICULTURISTS.

This chapter may conclude with a few words summarizing the effect which the conditions sketched in it and elsewhere in this volume have upon the economic condition of the class which so greatly preponderates in Vizagapatam, namely, the smaller agriculturists. The question is rendered more than usually difficult owing to the absence of agricultural statistics for more than nine-tenths of the area of the district.

It will be seen in Chapter VI below that arts, industries and manufactures are scarce, and consequently afford the people few alternative occupations when the seasons are unfavourable; but Chapter VIII shows that the rainfall is usually good except along the sea-board; that when it is not, emigration to Rangoon and Gódávari is the customary safety-valve; and that the ample communications with Burma, the deltas of the Gódávari and Kistna, and the grain-growing tracts in Jeypore suffice to prevent prices rising to excessive heights.

Were it otherwise the people would be poorer than they are, for zamindari tenure, without admitted occupancy right in the land, does not make for careful cultivation or the improvement of the soil. Doubtless statistics would show that the number of small holders of land is less in zamindari than in ryotwari land, but part of the reason for this lies in the fact that the zamindars do not encourage the pauper cultivator, preferring to let their land to men of substance. In none of the estates have the ryots an acknowledged fixity of tenure except in Vizianagram, where a re-settlement was lately carried out when the property was under Government management and the occupancy right of those ryots who agreed to the new rates was admitted. The assessments are not constantly or avariciously raised, but at irregular intervals they are enhanced by a few pies in the rupee to meet the extension of cultivation and the general rise in prices which has occurred, and when a man dies his patta is re-granted to his heirs (these documents are seldom renewed annually, as in the south) at a somewhat enhanced rate. But the chances of the occurrence of one or other of these events, or of a rival ryot applying (in accordance with a local custom which is well established) for an exchange of holdings with his neighbour on the ground that the latter's land is under-assessed, are sufficient to check the sinking of capital in improvements. Some of the zamindari pattas moreover contain ungenerous terms (such as a stipulation that no trees shall be felled and none planted without permission) and

CHAP. IV. Economic Condition of Agriculturists.

the custom of dividing the actual produce of wet lands (assessment on dry land is generally paid in money) between the zamindar and the tenant gives the former's officials chances of exacting perquisites. The general insignificance of the irrigation works, and the refusal of any remission in bad seasons, moreover renders wet cultivation less profitable than it might be, and forces the ryot to carry out repairs to irrigation works which in ryotwari tracts he would calmly leave to Government to effect. There is astonishingly little litigation between landlord and tenant under the tenancy law (Act VIII of 1865) and their relations are usually friendly enough; but the result of the system seems to be that the zamindari ryots in the plains of Vizagapatam are, as a body, much less prosperous than their fellows in southern ryotwari districts of equal fertility. It will be seen from p. 60 that thousands of them have emigrated to Gódávari, and from p. 194 that the receipts from income-tax and the sale of stamps are extremely small in the district; compared with the south, the houses are mean, the standard of comfort is low, and evidences of wealth in the shape of good clothes and gold jewellery among the women are strikingly slender. Outside the bigger towns, the women of the money-lending Kómatis (Baniyans, as they are called locally) are almost the only ones who wear gold ornaments of value. The Kómatis, the Pattu Sáles in some parts, and the Márváris in the large towns do nearly all the money-lending, and the rates they charge are not reduced in the same manner as further south by the competition of members of the agricultural castes or the benefits of chit associations or nidhis.

In the Agency, matters are on rather different ground. The system under which the Jeypore estate is administered is referred to in the account of it on p. 271 below and is fairly representative of the methods in the smaller properties. Contact with the outer world and the action of the Government officers who managed the estate during the recent minority have swept away many of the oppressive and inconvenient dues and assessments which used to be levied there, so that the taxes on houses, hearths, marriages and trades, which were in force as late as 1868, are things of the past, and the land assessments no longer include contributions of oil, skins, honey and so forth. Land is fertile and plentiful, firing is cheap, the rainfall is unfailing, the market for produce has been immensely widened by new roads, the ryot has usually a lenient and fixed assessment which is protected from violent enhancement by the fear of his decamping to rival estates, suits under the tenancy law are almost unknown, and if only ryotwari tenure could replace the mustájari (renting) system the people would have little to complain of. In the smaller estates things are sometimes managed differently. The pattas in Mádgole formally stipulate that the ryot shall send the zamindar the haunch of every deer shot and provide for miscellaneous payments of all kinds, and many of the cultivators of Páchipenta were recently driven to emigrate to Jeypore land because their plough and hoe taxes had been more than doubled arbitrarily. But on the whole the hill ryot is a cheery and well-nourished individual who can afford to dress his womenkind in bright cloths and load them with brass ornaments, keeps up to the local standard of comfort without undue effort, and every spring takes a clear month's holiday enlivened by songs, dances, beats for game, unlimited strong drink, and deep draughts of other pleasures of the flesh.

Two flies in this amber are the *Vetti*, or compulsory service, and the Sondi, the liquor-seller and money-lender. *Vetti* service is now becoming less universal, but while the Jeypore estate was under management Mr. H. D. Taylor reported that though this unpaid labour was really only demandable by custom by the Mahárája himself (and that too on payment of daily batta) yet the ámíns and lower revenue officials and the mustájars and others had come to exact it for the cultivation of their private land and did not even pay the labourer his batta.

The Sondis are a more serious evil. They are gradually getting much of the best land into their hands and many of the guileless hill ryots into their power. Mr. Taylor stated in 1892 that—

'The rate of interest on loans extorted by these Sondis is 100 per cent., and if this is not cleared off in the first year, compound interest at 100 per cent. is charged on the balance. The result is that in many instances the cultivators are unable to pay in cash or kind and become the *gótis* or serfs of the sowcars, for whom they have to work in return for mere batta, whilst the latter take care to manipulate their accounts in such a manner that the debt is never paid off. A remarkable instance of this tyranny was brought to my notice a few days since: a ryot some fifty years back borrowed Rs. 20: he paid back Rs. 50 at intervals and worked for the whole of his life and died in harness: for the same debt the sowcar claimed the services of his son, and he too died in bondage leaving two small sons aged 13 and 9, whose services were also claimed for an alleged arrear of Rs. 30 on a debt of Rs. 20, borrowed 50 years back, for which Rs. 50 in cash had been repaid in addition to the perpetual labour of a man for a similar period.'

CHAP. IV. ECONOMIC CONDITION OF AGRICULTURISTS.

This custom of *góti* is firmly established, and in a recent case an elder brother claimed to be able to pledge for his own debts the services of his younger brother and even those of the latter's wife. Debts due by persons of respectability are often collected by the Sondis by an exasperating method which has led to at least one case of homicide. They send Ghásis, who are one of the lowest of all castes and contact with whom is utter defilement entailing severe caste penalties, to haunt the house of the debtor who will not pay, insult and annoy him and his family, and threaten to drag him forcibly before the Sondi.

CHAPTER V.

FORESTS.

FORESTS—Government forests; beginnings of conservancy—Character of the forests; in Sarvasiddhi—In Pálkonda—And in Golgonda—Zamindari forests—The Jeypore forests; existing reserves—Destruction in former days—Situation and characteristics.

CHAP. V. FORESTS.

OF the forests of the district, Government owns only those in the three Government taluks of Golgonda, Pálkonda and Sarvasiddhi; and these are limited in extent and value.

Far the best growth is that which lies in the Jeypore zamindari and is thus outside direct State control, but in this estate (and also in the Vizianagram zamindari) steps have been taken in recent years (see below) to ensure some degree of protection against the wholesale destruction which has proceeded too long unchecked.

The worst enemy of the forests of the district has always been the system of cultivation practised by the hill people and called *kondapódu* or *pódu*. This consists in felling a piece of jungle, burning the felled trees and undergrowth, sowing dry grain broadcast in the ashes (without any kind of tilling) for two years in succession, and then abandoning the plot for another elsewhere.

Government forests; beginnings of conservancy.

The Government forests may be first referred to.[1] Those notified under section 16 of the Forest Act now consist of 213 square miles in Golgonda taluk, 62 in Pálkonda and 23 in Sarvasiddhi. In addition, about 530 square miles in the Golgonda Agency (the most valuable of all the Vizagapatam Government forests) and about 100 square miles in the Pálkonda Agency are protected by rules framed under section 26 of the Act.

As far back as 1865 Mr. Carmichael, the then Collector, drew the attention of the authorities to the value of the growth on the Golgonda hills, and suggested that it should be placed under the Conservator of Forests. He said that the reckless manner in which all the zamindari forests were being denuded made it the more imperative that Government should endeavour to conserve the few jungles which belonged to them. On this it was ordered

[1] In the account of these which follows I have received material assistance from Mr. W. Aitchison, District Forest Officer.

CHAP. V. FORESTS.

that a dépôt should be established at Narasapatam at which timber should be stocked for sale and that seigniorage rates should be charged on timber and bamboos brought down from the hills. The dépôt was never opened, however, and the seigniorage fees drove merchants and ryots to supply themselves elsewhere. In 1865–66 the charges for the establishment which collected the seigniorage were Rs. 410 and the revenue only Rs. 27, and in the next year the loss on working the system rose to over Rs. 900. The Conservator, Captain (afterwards Colonel) Beddome, thereupon made a spirited attempt to get the Government to transfer this unprofitable undertaking from his budget to the Collector's. He was unsuccessful; and his interest in the matter seems to have rapidly cooled in consequence.

Desultory action followed for many years until at length the Forest Act of 1882 rendered it possible to put matters on a more satisfactory footing. Progress was then, however, unfortunately checked by differences of opinion between the Collector and the new Forest department, and by doubts as to whether the Act could be extended to the forests in the Golgonda and Pálkonda Agencies; and it was only in 1886 that any definite policy was enunciated. It was then ordered that on the hills in Gólgonda taluk blocks should be selected in which unauthorized felling should be prohibited, and that in the rest of that Agency valuable timber should only be felled under license; that in Pálkonda Agency blocks should be selected and defined in which all cutting and *pódu* cultivation should be entirely forbidden; and that in Sarvasiddhi taluk areas not exceeding 5,000 acres in all should be selected for reservation. In the next six years, however, only one block was actually constituted a forest, and it was not until 1903 that reservation was complete. Conservation has thus had but a short trial in this district.

Character of the forests; in Sarvasiddhi.

Of the existing forests, those in Sarvasiddhi consist merely of the scrub growing on certain of the low, red hills with which that taluk is dotted. The two largest blocks are the Vémagiri and Peddapalli reserves, which are respectively 1,611 acres and 9,077 acres in extent; and working-plans have been sanctioned for these.

The former block is described as 'exhibiting in the highest degree the effect of unrestricted felling, grazing and browsing for many years' and as containing a crop 'similar to that of all the east coast forests' but possessing 'a variety of species remarkable for so miserable a growth.' The working-plan provides for the closure of the reserve for thirty years and for the regulation of the grazing during that period.

The Peddapalli reserve lies opposite Yellamanchili on the low, narrow range of red hills which run from the southern extremity of the district to near Kasimkóta. The growth in this is not quite so wretched as in Vémagiri. There is no real timber, but the slopes of the hill are covered with coppice varying in density according to the aspect, the incidence of grazing and the extent to which the forest was formerly denuded by *pódu* cultivation. Old inhabitants remember seeing *pódu* all over this range in former days. The crop is thinnest on the outer slopes next the cultivation, and densest in the interior valleys.

The working-plan divides the reserve into two circles, east and west. In the former of these about half the area is to be closed to felling for 20 years, while the other half is to be treated on the system known as 'coppice with standards' to meet the local demand for small timber, sugar-cane props and fuel. The latter circle (excepting 550 acres) has been divided into eight annual coupes which are to be felled, on the same system, for the supply of fuel to the railway companies at Waltair and the markets along the coast, when the exploitable age of the growth reaches 20 years. This necessitates the closure of the circle to felling for twelve years in each rotation. The working-plan also provides for the regulation of grazing and protection from fire.

In Pálkonda.

In Pálkonda the receipts from the forests, which lie chiefly on the Pálkonda hills, were included, up to 1886, in the lease of the taluk to Messrs. Arbuthnot & Co., and the Forest Act was only extended to the country in 1890. The inner valleys of the hills contain a good deal of sál (*Shorea robusta*) in patches, small but capable of improvement, and the outer slopes carry a scrub jungle full of seedlings of ironwood (*Xylia dolabriformis*), satinwood (*Chloroxylon Swietenia*) and other good trees. But the whole area is so liable to fires and has been so ruined by long-continued *pódu* cultivation that there is little growth left, while reservation is restricted by the necessity of leaving the hill people a sufficient area on which to practise this *pódu*. The largest reserves are Barnakonda (13,517 acres), Kadagandi (11,064), Antikonda (6,969) and Pálkonda (4,580). Of these, perhaps the least promising is the last, all of it having been felled at one time or another for *pódu*, and the northern slope being especially bad. Kadagandi, which includes a considerable belt on the plains, is probably the best of the reserves and is likely to increase in value.

For the areas in the Pálkonda Agency outside the tracts reserved under section 16 of the Forest Act, simple rules have

CHAP. V. FORESTS.

been framed under section 26 which, among other things, prohibit the felling or damaging of trees or the gathering of their produce without the Collector's permission; permit the special protection of special tracts from fire or grazing; empower the Collector to prohibit the felling of specified trees; and allow hill-villagers to fell free of charge any wood which they require for home consumption and to carry on *pódu* under certain restrictions.

And in Golgonda.

In Golgonda taluk the forests are also of two classes, those in the plains reserved under section 16 and those on the hills protected by rules framed under section 26 and similar to those in force in the Pálkonda Agency. The growth in the former resembles that in Sarvasiddhi taluk already referred to, the situation, soil, and circumstances of the two areas being very similar. Parts of two reserves near Narasapatam are being treated under a systematic working-plan to provide fuel for that town, while four small reserves which lie at the southern end of the taluk are being exploited for railway and other fuel as a complementary 'series' to the West Peddapalli working circle.

The forests on the Golgonda hills are some of the densest and most continuous in the whole district. On the edge of the plateau next the plains the villages are larger than elsewhere and *pódu* is frequent, but this seldom extends down the outer slopes and the further one travels inland the rarer does it become, until in the western part of the hills only isolated areas occur in the otherwise unbroken sea of jungle. The heaviest growth is in the valleys, and the tops of the numerous hills with which the plateau is dotted are usually bare except for a covering of long grass. The hill people require but little timber for their own domestic use, and as the plateau is inaccessible to carts no illicit removals to the plains are possible. The forests are in consequence as well protected as any in the Presidency, although they are not reserved under section 16 of the Act and no forest staff is stationed in them. The only real injury from which they suffer is that caused by fires.

Captain Beddome's report on this tract (and his description still applies) says—

'For the eastern coast the hills are very rich in forest vegetation, and I was surprised to find very considerable tracts of shola or moist forest land about most of the ravines and in the vicinity of the hill-streams. These tracts are not so rich in the number of species of trees, or in the endless variety of undergrowth, as similar tracts on our western coast, but the forest is evergreen and decidedly what would be termed shola, and is very rich in ferns; some fifty species having been observed, amongst which were three or four unknown to our western forests, though all of them Himalayan or Burmese ferns, and two very fine tree-ferns. The rattan abounds, moss was very abundant and at a much lower elevation than it is found in our western forests, and lycopods were common. The drier forests yield three sorts of bamboo and are very rich in valuable timber . . . . About fourteen miles to the south-west of Gúdem, and two miles from a small village called Marripákalu, I found a small tract of teak of superb growth. The area was perhaps not 200 acres, but has evidently been much curtailed by hill-cultivation and has occupied a larger area at some previous date. There were a good many trees seven to nine feet in girth and sixty or seventy feet high, with a perfectly straight trunk, and saplings were numerous. The tree was hardly observed at all elsewhere on the mountains; and it is curious that its area should be restricted.'

Among the most characteristic trees of these hills are the gall-nut (*Terminalia Chebula*), the *nalla maddi* (*T. tomentosa*), *Cedrela microcarpa*, a species of the valuable 'false cedar' which occurs in numbers near Gúdem, stunted *Buchanania latifolia*, which is found on grassy flats, *Pterocarpus Marsupium*, *Anogeissus latifolia* and *A. acuminata* on the banks of streams, while on the outer slopes are wide areas covered with bamboo.

The two largest reserves are Dárakonda, called after the prominent hill of that name, and Senivaram. They adjoin one another and clothe a conspicuous line of hills near the western boundary of the taluk, and together they are 122 square miles in extent. A novel working-plan, designed to secure the protection of the reserves from their worst enemy, was sanctioned for this area at the end of 1903. The two reserves used to suffer terribly every year from the fires which swept through them—generally started by careless travellers in the patches of long grass which clothe the tops of the hills and occupy the sites of deserted villages—and the plan proposes to protect them by enlisting the co-operation of the local people. To villages within the limits of which no fires occur in any year either money rewards or certain valued privileges (such as free grazing for a certain number of cattle, the right to collect minor forest produce, and permission to draw sago toddy) are granted by the District Forest Officer in person at his annual inspection; while where fires occur the privileges are withdrawn and the rewards withheld. Until 1905 the plan worked well, the villagers realizing that the Government were really anxious to stop the fires and appreciating the advantages to be gained by assisting the endeavour.

Zamindari forests.

In the forests in the Jeypore and Vizianagram zamindaris, conservation has lately been rendered possible by the introduction,

CHAP. V. FORESTS.

with the consent of the respective owners of those properties, of rules under the Forest Act. The Vizianagram forests consist, with the exception of a small area round about Anantagiri, of scrub jungles on the low hills in the plains, similar to those of Sarvasiddhi above referred to, and are not of great interest.

The Jeypore forests; existing reserves.

The forests of Jeypore, on the other hand, are the finest and most extensive in all the district. Reservation in these began in earnest in 1900, and up to date 61 blocks, aggregating 324 square miles or 2½ per cent. of the total area of the estate, have been reserved; while proposals for reserving an additional 125 square miles are now before the Agent (whose sanction to proposed reservations is necessary under the rules); [1] and another 597 square miles is undergoing the preliminary processes of selection, demarcation or survey under the care of the estate's Forest officer Mr. Eber Hardie.[2] The biggest of the reserved blocks is Dharangád, on the Rámagiri side of Jeypore taluk, which is 60,000 acres in extent, while two others in Malkanagiri taluk measure respectively 28,800 acres and 17,500 acres. Adjoining Dharangád are other blocks now under survey, and when these have been reserved there will be an unbroken stretch of 100,000, acres of sál forest in that corner of the estate.

Destruction in former days.

This action has not been taken a moment too soon, for the forests of the estate have already been grievously injured by unrestricted lopping, girdling, ringing, felling and burning.

As far back as 1872, Mr. H. G. Turner reported that the exclusive right to the timber of Malkanagiri had been leased by the then manager of the taluk, Bangára Dévi, for an inadequate sum to a man who had proceeded to 'cut down every stick of wood it would pay him to export. The forests in the neighbourhood of the Saveri are ruined.' Shortly afterwards he suggested that Government should lease the forests of the estate to preserve them from further denudation. He pointed out that the Indrávati and Saveri (which are the only two tributaries of the Gódávari which carry any considerable hot-weather supply and which are thus the mainstay of the second-crop cultivation in the Gódávari delta) were entirely dependent for their water upon the forests of Jeypore; and he declared that these latter were rapidly being wiped out of existence. He said—

'I can myself call to mind a score of hills that have been completely cleared of forest within five years. I have hunted bison in the rough

[1] The correspondence regarding the terms of the rules will be found in G.O., No. 433, Revenue, dated 9th July 1895, and the connected papers.

[2] Mr. Hardie has kindly checked and corrected the account of these forests which follows.

jungles that have now no vestige of existence. Old men point to country where there is now not a copse large enough to hide a sambhur for hundreds of square miles, and tell me that, in their youth, that land was covered with jungle. When civilization pushes back the wilder members of the hill-tribes into the yet unconquered jungle, they commence upon it by felling and burning virgin forest on the side of the hills. One would naturally imagine that they would attack the fertile valleys in the first instance. But these pioneers of civilization are generally without ploughs and they cannot keep down the grass with their hoes. The hill-felling will continue until every acre within the village bounds has been exhausted, and it is not till then that the ryot will begin to manure his low-lying lands. Nor will the hill-side be ever suffered to regain its lost function of supplying water for the country round about it; for, when its wood is nearly large enough to become of use in this way, some poor or lazy ryot will be attracted by the prospect of an easily raised crop, and will destroy the young jungle again. It is not easy to assess the enormous loss that the ryot entails on himself by these operations, for he grows his rice in terraces hollowed out of the water-courses that spring from the bottom of the slopes of these hills. Within my own circle of observation, I can point to one or two villages where some five years ago two crops were raised, but where there is now no water for the second.'

As a result of this letter Col. Beddome, the Conservator of Forests, was despatched to report upon the country. The verdict of this well-known authority was to the same effect. He said—

'This plateau (the 3,000 feet plateau) is wonderfully well watered by numerous streams, which all have their rise in the woods which more or less clothe all the small rising hills. These latter were all, at a very recent date, covered with fine forest, but this is fast disappearing owing to the ruinous system of hill cultivation. Numerous hills have already been turned into bare rocky waste, or are only clothed with a few date bushes or the poorest description of stunted growth; and if the present system of cultivation is allowed to go on unrestricted, the entire disappearance of all woodlands is only a question of time. Over the whole portion of the plateau visited I did not find a single patch of virgin forest, except here and there very small plots (scarcely over half an acre) where reservation had occurred on account of some sacred stone. Every acre has, at some time or other, been felled and burnt for hill cultivation, and is at the best only second growth; but most tracts have seen probably many rotations of this system, and, consequently, the forests are to be seen at every stage of deterioration. About the centre of the plateau the oldest growth anywhere observed by me was about forty or fifty years', and in almost all cases where I found forest above thirty years of age I was informed that it was marked for early destruction.

The woods are neither wholly evergreen nor wholly deciduous, but a mixture of both and similar to what is met with in some parts of

CHAP. V. FORESTS.

Coorg and Wynaad. They do not suffer at once in the same way as the heavy evergreen forests of the western side of the Presidency; the same growth more or less appears; not a thorny wilderness of quite different plants. The burning is (at first, at least) very superficial, and the stumps, or a greater portion of them, at once begin to grow again; and when the cultivation is abandoned, which it generally is after two years, the forest soon begins to recover itself. The evergreen trees suffer more than the others, and these are more or less absent at first, and for some years rank grass and much thorn and coarse undergrowth hold sway and fires periodically sweep through, and it is not till the growth arrives at an age of some twenty years or more that there is any chance of much humus being added to the surface soil, and then fires are soon excluded, seedlings have a chance, and shortly afterwards rattans and tree ferns appear. The evergreen trees increase in number, and the undergrowth quite changes its character, and species of acanthaceous shrubs (*Strobilanthes*) appear as in our moist western sholas.

This is a sketch of what occurs after the first felling of a virgin forest, or when the forest has been allowed forty or fifty years to recover. A virgin forest at this elevation is a fine sight; it is moist and shady, and tolerably open for walking through or for sport. Rattans and tree ferns, orchids, and moss abound. The trees are large, and there is much valuable timber. When a tract is allowed forty or fifty years to recover, it appears to return almost to its pristine vigour and form, and many seedling trees in time make way; and unless the base of the older trees be observed, a forester even might be deceived, and fancy that he was in a virgin forest. It is, however, only in a few tracts, chiefly on the eastern and western ghauts of the plateau where the hills form chaos, that the forests are allowed a rest of any long duration. About the more accessible and less densely-forested portions they are felled over every eight, ten, or fifteen years, and never have a chance of recovering. They have a wretched, stunted appearance, are very dry and more or less impenetrable from a tangled rank under-growth, and there are no seedlings; nothing, in fact, but the coppice growth, generally of only the quicker-growing but poorer sorts of timber. By the uninitiated these tracts are generally looked upon as having been *ab initio* of the same poor, stunted growth, but it is only the result of rotations of felling and burning and consequent poverty of the soil.

The south-west monsoon is very heavy on these hills, and when a tract of forest on the slopes of the hills, which rise all over the plateau, is felled and under cultivation, and before the forest again begins to grow, the denudation of soil is very great. The traces of this are everywhere apparent, and I had ocular demonstration of it on several occasions, as there was some very heavy rain whilst I was up. Besides this denudation, when these tracts are felled over at such short periods there is no virtue added to the soil by the decaying vegetation, and tree-growth cannot flourish: each rotation it is poorer and poorer till at last it disappears altogether.

I have nowhere in India seen this hill cultivation so systematically carried out. Directly all the forest within a certain radius has been felled and cultivated, the village is deserted and the cultivators move off to other tracts to carry on the same ruinous system. Numerous deserted villages may be seen all over the plateau; the site is almost always marked by a good many grand old tamarind, mango and champa trees, generally of about a hundred years' growth, and in most cases by a few tumbled down huts; these sites are probably always returned to periodically.'

This description of *pódu* cultivation and its effects is strictly applicable to the state of things which still prevails to-day. Wherever one travels through Jeypore, one sees wide tracts of hill-side, which once were forest-clothed, now covered only with blackened stumps, leafless dead trees, bare ash-covered soil and protruding barren rock. Mr. Willock wrote in 1890 that 'the destruction going on in the sál country beyond Naurangpur at present is most lamentable. Wherever one goes one sees huge areas, hundreds of acres in extent, covered with the remains of fine forests, ringed a year or two back to afford a site for two or three seasons' mixed cultivation of ragi, millet, niger and weeds, but chiefly the latter.'

The jungles have also suffered to a less extent from other wasteful habits of the hill man. He will lop a *Schleichera trijuga* tree out of all shape to collect the lac off its branches; hack the boughs off a *Terminalia Chebula* to save himself trouble in gathering its fruit; ring or fell a full-grown sál tree for the sake of the few pies' worth of dammar which results; and cut down a 50-feet teak tree to get a little honey from its upper branches.

Situation and characteristics.

The result of years of these reckless methods is that to-day the 3,000 feet plateau contains no considerable area of heavy jungle anywhere north of the line of the Machéru river. Rapidly dwindling patches survive, but their expectation of life is short. The jungle on Damuku, the big hill behind the Pottangi travellers' bungalow, for instance, still holds sambhur, but it is highly probable that in twenty years it will have disappeared. Round Koraput and Nandapuram the country is already so bare that even firewood is scarce, and it is difficult to believe that the hills ever carried any jungle at all.

The level country in the neighbourhood of Jeypore town and the hills between Náráyanapatnam and Bissamkatak contain sparse forest, ruined by constant *pódu* cultivation, but no large

CHAP. V. FORESTS.

timber is left in them except the mohwa, tamarind and jack trees which the hill people have spared for the sake of their fruit.

The only good growth remaining is that in the extreme north of the Bissamkatak and Gunupur taluks; in the country north of the Indrávati; in the west of Jeypore taluk round about Rámagiri; on the line of hills which separates this from the lower levels of Malkanagiri; and between Kondakambéru in this last taluk and the boundary of Hill Mádgole.

In the north of the Bissamkatak and Gunupur taluks grows the finest sál in the district. Except trees which were too big to transport, all which was near enough to the Vamsadhára river to be dragged thither by buffaloes, has long since been felled by the Reddi timber-contractors of Gunupur, and floated down on bamboo rafts to Kalingapatam in Ganjám district. A royalty on each raft used to be collected by the Gudári ámín. Difficulties of transport have, however, saved the more inaccessible sál. At Majjikóta, where the three main tributaries of the Vamsadhára meet, there is a waterfall, and the streams above this are full of rocky barriers. Consequently no floating is possible north of this point. Moreover the country to the east of the river, between it and Chandrapur and Bijápur, is too rough for timber-dragging. Further north, the sál in the Jagdalpur and Dongasúrada muttas has also escaped owing to its inaccessibility, and still includes trees as much as ten feet in girth.

The country to the north of the Indrávati, especially along the valley of the Tél, is one great forest with scattered cultivation in isolated glades. Here again there is much fine sál, and the difficulty of getting it out has preserved it from destruction. The tree makes a beautiful forest, for if it has a chance it eventually ousts other varieties and forms a jungle clear of undergrowth and consisting of tall, straight trunks topped with a heavy canopy of leaves. Round Umarkót grows the *Schleichera trijuga* on which the lac insect deposits its valuable secretions and here also, especially towards the Kálahandi side and near the frontier north-east of Raigarh, is some scattered teak of fair dimensions.

In the Rámagiri forests the sál again appears in strength, and at Mattupáda, near Rámagiri, are some saw-mills which were put up while the Jeypore estate was under management during the present Mahárája's minority.

On the range of hills which divides the Jeypore taluk from the lower Malkanagiri country is more fine sál; but just below them, along a line drawn from Pangam to Salimi, is the southern limit of the tree, and the most valuable timber in Malkanagiri itself is teak. The best places for this are some small tracts round Sikkapalli and Akkuru, and the banks of the Saveri, Potéru and Siléru rivers. But the Malkanagiri forests as a whole are disappointing, containing little (except to the east of Kondakambéru) but open sapling growth interspersed with wide swamps covered with high and almost impassable grass.

On the whole, therefore, the Jeypore forests, quite apart from their value to the streams which rise in the country, still form, in spite of the treatment they have undergone, a fine property which, if given a chance, will continually increase in value and is consequently well worth conserving in every way possible.

CHAPTER VI.

OCCUPATIONS AND TRADE.

OCCUPATIONS—Agriculture and pasture. ARTS AND INDUSTRIES—Jute-weaving—Cotton-weaving; carpets—Cloths—Made by Dombus in the Agency—On the plains by several castes—Silk-weavers' thread—Indigo—Jaggery—Oils—Tanning — Manganese-mining — Glass bangles — Snuff-boxes — Amulets—Metal-work; gold and silver—Brass and bell-metal—Iron—Ivory-work—Lacquer-work— Mats, etc. TRADE—Sea-borne trade—Road- and rail-borne trade—Mechanism of trade. WEIGHTS AND MEASURES —Tables of weight—Grain and liquid measures—Lineal measures.

CHAP. VI. OCCUPATIONS. Agriculture and pasture.

As in every other district in the Presidency, so in Vizagapatam, the proportion of the people who live by tilling the land and pastoral callings enormously outweighs the number of those who subsist by all other occupations put together. In the plain taluks the percentage of these people to the total population (70·5) is about equal to the average for the Presidency as a whole, but the figure in the Agency (84·2) is naturally much larger, and is the highest recorded in any part of Madras.

Agricultural methods have been referred to already in Chapter IV and it remains to consider here the callings which are connected with arts and industries and with trade. The ordinary village handicrafts are much the same as elsewhere and do not require specific mention.

ARTS AND INDUSTRIES.

The arts and industries of Vizagapatam are few and insignificant. The handicraft which employs the greatest number of the people is weaving. This consists of the weaving of jute and cotton, for all-silk fabrics are not made in the district, nor is wool ever woven. All the hundreds of blankets used in the Agency are imported.

Jute-weaving.

The local 'jute' is spun and woven into gunny-bags by steam at the mill at Chittivalasa near Bimlipatam referred to on p. 228 below. In three or four villages near Pálkonda and one or two round Anakápalle this same fibre is woven on hand-looms, by people of the Perike caste, into long strips of gunny, which are sold to the Kómati grain-traders and by them cut up and stitched into bags.

Cotton-weaving; carpets.

The cotton-weaving of the district resolves itself into the making of rugs and of apparel for men and women. Cotton rugs and carpets, used as hold-alls and for sleeping on, are made by Dévángas at Jámi in the Srungavarapukóta taluk. They are copied from the well-known Ádóni carpets and the pattern consists of stripes of red, white or blue. Aniline dyes are used.

Cloths.

The weaving of cloths for men and women to wear is similar in most respects to that done in other districts.

Made by Dombus in the Agency.

In the Agency, the only systematic work is that done by the Dombus, who make coarse white fabrics for use by either sex. The women of several castes, such as the Gadabas and Banda Porojas (see pp. 97 and 87), make their own clothes, largely from jungle fibre.

On the plains by several castes.

On the plains, cotton cloths are woven in hundreds of villages by Sáles, Padma Sáles, Pattu Sáles, Dévángas (most of whom are Lingáyats by faith) and Sálápus. The ryots often spin their own cotton into thread and then hand it over to the weavers to be made into cloths, but large quantities of machine-made yarn are used.

In the south, the chief weaving centres are Nakkapalli and Páyakaraopéta in Sarvasiddhi taluk, the Pattu Sáles in the latter of which turn out fabrics of fine thread, enriched with much gold and silver 'lace,' which are in great demand in the Gódávari and Ganjám districts. In the east of the district, there is a well-known collection of weavers round about Rázám, Siripuram and Pondúru, three neighbouring villages in the Pálkonda and Chípurupalle taluks. At Rázám coloured cloths for women are the chief product, and in the country round this village the white garments so universal elsewhere give place to coloured dress. These cloths are of very many patterns and colours, some of which are quite pleasing. Red, with yellow borders and ends; white, with red borders and ends; yellow; and dark blue with golden borders are perhaps the favourite colours, and the last of these is very becoming to brown skins. The cloths are sold locally and also sent in large quantities to Berhampur, Cuttack and even Calcutta. Most of the weaving is in the hands of Dévángas, but the dyeing of the thread is done with imported aniline and alizarine colours by the Balijas of Sigadam in Chípurupalle taluk and Balijapéta in Bobbili.

Silk-weavers' thread.

In Siripuram and Pondúru the Pattu Sáles make delicate fabrics from especially fine thread, called Pattu Sále *núlu*, or 'silk-weavers' thread,' which the women of their caste spin for them, and which is as fine as imported 150s. These are much valued by well-to-do natives for their softness and durability.

CHAP. VI. ARTS AND INDUSTRIES.

The weaving industry is on the decline throughout the district, except perhaps in Rázám, and the weaver castes are taking to other means of livelihood. Round Chípurupalle, for example, the Pattu Sáles have become experts in tobacco-curing and have made such profits that they are able to monopolise much of the trade and money-lending of the locality.

Indigo.

We may pass on to consider the other industries of the district which concern themselves with the utilization of its agricultural products.

Indigo-making used to be a great industry, especially in Pálkonda taluk, where during their lease Messrs. Arbuthnot & Co. greatly encouraged the growth of the plant. The whole taluk is still dotted with deserted indigo-vats and factories, but the trade has dwindled to almost nothing before the competition of the German synthetic dye.

Jaggery.

Messrs. Arbuthnot & Co. also at one time greatly promoted the growth of sugar-cane in Pálkonda, turning it into sugar at their factory at Chittivalasa which is now a jute mill.

The chief centre of the jaggery trade at present is Anakápalle, on the rich wet lands round which much cane is grown. Iron mills are always used there for pressing the cane, and in the jaggery season expensive metal-cutting lathes may be seen in sheds amid the wet land working at the repair of those mills. Messrs. Parry & Co. encourage the cultivation of cane by advances of money, and in the harvest season send down an agent who sets up a little laboratory and buys the jaggery according to its quality as determined by the polariscope. To improve this quality, the firm hires out to the ryots metal vessels for the storage of the juice to replace the earthen pots generally used (which set up fermentation) and instructs the ryots how to add lime to the juice while it is being boiled to prevent the wasteful 'inversion' of the sugar which goes on in the casual methods usually employed. The ryots, who are largely intelligent Gavaras, realise that attention to these instructions and processes means a better price for their jaggery, and follow them with care. Messrs. Parry & Co. send the jaggery to Sámalkót in the Gódávari district, where sugar, and afterwards arrack from the molasses, are manufactured from it by the Deccan Sugar and Abkári Company, of which they are the local managers.

Oils.

The oils used in the plains are practically all made in the usual wooden mills. The Telikulas and Tellis are the oilmonger castes. Until recently there was a European oil mill at Bimlipatam, but it did not pay and work there has now been stopped.

In the Agency, oils are made by squeezing the seeds between two boards. In the plains, imported kerosine is almost universally employed for lighting, but in the Agency castor and (more rarely) *ippa* oils are mostly used. The former is made by first roasting and then boiling the seed and skimming off the oil as it floats to the top; the latter by pressing the berries of the *ippa* tree which form after the flower has fallen. For cooking, gingelly (and to a less extent niger) oil is used both on the plains and in the Agency.

Tanning.

Tanning of hides and skins is carried on in several tanneries round Vizianagram and in one at Jeypore. The industry, as usual, is in the hands of Musalmans, and it presents no special points of interest.

Manganese-mining.

The minerals of the district afford but little employment to its people. The manufacture of salt is referred to on p. 183 below. Iron used to be extensively made from the local ores [1] and is still smelted on a small scale in a few places in the Jeypore country. Licenses have been granted for prospecting for graphite, which is much used for giving a finishing polish to the ordinary earthen pots of the district, but so far no commercial exploitation of it has been successful.

The only mineral, besides salt, which now provides occupation for any considerable body of people is manganese. The existence in the district of this substance was first brought to notice in 1850, when it was erroneously supposed to be an ore of antimony.[2] It was first mined in 1892 by the Vizianagram Mining Company, which owes its existence to Mr. H. G. Turner, Collector here from 1881 to 1889. This company has still practically a monopoly of the trade and is working at present at two principal centres; namely, Kódúr (including the adjacent villages of Garividi, Duvvám, Déváda and Sadánandapuram), three miles south-west of Chípurupalle, the mines in which were opened in 1892 and in 1904 produced 12,000 tons of ore; and Garbhám in the Gajapatinagaram taluk, where work was begun in 1896 and the output from which in 1904 was 41,000 tons. The mines are large open excavations—the biggest at Kódúr is a huge pit 105 feet deep and 88,000 square feet (over two acres) in extent at the bottom—and contain no underground workings. The ore occurs mainly in veins, which are visible on the surface and usually dip down without diminishing in richness. The ore and earth are taken to the top

[1] See *Report on the Iron Ores of the Madras Presidency* by E. Balfour, Madras, 1855.

[2] *Ibid.*, pp. 238–40.

of the excavation together (the work being usually done by contract), and the former is then hand-picked and sent by rail to Vizagapatam (the Kódúr ore goes from Garividi station), whence it is shipped to America, Middlesborough, Dunkirk and other places for use in the manufacture of steel and in chlorination processes such as those adopted at gold mines. Between 1900 and 1904 the output seriously declined owing to competition from newly opened mines in Russia, Brazil and elsewhere; and in 1904 the company was unable to pay any dividend. Since then, however, matters have taken a turn for the better, and the company is flourishing once more.

Glass bangles.

Bangles of the 'glass' made by melting down alkaline earths (some of which is imported from Nellore district) are made by Gázula Balijas in several villages round about Anakápalle, Yellamanchili and Chípurupalle; at Paidipálem, nine miles east of Narasapatam; and on a smaller scale at other places. The process of manufacture is the same as elsewhere, but sometimes the glass is coated outside with yellow lac, in which, while it is still hot, little bits of looking-glass are inserted. Somewhat similar bangles are made by the Sonkaris of Naurangpur. These yellow lac bangles and the imported kind made of moulded blue glass are characteristic adornments of the women of the south of the district.

Snuff-boxes.

Round Singapur in the Jeypore country neat little snuff-boxes, about two inches long and shaped like an almond, are made from fine-grained red and white stones which are found in those parts.

Amulets.

At Pedda Gummalúru in Sarvasiddhi taluk a Kamsáli makes little images of Ráma, Párvati, Hanumán, and other deities from sálagrámams. These are cased in gold or silver and worn round the neck as amulets.

Metal-work; gold and silver.

The work in gold and silver is usually done by this Kamsáli caste. At Rázám (and to a less extent at Párvatípur and Bobbili) these people make cups, rose-water sprinklers, small boxes and the like in silver, and their work is neatly finished. At Peddaponki in Bobbili taluk are manufactured waist-strings of twisted silver and gold which are called *góvatádu* and are known all over the district. The silver waist-belts and armlets made of a series of little chased plaques hinged together, which are also characteristic of this district, often exhibit excellent work. The best gold jewellery to be seen is that worn by the Gavara Kómati women. Their jewelled nose-studs and necklets are especially well chased.

The latter often represent rows of grains of rice or dholl, and are most effective.[1]

Brass and bell-metal.

Brass and bell-metal work is usually done by the Kancharis. In Párvatípur is a colony of the caste who speak Uriya, came long ago from Berhampur, and still marry with their kinsfolk in that town. Their work is held in much repute, especially the little vessels which they laboriously forge out of a single solid ingot by repeated re-heatings and hammerings. Anakápalle, Bobbili, Sómalingapálem near Yellamanchili, Anantavaram near Álamanda and Lakkavarapukóta are other centres for this industry.

The work consists, as usual, partly in casting vessels and then polishing them, and partly in making them out of sheets of metal which have to be shaped, soldered and hammered. A further branch of it in this district consists in the manufacture of the brass and copper jewellery which is so popular among many castes. This takes multifarious forms, among the most interesting of which are the heavy brass anklets and armlets which are cast in brass by the *cire perdue* process. In this process a core of clay is overlaid with wax moulded to the pattern desired, which is then covered with a coating of more clay. As soon as the latter has hardened, the whole is heated and the wax melts and runs away, leaving a hollow space into which the molten brass can pass and take the form assumed just before by the wax. In moulding the pattern, threads of wax (made by forcing the wax with a stick down a hollow bamboo ending in a perforated brass plate) are used to build up any required pattern, such as cables or spirals, while rosettes and the like are made by pressing the wax into brass dies.[2]

Most of the masses of heavy brass jewellery with which many of the women in the Agency are bedecked are made locally by Chitra Ghásis and Kodrus, but the lighter items, such as the little brass chains which some of them delight to hang from their ears, are manufactured in the plains and sent up to the hills by middlemen. German silver is rapidly cutting out brass and bell-metal as a material for these lesser ornaments.

Iron.

Besides the ordinary work in iron (such as the making of agricultural implements and tools), sugar-boiling pans are made at Anakápalle; knives, sword-sticks, etc., at Kódúr, eleven miles north-east of Chódavaram; tangis (axes) out of the native iron by the Lóháris round about Tentulakunti; and very excellent

[1] See Mr. E. B. Havell in *Journal of Indian Art*, v, 80.
[2] *Ibid.*, iv, 7 ff.

CHAP. VI.
ARTS AND INDUSTRIES.

spurs for fighting-cocks at Rámabhadrapuram on the Vizianagrám-Sálúr road.

Ivory-work.

At Vizagapatam two or three firms [1] manufacture for European clients fancy articles (such as chess-boards, photograph frames, card cases, trinket boxes and so on) from tortoiseshell, horn, porcupine quills and ivory. The industry is in a flourishing state and has won many medals at exhibitions. It is stated to have been introduced by Mr. Fane, Collector from 1859 to 1862, and to have then been developed by the Kamsális and the men of other castes who eventually took it up. The foundation of the fancy articles is usually sandalwood, which is imported from Bombay. Over this are laid porcupine quills split in half and placed side by side, or thin slices of polished bison, buffalo or stag horn, of tortoiseshell, or of ivory. The ivory is sometimes laid over the horn or shell, and is always either cut into geometrical patterns with a small keyhole saw or etched with designs representing gods and flowers. The etching is done with a small V-tool and then black wax is melted into the design with a tool like a soldering-iron, any excess being scraped off with a chisel, and the result is polished with a leaf of the *Ficus asperrima*. This gives a black design *sgraffito* on a white ground. The horn and porcupine quills are obtained from the Agency, and the tortoiseshell and ivory mainly from Bombay through the local Márváris.

The designs employed both in the etching and the fretwork are stiff, and suited rather to work in metal than in ivory, and the chief merit of this Vizagapatam work perhaps lies in its careful finish, a rare quality in Indian objects of art. The ivory is never carved now, but in the Calcutta Museum and elsewhere may be seen samples of the older Vizagapatam work which often contained ivory panels covered with scenes from holy writ executed in considerable relief.

Lacquer-work.

Lacquer-work of the usual kind is done at Nakkapalli in Sarvasiddhi taluk, at Chandanádu a few miles to the south of it, at Étikoppáka in Sarvasiddhi taluk, and at Lakkavarapukóta and Srungavarapukóta. Wood is turned on the ordinary primitive lathe and lac of various colours is then applied to it until the heat generated by the friction melts the lac and makes some of it stick to the wood. This is then polished with screw-pine leaves, bits of cloth, etc. The wood generally used is *ankudu* (*Wrightia tinctoria*). The Chandanádu and Nakkapalli work is the best,

[1] Golthy Kanniah, Gánulu Rámalingam and Chinna Víranna may be mentioned.

being very neatly finished and executed in tasteful colours. The articles made consist of cots, toys of various kinds for children, and small objects suited to European drawing-rooms, such as little boxes full of miniature lótas, tumblers, platters and the like.

At Naurangpur fancy objects, such as chains and fly whisks, are made of lac and are in some demand.

Mats, etc.

Mats, tatties, baskets, etc., are made from split bamboo in very many villages in the plains by Médaras, some Gúdalas and Godugulas, and by the wandering Yerukalas. The Yátas (the toddy-drawing caste) also make cheaper kinds from the leaves of the palmyra and date palms. In the Agency, this sort of work is not the exclusive function of one or two communities, but is done by most of the castes to supply their own needs.

TRADE.

Sea-borne trade.

The trade of the district divides itself into that carried by sea to and from its two ports and that carried by road and rail. The separate Appendix gives statistics of the former, from which it will be seen that in 1902–03 the imports at Bimlipatam were worth Rs. 9,79,000 and at Vizagapatam Rs. 3,11,000; and the exports respectively Rs. 32,17,000 and Rs. 10,71,000.

Although Vizagapatam is a better port than Bimlipatam, possessing a still-water channel in which surf boats can be loaded and unloaded afloat directly from the wharf, and although the fact that the railway runs down to it gives it all the manganese trade, yet Bimlipatam does a much greater export business for the reason that it lies nearer Vizianagram, the point through which all the carts from the Párvatípur and Jeypore Agencies must pass. Merchants who have brought their goods by cart all the way to Vizianagram naturally send them on by cart to the nearest port at Bimlipatam rather than transfer them to the railway to be railed to Vizagapatam. When the Vizianagram-Raipur line runs past the foot of the Jeypore ghát and on to Párvatípur, produce will travel by it direct to Vizagapatam port and Bimlipatam will no longer be able to obtain the lion's share of the export trade.

Of the average value of the imports at the two ports together in the five years ending 1902–03 (Rs. 14,97,000), more than half consisted of cotton twist and yarn (for the use of hand-loom weavers) or cotton piece-goods, and the only other item which amounted to as much as half a lakh was glass-ware. Of the average value of the exports in the same period (Rs. 50,16,000), gingelly seed and oil accounted for over 8 lakhs; other seeds for a similar sum; jaggery and hides and skins for over 7 lakhs each; the Vizianagram Mining Company's manganese ore for 6

CHAP. VI. TRADE.

lakhs; and jute, indigo and myrabolams for between 2 and 3 lakhs each.

Road- and rail-borne trade.

The trade carried by road is not registered at all, and the rail-borne traffic is lumped in the returns with that of Ganjám. It is therefore impossible to speak with certainty of the course or extent of either.

Excepting manganese and jute (which are exported by sea from Vizagapatam and Bimlipatam respectively, and so appear in the statistics of sea-borne trade), the cotton fabrics of Rázám, Siripuram and Pondúru (which are sent by rail to Ganjám, Cuttack and Calcutta), those of Nakkapalli and Páyakaraopéta (which go to Gódávari), the jaggery of Anakápalle (which is mostly exported to the Sámalkót distillery) and the tobacco and chillies of Chípurupalle taluk (which are sent to Ganjám and Cuttack), the chief items in the exports by road and rail from the plain taluks are the surplus stocks of the ordinary agricultural staples raised within them; while the principal imports are those necessaries of life which the district does not itself produce, such as kerosine, European piece-goods, sugar, and iron and other metals.

The trade with the Agency, however, is of a less ordinary description, since with its higher elevation and extensive jungles that country produces a number of articles which cannot be grown on the lower ground, and on the other hand its isolated position necessitates the export to it of many goods which are common enough in the plain taluks.

The chief exports from the Agency are its surplus grain (paddy, ragi, cholam, cambu, and red, green and black gram); the oil-seeds, gingelly, niger and mustard; saffron, turmeric, garlic and arrowroot; tamarind, soap-nut, ginger and 'long pepper'; honey and wax; horns, hides and skins; dammar and lac; marking-nut, myrabolams and other tanning barks; and *kamela* powder (obtained from the seed-vessels of the tree *Mallotus philippinensis*) and other dyes. The imports to the Agency include salt and salt-fish; chillies, tobacco and onions; jaggery, kerosine; cocoanuts, cotton twist and piece-goods; beads, bangles and coral; metals and metal utensils and jewellery.

Mechanism of trade.

In the plain taluks, the greater part of the trade is in the hands of the Kómati caste. Kápus, Balijas and some Pattu Sáles and Dévángas take a smaller share, while in the bigger towns are a few Márváris who assist in financing operations. The numerous weekly markets take a prominent part, as elsewhere, in collecting produce for export and in distributing imports to the villages. Judging from the bids for the right to collect the fees in these, the best attended are those at Kottavalasa in Vizagapatam taluk, Sálúr, Pálkonda and Párvatípur.

The last three of these owe some of their importance to the fact that they are situated near the foot of the hills and so are marts of hill-produce. All along the foot of the hills, from Krishnadévipet and Kondasanta in the south to Pálkonda in the north is a line of markets at which hill-produce is exchanged for the goods of civilization. On the hills themselves are many markets on the main lines of communication. On the Sálúr-Koraput road are Rállugedda and Damriput; between Jeypore and Malkanagiri is Mondiguda; between Jeypore and the Indrávati, Kebbedi, Kalliyaguda and Bobbiya; on the Kálahandi frontier is Maidalpur market; in the Párvatípur part of Jeypore is Ráyagada; and on the Vamsadhára to the north of Gunupur is the fair at Bhámini. In these and the numerous other markets (almost every important village has its own and the people date all events from them) barter is still the rule rather than the exception, cowries are still used as currency, and the people prefer the old ten cash and twenty cash copper dubs of the East India Company to any other coins which can be offered them.

The real business of import and export to and from the Agency is managed by the Kómatis of the low country and their agents. These men penetrate to the grain-producing centres, such as Kótapád and Naurangpur, and there see to the loading and despatch of the carts which have come up from the low country to take down the grain; they organize the operations of the many gangs of Brinjáris who drive pack-bullocks between this district and the Central Provinces, furnishing them at convenient centres (such as Sálúr and Párvatípur) with loads of salt, etc. to take to the hinterland, and giving them commissions for purchases of grain and so on to be made in return; and they conduct the distribution to the retail shop-keepers (such as Muhammadans, Dombus and others) of the imports from below.

WEIGHTS AND MEASURES.

The weights and measures of the district are more variable even than usual. The goldsmiths' table of weights is ordinarily as under :—

Tables of weight.

4 vísams (grains of paddy)	=	1 pátika.
2 pátikas	=	1 addiga.
2 addigas	=	1 chinnam.
30 chinnams	=	1 tola (180 grains).
24 tolas	=	1 seer.

CHAP. VI.
WEIGHTS AND MEASURES.

In Párvatípur and Ráyagada a seer contains only 22 tolas. The usual table of weights for other articles is :—

				lb.	oz.
2 chatáks	=	1 nauták	=	..	$1\frac{1}{4}$
8 nautáks	=	1 seer	=	..	10
5 seers	=	1 vísam (viss)	=	3	2
8 vísams	=	1 manugu (maund)	=	25	0
8 manugus	=	1 kantlám	=	200	0
20 manugus	=	1 putti or candy	=	500	0

But local variations abound (the seer being again 24 tolas in some places and 22 tolas in others) and special tables are often used for special articles, such as jaggery, wax, turmeric, cotton, etc. Moreover, the following table is used side by side with the other :—

				lb.
2 yébalams	=	1 padalam	=	$1\frac{1}{2}$
2 padalams	=	1 vísam	=	3
8 vísams	=	1 manugu	=	24
8 manugus	=	1 kantlám	=	192
20 manugus	=	1 candy	=	480

Grain and liquid measures.

In the grain measures (which are also used for liquids) the local variations again are legion. The usual table is :—

4 giddas	=	1 sóla		
2 sólas	=	1 tavva	=	$2\frac{1}{8}$ pints.
2 tavvas	=	1 adda or mánika	=	$4\frac{1}{4}$ pints.
4 addas	=	1 kuncham	=	17 pints.
20 kunchams	=	1 putti	=	$42\frac{1}{2}$ gals.
30 puttis	=	1 garce	=	1,275 gals.

Land is often measured by garces, puttis, and kunchams, a 'garce' of land being supposed to be the area which will produce a garce of grain. This extent is usually reckoned as two acres of wet land and four of dry.

Lineal measures.

The English inch, foot, yard, furlong and mile are coming into use, but the *ján* or hand's span, the *múra* or cubit (the length from the elbow to the top of the middle finger), and the *bára* or fathom, are more popularly employed for small lengths, while in the Agency the usual measure of distance is the *kós*, or distance which it is possible to walk before the leaves of a green twig carried along with one will wither. This last may be taken at about $2\frac{1}{2}$ miles, and four *kós* make one *ámada*. The weavers have special tables for measuring cloths.

CHAPTER VII.

MEANS OF COMMUNICATION.

ROADS—In the plains; their condition in 1850—Beginnings of extension—Their present condition—Chief lines of communication—Bridges—Roads in the Agency—Lammasingi ghát—Minamalúr ghát—Anantagiri ghát—Pottangi ghát and road to Jeypore—Roads on the Jeypore plateau—Lakshmipur ghát—Párvatípur-Ráyagada road—Roads in Gunupur Agency—Sítámpéta pass—Future extensions—Vehicles—Travellers' bungalows and chattrams. RAILWAYS—The Madras and Bengal-Nagpur lines—The proposed Vizianagram-Raipur line. LINES OF STEAMERS.

CHAP. VII.
ROADS.

THE roads of the district divide themselves into two groups; namely, those in the low country and those in the Agency. Except the Ittikavalasa-Jeypore line under the Public Works department, they are in charge of the local boards.

In the plains; their condition in 1850.

Even as late as forty years ago, the great want of the low country was roads. From 1825 to 1850 nothing was done, or next to nothing; the annual outlay on construction and repairs during that period averaging little more than Rs. 1,800. At the close of 1849 the Collector, Mr. Smollett, was requested to report on the roads of the Vizagapatam district. Mistaking, as well he might, the drift of the requisition, he submitted a carefully compiled statement of the roads available for shipping. On being set right, he explained that there was nothing to be said about the other kind of roads, there being 'not a mile of road in the district along which you can drive a gig or a pig.'

Beginnings of extension.

A beginning was made in 1851, when the line from Vizianagram to Bimlipatam was made by public subscription, the Rája contributing Rs. 5,000 out of the Rs. 8,500 required. Government built the bridge on this over the Góstani river at Chittivalasa, and it was washed away the same year. Between 1853 and 1855 about half a lakh was spent in earth-work, but the roads were not properly completed. Even 'the great northern trunk road,' which ran right through the district from Páyakaraopéta, past Anakápalle, Subbavaram and Chittivalasa, and thence parallel to the coast to Chicacole, entirely belied its high-sounding name at this time, being in some places entirely obliterated.[1] Bridges along it and cross roads connecting with it were

[1] Report on important Public Works for 1854, p. 31.

CHAP. VII. ROADS.

practically non-existent. To cross the rivers, carts had to be unloaded, taken off their wheels and ferried over on palmyra rafts.

The roads from Pálkonda to Párvatípur and to Chípurupalle, and the link between Vizagapatam and Anakápalle were next undertaken, but the want of funds occasioned by the Mutiny stopped their completion and they rapidly went to pieces. In 1860 the Deputy Chief Engineer said that 'with the exception of the road from Vizagapatam to Chittivalasa and thence to Vizianagram, there can hardly be said to be a thoroughly made road in the whole of the district.' In 1862 a little more activity was possible and (the Rája of Vizianagram having contributed Rs. 63,500 for the purpose) the roads from Vizagapatam and Vizianagram to Kásipuram, at the foot of the Anantagiri ghát referred to below, were undertaken. The idea at that time was to construct the main road to Jeypore up this ghát. In 1862–63 funds were allotted for the construction of the trunk road from Chittivalasa to Chicacole, 40 miles, and from Vizianagram to Chípurupalle; and thereafter progress was comparatively rapid.

Their present condition.

The condition of the existing roads is usually excellent, the red soil which covers the greater part of the district providing them with a solid foundation. Their milestones are equally substantial, being all built into the sides of solid pillars of masonry lest perchance the metal contractors should move them about and so make illicit profits.

Chief lines of communication.

The chief lines of communication are the trunk road from Páyakaraopéta to Chicacole, already mentioned, and the various cross roads which run from this to the sea on the one side and the gháts leading down from the Agency on the other. The map attached to this volume illustrates these better than any written description can hope to do. The more important of them are (*a*) that from Pólavaram on the coast to Narasapatam, and so to Kondasanta at the foot of the Lammasingi ghát to the Golgonda hills, (*b*) from Púdimadaka, through Anakápalle and Chódavaram, to Mádgole at the foot of the Minamalúr ghát to the Mádgole hills, (*c*) from Vizagapatam to Bodára (Bowdara) on the way to the Anantagiri ghát, (*d*) from Bimlipatam, through Vizianagram, to Sálúr and the Pottangi ghát to Jeypore, (*e*) the branch from this latter which takes off from it at Rámabhadrapuram and runs to Párvatípur, where it bifurcates and leads into the Agency to Ráyagada on the one side and Gunupur on the other, (*f*) the road from Párvatípur, through Pálkonda, to Chicacole in Ganjám, and (*g*) that from Vizianagram to Pálkonda, which goes on to the

Sítampeta pass through the Pálkonda Agency into the same district.

Bridges.

In two directions improvements might be effected to these roads; namely, by providing them with avenues, which are not plentiful at present, and by bridging some more of the many rivers and torrents which pour down from the hills across the line of all the main routes and sometimes greatly delay traffic.

The district no doubt already contains several fine bridges. The more important are those on the trunk road over the Sárada river near Anakápalle (ten arches of 30 feet span), over the Mahéndragedda (six arches of the same size) and over the Góstani at Chittivalasa (eleven similar arches); on the Vizagapatam-Bimlipatam road, that across the Gudilóvagedda (three arches of 40 feet span, built in 1883–84 at an outlay of Rs. 30,000); on the Srungavarapukóta-Bhímasingi road, that over the Mogadárigedda (four cut-stone arches of 30 feet span) and on the Púdimadaka-Mádgole road, that over the Sárada river (five girders of 60 feet each, built in 1901 at a cost of Rs. 72,000).

In 1887 a pontoon bridge was completed across the backwater at Vizagapatam, at the joint cost of the district board and the municipality, to facilitate communication with Anakápalle and the south. It consisted of 21 girders 20 feet long supported on steel pontoons 30 feet long, with a 40 feet opening in the centre for navigation, and was made by Messrs. Burn & Co. of Calcutta at a cost of Rs. 90,000. Up to 1894 it was in charge of the municipality, and afterwards of the district board. It was a failure. The salt-water so rapidly corroded the pontoons, in spite of every effort to protect them with paint, that by 1901 they were in places no thicker than stout paper, and notwithstanding constant and expensive repairs they began bursting one after the other. The idea of building a masonry bridge was mooted, but was given up in consequence of the great cost involved and the uncertainty regarding the requirements of the proposed harbour (see p. 327) in the backwater. Eventually in 1904 a ferry flat, purchased at a cost of Rs. 9,500 and worked by a submerged chain, replaced the pontoon bridge. This is hardly capable of coping with the present traffic southwards, even though the latter has greatly diminished since the railway was built.

Under-vent road-dams (which are cheaper than bridges, are less liable to be carried away by floods, and serve all purposes except during heavy freshes) are now being constructed across the Champávati at Gajapatinagaram and the Végavati on the road from Rámabhadrapuram to Párvatípur above mentioned.

CHAP. VII. ROADS.

The latter of these places is at present frequently cut off from Pálkonda by the Nágávali, which is a perennial stream carrying an immense body of water during floods, but a bridge is now to be built on top of the anicut which is being constructed over the river (see p. 106) and the two roads leading from Párvatípur to Pálkonda and to Gunupur respectively will be diverted and taken over this.

Roads in the Agency.

The roads in the Agency, with the single exception of that from Ittikavalasa to Jeypore, have all been made by the agency officers without professional assistance. For many years after the Jeypore estate was first entered by Government officers in 1863 (see p. 269) the amount granted for roads throughout it was only Rs. 13,000, of which Rs. 10,000 was for 'jungle-clearing' along the rough tracks which traversed it, the old rule being that 50 yards (the supposed effective arrow-range) should be cleared each side of a road. The annual allotment was slowly increased until in 1899 it reached Rs. 48,500 from Provincial funds and Rs. 10,000 from the Mahárája, special grants being occasionally made for special purposes. At first, it is clear, there was a want of system in the procedure, roads being made one year and left to go back to jungle the next; but latterly a series of five-year programmes have been drawn up and followed. The lines of road which have been completed may be conveniently referred to in their geographical order, beginning in the south of the district.

Lammasingi ghát.

On the Golgonda hills there are no roads practicable for carts. The chief ghát up to them is that from Kondasanta, nine miles north of Narasapatam, to Lammasingi. This was first regularly opened up in 1882, when Rs. 2,400 was spent upon it. Five years later the trace was much altered, with the idea of making the road practicable for carts, and was lengthened from eight miles to nine. In 1888 Government specially ordered it to be proceeded with, and by 1890 it was completed nearly to the top. Two years later it was made passable, with difficulty, for carts throughout; but though an estimate for improving it into a regular cart-road was prepared in 1895, this has never been carried out. The road is regularly maintained and more than one officer has expressed the opinion that it is more than good enough for the work it has to do. The rough track up these hills from Koyyúr to Peddavalasa is also kept in order.

Minamalúr ghát.

Proceeding northwards, the next ghát reached is that from Mádgole to Minamalúr on the Mádgole hills, fifteen miles (six on the plains) in length. This was begun in 1882, a rough trace of one in ten being cut. From Minamalúr, tracks run inland to Pádéru and Pádwa, and this ghát is the natural outlet for those parts. There are no cart-roads on the Mádgole hills. Though steep and not practicable for carts, the ghát is apparently much used, traffic returns [1] showing that over 800 carts a day pass over the bridge across the Sárada between Mádgole and Anakápalle.

Anantagiri ghát.

Thirty miles north-east of the Minamalúr track is the Anantagiri (or Gálikonda) ghát. This is so called from the village of Anantagiri near the top, at which the Rája of Vizianagram has a coffee-plantation, and from the great Gálikonda hill which overlooks it and is referred to on p. 6. When the Jeypore estate was first entered, in 1863, and it became necessary to construct a road from its capital to the plains, the original idea was to follow a line running from Vizagapatam, through Srungavarapukóta to Kásipuram (41 miles); thence four miles to Kottúr at the foot of the hills; up this Anantagiri ghát, ascending through Ráyavalasa (about eight miles) and Anantagiri (three miles further); over the watershed of Gálikonda, four or five miles up an easy gradient; down to Janamguda on the 3,000 feet plateau by a steep descent; and thence on *viâ* the Aruku valley, Pádwa, Handiput and Sogaru to Jeypore by the ghát starting down from Petta. The line from Kásipuram through Ráyavalasa was first traced by the old sibbandi force and improved upon by the company of Sappers then stationed in Jeypore, who also constructed part of the trace down the Petta ghát which had been marked out by Major Shaw-Stewart, R.E. In February 1863 the mortality and sickness among the Sappers was so heavy that Government recalled them. Lieutenant Smith, the first Assistant at Jeypore, nevertheless continued the work and made the 56 miles from Jeypore into an excellent bullock track. From 1866, however, he devoted his energy and funds to improving the alternative track *viâ* Pottangi and Sálúr, and the Anantagiri ghát was abandoned for many years.

The idea of completing it was revived in 1885 by Mr. H. G. Turner, the then Agent, who was much impressed by the capabilities of the Aruku and Pádwa country, the produce of which had no outlet. He intended to take the road from Sogaru to Jaitgiri, where it was to bifurcate, one branch running down to the north of the Malkanagiri taluk and the other through Dasmatpur into Rámagiri taluk. He began work on it in earnest in 1885–86, starting from Bodára (Bowdara), where the roads from Vizagapatam

[1] Kindly furnished by Mr. P. B. Arbuthnot, Local Fund Engineer.

CHAP. VII. ROADS.

and Vizianagram meet. Ten miles further on, at Kagalaméda, the ascent began, and ran up five miles to Damuku, the first shelf on the ghát, 2,000 feet above the sea. There the road entered the Ráyavalasa valley and proceeded by an easier ascent two miles to that village. From thence a sharp ascent led to Anantagiri, about 3,000 feet above the sea and four miles from Damuku. There an excellent bungalow, still standing, was built. From thence Mr. Turner worked out, and marked on the ground, a trace running along the stream to Dumariguda saddle; then up to Bispur saddle, the highest point, 3,650 feet; round the hill to the left, on a down grade; through a gorge, and so to the saddle above Baliaguda hamlet; below the cliffs of Grant's range, across the valley, to Karabolu; and thence to the west, out into the Aruku plains, near Madagada.[1] Up to 31st March 1887, Rs. 67,000 had been spent on the work, and carts could get to Anantagiri. The estimate for its completion was Rs. 86,000 more. In 1888, however, in spite of Mr. Turner's most earnest pleadings, Government declined [2] to allow any more money to be spent on this road, averring that it led only 'to a bare and sparsely populated plateau and will apparently be of little use except as a second alternative to the Sálúr-Pottangi road to Jeypore.'

Since then nothing has been done to carry on the road, and the only route across the range is an old bullock-track over Gálikonda. Even so, the traffic appears to be very considerable, as the returns show that over 800 carts a day travel from Bodára to Vizianagram and Vizagapatam. In 1892 Mr. Willock, then Agent, revived the proposal, pointing out [3] that the worst part of the ghát had already been done, that only 9½ miles remained to be completed, that the country to be tapped was very rich, and that the Pottangi-Koraput road was almost useless to it as hills and the troublesome Koláb river intervened. He considered that for Rs. 25,000 the track could be opened for cart traffic and that it could be made a really first-class road for an additional Rs 50,000. Government directed the Public Works department to furnish an approximate estimate of the cost of completing the work and the reply was that Rs. 42,000 would suffice; but funds were again refused. In 1897 Mr. Horne, and in 1902 Mr. Ayling, added other arguments [4] to those adduced by their predecessors,

[1] See p. 3 of G.O., No. 1970, Judicial, dated 15th September 1888.

[2] G.Os., No. 475, Financial, dated 12th April 1887 and No. 1541, Judicial, dated 20th July 1888.

[3] See G.O., No. 1027, Financial, dated 3rd October 1892.

[4] G.Os., Nos. 1308, Judicial, dated 8th September 1897; 1156, Judicial, dated 22nd July 1898; and 1886, Judicial, dated 12th September 1902.

but in 1898 Government had no money to spare and the present policy[1] is to complete first the other ghát between Náráyanapatnam and Lakshmipur referred to below.

Pottangi ghát and road to Jeypore.

The Pottangi ghát, the next to the north after the Anantagiri road, starts at Ittikavalasa, five miles from Sálúr, and runs to Pottangi on the 3,000 feet plateau, across this plateau to Koraput, and thence down to Jeypore. It is metalled and bridged throughout, is in charge of the Public Works department, and is the only cart-road from the plains to the Jeypore country.

From Ittikavalasa it rises sharply, with a gradient of about 1 in 17, for four miles; and then for five miles runs along an almost level trace to the picturesque bungalow in the feverish Sunki valley at the ninth mile. Thence for ten miles it keeps steadily up, at gradients varying from 1 in 16 to 1 in 20 with intervals of almost level ground, past Rállugedda, to the head of the ghát at the nineteenth mile; whence it descends, between 1 in 19 and 1 in 21, four miles to the wide valley of Pottangi, where there is another bungalow near the twenty-third mile. All this section runs through sparsely wooded and waterless hills, and the only places where water is obtainable in the hot weather are Sunki and Rállugedda. From Pottangi to Koraput the road undulates gently over red soil plains dotted with numerous small hills, and the country gets barer of vegetation every mile until at Koraput there is scarcely a forest tree to be seen in any direction. The stages are, Doliamba bungalow, thirty-third mile; Sembliguda bungalow, thirty-sixth mile (whence roads run north to Lakshmipur and south to Nandapuram); and Koraput, the head-quarters of the Divisional Officer and Superintendent of Police, fiftieth mile. Thence the road climbs sharply out of the hollow in which Koraput lies, and then descends over rather steep undulations to 58 miles 3 furlongs, at which point the beautiful ghát down to Jeypore, which runs through forest throughout, begins. This is on a gradient of 1 in 20, and ends at the sixty-first mile, whence the run in to Jeypore is two miles of level.

The construction of the section on the plateau was begun by Lieutenant Smith in 1866–67, and in 1869 it was definitely decided that the main route to Jeypore must follow this line. At the two ghâts at each end, however, several experiments were made before the existing routes were finally fixed upon. At the Pottangi end a bullock-track from Sunki to Páchipenta was first improved and by 1873 Mr. H. G. Turner, then Special Assistant

[1] G.O., No. 1540, Judicial, dated 16th October 1903, page 5.

CHAP. VII. ROADS.

Agent at Koraput, had constructed the ghát (which still sometimes goes by his name, but is otherwise known as the Tádivalasa ghát) from Pottangi to Tádivalasa on the plains. This was afterwards greatly improved, and it is still maintained and much used by pack-bullock caravans because the pasture and water on it are better than on the Ittikavalasa-Sunki-Pottangi road.

At the Jeypore end, Lieutenant Smith began by cutting the ghát from Koraput to Borigumma which is now known as the Ránigedda ghát and is a great favourite with cartmen going to Naurangpur and Bastar. It was not until later that Mr. Turner made a trace down to Jeypore. By 1874 carts, which a few years before had been unknown in any part of this country, could get (with difficulty) right through from Sálúr to Jeypore. In the next year the existing Pottangi ghát, which crosses the old Páchipenta route at several points, was begun under the care of Mr. Nordmann of the Public Works department. The difficulties were great: the upper staff were constantly down with malaria, and labour was scarce and shy. Colonel Sankey, the Chief Engineer, visited the work in 1880 (a bluff on it still bears his name) and stirred up those responsible; but it was not until 1883 that a carriage could be driven into Sunki, and even this result was due to special efforts made because it was thought that the Governor was coming to see the road. It was finished however in 1884 (the Sunki bridge was not completed until later), and the traffic which at once swarmed up and down it surpassed the highest expectations which had been formed, the cartmen travelling from the coast as far inland as Kótapád in search of grain. The 22 miles had cost Rs. 4,65,000, or Rs. 21,200 a mile, and the road was soon afterwards handed over to the Public Works department, which now maintains the 60 miles to Jeypore at a cost of Rs. 24,000 annually. Labour is scarce, the road is so narrow that the carts follow one another and wear deep ruts, the traffic is enormous (1,200 carts a day often pass a given point in 24 hours in the dry season) and the upkeep of the road is consequently not a simple matter.

In April 1886 Mr. H. D. Taylor, then in charge of the Jeypore estate, began the construction of a proper road on from Pottangi to Koraput, and next year the existing ghát thence to Jeypore (called at first 'the Jubilee ghát' because the Mahárája of Jeypore had contributed towards it in honour of the late Queen-Empress' Jubilee) was put in hand by him. The earth-work was completed in 1889 (one piece of blasting cost Rs. 5,000) and the

CHAP. VII. ROADS.

metalling in 1892. The Pottangi-Koraput section was completed by the Public Works department in 1895, at a cost of Rs. 3,08,000, except the iron girder bridge over the Kerandi river. This last was built on dry land on a narrow neck separating two points in the river's course and then a channel was dug to lead the river under it.

Roads on the Jeypore plateau.

Except this one through line (and its branches, already mentioned, from Sembliguda to Lakshmipur and Nandapuram, and that from Koraput to Lakshmipur, referred to below) there are no roads on the 3,000 feet plateau which are practicable for carts.

In the Jeypore plateau, however, which is 1,000 feet lower, there are several. The chief of these (see the map) is that which runs from Jeypore through Borigumma and Kótapád to the Bastar State and its capital Jagdalpur. From the latter place a good road leads to Raipur, which thus has through communication with the sea. From Borigumma this line goes on, over the Indrávati to Naurangpur, whence it is now being carried on to Pappadahandi. At this place it bifurcates, a rough track leading northwards through Dabugám, Bijápur and Umarkót to Raigarh; and a better road, which is now being further improved, passing through Maidalpur to the Kálahandi boundary, where it joins the road to Bhavánipatnam, the capital of that State.

From Jeypore an inferior road runs southwards, over the Koláb (which badly needs bridging) to Boipariguda (whence a track leads off to Rámagiri) and Kollar, down a ghát to Góvindupalle, and thence to Malkanagiri. Up to this last place it is just practicable for carts, but thereafter it degenerates into a rough track running on to Mótu, at the junction of the Saveri and the Siléru rivers.

Lakshmipur ghát.

Returning again to the plains and going northwards from Sálúr, one finds no ghát up to the plateau until Párvatípur is reached. From this place a road (made in 1895–96 at a cost of Rs. 13,500 to replace the old track, which crossed the Janjhávati no less than 21 times) runs westwards through Álamanda and Bandigám to Náráyanapatnam (a very malarious spot), whence a ghát is being made up the comparatively easy incline which leads to Lakshmipur on the 3,000 feet plateau. This latter place is already connected (see above) with Koraput by a road practicable for carts and it is thought that when the railway is opened to Párvatípur much of the produce of the Jeypore level will use this route to reach it.

CHAP. VII. ROADS.

Párvatípur–Ráyagada road.

From Párvatípur a cart-road runs northwards to Ráyagada and thence six miles further to Komatlipéta, where the tracks to Bissamkatak and Kalyána Singapur branch off from it. This was first traced in the fifties of the last century by the Public Works department, and was much improved by Mr. Willock in 1875. In 1892 the line was resurveyed and a proposal (made by Mr. Goodrich in 1875) that the Kumbikóta-gedda near Ráyagada should be crossed by a bridge at a point where (see p. 301) it runs in a deep and narrow gorge, instead of at the usual ford, was revived by Mr. Willock. Special allotments for the road were made by Government and from the funds of the Jeypore estate (which was then under management during the present Mahárája's minority), and in 1897 the work was completed at a cost of Rs. 75,300. The bridge over the Kumbikóta gedda, the central span of which is an iron girder 76 feet long and 95 feet above the bed of the stream, was completed in 1900 after much trouble with drunken and absconding workmen. It cost Rs. 22,730 and has been invaluable in removing the most serious obstacle to traffic along this route.

Roads in Gunupur Agency.

From Párvatípur a metalled road leads to Kurupám, whence a cart-track goes on to Gunupur; and from the latter place another track runs north to Gudári and a third through Durgi, near the Kailásakóta hills, to Bissamkatak. None of these three is now of much importance, but they will be greatly used as soon as the railway reaches Párvatípur.

Sítámpéta pass.

The last road in the Agency which need be referred to is the Sítámpéta pass running from Pálkonda, through the Pálkonda hills, to the Ganjám district. This was first properly cleared under a system suggested [1] in 1835 by Sir Frederick Adam, then Governor of Madras, when he came to the district in consequence of the disturbances which gave rise to Mr. Russell's deputation (see p. 57). In May 1836 the Collector leased out 23 patches of land, forming a belt along either side of the road, to 23 mokhásadárs free of kattubadi on condition [2] that they kept them clear of jungle. On these cleared belts seven small villages eventually sprang up which for many years were known as the 'road villages.' In 1886 it was found that the land had mostly been alienated and that the services were not performed, and the grants were accordingly resumed. The road is practicable for carts.

[1] See his Minute on pp. 64–5 of Vol. I of Mr. Russell's report and the orders on p. 86 thereof.

[2] For details, see G.O., No. 2781, Judicial, dated 1st December 1887, p. 42.

Future extensions.

Though there are thus several excellent lines of road through the various parts of the Agency, much more might undoubtedly be done. There are still large tracts in which no cart has ever been seen and the people are actually afraid of them. A case recently occurred in which the only hill man who could be induced to get into the first cart which arrived on a new road was a Dombu whose ideas had been widened by a compulsory journey to the Vizagapatam jail! In particular, when funds become available, the country round Pádéru, Pádwa and Aruku requires an outlet to the plains. The difficulty is want of money. The recent introduction of the Local Boards Act (see p. 212) into parts of the Agency will bring in some Rs. 35,000 from land-cess and tolls, but a contribution of an equal amount from Provincial funds (in addition to the Rs. 24,000 already allowed for the maintenance of the Ittikavalasa–Jeypore road) will be necessary, and even then only about Rs. 8,000 per annum will be available for new works above the ghâts. The advantage formerly urged in favour of opening up Jeypore—that it would serve as a granary to Vizagapatam in times of scarcity—has been already sufficiently secured by the Pottangi ghát and the extension of the road thence to the Bastar frontier.

Vehicles.

The country carts of the Vizagapatam district are somewhat smaller and lighter than those of the south and usually have only wooden axles. The oxen hardly ever have nose-strings, or even ropes to their horns, as in the south, and if they shy or bolt the driver is powerless. The carts which fetch down grain from the trans-ghát country carry a kind of huge sarcophagus, three feet high and seven long and capable of holding a third of a garce, made by the Médaras of bamboo wattle smeared inside with clay, and the grain is poured loose into this, gunny-bags not being used. In the Jeypore plateau one meets the smaller wains from Bastar, which have little wheels with broad fellies or solid wooden wheels studded along the rim with big nails.

The palanquin is still common in the Agency, but may only be used by those to whom the Jeypore Mahárája has granted permission. The carriers are almost always Gadabas and many of them own inams requiring this service of them. *Kávadis* (baskets slung on either end of a bamboo carried across the shoulder) are much used for lighter loads, and are so popular both in the plains and the Agency that a man will use them even for the lightest loads (when taking out his dinner to the fields, for example) instead of carrying them on his head, as would be done in the south. Manure, etc., is often carried on to the land on a kind of

CHAP. VII. ROADS.

rude sledge made of two bamboos tied together at one end and fitted with a yoke at the other, between which is placed a large basket. The contrivance is pulled along by cattle, and is called *sarugudu*.

Travellers' bungalows and chattrams.

A list of the travellers' bungalows in the district, with particulars of the accommodation available in each, will be found in the separate Appendix to this volume. The local boards maintain eighteen chattrams for native travellers, five of which possess small endowments. In Vizagapatam town, near the old parade-ground, is 'the Turner Chattram' founded in 1894 as a memorial of Mr. H. G. Turner, Collector and Agent from 1881 to 1889. The site was the gift of the late Mahárája Sir Gajapati Rao and the Rs. 33,000 spent on the building was raised by public subscription. In April 1898 the institution was handed over to the municipal council, which now administers it.

RAILWAYS. The Madras and Bengal-Nagpur lines.

The district is traversed from south to north by a broad-gauge line which was built by the State and is now worked as far as Waltair by the Madras Railway Co., and from thence onwards by the Bengal-Nagpur Railway Co. The former section (61 miles) was opened to traffic in 1893 and the latter (76 miles) in the following year. This line enters the district at Páyakaraopéta by a bridge of four spans of 100 feet across the river which forms the boundary between Vizagapatam and Gódávari, and passes to Anakápalle (crossing the Sárada on a bridge of six spans of 100 feet), Waltair, and the beach at Vizagapatam. Returning on its tracks for a short distance, it makes a détour to avoid the Simháchalam hills and goes on over the Góstani (five spans of 100 feet) to Vizianagram and thence across the Champávati near Nellimarla (four similar spans) to the boundary of the district on the Lángulya river opposite Chicacole.

The proposed Vizianagram-Raipur line.

Another line, which has long been projected, was first surveyed in 1881, and is at last to be actually begun is that from Vizianagram to Raipur in the Central Provinces, *viâ* Gajapatinagaram, Bobbili, Párvatípur, Ráyagada and the Kalyána Singapur valley, through the ghâts near Satikóna by a tunnel 1,000 feet long and 1,388 feet above the sea, and so into the Central Provinces by the valley of the Tél river. The length in this district will be 133 miles. The original 1881 survey was made by Mr. K. F. Nordmann and his report (G.O., No. 2366, Public Works, dated 13th September 1882) stated that the difference between the cost of following the above route and of carrying the line by the alternative alignment up the Pottangi ghát, down to Jeypore, and thence northwards *viâ* Naurangpur was slightly in favour of the latter route, which, though steeper, was shorter. The country alongside this latter is also richer than the Ráyagada valley, where there is little irrigated land. The authorities however considered that the difficulties of the ghâts up to Pottangi and down to Jeypore would probably prove more considerable than was anticipated and that the cost of working trains up the heavy inclines on that line would be great, and preferred the easier route now finally selected. Mr. Nordmann suggested that, if this was chosen, a road should be carried from Naurangpur eastwards to Ráyagada to tap the rich wet area round the former place and Kótapád, but this would have to cross a saddle 2,700 feet above the sea and about 25 miles of it would be within the Kálahandi State. An easier line would probably be that from Kalyána Singapur to Maidalpur and thence through Pappadahandi to Naurangpur.

Connected with the new line is the question of the construction of a harbour at Vizagapatam (see p. 327)—or perhaps Bimlipatam — for the export of the produce of the Central Provinces which is expected to pour down to the sea. Calcutta is said to have already as much trade as it can cope with, and an alternative outlet is considered necessary on this ground alone. The steps which should be taken, and the agency and funds which should be employed, are now under consideration.

LINES OF STEAMERS.

Vizagapatam and Bimlipatam are regularly visited by the boats of the British India Steam Navigation Co., and Clan Line steamers call at intervals at the former place for the manganese (see p. 125) from the Garividi mines. Within recent memory a regular fleet of schooners, owned and manned by natives, used to ply from Vizagapatam, and boats of this class were built in the backwater there, but the steamers have now captured all the trade to Burma and the coasting traffic is monopolized by the railway.

CHAPTER VIII.

RAINFALL AND SEASONS.

RAINFALL. FAMINES AND SCARCITIES—In 1790-92—In 1824—In 1865-66—In 1871-72—In 1876-78—In 1885-86—In 1889—In 1896-97—The relief granted—Private charity and Government loans—Cost to the State—Resisting power of the district. FLOODS AND STORMS — Storm of 1700 -- Of 1749—And of 1752—Cyclone of 1867—Flood and cyclone of 1870—Flood of 1872—Cyclone of 1876—Two cyclones of 1878. EARTHQUAKES.

CHAP. VIII. RAINFALL.

STATISTICS of the rainfall at the various recording stations in both the plains and the Agency, and for the district as a whole, are given below for the dry weather (January to March), the hot weather (April and May), the south-west monsoon (June to September), the north-east monsoon (October to December) and the whole year. The figures shown are the averages of those recorded between 1904 and the earliest year in which rainfall was systematically registered at each station.

Station.	Years recorded.	January to March.	April and May.	June to September.	October to December.	Total.
Koraput Division.						
Jeypore	1882-1904	0·94	4·18	64·61	5·40	75·13
Koraput	1877-1904	0·93	3·96	48·95	5·50	59·34
Malkanagiri	1882-1904	0·56	3·08	58·12	4·70	66·46
Naurangpur	1882-1904	0·83	3·56	55·99	3·90	64·28
Pádwa	1882-1904	1·55	7·69	37·18	7·28	53·70
Pottangi	1883-1904	1·69	6·08	44·81	10·12	62·70
Narasapatam Division.						
Anakápalle	1870-1904	0·71	2·90	21·34	11·44	36·39
Narasapatam	1870-1904	1·64	5·21	24·37	11·54	42·76
Pólavaram	1895-1904	1·98	2·89	17·06	9·28	31·21
Yellamanchili... ...	1870-1904	1·00	3·45	20·55	12·37	37·37
Chódavaram	1870-1904	1·39	4·58	25·42	12·57	43·96
Párvatipur Division.						
Bissamkatak	1890-1904	1·59	5·92	36·46	4·06	48·03
Bobbili	1884-1904	1·88	3·91	28·56	7·72	42·07
Gunupur	1882-1904	2·02	4·96	34·89	6·05	47·92
Párvatípur	1870-1904	1·90	4·55	30·98	8·69	46·12
Ráyagada	1877-1904	1·29	5·35	32·30	5·92	44·86
Sálúr	1870-1904	1·40	4·39	26·83	10·96	43·58

Station.	Years recorded.	January to March.	April and May	June to September.	October to December.	Total.
Vizagapatam Division.						
Bálacheruvu	1870–1904	1·07	2·92	19·92	14·97	38·88
Srungavarapukóta ..	1884–1904	1·74	4·22	27·67	8·99	42·62
Waltair	1870–1904	1·04	3·27	19·95	15·60	39·86
Vizianagram Division.						
Bimlipatam	1870–1904	0·95	2·66	18·55	13·58	35·74
Kónáda	1895–1904	1·07	2·50	19·80	10·11	33·48
Chípurupalle	1870–1904	1·00	2·78	25·29	11·62	40·69
Kuppili	1870–1904	1·05	3·29	21·64	13·48	39·46
Gajapatinagaram ...	1884–1904	1·26	3·72	24·64	8·24	37·86
Pálkonda	1870–1904	1·50	4·13	32·60	8·19	46·42
Vizianagram	1870–1904	1·63	3·38	24·88	12·74	42·63
District average. Plains.	......	1·29	3·72	24·05	12·00	41·06
District average. Agency.	......	1·29	5·11	44·43	6·29	57·12

It will be seen that the average annual fall in the plains is 41 inches, and in the Agency as a whole 57 inches. The wettest part of the district is the strip beyond the 3,000 feet plateau (Jeypore, Malkanagiri and Naurangpur taluks) in parts of which the fall is 75 inches, of which no less than 65 inches is brought by the south-west monsoon; next comes the 3,000 feet plateau itself (Koraput, Pádwa and Pottangi) with an average of 59 inches; then the lower Párvatípur Agency (Bissamkatak, Gunupur and Ráyagada) with 47 inches; after that the submontane stations on the plains (such as Chódavaram, Sálúr and Pálkonda) with 44 inches; and last those on the coast, average 37 inches, of which Pólavaram (only 31 inches) is the most unfortunate of all. It will thus be noticed that the fall decreases steadily in these tracts according as each is further and further removed from the point where the south-west monsoon first strikes the district. This current parts with the chief portion of its moisture in the tract it reaches first, and has little left for those over which it passes later on.

In the case of the north-east monsoon the conditions are reversed; and while places on the coast, like Waltair and Bimlipatam, get from 14 to 16 inches, Jeypore and Naurangpur, beyond the gháts and the last to be reached by the current, only get from 4 to 6 inches. This monsoon, however, is of much less importance to the welfare of the district than the south-west.

CHAP. VIII. RAINFALL.

Violent fluctuations in the amount received are usual in all parts of the district. In Jeypore the annual fall has varied from 46½ inches in 1901 to 105 inches in 1890; in Koraput it has ranged between 40 inches in 1899 and 84 in 1893; in Bissamkatak between 36 inches in 1899 and 65 in 1903; in Chódavaram between 24 inches in 1900 and 80 in 1878; and in Pólavaram between 19 inches in 1896 and 44 inches in 1903. In the plains as a whole the heaviest fall on record is the 70·90 inches of 1878 (the year of the disastrous cyclone referred to below) and the lightest the 24·98 inches of 1896; while in the Agency the maximum known was the 72·88 inches of 1893 and the minimum the 41·32 of 1879.

FAMINES AND SCARCITIES.

The district has suffered but little from famines and scarcities

In 1790-92.

In common with the rest of the north of the Presidency, it experienced a serious dearth of food between November 1790 and November 1792. In April 1791, 1,200 persons were stated to have died of starvation in the neighbourhood of Vizagapatam, and the transit duties on grain were suspended and the Chief and Council issued supplies gratis to the poor from the public stores.

In 1824.

The failure of the two monsoons of 1823 resulted in nearly half the wet land being left uncultivated and in the dry land crops suffering greatly, so that early in 1824 the price of grain was double the normal. The importation of food-stuffs was encouraged by the removal of the transit duties and the grant of a bonus, employment was given by the State to a number of persons, and the opening of a relief dépôt was sanctioned. In October 1824 good rain fell, prices declined and all fears subsided.

In 1865-66.

The effects of the Orissa famine of 1865–66 were somewhat felt in Vizagapatam, prices rising to famine rates; cholera, small-pox and cattle disease being prevalent; and some emigration to Burma taking place. But grain was sent down by sea in large quantities from Balasore, and by road from Chicacole and Kimedi, and there was little severe suffering.

In 1871-72.

The north-east monsoon of 1868 failed, and some anxiety prevailed until the south-west rains of 1869 proved to be favourable.

In 1871 distress threatened, and Mr. G. Thornhill, Member of the Board, was deputed in November to report on the state of the district and of Ganjám. Between that date and the middle of 1872, when all pressure was over, some Rs. 75,000 were spent upon relief-works in this district, considerable emigration to Gódávari took place, and the Mahárája of Vizianagram authorized the expenditure of two lakhs on irrigation works in his estate. The distress was never really serious.

In 1876–78.

The great famine of 1876–78, which wrought such terrible havoc in the south of the Presidency, was hardly felt in Vizagapatam. Prices rose, no doubt, in consequence of the exportation of grain to the affected areas, and cholera was more than usually prevalent, but the remissions granted in the two Government taluks of Golgonda and Sarvasiddhi amounted to less than Rs. 20,000 and in only one month were there more than 1,000 persons in receipt of relief. The two cyclones of 1878 mentioned below did far more harm, in fact, than the famine.

In 1885–86.

The season of 1885–86 was especially unfavourable, and in the two Government taluks remissions amounting to Rs. 70,000 were necessary.

In 1889.

Yet in 1889, the year of 'the Ganjám famine,' Vizagapatam escaped almost entirely. This was owing to large imports of grain by sea, and by land from Gódávari and the Jeypore country, and to an increase in the usual emigration to Burma for the paddy harvest and to Gódávari for silt-clearing in the canals and work on the Nizam's railway to Bezwada, which was then approaching completion.

In 1891–92 there was again considerable scarcity of food; but the district was saved by the grain which poured down from Bastar and Jeypore by the new ghát road to the latter, and relief-works were never necessary.

In 1896–97.

In 1896–97 occurred the last famine which the district has witnessed. Conditions were aggravated by the prevalence of wide-spread distress in other parts. The north-east monsoon of 1896 was an absolute failure, the fall in the littoral tracts being less than an inch against an average of 13 inches. Though the area sown, both wet and dry, was not much below the average, the outturn was very inferior. Large imports of grain took place by rail, and even more came in by road from the Jeypore country, as much as 70,000 tons arriving altogether between January and October; but the price of ragi rose in the affected area of the district from 29 seers the rupee in August 1896 to 11 seers in July 1897. Emigrants to Burma increased from the normal of 7,000 to about 20,000 and the movement to Gódávari, though not actually enumerated, was known to be equally in excess of the ordinary. Pasture became very scarce, grass being sold at Vizagapatam at 7 annas the bundle against the usual price of 1 anna, but the forests were thrown open for grazing and the mortality among cattle was apparently slight.

CHAP. VIII. FAMINES AND SCARCITIES.

The relief granted.

Relief-works were opened in March 1897, but (see the figures below) were sparsely attended until the south-west monsoon threatened also to fail, when people crowded to the works and in addition gratuitous relief was necessary on a considerable scale. In August, however, the district recovered almost as suddenly as it had declined. The report on the famine explained this by saying that—

'The cause of the sudden demoralization may be ascribed to the almost perpetual immunity from famine that the district has enjoyed Even in 1876–78 it escaped practically scatheless. The break-down in the present year appears to have been due to the fact that, while the people realised that a disaster was impending, they had no experience of its nature or of the extent to which they could rely upon the help of the State, and consequently exaggerated the unknown danger before them. It may also, perhaps, have been due to the belief, which prevailed throughout the Presidency, in a prophecy that the last three years of the current Hindu cycle ending with 1900 would be years of famine and pestilence ending in a general débâcle, in which caste would disappear.'

Part of the sudden crowding to the works was also doubtless due to the high rates of wages which were being paid at them, and much of the sudden recovery to the excellence of the rain in August and September. The parts of the district which were earliest and most severely affected were the taluks of Bimlipatam, Vizagapatam and Sarvasiddhi, and parts of Anakápalle and of the Vizianagram zamindari. But eventually the whole of the plains portion of the district and the Pálkonda Agency were included in the area of distress.

The average numbers on relief in the district during the famine and the price in seers per rupee of ragi in each month in the affected taluks are shown below :—

Month and year.	Average number of people relieved during each month.				Price of ragi in seers per rupee.
	On relief works.	Weavers.	On gratuitous relief.	Total.	
March 1897 ...	3,042	...	394	3,436	21·0
April " ...	10,616	...	1,946	12,562	15·7
May " ...	12,992	...	2,711	15,703	14·2
June " ...	15,132	698	9,630	25,460	11·2
July " ...	20,461	5,139	27,878	53,478	10·8
August " ...	12,935	7,599	13,522	34,056	12·4
September " ...	5,834	6,637	4,534	17,005	12·2

Weavers were relieved by making them advances of material and taking over the fabrics woven therefrom at rates which left the workers sufficient for their maintenance during the time spent in weaving them.

Private charity and Government loans.

From the Indian Famine Charitable Relief Fund, Rs. 1,42,000 were received for expenditure in the district, and nearly the whole of this was laid out in setting up afresh with cattle, seed etc. those who had suffered most severely by the distress. The Mahárája of Bobbili and Mahárája Gajapati Rao were conspicuous by their charity during the famine, and their example was followed by the Vizianagram estate and several prominent people in the district. The amounts advanced by Government comprised Rs. 6,030 under the Land Improvement Loans Act and Rs. 1,42,616 under the Agriculturists Loans Act. Of the latter sum, the greater part was spent on the purchase of cattle and seed-grain when the distress was over.

Cost to the State.

The loss to the State from remissions of land revenue was Rs. 1,53,000 and from other causes Rs. 15,900. The direct expenditure on the famine amounted to Rs. 4,48,695 (of which Rs. 2,15,900 were laid out on works and Rs. 1,26,900 on gratuitous relief) and the indirect expenditure to Rs. 10,823. The total cost to the State was thus some 6½ lakhs.

Resisting power of the district.

The power of the district to withstand the attacks of famine is above the normal. Labour is available in the fields for nearly ten months out of the twelve. As a late Collector put it :—

'In the Deccan, I believe, there is little besides the one big harvest of the staple dry crop. Here there is cultivation and harvesting of some kind going on almost all the year. With the first good showers in May ploughing of dry lands and sowing of ragi and cambu in seed-beds commences, and in June transplantation of these crops is in full swing. Even earlier than this, if showers have been received, gingelly has been sown. As soon as transplantation of dry crops is over, should the south-west monsoon set in, wet lands are ploughed and paddy seed sown. At the end of July paddy transplantation begins and continues through August. Hardly is that over when the ragi and cambu harvest commences and is carried on through September. Gingelly is meanwhile being reaped in August and September and korra, vuda, and sámai in August. When the ragi and cambu is off the ground, dry lands are immediately prepared again and sown with grams and pulses—or a second crop of ragi or with cholam. Then follows the north-east monsoon in October, and very soon after that is over early paddy commences to be harvested Ragi, sown at various periods, is being cut all this time. The big paddy harvest commences in November and extends into December. Then follows the cold

CHAP. VIII. FAMINES AND SCARCITIES.

weather cultivation of ragi, chillies &c. under wells, and the harvesting of grams and pulses. Indigo is sown as soon as the paddy is off the ground, and sugar-cane is harvested up to March. When this is over, it is almost time to sow gingelly again, so that in fact it is only for about two and a half months from March to May that agriculture of some kind is not proceeding to a considerable extent.'

Moreover, as has been said, emigration to Burma and Gódávari is an established custom.

Irrigation sources, if seldom on a large scale, are numerous, and some of them have their sources in the forests on the Gháts and so benefit from the heavier rainfall received there—though the effect of the reckless felling of those jungles is becoming very perceptible in the diminished volume and constancy of their flow.

Communications are also excellent. From one end of the district to the other runs a railway which links it with Bengal on the north and the Gódávari and Kistna deltas on the south; its two ports enable grain to be brought to it from Rangoon; and the roads from Párvatípur to Ráyagada and from Sálúr across the 3,000 feet plateau to Jeypore and Naurangpur render available in case of need immense areas of grain land wherein the rains scarcely ever fail. At the beginning of 1906 the high prices occasioned by the shortage in other parts of India resulted in an almost continuous string of grain-laden carts—1,200 a day were counted—pouring down from the Jeypore country by the ghát leading to Sálúr.

FLOODS AND STORMS.

Though Vizagapatam has usually escaped the ravages of famine, it has experienced more than its share of floods and storms.

Storm of 1700.

A letter from Vizagapatam to the Madras Government dated April 28th 1700 said—

'On the 18th here happen'd a more dreadful Storme from the No: East which lasted 3 days and did much damage to the country, and the Sea was so boystrous and came in at the rate that most of the rivers overflowed, and Struck a great terror in the Inhabitants that the country would be dr wned, all vessels in the Sea along this coast were lost and many in the rivers by the force of the currant and tides, and Mr. holcombes Ship Fleetwood bound for bengall, with a large grab that was in our road, was drove a Shear and Stav'd, but thro: Gods mercy most or all the goods Saved w:th the greatest part of the wreck.'

Of 1749.

In 1749 another storm 'greatly affected the Merchants of this place by the loss of 14 or 15 vessells, which we are affraid will much diminish our customs.'

And of 1752.

Three years later, yet another storm drove ashore a ship lying in the roads, sank some of the vessels in the river and damaged others, and caused immense havoc inland. Kasimkóta and Anakápalle had 'little left of them,' and Vizagapatam 'in general was in ruin, scarce a House with its roofing and few with the walls standing. Our people have been employed ever since in Burying the Dead Bodies both of men and cattle which were left in the Town as the waters went off.'

Cyclone of 1867.

On the night of the 29th September 1867 a cyclone passed over Vizianagram and its neighbourhood (the wind coming first from the north-west and afterwards from the south-east) which blew the lantern off the Santapilly lighthouse and was reported to have damaged every single tiled and thatched building in the town and cantonment of Vizianagram, swept the roof off the church, blown down hundreds of trees, and torn the branches and leaves off those which it could not uproot.

Flood and cyclone of 1870.

On the 23rd to 25th October 1870 unusual rain fell in the centre of the district and caused a flood. At Vizianagram 16 inches were registered in 36 hours, and at Bimlipatam there were three feet of water on the salt platforms and the police constables had to climb on the roof of their lines to save their lives.

Twelve days later a furious cyclone swept over the district, the centre of it being near Vizagapatam.

It began from the north-north-east at 11 P.M. on November 4th, and ended at 5 A.M. next morning from the east-south-east. At Vizagapatam the sea rose and swept over the beach road, doing damage to the extent of Rs. 3,500 ; smashed up many of the masúla boats on the beach ; and flooded the lower parts of the town, drowning six people and doing Rs. 6,000 worth of damage to municipal property. The wind almost levelled with the ground the temporary jail and the lines of the native regiment (one life was lost in the latter) and blew down the belfry of the church at Waltair. The anemometer at Mr. A. V. Narasinga Rao's observatory recorded that the gale was travelling at the rate of 100 miles an hour, and then one of its cups was blown off. Anakápalle town was flooded, the water being up to the parapet of the bridge over the Sárada river, and throughout the path of the cyclone trees and houses were blown down, and roads and bridges were damaged.

Flood of 1872.

In June and July 1872 heavy rain fell in the hills. The Indrávati rose and swept away 25 villages on its bank, the inhabitants escaping with their smaller personal property but losing their grain and cattle, and the Vamsadhára demolished the bungalows at Gudári and Gunupur, as well as other property.

CHAP. VIII. FLOODS AND STORMS.

Cyclone of 1876.

One of the worst cyclones the district has ever known occurred on the 7th and 8th of October 1876. At Vizagapatam it lasted from 4 P.M. on the 7th until 9 A.M. on the 8th, and fifteen inches of rain fell in eighteen hours. The centre (or calm area) of it passed over Bimlipatam and Vizianagram, travelling at the rate of three miles an hour. At the latter place the wind first blew from the north and north-east; then a perfect calm, lasting half an hour, followed; and then the gale suddenly sprang up from the opposite direction with even greater violence than before. These two towns naturally suffered less than the areas on either side of them. A fine French ship, the *Jules Rose*, was driven right across the Santapilly reef by a storm-wave going westwards, and her bottom was torn out and two of her crew drowned. The storm-wave rushed up the mouth of the backwater at Vizagapatam and the level of the backwater rose eight feet, the lower parts of the town were flooded, many boats were smashed, 600 houses collapsed and 30 lives were lost. The temporary jail and the infantry lines were again almost levelled with the ground by the wind, the rain got into the Collector's office and destroyed a great quantity of records, and the new dome of Mr. Narasinga Rao's observatory—a corrugated iron structure twelve feet in diameter and nine feet high which had been placed in position but not riveted down—was blown a distance of 33 feet. Buildings, trees, roads, and channels suffered everywhere, one-fourth of the salt stored in the pans was destroyed, and the bridges over the Góstani at Chittivalasa and over the Lángulya at Chicacole were washed away. The latter was choked by trees and other débris, the strong wind blowing up the stream would not let the water get away, and finally a high wave ran up the river and completed the destruction, the six centre arches collapsing.[1]

Two cyclones f 1878.

In the autumn of 1878 two cyclones occurred on the coast within a month of one another, the first on the 5th of November and the second on the 6th to the 8th of December. The latter was the most disastrous the district has ever seen, as it was accompanied by very heavy rainfall (30 inches along the seaboard and twelve inches at the foot of the Gháts) which, coming at a time when the tanks were already brim full, caused floods which breached almost every large tank in the district and drowned hundreds of cattle and persons. The rain was heaviest in the Mádgole and Golgonda hills and consequently the damage was worst in the valley of the Sárada river. This stream was already

[1] For more details and many scientific observations and particulars, see *Report on the Vizagapatam and Backergunge cyclones of October 1876* by Mr. J. Eliot, late Meteorological Reporter (Bengal Secretariat Press, 1877).

FLOODS AND STORMS.

running full from bank to bank when every one of its tributaries came down simultaneously in flood. It rose twelve feet above the level of ordinary freshes and inundated the whole of its valley. The fine bridge over it near Chódavaram was swept away and that at Anakápalle (the parapet walls of which were 1½ feet under water) was only saved by the road on either side of it breaching. Most of the best tanks in the Golgonda taluk were breached ; the rice crop in the Anakápalle plain was almost a total loss ; and in that town 987 houses and 149 cattle were destroyed and 29 lives were lost. In the Sárada valley as a whole, 414 persons, about 5,000 cattle, and 25,000 sheep and goats were drowned. Many of the bodies were swept out to sea. Some of the survivors were living on trees and house-tops for three days. A large French steamer, the *Coromandel*, was driven ashore at Vátáda and a French barque, the *Quatre Cœurs*, at Rájayyapéta. The damage to roads and to Government buildings and irrigation works in the district was estimated at Rs. 80,000.

EARTHQUAKES.

Earthquakes have been reported as occurring in the district on the 6th January 1827, 24th August 1859, 19th December 1870 and 31st December 1881, but none of them did any damage.

CHAPTER IX.

PUBLIC HEALTH.

GENERAL HEALTH—Malaria—Cholera—Small-pox—Vital statistics. MEDICAL INSTITUTIONS—Civil hospital at Vizagapatam—Institutions at Bimlipatam—Pálkonda—Vizagapatam—Vizianagram—And Bobbili—The Waltair Lunatic Asylum.

CHAP. IX. GENERAL HEALTH.

EXCEPT for the malaria of the Agency, the district is healthy enough and is not known for the special prevalence of any particular diseases. Elephantiasis used to be common in Bimlipatam and Vizagapatam, but has been checked since more care has been taken regarding the water-supply. Beri-beri prevails along the coast. Leprosy is brought into prominence by the leper asylums the Schleswig-Holstein Mission has established at Jeypore and Sálúr, but is not really more common than in the average district.

Malaria.

Malaria prevails throughout the whole of the Agency. The worst localities are perhaps the Bissamkatak side, the Malkanagiri taluk and the Golgonda hills. The worst season of the year for the disease is undoubtedly in the rains, which is contrary to the usual rule in such matters. The least unhealthy period is from November up to the first thunderstorms of April. Malaria is as bad in spots which are open, elevated and free from jungle (such as Koraput) as in those (like Jeypore town) which lie low in situations shut in by hill and jungle. Black-water fever is common among European residents in the hills. The hill people themselves seem to suffer little from malaria. If they ever do contract the disease they take no medicine, but fast and offer sacrifices to the local deity, beginning with fowls and going upwards through pigs to goats and at last to buffaloes, until either the fever leaves them or they realize that it is their fate to have to bear it.

Cholera.

Cholera has usually been most severe when the seasons have been most adverse. In 1866 the deaths from it numbered 11,695; in 1877, 6,923; in 1878, 4,456; in 1889, 7,065; in 1892, 3,229; and in 1897, 5,103. In 1906, on the other hand, though the season was good the disease was particularly virulent, 9,685 deaths (a record) occurring up to the end of August. Doubtless on the plains the general increase in sanitary knowledge has much to do with the general decline in mortality from cholera which has occurred, but in the hills things differ, and villagers have been known to propose the imprisonment of the neighbouring wizard as the only method of checking an epidemic.

Small-pox.

Mortality from small-pox, as elsewhere, fluctuates violently in accordance with no very obvious principles. The worst years in recent times have been 1884–86, 1889, 1892–93 and 1898, the deaths in which averaged about 1,200. Vaccination is compulsory only in the four municipalities and in nine of the unions.

Vital statistics.

Statistics of the recorded rates of births and deaths in the plain taluks in recent years will be found in the Appendix. Registration of these events is compulsory in eleven of the fifteen unions and in sixteen other villages.

MEDICAL INSTITUTIONS.

The medical institutions of the district comprise 31 hospitals or dispensaries, of which only three contain no accommodation for in-patients. Of these, three—those at Gunupur, established in 1869, Ráyagada, opened in 1887, and Bissamkatak (1888)–are in the Agency and are maintained by the Párvatípur taluk board; four—those at Jeypore (1887), Naurangpur (1890), Malkanagiri (1899) and Pádwa (1904)—are similarly in the Agency but are kept up by the Koraput District Board; three—those at Bimlipatam (1871), Anakápalle (1879) and Vizianagram (1901)—are maintained by the respective municipalities; five—two each at Vizagapatam (1845 and 1894) and Vizianagram (1860 and 1905) and one at Bobbili (1896)—are supported partly or wholly from private benevolence; while the remaining 16 in the margin are financed by the taluk boards. Statistics of the attendance at, and cost of, those of these institutions which are managed officially will be found in the Appendix to this book.

Institution	Year
Pálkonda	1869
Sálúr	1875
Párvatípur, Bobbili	1876
Yellamanchili, Narasapatam, Chódavaram	1878
Chípurupalle, Srungavarapukóta	1879
Gajapatinagaram	1882
Jámi	1890
Nakkapalli, Rázám	1891
Víraghattam	1892
Pondúru	1899
Kurupám	1901

Civil hospital at Vizagapatam.

Of all of them, the oldest and the most important is the civil hospital at Vizagapatam. This began with a dispensary originated in 1845 under leave from the Court of Directors, and was at first located in a rented house 'nearly in the centre of the town' and adjoining 'the building now occupied as a military hospital'. By the end of 1857 it was removed to a new building costing Rs. 17,200, of which sum Rs. 10,225 had been made up by public subscription (the Rájas of Vizianagram and Bobbili and the Godé

CHAP. IX.
MEDICAL INSTITUTIONS.

family figuring prominently) and Rs. 6,975 had been given by Government.

Up to 186 the poor ward in the dispensary seems to have been maintained at the cost of Government, but in that year the then Rája of Vizianagram gave the institution Rs. 20,000 in public securities, the interest on which, together with contributions from local funds (Rs. 2,800) and the municipality (Rs. 2,600), is still utilized for its upkeep. It now blossomed into a civil hospital and was placed under the care of a local committee of which the Collector was *ex-officio* President and the District Surgeon *ex-officio* member. This body still controls its destinies. Subsequently several small detached cottages were constructed round the main building by private benefactors, a dispensary has been recently erected by M.R.Ry. A. V. Jagga Rao, and Government has added a septic room, an operation theatre and a maternity ward. A medical school is now connected with the institution and Mahárání Lady Gajapati Rao has promised to erect a building for this. The foundation stone was laid not long back by Lord Ampthill.

Institutions at Bimlipatam.

The next oldest dispensary is that at Bimlipatam, which was established in 1862 on the motion of the European residents in the town. The building for it cost about Rs. 5,300, of which half was subscribed and half granted by Government, and the cost of upkeep was similarly shared. A committee of residents managed the institution at first, but it was vested in the municipal council in 1876.

Pálkonda.

The Pálkonda hospital was opened in 1869 on the motion of the manager to the renters of that taluk, Messrs. Arbuthnot & Co.

Vizagapatam.

Of the five institutions which have been mentioned as being kept up partly by private benevolence, one is the civil hospital at Vizagapatam already referred to. The Victoria Gosha Female Hospital at the same town is located in a building bought for it by the late Mahárája Sir Gajapati Rao, who also contributed largely to the maintenance of the institution during his lifetime.

Vizianagram.

The two hospitals at Vizianagram are kept up respectively by the Rája and his adoptive sister. The former seems to have been started as far back as 1860 as a dispensary for the Rája's own followers, and has gradually been raised to its present excellent condition. The latter, which is for gosha women and children, is one of the best buildings of its class in the mufassal, stands in a large, stone-walled compound with an imposing gateway on and over which is inscribed the name of the founder, consists of four wings and cost over Rs. 40,000.

And Bobbili.

The women and children's hospital at Bobbili was built by the present Mahárája in 1895, entirely at his own cost, and was handed over by him to the local board together with an endowment of Rs. 20,000 in securities, the interest on which is utilized for its maintenance.

The Waltair Lunatic Asylum.

The Lunatic Asylum at Waltair originated in the accidental fact that in 1862 seven non-criminal lunatics had been committed to custody all at once. There being no proper place for them, the District Magistrate was allowed to rent a small house for them, wherein they lived, guarded by constables and waited on by convicts. The question of providing mufassal asylums was thus raised; and one was sanctioned for Vizagapatam, among other places. Meanwhile a larger building was rented, which became a recognized asylum for the Northern Circars and had a regular board of visitors.

The existing buildings at Waltair were completed in 1871. At present they contain accommodation for 96 patients, while the daily average strength is 76.

CHAPTER X.

EDUCATION.

CENSUS STATISTICS—Education by religions and taluks. EDUCATIONAL INSTITUTIONS—The Rája's College at Vizianagram—The Mrs. A. V. Narasinga Rao College—Upper secondary schools—Lower secondary schools—Other public schools—Sanskrit schools—Schools for girls—Schools for backward classes.

CHAP. X. CENSUS STATISTICS.

THE separate Appendix to this volume gives the more important of the statistics of the state of education in Vizagapatam according to the last census and the returns of the Educational department. The census figures showed that the number of the people in the Agency who could read and write was less even than the miserable average for all the three Agencies (one per cent. of the inhabitants), and that the dwellers in the plain taluks were considerably more illiterate than the people of any other district in the Presidency. Only three people in every hundred of the latter can read and write and only four girls in every thousand. This district has always been a byword for its illiteracy. The Uriya Bráhman takes less kindly to letters than his Tamil- and Telugu - speaking fellow-castemen, and the Telugu Bráhmans are already so liberally provided with posts as scribes and Levites to the numerous zamindars, and with whole and minor inams granted them by the ancestors of these gentlemen, that they have little need to trouble themselves to pass examinations qualifying for Government service.

Some of the hill folk have been reported to believe that if a highlander dares to learn to read and write his eyes will drop out and his head burst into a thousand pieces, but the usual attitude is mere apathy and is typified by the Khond who asked 'What's the good of education? Will it bring me food?' Hill villages often consist of only a hut or two, and are scattered and distant from the schools; hill school-masters are seldom the best of their class and are usually ignorant of the hill languages; and the inspecting staff displays little anxiety to visit the hills frequently. In 1905 Government approved certain proposals to remedy matters made by a conference of the local officials chiefly concerned,[1] but it is too soon yet to say what results will follow.

[1] G.O., No. 367, Educational, dated 31st May 1905.

CHAP. X. CENSUS STATISTICS.

Meanwhile the Khond is commercially at the mercy of the wily Sondi and the cringing Dombu.

Telugu is the language chiefly known by the few who are literate. In the plains eleven per cent. of these people could read and write English at the time of the last census, and in the Agency three per cent., but this latter figure is made up almost entirely of officials.

Education by religions and taluks.

Of the followers of the three chief religions, the Christians of both sexes are the best educated, then come the Musalmans, and the Hindus bring up the rear. Of the various taluks Vizagapatam naturally contains the largest number of literates and Vizianagram the next largest. Golgonda is the most backward, actually ranking below the most advanced of the purely agency taluks, Gunupur.

EDUCATIONAL INSTITUTIONS.

The district boasts two colleges; namely, the first-grade institution maintained by the Rája at Vizianagram and the second-grade Mrs. A. V. Narasinga Rao College at Vizagapatam.

The Rája's College at Vizianagram

The former of these began as a school in 1857, when it contained two branches, one for Bráhmans and Kshatriyas and the other for boys of other castes. These were amalgamated in 1859; nine years later a matriculation class was opened; in 1877 the institution was made a second-grade college; and in 1883 it was raised to the first grade. An inscription on the foundation stone of the southern extension of the main building shows that this was laid by Lord Wenlock in October 1894. The Rája bears the whole cost of the institution, at present about Rs. 16,000 per annum. Some 80 youths, almost all of them Bráhmans, are reading in the college classes.

The Mrs. A. V. Narasinga Rao College.

The Mrs. A. V. Narasinga Rao College at Vizagapatam originated in a school called 'the Anglo-Vernacular school' which was founded in 1860 by Mr. Grant, Inspector of Schools (subsequently Sir Alexander Grant, Director of Public Instruction, Bombay), Mr. E. Fane, Collector of the district from 1859 to 1862, M.R.Ry. (afterwards Mahárája) G. N. Gajapati Rao and M.R.Ry. C. Venkatasvámi Náyudu. The leading zamindars of the district, especially Vizianagram and Bobbili, and Mahárája Sir Gajapati Rao contributed liberally towards the school for many years. In 1878 it was raised to the status of a second-grade college and affiliated to the Madras University, and its name was then changed to 'the Hindu College.' In 1892 the late M.R.Ry. A. V. Narasinga Rao of Vizagapatam, who had married into the Godé family referred to on p. 219 below, bequeathed a lakh of rupees (besides a building fund of Rs. 15,000) for a college to be called after his

CHAP. X. EDUCATIONAL INSTITUTIONS.

wife, and the managing committee of this bequest took over the Hindu College on 1st April 1899 as a basis for the construction of such an institution. An imposing new building of stone is being now constructed to house it. A hostel for 50 students has already been opened. About 50 boys, most of them Bráhmans, are reading in the college classes.

Upper secondary schools.

Both these colleges contain upper secondary departments, that attached to the latter of them having as many as 450 boys on its rolls. There are five other schools of that grade for boys; namely, the municipality's high school at Bimlipatam, the two kept up in Vizagapatam by the London Mission and the Roman Catholic Mission, the Mahárája's school at Bobbili (founded in 1865), and a private institution—the Ripon Hindu Theological school at Vizianagram. The London Mission school arose from the amalgamation, in 1845, of their smaller institutions. That of the Catholic Mission is known as St. Aloysius' and its 180 pupils are practically all of them Europeans, Eurasians or Native Christians. The staff consists of seven European priests, four Brothers and two lay teachers, the industrial and technical classes are a special feature, and the institution boasts a band and a cadet corps 60 strong. The Mahárája's school at Bobbili accepts no aid from public funds.

Lower secondary schools.

English lower secondary schools number twelve, of which one is supported by the Anakápalle municipal council; eight, those at Narasapatam, Yellamanchili, Kasimkóta, Chódavaram, Pálkonda, Jeypore, Gunupur and Párvatípur, are kept up by the local boards; one, at Sálúr, is managed by the Lutheran Mission there; another, at Bimlipatam, belongs to the Canadian Baptists; and the twelfth, at Vizianagram, is managed privately. The two last receive no aid from Provincial or local funds. The two schools in the Agency are shown in the official returns as being specially maintained for aboriginal and hill tribes, but of their 280 pupils none appear to belong to either of these classes.

Other public schools.

Government maintains training-schools for masters at Vizagapatam and Gunupur, and one for mistresses and a medical school at Vizagapatam. Several of the schools have technical classes, those at St. Aloysius' teaching telegraphy, shorthand, type-writing and freehand drawing.

Sanskrit schools.

Sanskrit or Véda schools numbering 21 and costing Rs. 5,000 annually appear in the official returns. Chief among them are that maintained by the Rája at Vizianagram, in which 60 students are taught at an annual outlay of Rs. 3,000, and that at Sálúr referred to on p. 307. It is interesting to note that in several villages in the district the ancient system of imparting instruction in the Védas still survives, the Bráhman teacher receiving the pupils into his house, supplying them with food and otherwise treating them as members of his own family until they have reached the requisite stage of erudition, and requiring them, in return, to discharge certain minor duties about the house.

Schools for girls.

The most advanced school for girls in the district is that belonging to the Roman Catholic Mission and located in the striking-looking building erected by Bishop Clerc opposite the Waltair railway-station. In this and its branch in the fort, 180 girls are under instruction by about a dozen nuns and several lay teachers. The classes go up to the matriculation standard, and besides the day school there is a large boarding establishment and a special school for pupils whose parents can afford to pay for separate accommodation, all located in different parts of the spacious building. There are also seven lower secondary vernacular schools for girls in different parts of the district, the two largest being those for caste girls kept up by the London and Roman Catholic Missions in Vizagapatam and Vizianagram respectively, both of which contain over 200 pupils.

Schools for backward classes.

Besides the Jeypore and Gunupur schools already referred to, 130 primary schools are maintained in the Agency specially for hill tribes. Of the 2,700 pupils in these, 30 per cent. are reported to belong to those classes. The highlanders, as has been already stated, do not take kindly to books, and the danger is that the schools will be attended less by them than by the sons of the alien or lower castes who cheat and overreach them, and will result, not in the enlightenment of the backward races, but in conferring additional intelligence on that section of the population which already preys upon them more than is good. About 1,000 'Panchamas' are under instruction at schools kept up specially for their kind. The percentage of scholars to the population of these people of school-age is, however, lower than anywhere in the Presidency except on the conservative west coast.

CHAPTER XI.

LAND REVENUE ADMINISTRATION.

REVENUE HISTORY—Early systems—Practice under the Musalmans—The exactions of the zamindars—Beginnings of the Company's administration—The Permanent Settlement; the instructions issued—The action taken—The general results—The formation of the three Government taluks—The existing revenue settlement in these—Principles followed—Rates prescribed. INAMS. EXISTING DIVISIONAL CHARGES. APPENDIX, List of Chiefs in Council and Collectors.

CHAP. XI. REVENUE HISTORY.

NINE-TENTHS of Vizagapatam is zamindari land and the three Government taluks only came under direct administration in comparatively recent times. The history of the land revenue administration of the district is consequently simpler than usual.

Early systems.

Regarding the revenue systems followed by the ancient Hindu rulers and their successors the Musalman kings of Golconda and the Subadars of the Deccan at Hyderabad with their subordinate Faujdars at Chicacole, only the very scantiest information survives.

The earliest authoritative account is the report of 1784[1] of the Committee of Circuit on 'the Kasimkóta division of the Chicacole circar,' as the country was then styled. This says:—

'The ancient and present mode of making the collections we understand to be widely different. The one formerly in use under the native princes, when troops and servants were paid in necessaries instead of coin and before there were large exports and returns of money, was an *equal* division of the produce between the Rája and the cultivator, the latter defraying all village and collection expenses. The quantity of the crop was determined by a valuation made by indifferent persons just before the harvest and in the presence of the public servants and the inhabitants. This estimate being registered by the karnam, the Circar servants, after the grain was trodden out, received the Government moiety.'

This agrees roughly with the practice which also anciently obtained (at least in theory) in the southern districts of the Presidency under Hindu rule; there the *swatantrams*, or fees to village officers, were usually first subtracted from the total crop, and the remainder was then equally divided between the government and the ryot.

[1] This is available in print, and contains a mass of statistical and other information of interest.

The actual collection of the revenue in Vizagapatam was apparently in the hands of a number of local chiefs (who were also expected to keep their charges free from disturbance) supervised by superior officers who kept accounts of their own as checks.

Practice under the Musalmans.

After the arrival of the Musalmans, these chiefs were allowed to retain their positions; but [1] they were not acknowledged by their masters as independent or tributary rulers, or even as having any property in the land. They were 'accountable managers and collectors, and not lords and proprietors of the land.' They were allowed, in return for the due performance of their duties, rent-free lands, fees on the crops, the customs dues and a quit-rent on houses, which amounted together to about ten per cent. on their collections. It was not until a late period of the Musalman government that they received the name *zamindars*, which with its literal meaning of 'possessors of land' gave colour to the erroneous idea that they had an hereditary right to the soil. In accordance with eastern tendency, their offices gradually became hereditary, and in at least two cases (Bobbili and Vizianagram) their descendants still hold land originally allotted them.

The Committee of Circuit says that these zamindars eventually—

'Set aside the former usage and, after ascertaining by measurement the quantity of the arable land, imposed a fixed rate of Rs. 10 per garce called sist, the payment of which was to entitle the labourer to the unrestricted disposal of his whole crop. This alteration, favourable as at first sight it may appear to the inhabitant, was established solely for the convenience and profit of the zamindar, as it enabled him to take one kist of the collections in advance, and served as a foundation whereon to calculate any further assessments. Soon after, when the land was supposed to be improved, the *malavati* was added at the rate of 100 and 150 per cent. on the sist, and thenceforward considered as a fixed payment. The *nazzar*, which is taken in plenteous years, is an exaction not fixed, but generally at the rate of 50 per cent. on the sist. The *bilmakta* is an appraisement of poor ground producing only small grain, by which the same is rented for a specific sum and not liable to any other imposition excepting the *sari*, which was originally the zamindar's allowance from the Mughal darbar of 10 per cent. on the collections in reward for preserving good order and encouraging cultivation. These assessments reduced the labourer's share to about *one-third* of the produce.'

[1] *Fifth Report on the affairs of the East India Co., 1812* (Madras, 1883), ii, 6. A very elaborate account of the Musalman revenue system will be found in Mr. Grant's 'Political Survey of the Northern Circars' appended to this.

CHAP. XI.
REVENUE HISTORY.

The exactions of the zamindars.

Even this small proportion was still further whittled down in the greater part of the district. The Committee says—

'The zamindars have introduced other changes which have curtailed the labourer's real share to barely *one-fifth* of the harvest. We find that since the decline of the Musalman government the zamindars, experiencing a greater liberty than before, have indulged themselves in indolence, and, entrusting their parganas to renters, have delegated the full extent of their own authority to them. And, although they cannot but be sensible of the impositions to which they are exposed and of the hardships and sufferings of the labourers, they still allow them to continue their collections in specie without requiring the estimated accounts of produce which, if taken, would clearly ascertain all abuses and oppressions.'

In the havíli (literally, 'neighbouring') land (an area producing a revenue of 3¾ lakhs and consisting of the old demesne or household property of the sovereign, or tracts near towns specially appropriated by the Musalmans to the payment of their troops and establishments) the land revenue had always been under the immediate management of the local Faujdars. There, says the Committee—

'It has been customary to receive Government's share of the produce in specie, but the proportions have always been ascertained by a yearly valuation of the crop, one-third being allowed the fixed inhabitants, two-fifths to strangers, and one-half to Telingis and those who cultivate dry grain. Previous, however, to dividing the shares, one rupee per garce upon the whole was collected by the Circar. The repair of tanks and water-courses fell to the share of Government.'

Besides the assessments on land, the government obtained a revenue from the sale of monopolies of such articles as salt, arrack and betel-leaf, from customs on imports and exports by sea and land (sayar), and by taxes on trades (moturpha). The land-customs became so excessive (Rs. 167 for every 100 bullock-loads between Kálahandi and the coast) that the Brinjáris ceased to visit the low country; and the taxes on trades had grown so high that, says the Committee—

'Numbers have adopted a new mode of life or been compelled to forsake their ancient habitations, on their property being seized to discharge these unusual taxes; and we can add from our own observation that the evident appearance of extreme indigence extending almost universally over the circar strongly indicates the long continuance of a series of hardships and exaction.'

Beginnings of the Company's administration.

Though the establishment of the British settlement at Vizagapatam dates from the seventeenth century, it was not, as has been seen (p. 34), until 1765 that the Company acquired the territory outside its limits. In 1769 this was placed under the existing Chief and Council at Vizagapatam. They found that the land of the district was then divided into the two classes already described; namely, that under the zamindars and the havíli land. The former, practically all of which had become tributary to, or was in the hands of, the Rája of Vizianagram, they assessed at a fixed sum, 'very inadequate to his receipts,' and the latter, in accordance with customary practice, they leased out to a renter, who for several years was Sítaráma Rázu, the brother and díwán of the Rája of Vizianagram.

The Chief and Council, it is clear, were corrupt and inefficient; and under their charge the country retrograded rather than improved. The administration of the havíli land was especially lax, and the Rája's under-renters were allowed to juggle with the commutation rates of produce in a way which absorbed much of the ryot's profits. In 1776 the Madras Government despatched a Committee of Circuit consisting of five of the Council (which then contained nineteen Members) to enquire into the state of the Northern Circars, and the revenue system there, including the suitability of the payments made by the zamindars. The Committee had made some progress when, in February 1778, Sir Thomas Rumbold (who is said to have begun life as a waiter at White's Club) became Governor of Madras. He ordered that the zamindars should be sent for to Madras, where the information required could be at once obtained and details of peshkash settled with them in person. A considerable number of them came to the Presidency accordingly and there, says Mill's history, 'in every case the Governor alone negotiated with the zamindars and regulated their payments; in no case did he lay the grounds of his treaty before the Council; in every case the Council, without enquiry, acquiesced in his decrees.' Sir Thomas Rumbold was charged with having conducted these negotiations corruptly, and in 1781 he and two Members of his Council were dismissed while several others were degraded.

The Committee of Circuit was revived in 1783 and continued its labours until 1788. Its report of 1784 on this district has already been referred to. This condemned the existing system in the strongest terms. Referring to the zamindari land, it spoke with indignation of the oppressions of Sítaráma Rázu, the díwán of Vizianagram, which had resulted in the ryots having to hand over to the Circar all their paddy and subsist on the coarser grains, to suffer constant ejectment from their holdings and to resort to borrowing from money-lenders to pay their kists, which

CHAP. XI. REVENUE HISTORY.

fell due before the crop was ripe; and it wound up by saying 'notwithstanding the abundant advantages enjoyed by Government, we have discovered no traces in return of protection, assistance, or attention to the cultivation. The villages are composed of wretched hovels, the people meanly clothed, and meagre through the extremes of labour and hard fare, the soil in many parts overrun with shrubs and the tanks in the very worst repair.' The account of the administration of the havíli land was even more unfavourable, and Mr. Oram, one of the most active of the members of the Committee, was appointed in 1787 to superintend the administration of this independently of the Chief and Council.[1] A few months afterwards, he was succeeded by special European Collectors, who managed the havíli under the immediate orders of the new Board of Revenue which had been established the year before. They rented out some portions of it and managed the rest under amáni, receiving the assessment in kind. The old abuses and irregularities consequently somewhat decreased and the ryots advanced in prosperity. In 1792, however, these Collectors were partly subordinated to the Chiefs in Council, and the natural result was 'continual collisions of authority and of opinions between the Board of Revenue and the provincial establishments.'

In the same year Lord Cornwallis, then Governor-General, advocated with characteristic energy the total abolition of the Chiefs in Council in the Northern Circars and the substitution throughout that area of Collectors subordinate to the Board of Revenue. He said—

'It is now thirty years since the Company became possessed of the Circars; and at this moment their influence is very little, if at all, better established than it was the first day. The zamindars still keep the same troops and exercise the same authority, within their respective districts. The oppressions they commit are, we believe, in no way abated; and their engagements to the Company are as ill-performed as they have been at any period.'

In 1794, accordingly, the Chiefs and Councils were abolished by a proclamation (which, after the fashion of those times, improved the occasion by a lengthy homily on the reciprocal duties of Collectors and zamindars) and Vizagapatam was arranged into three 'divisions' each under a Collector.

Meanwhile, in 1793, the Vizianagram estate, which comprised almost all the present district except the havíli land, had been sequestrated for arrears (see p. 50), and in 1794 the Rája of Vizianagram had been killed at the battle of Padmanábham.

[1] *Fifth Report*, ii, 19.

In 1796 the zamindars who had been dispossessed by him were recalled and given temporary leases for their ancient estates during their good behaviour, the Anakápalle taluk and some adjacent tracts were transferred from the Vizianagram estate to the havíli land; and the rest of the late Rája's property was rented at an enhanced peshkash, also temporarily, to his son. The limits and designations of the three divisions into which the district had been arranged were revised in the same year and then stood as follows: (*a*) 'the First division,' which included the Vizagapatam and Kasimkóta havíli land; (*b*) 'the Second division,' comprising the Vizianagram estate and the restored zamindaris; and (*c*) 'the Third division,' made up of the Chicacole and Tekkali havíli land and the Kimedi zamindari, the two latter of which now form part of Ganjám.

The zamindaris, with few exceptions, were subsequently leased for sums which varied every year and were seldom punctually paid. The havíli land was treated on no fixed principles and the settlements constantly varied. For the most part it was let out annually village by village to the headmen, the Government share of the produce being commuted into money at current or average prices; but this arrangement was based on no survey, and was therefore imperfect, and it did little to protect the cultivators from oppression by the headmen.

The Permanent Settlement; the instructions issued.

The evils arising from these fluctuating and temporary arrangements hurried on the introduction of the Permanent Settlement, which at this time was in high favour in Bengal and was being forced upon Madras by the Government of India.

The elaborate instructions of the Board of Revenue to Collectors in the Northern Circars regarding the methods of arranging this settlement were issued in October 1799. Briefly epitomized, these directed that the existing zamindars should be constituted proprietors of their estates upon a permanent peshkash, and that the havíli land should also be carved up into properties which should be similarly settled in perpetuity and sold by auction. In calculating the peshkash the statistics of gross revenue given by the Circuit Committee were to be taken as the general standard, and, after deducting from these the receipts from land-customs, abkári and salt (which were thenceforth to be taken under Government administration) and excluding all inams except those enjoyed by the village establishments and all allowances made for the upkeep of police, the demand was to be fixed at not less than two-thirds (taking all the estates together) of the remainder. Uncultivated arable and waste lands were to

CHAP. XI. REVENUE HISTORY.

be given over to the zamindars free of additional assessment. In the case of the havíli land, the Circuit Committee's figures of revenue were also to be checked by a comparison with the actual collections of the preceding thirteen years, and in addition such factors as the quality of the irrigation in the new estates and their proximity to the markets at the ports and towns were to be taken into consideration.

The action taken.

The Collectors of the three divisions of the district were directed to report upon the estates which should be constituted in their several charges and the peshkash which should be laid upon each; and their replies, available in print, are valuable papers. The Collector of the First division, Mr. Robert Alexander, divided his charge, which comprised the havíli land of Vizagapatam and Kasimkóta, into the seventeen proprietary estates noted in the margin.

Anakápalle	Panchadhárala
Dimila	Ráyavaram
Godicherla	Sarvasiddhi
Kasimkóta	Srírámpuram
Kondakarla	Uppáda
Kottakóta	Uratla
Mélupáka	Vémulapúdi
Munagapáka	Waltair
Nakkapalli	

He stated that the land revenue was collected in three forms called sist, *bilmakta* and *bhágam*. The sist was a nominal sum entered in the patta; and when the crop was nearly ripe it was valued by the Circar servants and an enhancement, called *malavati* and calculated on the condition of the crop, was added to the sist. This was often most unjustly assessed, and sometimes actually exceeded the whole value of the crop. The *bilmakta* was a fixed money rent, levied for the most part on high-level land and tracts long left uncultivated, and was not common. Most of the land was assessed on the *bhágam*, or sharing, system. The share taken by the Government varied with the nature of the ground and the condition and caste of the ryot. Rajputs, Velamas, and cultivators from other parts who took over land which the inhabitants of any village were unable to cultivate themselves, were allowed a half share of the crop; but the ordinary ryot only received a third. Mr. Alexander said this one-third was a most inadequate proportion, much less than inamdars gave to their tenants, and productive of discontent, restlessness and emigration. He considered that the new proprietors should be allowed not less than ten, nor more than twenty, per cent. of the calculated revenue of their estates.

The total permanent assessment on the seventeen estates was fixed at Rs. 3,18,710. They were sold by auction in 1802 and, except Waltair, were all bought by the Rája of Vizianagram, the price paid being Rs. 1,62,846.

In the Second division of the district there were at this time the sixteen ancient zamindaris named in the margin. These were handed over to their existing owners at a total peshkash of Rs. 8,02,580 per annum. Little was then known of Jeypore and the other hill zamindaris, and their peshkash was fixed very low. Even in 1819, Mr. Thackeray, the well-known Member of the Board of Revenue, dismissed them from detailed consideration as being 'a wide tract of hill and jungle, inhabited by uncivilized and indeed unconquered barbarians: their climate and their poverty have secured them from conquest. No great native Government ever seems to have thought this tract worth conquering. It has been left as a waste corner of the earth to wild beasts and Conds. Nobody seems even to know the boundary. This tract has never been explored: there is a blank left here in the maps.'

Ándra	Mérangi
Belgám	Páchipenta
Bobbili	Pálkonda
Chemudu	Sálúr
Golgonda	Sangamvalasa
Jeypore	Sarapalli-Bhímavaram
Kásipuram	Vizianagram
Kurupám	
Mádgole	

In the Third division twenty estates were carved out of the Chicacole and Tekkali havíli land, of which the six in the margin are now included in this district. The peshkash on these was fixed at Rs. 67,931 and they were sold by auction for Rs. 84,589. The Rája of Vizianagram bought Kuppili, Honzarám and Siripuram.

Honzarám	Siripuram
Kintali	Ungaráda
Kuppili	
Shérmuhammadpuram	

Early in 1803, the Parlákimedi estate and the Tekkali havíli land were transferred to Ganjám, the southern boundary of which became the last part of the course of the Lángulya, and the Vizagapatam district, consisting of the sixteen zamindaris and twenty-three proprietary estates mentioned above, was put in charge of a single Collector. Its boundaries have not since undergone any noteworthy change except by the transfer to Gódávari of the Uppáda estate and of the Dutsarti and Guditéru muttas of Golgonda after the Rampa rebellion referred to on p. 250 below.

The general results.

As has already been narrated in Chapter II above, the general results of the permanent settlement were disappointing. The new system took no account of the abrupt change it necessarily effected in the position of the zamindars, who were reduced at one stroke from the position of feudatory chiefs to that of farmers

CHAP. XI. REVENUE HISTORY.

of the revenue, liable to ejectment from their properties if they failed to pay their peshkash, subject to petty indignities from a horde of insolent subordinates and obliged to conform to a series of new regulations and laws. For years the zamindars were in a chronic state of discontent and disaffection, and at last, in 1832, the disturbances in this district and in the Parlákimedi zamindari of Ganjám rose to such a height that, as has been recounted on p. 57, Government were compelled to appoint Mr. Russell as Special Commissioner to repress them, arming him with extraordinary powers and a large military force. The action he took against the three most obstreperous of the malcontents—Vírabhadra Rázu of Kásipuram, Páyaka Rao of Páyakaraopéta and the zamindar of Pálkonda—is referred to in the account of those places in Chapter XV below.

The formation of the three Government taluks.

In 1833 the Pálkonda zamindari was forfeited for rebellion and (with the Honzarám proprietary estate, which had been bought in by Government at a sale for arrears in 1811) was made into the existing Government taluk of Pálkonda.

The proprietary estates of Sarvasiddhi and Vémulapúdi and the Rájala subdivision of Panchadhárala (Chípurupalle) had already been bought in for arrears in 1831; in 1833 Kottakóta, and in 1837 Golgonda (see p. 249), suffered a like fate; while in 1844 Ráyavaram was transferred to Government by its owner and Kondakarla, Dimila and the Kottúr and Veluchúru-Kodúr subdivisions of Panchadhárala were also bought in for arrears. Golgonda, Kottakóta and Vémulapúdi were formed into the existing Government taluk of Golgonda and the other estates made up the Sarvasiddhi taluk. Some account of the others of the sixteen ancient zamindaris and twenty-three proprietary estates included in the district at the permanent settlement which still survive as such, will be found in Chapter XV below and may be traced through the index. Of the fourteen ancient zamindaris which remained after Pálkonda was forfeited and Golgonda sold up, two (Belgám and Mérangi) were afterwards partitioned and one (Chemudu) passed by sale from the family of the holder at the permanent settlement. The other eleven have been declared by Act II of 1904 to be inalienable and impartible. They descend to the eldest son. The proprietary estates, which follow the ordinary Hindu rules of co-parcenary, have in some cases been bought and sold, amalgamated and divided, in a somewhat bewildering manner.

Since 1834 the district has twice been placed under a Special Commissioner owing to exceptional circumstances. In 1849, in consequence of the heavy arrears of peshkash which had accrued, Mr. (afterwards Sir Walter) Elliott was appointed under a special Act (X of 1849) as Commissioner with the powers of a Board of Revenue, and the appointment continued until 1856. In February 1881 Mr. Carmichael, who was then a Member of Council, was made Special Commissioner to 'take the chief direction of affairs' throughout the tracts affected by the Rampa rebellion and in the Agencies of Ganjám and Vizagapatam, and was given special powers therein His report was published in November of the same year.

The existing revenue settlement in these.

As a result of Mr. Russell's mission, an Act (XXIV of 1839) was passed which (see p. 196) excluded the hilly portions of Golgonda and Pálkonda taluks (among other areas) from the operation of much of the ordinary law of the land, and the peculiar conditions existing in these tracts have always necessitated wide differences between the revenue methods introduced into them and into the rest of these two taluks.

When the Government took over these taluks and Sarvasiddhi, no immediate change was made in the settlements in force, the tenures in the hills remaining unaltered and the ryots in the plains being required to pay the same assessments as at the time of the forfeiture or purchase, and new cultivation being charged the rates obtaining on adjoining land. In 1883, however, a beginning was made with the first scientific survey and settlement of Sarvasiddhi and the low country in Golgonda and Pálkonda, and orders on the settlement of all three tracts were passed in 1889.

Principles followed.

This settlement was conducted on the usual principles. The soils were classified and grouped under the two main heads of black régada and red ferruginous, and were further subdivided into clays, loams and sands. The proportion in which each of these was found to occur in each of the three taluks has already been shown on p. 13 above.

For purposes of dry assessment, the villages were arranged into two groups, the first of which included 99 of the 127 villages in Pálkonda and the whole of Sarvasiddhi taluk, and the second the whole of Golgonda and the remaining 28 villages of Pálkonda, which were in remote situations under the hills, inaccessible to ports and markets, unhealthy, and exposed to damage from wild animals.

For purposes of wet assessment four classes of irrigation sources were distinguished ; namely,

CHAP. XI.
REVENUE HISTORY.

(1) All irrigation under the Nágávali channels; under tanks directly fed by them and rain-fed tanks of eight months' supply and upwards; under the Suvarnamukhi; and under the Godári anicut on the Sárada and the Kondakarla áva supplied therefrom (see p. 105);

(2) Irrigation under the other Sárada channels, the Varáha channels, tanks indirectly fed by the Nágávali channels, rain-fed tanks of five to eight months' capacity, the hill streams Votti-gedda, Jamparakótagedda, Malligedda, Potulagedda, Onigedda and Boddéru, and the Komaravólu áva;

(3) Irrigation under rain-fed tanks of from three to five months' capacity and ordinary hill streams; and

(4) Irrigation under tanks of less than three months' capacity and drainage sources.

The crops taken as standards for estimating outturns were paddy for all wet land, and, for dry land, ragi in Pálkonda and cambu and ragi in conjunction (in the proportion of two to one) for Golgonda and Sarvasiddhi. The commonest dry crop in Pálkonda was indigo, which was grown in such large quantities for the supply of Messrs. Arbuthnot and Co.'s factories that it occupied nearly half of all the dry land, but it was considered unsuitable as a standard crop. The outturn of paddy was estimated (on the basis of experiments made in other districts) to range, according to the nature of the soil and irrigation, from 400 to 1,000 Madras measures per acre; of cambu, from 130 such measures to 400; and of ragi from 140 to 375 measures. These outturns were commuted into money at a rate based upon the average of the prices prevailing during the 20 non-famine years immediately preceding the year of settlement, and the result was reduced by 15 per cent. to allow for cartage to markets and merchants' profits. The commutation rates thus arrived at worked out to Rs. 105 for paddy, Rs. 114 for cambu, and Rs. 126 for ragi, per Madras garce of 3,200 Madras measures. From the value of the crop so obtained, the expenses of cultivation (which were calculated to be one-third more than those of Ganjám in the case of wet land and one-fifth more in that of dry) were deducted, and in addition a further reduction of one-fifth was made on both wet and dry land to allow for vicissitudes of season and the inclusion within the survey fields of unprofitable areas, such as paths, banks, and small channels. The remainder was assumed to be the net yield per acre, and half of this was taken as the Government share.

CHAP. XI. REVENUE HISTORY.

Rates prescribed.

The acreage rates so arrived at are given in the margin. Only four per cent. of the wet land in the three taluks was assessed at the highest wet rate and only two per cent. of the dry land at the two highest dry rates. The percentages of the assessed area in each taluk assessed at each of the rates has been given in detail already on p. 100 and further figures will be found in the separate Appendix to this volume. The table subjoined shows at a glance the general effect of the survey and settlement on wet and dry land respectively in each of the three taluks; namely, the difference in the cultivated area disclosed by the survey and the enhancement or reduction of the assessment brought about by the settlement :—

Wet.		Dry.	
RS.	A.	RS.	A.
8	...	3	...
7	..	2	8
5	8	2	...
4	8	1	8
3	8	1	4
2	8	1	...
2	...	...	12
		...	8
		...	6

Taluk.	Wet land.		Dry land.		Total.	
	Percentage difference in		Percentage difference in		Percentage difference in	
	Extent.	Assessment.	Extent.	Assessment.	Extent.	Assessment.
Golgonda	+ 15	+ 20	+ 35	+ 18	+ 30	+ 20
Pálkonda	+ 32	+ 21	+ 89	− 2	+ 48	+ 18
Sarvasiddhi	+ 4	+ 20	− 18	− 18	− 9	+ 9

The increase in wet assessment here shown includes the charge for second crops. Double-crop land is charged a consolidated rate covering any number of crops which may be grown. This consists of an addition to the single-crop assessment of one third in the case of land under sources of irrigation placed in the first of the four groups mentioned above, one-fourth for that under second-class sources, one-fifth for third class and one-sixth for fourth class.

It had long been held that the dry land in Pálkonda was over-assessed (nearly one half of the arable dry area was unoccupied at the time of the settlement) and that the wet land (only 660 acres of which was waste) had been too leniently treated. In Sarvasiddhi, the former rates on both wet and dry land, which had been fixed during the time the taluk was zamindari land, were in many cases excessive.

INAMS.

Inams were lavishly granted in the district during the lax administration of the Musalmans, especially in the havíli land.

CHAP. XI.
INAMS.

The Circuit Committee says that the Rája of Vizianagram resumed numbers of these when he rented that tract and even seized 'the whole of the free gift lands to the Bráhmans and others excepting those of village servants.' But hardly any of the inams were properly authorized grants; 'very few bear the seal of the Hyderabad darbar, which we consider absolutely necessary to authenticate such deeds, and most appear to have been granted to mullahs, servants and dependents of the Nawábs, who, however absolute upon the spot from their military command and the distance of their court, being in fact nothing more than renters, could not be legally empowered to make any alienations of the Sirkar lands.'

The Inam Commission visited this district in 1862. It did not touch inams in Jeypore (these are shortly referred to in the account of that estate on p. 272 below) but dealt with those in the three Government taluks and in the other estates, more than half of which were included in the Vizianagram zamindari. The procedure followed is set out in detail in the Inam Commissioner's instructions printed in G.O. No. 647, Revenue, dated 24th March 1862, and is too elaborate to be embodied here in detail. By the terms of the permanent settlement, the reversionary right in inam tenures then in existence was reserved to Government, though the kattubadi on them was included in the assets of the estates and is payable to the zamindars and proprietors. The Inam Commission's rules allowed most of the inamdars to enfranchise their grants from the risk of this reversion by the payment of a certain annual quit-rent which was fixed according to circumstances and did not vary thereafter. Inams granted for services no longer required were enfranchised compulsorily. This latter course was followed with the old grants for military police services (which still existed in large numbers), the enfranchisement being on a quit-rent equal to half the full assessment. The inams in the Vizianagram estate had been examined between 1835 and 1838 when the estate was under Government management, and the kattubadi in their case was usually fixed at the difference between the then quit-rent and the full assessment. Mokhásas, which were held on honorary and almost nominal service tenure, were enfranchised at a fourth of the assessment; village police inams in zamindaris at five-eighths; tank-digging grants at one-fourth, and so on. Certain 99 years' grants for house and garden land in Waltair, granted by the Chiefs about 1790, were enfranchised at one-fourth or one-half of their then value. Village service inams in the Government taluks were not enfranchised till 1891–92. Similar grants in proprietary estates are now being

CHAP. XI. INAMS.

enfranchised at a quit-rent equal to the full assessment minus the existing jodi.

EXISTING DIVISIONAL CHARGES.

The manner in which Golgonda, Pálkonda and Sarvasiddhi became Government taluks has already been referred to. In 1859, in spite of the Collector's protests, the first and last of these were ordered to be amalgamated and made into one taluk called Narasapatam, with head-quarters at that place. But the plan was a failure, and in 1863 the old arrangement was restored.

In the same year the Jeypore estate was brought for the first time, in the circumstances set out later (p. 269), under direct administration.

In 1875 the divisional charges were as under :—

Collector. (Vizagapatam.)	Principal Assistant Collector. (Narasapatam.)	Senior Assistant Collector. (Párvatípur.)		Special Assistant Agent. (Koraput.)
Vizagapatam.	Golgonda.	Párvatípur.	Pálkonda.	Koraput.
Bimlipatam.	Anakápalle.	Bobbili.	Ráyagada.	Jeypore.
Chípurupalle.	Sarvasiddhi.	Gajapati-nagaram.	Sálúr.	Naurangpur.
Srungavarapukóta.	Víravilli.	Gunupur.	Vizia-nagram.	Malkanagiri.

In 1882, in accordance with recommendations made by Mr. Carmichael when Special Commissioner in connection with the Rampa rebellion, three new deputy tahsildars' divisions were ordered to be constituted with head-quarters at Páderu, Pottangi and Bissamkatak. The two first of these came into being in 1883 and the last in 1884. Páderu was placed under the Principal Assistant for some time, but in 1893 the Pádwa taluk was constituted in its place and given to the Special Assistant.

In 1883 a new Deputy Collector was sanctioned for the district and after some discussion he was put in charge of Bimlipatam and Chípurupalle from the Collector's division and Gajapatinagaram, Pálkonda and Vizianagram from the Senior Assistant's. Nine years later a Covenanted Civilian was placed over the division so formed.

In 1888 another Deputy Collector was appointed to relieve the Collector of the direct care of the two taluks, Srungavarapukóta and Vizagapatam, which remained under him, and the divisional charges thus constituted (which have already been set out on p. 2 above) still exist. The head-quarters division is the only one which is in charge of a Deputy Collector.

CHAP. XI.
APPENDIX.

APPENDIX.

List of the Chiefs in Council and Collectors of Vizagapatam.

Name.	Date of appointment.	—
CHIEFS IN COUNCIL OF VIZAGAPATAM FACTORY.		
George Ramsden	1st Aug. 1682 ...	Suspended 24th March 1683; appointed Second in Council 5th March 1685.
Richard Browne	14th April 1684 ...	Resigned in July 1688.
John Stables	12th July 1688 ...	Murdered in the sack of the factory in 1689.
Daniell Dubois	17th Sept. 1690 ...	Suspended in April 1692 and dismissed in June.
Simon Holcombe	30th June 1692 ...	Died at Vizagapatam 21st May 1705. His tomb stands in the old cemetery there.
Stephen Trewen	12th June 1705 ...	Died at Vizagapatam on 30th May 1706.
Francis Hastings	17th June 1706 ...	Was Second in Council. Afterwards acted as Governor of Fort St. George from 18th January 1720 to 14th October 1721.
William Jennings	29th June 1714.	
Robert Symonds	12th May 1715.	
Sandys Davis	8th Jan. 1728 ...	Died 14th May 1734 at Vizagapatam, where his tomb may be seen in the old cemetery.
John Sanderson	29th May 1734.	
Charles Simpson	4th Jan. 1739 ...	Died at Vizagapatam on 4th April 1741. His tombstone is in the old cemetery.
John Stratton	18th May 1741.	
Richard Prince	6th June 1743 ...	Took charge on October 13th.
Thomas Saunders	3rd Oct. 1748 ...	Took charge on 30th December. Appointed Governor of Fort St. David (then the head settlement on the coast—Madras being in the hands of the French) on 21st September 1750 and became Governor of Madras on the restoration (on 5th April 1752) of that town to the position of capital.

List of the Chiefs in Council and Collectors of Vizagapatam—cont.

Name.	Date of appointment.	——
CHIEFS IN COUNCIL OF VIZAGAPATAM FACTORY—*cont.*		
Robert Goodere...	20th Oct. 1750.	
George Pigot	23rd Dec. 1751 ...	Afterwards became Lord Pigot and Governor of Madras.
Charles Boddam	2nd Sept. 1754.	
John Lewin Smith	5th July 1756.	
William Perceval	3rd March 1757 ...	Vizagapatam was captured by the French during his time and he was a prisoner on parole in Bengal.
John Andrews	9th Oct. 1758.	
Thomas Heath	21st April 1759.	
John Smith	29th March 1763.	
CHIEFS IN COUNCIL OF VIZAGAPATAM DISTRICT.		
John Andrews	27th July 1769.	
George Stratton	10th Aug. 1772 ...	Afterwards Member of Council at Fort St. George. Was instrumental in the arrest of Lord Pigot, the Governor, and made himself Governor on 24th August 1776. Suspended, 31st August 1777.
Samuel Johnson	26th Sept. 1775.	
Morgan Williams	17th Sept. 1777.	
Alexander Davidson	27th March 1778 ...	Provisional Governor of Madras from 18th June 1785 to 6th April 1786.
James Henry Casamajor ...	21st May 1780.	
Morgan Williams	1st March 1782.	
Claud Russell	24th July 1782 ...	Son-in-law of Lord Pigot.
Alexander Davidson	24th March 1789 ...	Died at Vizagapatam on 20th September 1791 about two months after his wife. Both are buried in the old cemetery beneath flowery epitaphs of the kind then in fashion.
John Chamier	21st Oct. 1791 ...	The last of the Chiefs, the designation being abolished on 20th November 1794.

CHAP. XI. APPENDIX.

List of the Chiefs in Council and Collectors of Vizagapatam—cont.

Name.	Date of appointment.	—
COLLECTORS OF VIZAGAPATAM DISTRICT—*cont.*		
John Snow ... ... Nathaniel Webb ... ... Michael Keating	20th Nov. 1794 ...	Collectors of the three divisions into which the district was now arranged.
William Brown	6th Feb. 1796 ...	Collector of the new Second division of the district, afterwards called the First division. Was succeeded by Mr. Robert Alexander on 19th August 1800.
Nathaniel Webb	March 1796 ...	Collector of the First, afterwards called the Second division, which was amalgamated with the First division and placed under Mr. Alexander in July 1802.
Michael Keating	March 1796 ...	Collector of the Third division. Was relieved in July 1797 by Mr. Andrew Scott, who in his turn was succeeded by Mr. Peter Cherry on 30th August 1800.
Hon. Leveston Granville Keith Murray.	13th May 1803 ...	First Collector of the whole district.
Charles Henry Churchill ...	30th April 1805 ...	Died at Vizagapatam on 16th April 1811.
Charles Hyde	24th July 1811 ...	Transferred to South Arcot, where his name is still remembered. See the *Gazetteer* of that district.
John Smith	23rd Feb. 1813 ...	Died on 20th June 1824 at Vizagapatam and is buried under an imposing monument in the Regimental Lines Cemetery.
Robert Bayard	29th June 1824.	
Henry Gardiner	25th Aug. 1826.	
William Mason	18th Dec. 1832 ...	Died at Vizagapatam on 2nd July 1834 and lies buried in the Regimental Lines Cemetery.

List of the Chiefs in Council and Collectors of Vizagapatam—cont.

Name.	Date of appointment.	—
COLLECTORS OF VIZAGAPATAM DISTRICT—*cont.*		
William Urquhart Arbuthnot.	3rd July 1834.	
Arthur Freese	20th Jan. 1835.	
William Urquhart Arbuthnot.	29th March 1837 ...	From 26th November 1839, the Collector became also Agent to the Governor for the territories brought under Act XXIV of that year.
Patrick Boyle Smollett ...	6th Jan. 1842.	
William Urquhart Arbuthnot.	20th Dec. 1843 ...	Resigned the service in 1846; appointed to Secretary of State's new Council in 1858. Died 1874.
Patrick Boyle Smollett ...	20th Feb. 1846.	
Andrew Robertson	14th Sept. 1850.	
Patrick Boyle Smollett ...	1st May 1855.	
Charles William Reade ...	21st July 1857.	
Edward George Robert Fane ...	7th Oct. 1859.	
David Freemantle Carmichael.	11th March 1862 ...	Afterwards Member of Council from 30th August 1878 to 9th December 1883. Appointed Special Commissioner to enquire into the Rampa rebellion of 1881.
John Henry Master	20th April 1867.	
James Innes Minchin	21st April 1868.	
Robertson John Melville ...	21st Jan. 1870.	
John Read Daniell	24th April 1873.	
Alexander McCallum Webster.	13th May 1874.	
Harry St. Aubyn Goodrich ...	19th Sept. 1874.	
Robertson John Melville ...	3rd Nov. 1876.	
Harry St. Aubyn Goodrich ...	15th Feb. 1877.	
John Lee-Warner	16th April 1879.	
Octavius Butler Irvine ...	26th Sept. 1879 ...	Died at Vizagapatam on the 14th March 1880 from wounds inflicted by a panther.
John Henry Garstin	16th March 1880 ...	Afterwards C.S.I. and Temporary Governor of Madras from 1st December 1890 to 22nd January 1891.
Henry Gribble Turner ...	11th June 1881 ...	Most of his previous service had been spent in this district.
Evans Charles Johnson ...	23rd April 1883.	
Henry Gribble Turner ...	28th April 1884.	
William Alexander Willock ...	7th April 1889.	

List of the Chiefs in Council and Collectors of Vizagapatam—cont.

Name.	Date of appointment.	——
COLLECTORS OF VIZAGAPATAM DISTRICT—*cont.*		
Edward Sidney Laffan ...	16th May 1891 ...	Went to Madras on sick leave on 22nd September and died there four days later. Is buried in St. George's Cathedral Cemetery.
William Alexander Willock ...	14th Nov. 1891.	
Francis D'Arcy Osborne Wolfe-Murray.	22nd Feb. 1894.	
Leslie Creery Miller	25th June 1895.	
William Alexander Willock ...	5th Nov. 1895.	
William Ogilvie Horne ...	10th April 1896.	
William Book Ayling	7th June 1901.	
Richard Hamilton Campbell ...	12th Dec. 1902.	

CHAPTER XII.

SALT, ABKÁRI AND MISCELLANEOUS REVENUE.

SALT—The existing factories—The supply produced—The Oriental Salt Company—Earth-salt—Fish-curing yards. ABKÁRI AND OPIUM—Abkári in the Agency—Toddy—Spirit—Abkári in the ordinary tracts; arrack—Toddy—Opium—Hemp-drugs. CUSTOMS—Sea-customs—Land-customs. INCOME-TAX. STAMPS.

CHAP. XII.

SALT.

BEFORE the permanent settlement was carried out in 1802, the Company owned certain salt pans in the havíli lands and the zamindars had others within their properties. Regulation XXV of 1802 excluded from the assets of the zamindaris all profits on the manufacture of salt, and Regulation I of 1805 established the Government monopoly in that article which still subsists.

The existing factories.

The existing salt-factories (going down the coast from north to south) are Kuppili, Kónáda, Bimlipatam, Karása, Bálacheruvu and Pólavaram. Of these, the two last and the part of Karása called 'the Karása extension' are monopoly factories; that is, the pans in them are worked by license-holders who are required to hand over to Government, on receipt of a stated rate per garce called the *kudivάram*, all the salt they make. The rates of this *kudivάram* are so calculated as to make it cover all the expenses of manufacture and leave a reasonable profit besides. They are not often altered, but may be varied to meet changes in the cost of manufacture, such as a rise or fall in the general rate of wages.

The license-holders, as elsewhere, are each required to manufacture a stated quantity of salt known as the *dittam*, which is fixed at the beginning of the season by the Salt, Abkári and Customs department after consideration of the stocks in hand and other local circumstances. Failure to manufacture this *dittam* may be visited with the penalties in section 25 of the Salt Act, which include fines and the suspension or cancellation of the license, but the more severe of these punishments are very rarely inflicted.

The other factories are excise factories; that is, those who hold licenses to make salt in them are allowed, subject to certain restrictions, to make any quantity they choose and dispose of it how and when they like after they have paid to Government the

CHAP. XII. SALT.

excise duty upon it and a small cess to cover the interest on the capital cost of permanent works carried out by Government to facilitate storage and manufacture.

The supply produced.

The salt made at Kuppili and Bimlipatam is lighter than that produced in the other factories, and consequently—since salt is bought by merchants at the factories by weight and sold retail in the bazaars by measure—it fetches a better price. This is especially the case at Kuppili, although the product there gives indifferent results on analysis. The Bálacheruvu salt used to be the best in appearance, consisting of large (but brittle) crystals, but of late the factory has not been regularly worked and the quality has declined. The Karása salt is the worst, both in size and colour. In the old days when large numbers of Brinjári gangs came right down to the coast to fetch salt for Bastar and Raipur, they used to prefer the salt manufactured at Naupada in Ganjám, which consists of large and hard crystals which will stand transport by pack-bullocks without wastage, to the more brittle kinds made in the factories in this district. These Brinjári gangs still transport large quantities of salt to the country beyond the gháts, but they no longer come to the pans in the same numbers as formerly. Much of the salt is carried in carts through the low country and sold to the Brinjáris at places at the foot of the hills or where the cart roads stop, such as Párvatípur, for example, and Naurangpur.

The Kónáda and Bimlipatam factories are small affairs; Pólavaram is comparatively new; and Bálacheruvu suffers from want of labour and from its distance from the railway; but the Karása factory is a fine one, capable of much extension.

Figures of the manufacture and sales at each of these places in recent years are given in the separate Appendix to this volume. They supply (*a*) parts of Orissa and the inland country behind it, sharing the market with salt imported through Calcutta, and with Bombay salt brought by the Bengal-Nagpur railway to Sambalpur and the adjacent country; (*b*) the plains of Vizagapatam and parts of Ganjám; (*c*) the Jeypore country above the gháts, to which Bombay salt does not penetrate; and (*d*) the portion of Bengal and the Central Provinces which are accessible from the great route through the Ráyagada valley and are yet beyond competition from Bombay.

The Oriental Salt Company.

In 1896 Messrs. Stuart, Hall & Co., a branch of Messrs. Hall, Wilson & Co., who had leased part of the Karása factory, attempted so to purify and improve the local salt as to render it able to compete with the imported 'Liverpool' salt in the

Calcutta market. They sifted the Karása product, sold the larger crystals in the local market in the ordinary way and then treated the smaller siftings with a concentrated brine containing a small proportion of carbonate of soda. The latter reacted upon the chlorides of magnesium and calcium in the salt, forming carbonates of magnesium and calcium (which could be removed) and chloride of sodium, or common salt. The product thus purified was dried by centrifugals and became an exceedingly white salt which was much less hygroscopic than the ordinary variety. This process was patented and in 1898 the Oriental Salt Company, Limited, was formed to work it. The company carried on operations at Naupada in Ganjám, Jagannaikpur (Jagannáthapuram) in Gódávari and Covelong in Chingleput, as well as at Karása. The venture, however, was not a commercial success and in December 1904 the shareholders decided voluntarily to wind up the company. Messrs. Hall, Wilson & Co. have been recognized as receivers for the debenture-holders, and still carry on work at Naupada.

Earth-salt.

All along the shore of the district are extensive salt swamps, the nine largest covering an area of 50 square miles. In these much spontaneous salt effloresces and this was at one time extensively consumed by the poorer classes. These people used also to scrape up the salt-earth found in the swamps and lixiviate it with water to obtain the salt from it. The problem of preventing these practices in so large an area was for many years one of great difficulty, and in 1865 a special Deputy Collector was appointed to endeavour to suppress the traffic. He reported soon afterwards that he believed that the quantity of this illicit salt consumed was larger than the amount of Government salt sold at all the factories, and said that the spontaneous salt and the salt-earth were openly collected in broad daylight in *kávadis* by bodies of men a hundred strong, and were even raided by people with carts. A doubt arose soon afterwards as to whether mere possession of salt-earth was an offence under the existing law, and this checked the preventive measures; but in 1872 prosecutions were revived and no less than 10,000 maunds of earth-salt were seized and as many as 2,000 persons were punished. The next year a special preventive force was entertained, but it was not strong enough to cope adequately with the difficulty and even in 1875–76 as much as 9,500 maunds of illicit salt were seized.

The manufacture of illicit salt has now practically ceased. Some of the swamps have become covered with blown sand and

CHAP. XII. SALT.

the increase in population has led to the cultivation of others of the saline areas.

Fish-curing yards.

There are in the district fifteen fish-curing yards, controlled by Government, in which salt is supplied duty free to be utilized in curing fish. The quantity of fish cured annually in these is about 57,000 Indian maunds. It is consumed throughout the district.

ABKÁRI AND OPIUM.

The abkári revenue consists of that derived from arrack, foreign liquor, toddy and hemp-drugs. Statistics regarding each of these items, and also concerning opium, will be found in the separate Appendix.

For abkári purposes, the district was long treated as consisting of three different zones in which three different systems of administration were required; namely, the Agency, the interior taluks and the littoral tracts; and even at present the system of administration in the Agency differs widely from that in the plains.

Abkári in the Agency.

In the former (except in a few villages along the foot of the hills, chiefly in Golgonda taluk) the Abkári Act I of 1886 is not in force, the officers of the Abkári department have no jurisdiction, and matters are directly administered by the Agent and his subordinates.

Toddy.

In this tract, unlike the rest of the district, there are no restrictions whatever upon the manufacture and consumption of toddy.

Except in Malkanagiri, where palmyra palms are plentiful, toddy is obtained there from the sago-palm (*Caryota urens*), date and cocoa palms being rare and never tapped. A rough ladder, consisting of a stem of bamboo with the branches on either side of it cut short so as to make steps, is lashed to the tree and left there permanently, and the owner climbs up whenever he or his require a drink. The people do not know how to climb palms in the method followed by the Shánáns of the southern districts. The tree is tapped in the same way as a palmyra, the end of the flower spathe being cut off and a pot suspended below to catch the sap as it exudes.

Spirit.

Though the manufacture of toddy has always been unrestricted in the Agency, a fair amount of revenue has always been extracted from the consumption of spirit there, but methods of administration have always differed widely from those followed in the plains.

The early system in Jeypore was particularly simple: the estate was rented as a farm, the Rája bought it, and he then collected the revenue by imposing what amounted to a poll-tax on all the inhabitants—whether they sold or drank liquor or not—graduated according to their supposed means. In 1868 Government got to know of this, and indignantly took the farm under their own management. Improvements in the system were not so easy to effect, however, as at first sight appeared; for the hill people know of several forms of strong drink all of which can easily be made at home; and even if it had been possible to stop the manufacture of these in the thousands of scattered huts dotted about the hundreds of jungly and secluded valleys in the Agency, the coercion necessary would speedily have driven the hill men to resistance.

The most popular of these drinks is the liquor distilled from the blossom of the *Bassia latifolia*, called *ippa* in Telugu and *mohwa* in Uriya. This tree flowers in the month of Chaitra (March and April). The people burn the grass under the trees beforehand, so as to facilitate the gathering of the blossoms, and when these fall they turn out and collect them. If the blossoms are dried in the sun they will keep good for some weeks; and if they are fried and then pressed into balls (the frying makes them sticky) they will keep a couple of years. Some of them are mixed with jaggery and eaten, some are sold to the Sondis (see below) to be distilled into spirit, and in parts of the Agency (*e.g.*, the Savara and Kuttiya Khond hills) some are retained for distillation at home. This latter process is simple. The flowers are soaked in water for three or four days and are then boiled with water in an earthenware chatty. Over the top of this is placed another chatty, mouth downwards, the join between the two being made air-tight by being tied round with a bit of cloth and luted with clay. From a hole made in the upper chatty a hollow bamboo leads to a third pot, specially made for the purpose, which is globular and has no opening except that into which the bamboo pipe leads. This last is kept cool by pouring water constantly over it, and the distillate is forced into it through the bamboo and there condenses.

Besides *ippa* liquor the hill people brew beer from rice, sámai (the millet *Panicum miliare*) and ragi. They 'mash' the grain in the ordinary manner, add some more water to it, mix a small quantity of a ferment with it, leave it to ferment three or four days, and then strain off the grain. The beer so obtained is often highly intoxicating, and different kinds of it go by different names, such as *londa*, *pandiyam* and *maddikallu*. The ferment which is used is called the *sáraiya-mandu* ('spirit drug') or

CHAP. XII.
ABKÁRI AND OPIUM.

Sondi-mandu ('Sondis' drug') and can be bought in the weekly markets. There are numerous recipes [1] for making it, but the ingredients are always jungle roots and barks. It is sold made up into small balls with rice.

This beer is the common drink in places where the *ippa* tree is rare, such as the Pádwa and Koraput taluks (where the *ippa* tree is plentiful, as in Gunupur taluk, it is almost unknown), and seems a harmless kind of beverage. Sometimes, however, the fermented grain is afterwards distilled, and the spirit so made is potent enough.

At first the authorities endeavoured to administer the liquor revenue directly, under amáni, but gradually the renting system was reverted to everywhere except in Malkanagiri, Kótapád and Naurangpur. It was tried, indeed, in these also in 1880, but was a miserable failure. Both in the rented and the amáni taluks the methods followed were much the same. Strong waters made for home consumption were entirely exempt from taxation, but manufacture for sale was only permitted under a license. Each retail shop had its own still alongside, and the license covered both. This system is necessary in a country which is too rugged to admit of easy transport from a central distillery to outlying shops, and in which strong drink transported by a highlander through highland villages would be unlikely to reach its destination without paying heavy toll *en route*.

After ten years of renting, the pendulum swung back again and the amáni system rose once more into favour. In 1893, in the amáni taluks, the right to distil and to sell in the same licensed premises was, for the first time, sold separately; in 1897 this policy was extended to the whole of the Agency except the Gunupur farm; in 1901 this farm was abolished; and at present the right to distil and sell is separately sold throughout the agency tracts except in 36 villages (mainly in Golgond taluk) which, for abkári purposes, are included in the ordinary tracts. The stills make liquor both from *ippa* flowers and from grain.

To prevent smuggling from the Agency to the rest of the district, where the price of spirit is higher, a preventive belt, five miles wide, was established in 1890 along the frontier between the two; and in this no shops or stills may be set up.

[1] One given on p. 264 of Mr. Carmichael's *Manual* contains 23 ingredients; compare Mr. H. G. Turner's letters in G.O., No. 532, Revenue, dated 2nd May 1874.

CHAP. XII. ABKÁRI AND OPIUM.

The actual shop-keepers and still-owners in the hills, especially in the Párvatípur and Pálkonda Agencies, are usually immigrants of the Sondi caste, a wily class who know exactly how to take advantage of the sin which doth so easily beset the hill man and to wheedle from him, in exchange for the strong drink which he cannot do without, his ready money, his little possessions, his crops, and finally his land itself. Statistics of the arrack rentals for the last decade in the Koraput division exhibit a marked increase and go to show either that the shops were sold for much less than their value in former years or, perhaps, that drinking there is more prevalent than it was; but in the Párvatípur Agency it is stated that extended communications and contact with the outer world are gradually teaching the hill people restraint in this matter, and that even the Chaitra Saturnalia (see p. 72) shows signs of decreasing in vehemence.

Abkári in the ordinary tracts; arrack.

Outside the agency tracts, abkári administration usually consisted at first in dividing the country into farms and selling by auction the right to collect the arrack and the toddy revenue in them. The two were kept quite distinct and were sold separately. From 1830–31 to 1860–61 the receipts were almost stationary, fluctuating between Rs. 60,000 and Rs. 67,000; in 1868–69 they rose to a lakh; and in the next year the farms sold for as much as Rs. 1,71,000. This, however, was more than they were worth, and several of the purchasers went bankrupt in consequence.

In 1872 the excise system (under which the revenue is collected in the form of a duty, levied at the distillery, on every gallon of liquor issued for consumption) was introduced in the case of arrack for a term of three years. Mr. Minchin of Aska in Ganjám undertook the supply of the liquor, and sent that required for the Gunupur and Ráyagada Agencies (which were included with the plain taluks) by road through Chicacole, and supplied the rest of the district through Bimlipatam, whither the liquor was brought down by sea. His contract included also the monopoly of the manufacture and sale of toddy, but he was allowed to sub-rent this on condition of paying to Government three-quarters of the sum for which he leased it. An attempt was at first made to give the Aska liquor, which was distilled from jaggery, the peculiar flavour popular in this district by mingling with it a little rice arrack; but this did not meet the public taste and eventually it became necessary to mix with it as much as a fourth part of rice spirit. Even then, this arrack was never as popular as that made in the country stills, and on this

CHAP. XII. ABKÁRI AND OPIUM.

account Mr. Minchin was allowed to sub-rent Gunupur, Ráyagada and the Sálúr and Pálkonda Agencies on the same terms as the toddy farms. Numerous other difficulties also cropped up,[1] chief among them being the smuggling of *ippa* arrack from the Agency into the interior taluks at the foot of the hills.

In 1875 another triennial lease was granted to Mr. Minchin for the arrack supply, but the toddy farms were sold separately. Smuggling continued and eventually led to the entire breakdown of the excise system in the interior taluks. They were accordingly first leased out to Mr. Minchin and supplied on the old system of scattered stills, and afterwards, in 1878–79, rented out by public auction in four[2] farms to others, who manufactured two strengths of rice or *ippa* liquor (30° and 60° underproof respectively) at sanctioned stills and sold it at fixed shops. This step only transferred, and did not abolish, the smuggling: it was now systematically carried on from this rented belt into the littoral taluks in quart bottles, the provisions of the then abkári law making it no offence to transport arrack in quantities of one quart or less.

This system was overthrown by the introduction of the existing Abkári Act, which not only stopped 'the quart system', as it was called, but rendered the salt preventive staff available for the enforcement of the abkári law. At the beginning of 1888 the excise system was once more tried in these inland taluks, but the right of supply was given to native renters both there and in the littoral taluks, and Mr. Minchin's connection with the district, which had lasted for sixteen years, ceased.[3]

The supply of arrack to the district has for the last twelve years been in the hands of a native firm, known as the Vizagapatam Commercial Corporation, which makes the spirit from sugar-cane jaggery at their distillery at the district head-quarters. Since 1890 the issue of rice spirit has been discontinued, and this has done much to check the smuggling from the Agency tracts which was formerly such a difficulty, as illicit liquor can now be recognized at once. The system of supply of country spirit at present in force is known as the contract distillery supply system, under

[1] See G.Os., Nos. 561, Revenue, dated 6th May 1874, and 332, dated 2nd March 1875.

[2] Consisting of (i) Gunupur and Ráyagada taluks, (ii) Gajapatinagaram, Sálúr and Bobbili, (iii) Párvatípur and Pálkonda and (iv) Víravilli and Srungavarapukóta.

[3] A fuller history of abkári administration in Vizagapatam during this period will be found in G.O., No. 1005, Revenue, dated 19th December 1889.

which the exclusive privilege of manufacture and supply is disposed of by tender and the prices to be charged at the distilleries, warehouses and wholesale dépôts are fixed by Government. The right to sell retail is sold separately, and shop by shop, by auction every year.

Toddy.

In the ordinary tracts the toddy revenue is managed on the tree-tax system, under which a tax is levied on every tree tapped. This was first introduced into certain of the taluks in October 1892. The right of retail sale at the shops approved by Government is in some cases sold annually by auction, or, more generally, on payment of fixed fees.

Toddy is obtained from the palmyra and date palms. The cocoanut is never tapped. The toddy-drawers are usually of the Yáta and Segidi castes. Their methods are the same as usual, the palmyra being tapped by cutting off the end of the flower spathe, and the date palm by making an incision like an inverted V close under the crown of leaves. In the zamindaris little care is taken to see that date trees are not overtapped, and hundreds of them may be seen ruined and even killed by excessive tapping.

Sweet toddy tapping is almost unknown. A little jaggery is made from palmyra toddy in two or three villages round Púdimadaka in the Sarvasiddhi taluk, but so far the industry is small. Date toddy is not used in this way.

Opium.

The opium consumed in the district is all supplied from the Rajahmundry warehouse. The drug is generally eaten, maddat (the smoking mixture) being little in demand. On the plains the system of supply is the same as elsewhere. In the Agency, however, special conditions formerly resulted in special rules.

The Opium Act I of 1878 came into force on the 1st July 1880 and occasioned an immediate and abrupt rise in the price of the drug. In the Agency it went up from five (and even six) tolas a rupee to two tolas, and in some places none was procurable for love or money. The people in the Golgonda Agency, where almost everyone—men, women and children—eats opium, believed that Government had imposed the tax as a punishment for the Rampa rebellion, which was just over. The craving for a narcotic to which they had been habituated from childhood but could no longer afford, and the deprivation of what they believed to be a panacea against malaria, dysentery and other hill diseases, rendered them openly discontented and restless, and the then Agent, Mr. Garstin, thought that special measures were necessary and suggested that Government should forego part of the

CHAP. XII. ABKÁRI AND OPIUM.

usual opium duty so that the agency people might be able to have their daily dose without paying very much extra for it. This was agreed to, and from April 1881 opium of varying qualities was supplied by Government to licensed retailers, who sold it to the public at prices ranging from 5 to 3½ tolas per rupee, against the rate of two tolas which obtained in the low country. In 1882 the minimum price was raised to four tolas, and in 1883 to 3½ tolas, and this latter figure enabled Government to charge the usual duty in full and to hand over the whole business of supply to a monopolist from April 1884. Later on, the price was enhanced to three tolas, and in 1888–89, at Mr. H. G. Turner's suggestion, it was increased to 2½ tolas in all parts of the Agency except Malkanagiri taluk and the Golgonda and Mádgole hills. Mr. Turner was strongly of opinion that the opium habit was doing great harm among the Telugu hill folk in the south of the Agency; and he contrasted their physical condition and energy most unfavourably with those of the Uriyas further north, who are much less addicted to the drug. He did not believe that opium was in the least necessary to health, but held that on the contrary the people spent upon it money which would have been better laid out on food or warm clothes. He pointed out that opium-eaters required continually increasing doses as they got on in years, and that the habit was so universal that nursing mothers even rubbed the drug on their nipples before giving their babies the breast.

Two years later the price in the three excepted tracts above mentioned was raised, at Mr. Willock's suggestion, to the rate obtaining elsewhere in the Agency, namely, 2½ tolas per rupee; and in 1904 the rate throughout the district was enhanced to its present figure, 2¼ tolas.

Retail supply is effected through vendors, who are granted licenses free in shops where the total annual sales are less than 1,000 tolas; pay Rs. 15 and Rs. 30 respectively if the sales are between 1,000 and 2,000 tolas and 2,000 and 3,000 tolas; and purchase the license by auction, subject to a minimum of Rs. 40, where the sales are more than 4,000 tolas annually. The consumption is greater than in any district except Gódávari, and the incidence of revenue per head of the population higher than anywhere except that district, the Nilgiris and Kistna.

Hemp-drugs.

In the Agency, the cultivation of the hemp plant is under no restrictions, but assertions on the part of officers of the Central Provinces that ganja was smuggled thither from the Jeypore zamindari, especially from the neighbourhood of Maidalpur, have

CHAP. XII. ABKÁRI AND OPIUM.

recently been met by the prohibition of the export of the drug from the estate.[1]

In the plains the sale of ganja is controlled on the system usual elsewhere. The drug is generally supplied from the Daggupád storehouse in Guntúr district, but a proportion of it comes from Kaniyambádi in North Arcot, where the crop grown on the Javádi hills is stored. Comparatively little is used in the district, and the consumers are largely religious mendicants and others from northern India, some Musalmans, and followers of the Rája of Vizianagram who picked up the habit when resident with former chiefs of that family at Benares.

CUSTOMS. Sea-customs

Since April 1900, the collection of sea-customs has devolved, as elsewhere, upon the Salt, Abkári and Customs department. Of the two ports in the district, Bimlipatam contributes somewhat the larger proportion of the small amount of export duties which are realized, and Vizagapatam the greater share of the import duties. These latter average about Rs. 5,500 annually at that port.

Land-customs.

No land-customs are collected anywhere in the district now, but as late as 1860 almost every zamindar in the district levied on all travellers and traders passing through his property varying fees which (though often described as charges for protection, for pasturage, for the use of halting-places, and so forth) were in reality transit duties pure and simple. Varying rates were demanded for each kávadi-load, pack-bullock and cart, and in Jeypore a tax of three or four pies a bullock was stated to give the Rája an income of Rs. 2,500 per annum.[2] These duties were not included in the assets on which the peshkash was originally fixed in these estates, and their eventual abolition (in 1863) involved no compensation. The Brinjári pack-bullock traders gave a pitiable account of the hardship they involved. 'We never knew', they said, 'the amount we should have to pay. In the morning we were taxed; in the evening we were taxed. Our bullocks were detained, our merchandise seized. Tigers and wild beasts are dangerous, but the Rája's robbers are even more to be dreaded.'

INCOME-TAX.

The Income-tax Act is not in force in the Agency.

In the plain taluks the tax is levied and collected in the usual manner. Statistics will be found in the separate Appendix to this volume. In the triennium ending with 1904–05 the proportion borne by the tax-payers to the total population

[1] G.O., No. 515, Revenue, dated 5th June 1905.

[2] G.O., No. 576, Political, dated 30th August 1859.

CHAP. XII. INCOME-TAX.

was smaller than in any other district in the Presidency, and the incidence of the tax per head of the population was lower than in any other except South Arcot and Salem, the figure being only 6 pies against an average for the Presidency, excluding Madras City, of 10½ pies. Only 25 per cent. of the assessees paid tax at the higher rate of 5 pies per rupee, against a similar Presidency average of over 37 per cent.

The zamindars and owners of proprietary estates in the district formerly levied for many years a profession tax, called moturpha and graduated on no very fixed principles, on certain classes of people resident within their properties. In 1861 this was stopped, compensation being paid to those of the zamindars and proprietors in fixing whose peshkash the proceeds of this tax had been included among the assets of the estate.

STAMPS.

Both judicial and non-judicial stamps are sold on the system usual elsewhere. The Stamp Act is in force in the Agency. Statistics of the receipts will be found in the Appendix, and it will be seen that they are very small. Its revenue from this source has often been held to be an index of the prosperity of a district, since where trade is large and business brisk non-judicial stamps are largely required, while where the people have money in their pockets they are usually fond of spending it on litigation and the sale of judicial stamps accordingly increases. If this test be a true one, Vizagapatam as a whole is the poorest area in the Presidency, since, including the Agency, the revenue there per 1,000 of the population both from judicial and non-judicial stamps, and both in the year 1904–05 and the six years ending therewith, was lower than in any other Madras district. There are however certain special reasons why the stamp revenue there should be low, among them the infrequency of communications and the backwardness of the people in a large part of the district.

CHAPTER XIII.

ADMINISTRATION OF JUSTICE.

FORMER COURTS. COURTS AND LAWS IN THE AGENCY—Limits of the Agency—Agency rules—Laws in force in the Agency. CIVIL JUSTICE ELSEWHERE—Existing courts—Amount of litigation—Registration. CRIMINAL JUSTICE—The various tribunals—Former meriah sacrifices—Crime and criminal castes. POLICE. JAILS. APPENDIX, Laws in force in the Agency.

CHAP. XIII.

FORMER COURTS.

THE report of 1784 of the Circuit Committee throws a lurid light on the judicial methods in force in the district before the arrival of the British. 'During the Muhammadan government an adálat was established at Chicacole in which the ámildar, nominally the Faujdar, was supposed to preside. But he appears to have disposed of the authority and profits, which were established at 25 per cent. on the amount of property.' Petty disputes were settled by pancháyats or by the heads of villages, the Hindus preferring this method to recourse to a Musalman court. After the dissolution of Musalman rule, no regular courts of justice existed, 'the renter's decision being the only resource of the injured, so that those who have money generally escape by a well-applied present, while the poor, who are perhaps the really aggrieved, frequently undergo a corporal punishment. This authority leaves the renter frequently judge and party in his own cause; therefore an equitable distribution of justice is not to be expected.'

The earliest British court in the settlement at Vizagapatam appears to have been that established in 1742 by an order that the Council do 'meet regularly at the Choultry for administering justice to the inhabitants.' Confinement, 'whether to the Choultry, the Cockhouse, the person's private house or elsewhere,' required the sanction of a majority of the Council and had to be reported at once to the authorities at Madras.

At the beginning of the last century Lord Cornwallis' system of civil and criminal courts was introduced in this Presidency and since then the general history of the administration of justice has been the same in Vizagapatam as in other districts, with the one exception of the establishment in the Agency of the special judicial system which still obtains there.

COURTS AND LAWS IN THE AGENCY.

As a result of the constant disturbances in Vizagapatam and Ganjám which at length, at the end of 1832, necessitated, as already (p. 57) related, the despatch of Mr. Russell as Special

CHAP. XIII.
COURTS AND LAWS IN THE AGENCY.

Commissioner with a force of troops, an Act (XXIV of 1839) was passed on Mr. Russell's advice which enacted that in this district (and also in Ganjám) 'the operation of the rules for the administration of civil and criminal justice, as well as those for the collection of the revenue, shall cease to have effect, except as hereinafter mentioned, within the undermentioned tracts of country' and that 'the administration of civil and criminal justice (including the superintendence of the police) and the collection and superintendence of the revenues of every description, within the tracts of country specified, . . . shall be vested in the Collector of Vizagapatam and shall be exercised by (him) as Agent to the Governor of Fort St. George.'

Limits of the Agency.

The tracts in this district which were thus removed from the jurisdiction of the ordinary courts and laws and constituted the Agency, were the zamindaris and taluks noted in the margin. In other words, some seven-eighths of the whole district (all of it except the old havíli land) was turned into a non-regulation area and placed under a special system of administration. The remainder was subordinated, in judicial matters, to the Civil and Sessions Judge of Chicacole, with a sub-court at Vizagapatam and a district munsif at Ráyavaram.

Zamindaris.

Vizianagram.
Bobbili.
Jeypore.
Kurupám.
Sangamvalasa.
Chemudu.
Páchipenta.
Ándra.
Sarapalli-Bhímavaram.
Sálúr.
Mádgole.
Belgám.
Mérangi.

Taluks.

Pálkonda.
Golgonda.

In June 1863, in view of the improved condition of the district, the zamindaris of Vizianagram (except Kásipuram estate) and Bobbili, and the taluk of Pálkonda, were restored by notification to the ordinary jurisdiction and placed under the newly-constituted Civil and Sessions Court at Vizagapatam. In December 1864, in consequence of the heavy work thrown on the Agent by the civil cases arising in so large an Agency, a further reduction in its limits was made by the exclusion from it of the estates noted in the margin; while in December 1868 that part of Golgonda taluk which lay below the Gháts and between them and the east of the river Boddéru was retransferred to the ordinary jurisdiction. Since then no alterations in the limits of the Agency have occurred.

Zamindaris.

Kurupám (except the Gumma and Konda muttas).
Sangamvalasa.
Chemudu.
Páchipenta (below the Gháts).
Ándra.
Sarapalli-Bhímavaram.
Sálúr.
Mádgole (below the Gháts).
Belgám.
Mérangi (except the Mondenkallu and Konda muttas).

Taluk.

Golgonda (except the hill muttas).

Agency rules.

Act XXIV of 1839 empowered the Government of Madras to prescribe such rules as they might deem proper for the guidance of the Agent and his subordinates in judicial and other matters; for the determination of the extent to which his decision in civil suits should be final or subject to appeal to the High Court; and for the regulation of the manner in which the same tribunal should deal with his judgments in criminal cases. The rules accordingly framed originally left civil cases to be tried by pancháyats, but they have since been frequently revised, and as they stand at present they direct that civil suits shall be heard by the revenue officers, but lay down a course of procedure simpler than that prescribed by the Civil Procedure Code, which is not in force in the Agency. They empower the district munsifs (who are the deputy tahsildars) to try suits up to Rs. 500 in value, the Divisional Officers (who have the civil powers of sub-judges) those between Rs. 500 and Rs. 5,000, and the Agent those above the latter sum in value. Criminal justice is administered as elsewhere, both the Penal Code and the Criminal Procedure Code being in force, except that there is no trial by jury. The deputy tahsildars are sub-magistrates, the Divisional Officers have first-class powers, and the Agent is the Sessions Judge and is aided by the senior Civilian Divisional Officer, who is made an Additional Sessions Judge.

Laws in force in the Agency.

The wide terms of Act XXIV of 1839 (which has both retrospective and prospective effect) coupled with the uncertainties of the two subsequent enactments of 1874 called the Laws Local Extent Act and the Scheduled Districts Act, led to much doubt as to what laws were actually in force in the Agency, and in 1898, after prolonged correspondence with the Government of India, was published the first of a series of notifications under the Scheduled Districts Act which did much to set the matter at rest. The Appendix to this chapter shows the Acts which have now been so notified to be in force there (or, there being no doubt in the matter, have by executive order been declared to be so in force), but the notifications are not decisive of the question whether an enactment not included in them is or is not in force.

CIVIL JUSTICE ELSEWHERE.

Existing courts.

Outside the Agency, the civil tribunals are of the usual four grades, namely, the courts of village and district munsifs and of the recently-appointed sub-judge, and the District Court. Their powers and jurisdiction are the same as elsewhere. Statistics regarding the work done by them will be found in the separate Appendix to this volume.

CHAP. XIII.
CIVIL JUSTICE ELSEWHERE.

As elsewhere, the value of the suits tried by the village munsifs is seldom above Rs. 20. The system of trial by Bench Courts under section 9 of the Village Courts Act I of 1889 has been introduced in seventeen of the larger villages. There are now six district munsifs; namely, at *Yellamanchili* with jurisdiction over the taluks of Sarvasiddhi and Golgonda; *Vizianagram*, for Vizianagram and Gajapatinagaram; *Chódavaram*, for Víravilli and Srungavarapukóta; *Párvatípur*, for Párvatípur, Bobbili and Sálúr; *Vizagapatam*, for Vizagapatam, Bimlipatam and Anakápalle; and *Rázám*, for Chípurupalle and Pálkonda. The Chódavaram munsif was transferred to that station from Bimlipatam in 1889, in which year a redistribution of the munsifs' charges was carried out.

The jurisdiction of the District Court extends over all but the agency portion of the district.

Amount of litigation.

Including the Agency, Vizagapatam is almost the least litigious area in Madras. The number of suits filed is only one for every 275 of the population against one for every 117 in the Presidency as a whole, and Anantapur is the only district in which the proportion is lower. This result is due partly to the poverty of the mass of the population, partly to the fact that the numerous inhabitants of the hills have not yet acquired the taste for squabbling over their rights in the courts, and partly to the marked infrequency of suits under the Tenancy Act. Though nine-tenths of the district is zamindari land, a ten years' average of the cases filed under that enactment in this district works out to less than 200, while in Kistna and Tanjore, with far smaller areas of zamindari estates, it was eight times that number.

Registration.

The Registration Act does not extend to the Agency. Outside that area, the registration of assurances is managed on the usual lines. Besides the District Registrar at Vizagapatam there are thirteen sub-registrars, who are stationed at the head-quarters of the remaining ten non-agency deputy tahsildars and of the three tahsildars.

CRIMINAL JUSTICE.
The various tribunals.

The criminal tribunals are of the same classes as elsewhere. The village magistrates in the three Government taluks possess the usual powers in respect to petty cases arising within their villages, and in an ordinary year about half of them make use of these. Benches of magistrates in the four municipalities of Anakápalle, Bimlipatam, Vizagapatam and Vizianagram possess the usual powers with respect to certain minor kinds of offences committed within those places. The Towns Nuisances Act has been extended to seventeen other villages and is also put in force on the Simhāchalam hill during the two chief festivals at the famous temple there. The great bulk of the second and third class cases are, however, heard by the tahsildar- and sheristadar-magistrates at Narasapatam, the stationary sub-magistrates at Pálkonda and Yellamanchili, and the deputy tahsildars in charge of the other (zamindari) divisions in the district.

The Divisional Magistrates and the District Magistrate (and also the Treasury Deputy Collector) have the usual first-class powers and the Court of Session possesses the same authority as elsewhere throughout the non-agency portion of the district.

Former meriah sacrifices.

Of the grave crime committed in the district, that which has attracted the most attention is the former practice of meriah, or the sacrifice of human victims to propitiate the Earth Goddess and other deities. Its existence was discovered by Mr. Russell, the Special Commissioner, in 1836. Enquiries showed that it was common in Jeypore. By Act XXI of 1845 an officer called the Agent for the suppression of Meriah Sacrifices was placed in charge of the country where the custom prevailed, both in this and other Provinces. The first Meriah Agent was Captain Macpherson, whose monograph on the Khonds is so well known, and the Agency continued in existence until 1861. The following account in Mr. Frazer's *The Golden Bough* well summarizes, from the reports of these Agents and others, the chief characteristics of the custom :—

'The sacrifices were offered to the Earth Goddess, Tari Pennu or Bera Pennu,[1] and were believed to ensure good crops and immunity from all disease and accidents. In particular, they were considered necessary in the cultivation of turmeric, the Khonds arguing that the turmeric could not have a deep red colour without the shedding of blood. The victim or Meriah was acceptable to the goddess only if he had been purchased, or had been born a victim—that is, the son of a victim father—or had been devoted as a child by his father or guardian. Khonds in distress often sold their children for victims, 'considering the beatification of their souls certain, and their death, for the benefit of mankind, the most honourable possible.' A man of the Panua (Páno) tribe was once seen to load a Khond with curses and finally to spit on his face, because the Khond had sold for a victim his own child, whom the Panua had wished to marry. A party of Khonds, who saw this, immediately pressed forward to comfort the seller of his child, saying, "your child has died that all the world may live, and the Earth Goddess herself will wipe that spittle from your face." The victims were often kept for years before they were

[1] Not exclusively, as will appear below.

CHAP. XIII. CRIMINAL JUSTICE.

sacrificed. Being regarded as consecrated beings, they were treated with extreme affection, mingled with deference, and were welcomed wherever they went. A Meriah youth, on attaining maturity, was generally given a wife, who was herself usually a Meriah or victim; and with her he received a portion of land and farm-stock. Their offspring were also victims. Human sacrifices were offered to the Earth Goddess by tribes, branches of tribes, or villages, both at periodical festivals and on extraordinary occasions. The periodical sacrifices were generally so arranged by tribes and divisions of tribes that each head of a family was enabled, at least once a year, to procure a shred of flesh for his fields, generally about the time when his chief crop was laid down.

'The mode of performing these tribal sacrifices was as follows. Ten or twelve days before the sacrifice, the victim was devoted by cutting off his hair, which, until then, had been kept unshorn. Crowds of men and women assembled to witness the sacrifice; none might be excluded, since the sacrifice was declared to be for all mankind. It was preceded by several days of wild revelry and gross debauchery. On the day before the sacrifice the victim, dressed in a new garment, was led forth from the village in solemn procession, with music and dancing, to the Meriah grove, a clump of high forest trees standing a little way from the village and untouched by the axe. Here they tied him to a post, which was sometimes placed between two plants of the sankissar shrub. He was then anointed with oil, ghee, and turmeric, and adorned with flowers; and 'a species of reverence, which is not easy to distinguish from adoration' was paid to him throughout the day. A great struggle now arose to obtain the smallest relic from his person; a particle of the turmeric paste with which he was smeared, or a drop of his spittle, was esteemed of sovereign virtue, especially by the women. The crowd danced round the post to music, and, addressing the earth, said "O God, we offer this sacrifice to you; give us good crops, seasons, and health."

'On the last morning the orgies, which had been scarcely interrupted during the night, were resumed and continued till noon, when they ceased, and the assembly proceeded to consummate the sacrifice. The victim was again anointed with oil, and each person touched the anointed part, and wiped the oil on his own head. In some places they took the victim in procession round the village, from door to door, where some plucked hair from his head, and others begged for a drop of his spittle, with which they anointed their heads. As the victim might not be bound nor make any show of resistance, the bones of his arms and, if necessary, his legs were broken; but often this precaution was rendered unnecessary by stupefying him with opium. The mode of putting him to death varied in different places. One of the commonest modes seems to have been strangulation, or squeezing to death. The branch of a green tree was cleft several feet down the middle; the victim's neck (in other places, his chest) was inserted in the cleft, which the priest, aided by his assistants, strove with all his force to close. Then he wounded the victim slightly with his axe, whereupon the crowd rushed at the wretch and cut the flesh from the bones, leaving the head and bowels untouched. Sometimes he was cut up alive. In Chinna Kimedy he was dragged along the fields, surrounded by the crowd, who, avoiding his head and intestines, hacked the flesh from his body with their knives till he died. Another very common mode of sacrifice in the same district was to fasten the victim to the proboscis of a wooden elephant, which revolved on a stout post, and, as it whirled round, the crowd cut the flesh from the victim while the life remained.[1] In some villages Major Campbell found as many as fourteen of these wooden elephants, which had been used at sacrifices. In one district the victim was put to death slowly by fire. A low stage was formed, sloping on either side like a roof; upon it they laid the victim, his limbs wound round with cords to confine his struggles. Fires were then lighted and hot brands applied, to make him roll up and down the slopes of the stage as long as possible; for the more tears he shed the more abundant would be the supply of rain. Next day the body was cut to pieces.

'The flesh cut from the victim was instantly taken home by the persons who had been deputed by each village to bring it. To secure its rapid arrival, it was sometimes forwarded by relays of men, and conveyed with postal fleetness fifty or sixty miles. In each village all who stayed at home fasted rigidly until the flesh arrived. The bearer deposited it in the place of public assembly, where it was received by the priest and heads of families. The priest divided it into two portions, one of which he offered to the Earth Goddess by burying it in a hole in the ground with his back turned, and without looking. Then each man added a little earth to bury it, and the priest poured water on the spot from a hill gourd. The other portion of flesh he divided into as many shares as there were heads of houses present. Each head of a house rolled his shred of flesh in leaves, and buried it in his favourite field, placing it in the earth behind his back without looking. In some places each man carried his portion of flesh to the stream which watered his fields, and there hung it on a pole. For three days thereafter no house was swept; and, in one district, strict silence was observed, no fire might be given out, no wood cut, and no strangers received. The remains of the human victim (namely, the head, bowels, and bones) were watched by strong parties the night after the sacrifice; and next morning they were burned, along with a whole sheep, on a funeral pile. The ashes were scattered over the fields, laid as paste over the houses and granaries, or mixed with the new corn to preserve it from insects. Sometimes, however, the head and bones were buried, not burnt.'

The Meriah Agency appears first to have visited Jeypore in 1851, in which year Lieutenant-Colonel Campbell toured through

[1] One of these diabolical contrivances is now in the Madras Museum.

CHAP. XIII. CRIMINAL JUSTICE.

the country. At Bissamkatak he found in the house of the Tát Rája a boy who was being kept ready for sacrifice to the god of battles in the event, daily expected, of an outbreak of hostilities between the Tát Rája and his suzerain the Rája of Jeypore. At Ráyabijji (which, with its neighbour Chandrapur, was one of the chief strongholds of the custom and where an outpost of sibbandis was accordingly established) he rescued 69 meriahs, and at Gudári 46. In the hills north-east of the latter place his camp was attacked by some 300 Khonds, but they were driven off. In 1851–52 and 1852–53, 77 male and 115 female meriahs were rescued in this district, as well as 14 male and 8 female pússias, or children of female meriahs married temporarily to Khonds. Other reports show that on the site of the old fort at Rámagiri a victim was sacrificed every third year. The poor wretch was forced into a hole in the ground, three feet deep and eighteen inches square, at the bottom of which the goddess ('Goorbone-shanny') was supposed to dwell, his throat was cut and the blood allowed to flow into the hole, and afterwards his head was struck off and placed on his lap and the mutilated body covered with earth and a mound of stones until the time for the next sacrifice came round, when the bones were taken out and thrown away. In this taluk a sacrifice was also performed in 1855 to secure the release of the pátro, who had been confined by the Jeypore Rája. At Malkanagiri periodical sacrifices occurred at the four gates of the fort (see p. 281) and the rāni had a victim slain as a thank-offering for her recovery from an illness. In 1861 several sacrifices were made to celebrate the Jeypore Rája's recent succession to the estate and a girl was offered up in Jeypore itself to stay an epidemic of cholera. Sati was also openly practised, supposed sorceresses and witches were constantly put to death with the general approval of the people, and round Ráyagada infanticide was common.

Goats and buffaloes nowadays take the place of human meriah victims, but the belief in the superior efficacy of the latter dies hard and every now and again revives. When the Rampa rebellion of 1879–80 spread to this district, several cases of human sacrifice occurred in the disturbed tracts. In 1880 two persons were convicted of attempting a meriah sacrifice near Ambadála in Bissamkatak; in 1883 a man (a beggar and a stranger) was found at daybreak murdered in one of the temples in Jeypore in circumstances which pointed to his having been slain as a meriah; and as late as 1886 a formal enquiry showed that there were 'ample grounds for the suspicion' that the kidnapping of victims still went on in Bastar.

Crime and criminal castes.

The Jeypore country had so long been in a state of anarchy that for some time after the police were first posted there in 1863 daring and violent crime continued to be common. In 1864, to give only one instance, two paiks at Naurangpur fought a duel with broadswords in open daylight in one of the streets there to settle a dispute between their wives about a well, and one of them had his head taken off at one swoop of his opponent's weapon. To render them more deterrent, sentences of death used always to be carried out publicly at the head-quarters of the taluk.

At present, crime in the district may be said to be light and (except in the Agency) robberies, cattle-thefts and dacoities are uncommon. In the Golgonda Agency, however, crime (even petty theft) is practically unknown. In the low country, offences are especially rare in the south, the only castes which give trouble there being the gangs of Nakkalas or Yánádis who have settled permanently near Kottakóta and Makkavárapálem. They travel about to Sarvasiddhi taluk and the Gódávari district, but they usually confine themselves to sneaking kinds of crime, such as petty house-breakings and thefts of crops or the contents of carts, and do not perpetrate dacoities. Another wilder section of them haunts the country between Pálkonda and Párvatípur, living in temporary huts in the jungles. They are said to be called Nakkalas either because of their eating jackals or from their slinking ways. They live partly by making date mats and snaring small game, and are said to have a thieves' slang of their own. The Málas and Yátas (toddy-drawers) are also responsible for a good deal of the crime in the southern corner of the district.

Further north, in the centre of the plain country, the Yátas again contribute to the total, and in some villages (*e.g.*, Ballanki and Bánádi of Srungavarapukóta and Gópálapatnam of Vizagapatam) are coteries of Mádiga housebreakers. But the greater part of the offences are committed by the Konda Doras, who differ from their namesakes of the hills in not eating beef and in other respects, and are nominally cultivators. Some villages (*e.g.*, Nílamrázupéta of Vizianagram and Chinnabántupalli of Gajapatinagaram) are almost exclusively inhabited by these people. They travel widely in search of loot; and where they are thickest they have persuaded the villagers to employ some of their numbers as watchmen under an implied promise of exemption from open molestation.

Still further north, in the Párvatípur country, the Paidis (Paidi Málas) do most of the crime. They are more daring and violent than any of the castes yet mentioned, often committing dacoities on the roads. Like the Konda Doras, they have induced

CHAP. XIII. CRIMINAL JUSTICE.

some of the people to employ watchmen of their caste as the price of immunity from theft. They are connected with the Dombus of the Ráyagada and Gunupur taluks, who are even worse. These people dacoit houses at night in armed gangs of 50 or more with their faces blacked to prevent recognition. Terrifying the villagers into staying quiet in their huts, they force their way into the house of some wealthy person (for choice the local Sondi, liquor-seller and sowcar—usually the only man worth looting in an agency village and a shark who gets little pity from his neighbours when forced to disgorge), tie up the men, rape the women and go off with everything of value. Their favourite method of extracting information regarding concealed property is to sprinkle the house-owner with boiling oil.

In the east of Gunupur the Savaras commit much cattle-theft, partly, it is said, because caste custom enjoins big periodical sacrifices of cattle to their deceased ancestors.

The Khonds here and in Bissamkatak also steal cattle, especially those belonging to Brinjári gangs, in an open manner for the sake of their flesh. In 1898, at Deppiguda near Gudári, a party of them attacked four constables who were patrolling the country to check these thefts, thrashed them, and carried off all their property and uniforms. Efforts to arrest these men resulted in the inhabitants of their village fleeing to the hills; and for a time it looked as if there was danger of others joining them and of the Khonds 'going out.'

Throughout the Jeypore country proper, the Dombus (and some Ghásis) are by far the most troublesome class. Their favourite crime is cattle-theft for the sake of the skins, but in 1902 a Dombu gang in Naurangpur went so far as to levy blackmail over a large extent of country and defy for some months all attempts at capture. The loss of their cattle exasperates the other hill folk to the last degree and in 1899 the naiks (headmen) of sixteen villages in the north of Jeypore taluk headed an organized attack on the houses of the Dombus, which, in the most deliberate manner, they razed to the ground in some fifteen villages. The Dombus had fortunately got scent of what was coming and made themselves scarce, and no bloodshed occurred. In the next year some of the naiks of the Rámagiri side of Jeypore taluk sent round a jack branch, a well-recognized form of the fiery cross, summoning villagers other than Dombus to assemble at a fixed time and place, but this was luckily intercepted by the police. The Agent afterwards discussed the whole question with the chief naiks of Jeypore and south Naurangpur.

They had no opinion of the deterrent effects of mere imprisonment on the Dombus. 'You fatten them and send them back,' they said, and they suggested that a far better plan would be to cut off their right hands.

They eventually proposed a plan of checking the cattle-thefts which is now being followed in much of that country. The báranaiks, or heads of groups of villages, were each given brands with distinctive letters and numbers and required to brand the skins of all animals which had died a natural death or been honestly killed; and the possession by Dombus, skin-merchants or others of unbranded skins is now considered a suspicious circumstance the burden of explaining which lies upon the possessor. Unless this or some other way of checking the Dombus' depredations proves successful, serious danger exists that the rest of the people will take the matter into their own hands, and as the Dombus in the Agency number over 50,000 this would mean real trouble.

Attacks upon supposed sorcerers are still not uncommon in the Agency. In one instance a wizard's front teeth were pulled out by the local blacksmith to render him unable to pronounce his spells with the distinctness requisite to real efficacy (a similar case also occurred recently at Bimlipatam, the teeth being there knocked out with a stone); and in another, three Khonds whose dead brother's chest refused to burn on the funeral pyre killed the man who they therefore thought must have bewitched him, hacked the chest from the corpse, burnt it, and then gave themselves up to the police. The practice of carrying the handy axes called tangis, which is universal in the Agency, and the fondness of the hill man for strong waters lead to many cases of grievous hurt in sudden quarrels.

Two of the chief difficulties with which the police have to igntend are the general ignorance of the Khond, Savara, Gadaba and other tribal languages, and the opportunities for escape afforded by the propinquity of the Bastar and Kálahandi States.

POLICE.

Up to the time of the permanent settlement, such police as existed were under the orders of the zamindars and renters and were paid by grants of land. In the larger towns kotwáls were appointed to the immediate charge of them. Between 1802 and 1816 the village police were under the District Magistrate, who was then the same officer as the District Judge and did no touring. This system was a failure. The transfer of the force to the charge of the Collector effected some improvement, but the men were badly paid and had revenue, as well as police, duties.

CHAP. XIII. POLICE.

Companies of sibbandis were maintained to keep order in certain tracts, notably Golgonda. The present police force was organized gradually from 1861 onwards under Act XXIV of 1859, many of the former establishment (whose inams were enfranchised in 1862) joining the new department, and the sibbandi corps being incorporated with it. The town police were maintained, but on a different basis, being paid from municipal funds for some years.

There are now two Superintendents and three Assistant Superintendents in the district. One Superintendent (whose appointment was sanctioned in 1864) has charge of the Koraput division and is helped by an Assistant who usually has immediate control of the Jeypore and Malkanagiri taluks; and the other takes the rest of the district and has Assistants at Narasapatam and Párvatípur who take off his shoulders the direct charge of all but the five taluks noted in the margin. Statistics of the force appear in the separate Appendix. The risk of trouble in the Agency necessitates the upkeep of four bodies of reserve police (who are dressed in a workmanlike khaki uniform with putties and green turbans and are armed with Lee-Metfords) at Vizagapatam, Párvatípur, Koraput and Chintapalle in the Golgonda Agency. This last reserve was established after the fitúri of 1886 (see p. 251) by concentrating the stations formerly existing at Koyyúr, Lammasingi and Gúdem.

Bimlipatam.
Chípurupalle.
Gajapatinagaram.
Vizagapatam.
Vizianagram.

JAILS.

The district possesses 23 sub-jails, one at the head-quarters of each of the sub-magistrates except Vizagapatam, in which latter place the District Jail accommodates the under-trial prisoners.

The Koraput sub-jail contains accommodation for as many as 87 prisoners, is under the charge of the Assistant Surgeon and sends its returns to the Inspector-General of Prisons, instead of to the District Magistrate. It was originally enlarged in 1873–75 at a cost of Rs. 7,000 on the motion of Mr. H. G. Turner, then Divisional Officer at Koraput, who represented with much earnestness (what had long been well known) that hill men dreaded being sent to the Vizagapatam jail as much as ordinary criminals feared transportation across the seas, and also died in large numbers from the abrupt change of climate. When he became Agent, Mr. Turner proposed that the building should be reconstructed in pucka material and enlarged still further, and in 1892 estimates were sanctioned accordingly. The work was completed by 1896 at a cost of Rs. 15,000 and short-term convicts from the hills are now confined here instead of being sent down to Vizagapatam.

The same consideration for the hill convict which had prompted the enlargement of the Koraput sub-jail led to the construction of the jail at Párvatípur. Work was begun in 1864, but after Rs. 11,000 had been spent, the plan of the construction was condemned on the ground that the outer wall was too near the buildings inside and that the central space was insufficient for proper ventilation owing to much of it being blocked up by a warder's tower. Meanwhile, from 1873, the buildings were used for the sub-jail, sub-magistrate's cutcherry, and Divisional Officer's office. In 1875 it was ordered that the outer wall should be put back and the warder's tower removed; and in 1880 the jail was at last occupied. It was abandoned again fifteen years later on the grounds that good medical attendance was not procurable, that it was too far from the rail to be properly supervised, that the site was unhealthy and the jail infected with the dysenteric taint and that though it was intended for hill convicts it was so far from the hills that prisoners in it suffered just as much as those who were sent to Vizagapatam. The buildings are at present unoccupied except by some of the stores belonging to the Nágávali project referred to on p. 106 above.

The Vizagapatam District Jail was originally located in the ground floor of the building now occupied by the District Court. In 1839 an upper storey was added to this and the sub-court placed therein. In 1863 obstinate cholera broke out in the jail, the building was condemned and the prisoners were removed into sheds elsewhere. In 1864 the present jail was begun and it was finished in 1872; but it was then pronounced too small and was not occupied. In 1877 estimates for greatly enlarging it were sanctioned, and it was first used after the completion of the extensions in 1878–79. It is now to be rebuilt on the cellular system.

APPENDIX.

Laws in force in the Agency.

Year.	No.	Short title or subject.	Extent of application.
		(a) REGULATIONS OF THE MADRAS CODE.	
1802	XIX	Prohibition of Loans by Covenanted Civil Servants.	The whole.
	XXV	Revenue Settlement	Do.
	XXVI	Sale and sub-division of malguzari land.	Do.
1808	VII	Power to establish Martial Law ...	Do.
1819	II	State Prisoners	Do.
1822	IV	Rights of Cultivators	Do.
	VII	Appointment and removal of Native Officers.	Do.
	IX	Malversation: Collectors: Embezzlement: Appeals.	Do.
1828	VII	Subordinate and Assistant Collectors.	The whole except section 6.
1829	V	Hindu Wills	The whole.
1830	I	Sati	Do.
1831	V	Salt; Tobacco; Stamps	Do.
1832	III	Limitation under Regulation IX of 1822.	Do.
		(b) ACTS OF THE GOVERNOR OF FORT ST. GEORGE IN COUNCIL.	
1864	II	Recovery of arrears of Revenue ...	The whole.
	III	Abkári	In tracts to which Act I of 1886 has not been extended.
1865	VI	Official Seals	The whole.
	VII	Cess for Irrigation	Do.
	VIII	Recovery of Rent	Do.
1866	V	Labour Contracts with Natives ...	Do.
1867	I	General Clauses Act ...	Do.
1869	III	Empowering Revenue officers to summon witnesses.	Do.
1871	II	Explaining Madras Act VIII of 1865, section 11, clause 4.	Do.
1873	I	Wild Elephants	Do.
1876	I	Assessment of Land Revenue ...	Do.
1882	V	Forests	Do.
1884	III	Revenue arrears (amending Madras Act II of 1864).	Do.
	V	Local Boards	See G.O., No. 124 L., 4th February 1905.
1886	I	Abkári	See G.Os., Nos. 181, 4th March 1890; 659, 31st July 1897; 120, 15th February 1899; and 62, 30th January 1900, Revenue.

Laws in force in the Agency—cont.

Year.	No.	Short title or subject.	Extent of application.
		(b) ACTS OF THE GOVERNOR OF FORT ST. GEORGE IN COUNCIL—*cont.*	
1890	III	Local Boards: Rent Recovery (amending Madras Acts V of 1884 and VIII of 1865).	The whole.
1896	V	Repealing Madras Act III, 1882 ...	Do.
		(c) ACTS OF THE GOVERNOR-GENERAL IN COUNCIL.	
1837	IV	The Property in Land Act, 1837.	The whole.
	XXXVI	Criminal Jurisdiction, Madras ...	Do.
1838	XXV	The Wills Act, 1838	Do.
1839	VII	Sale of distrained property by Tahsildars.	Do.
	XXIV	Ganjám and Vizagapatam ..	Do.
	XXIX	The Dower Act, 1839	Do.
	XXX	The Inheritance Act, 1839 ...	Do.
	XXXII	The Interest Act, 1839	Do.
1841	XXIV	The Illusory Appointments and Infants Property Act, 1841.	Do.
1843	V	The Indian Slavery Act, 1843 ...	Do.
1847	XX	The Indian Copyright Act, 1847 ...	Do.
1850	XII	The Public Accountants' Defaults Act, 1850.	Do.
	XVIII	The Judicial Officers Protection Act, 1850.	Do.
	XIX	The Apprentices Act, 1850 ...	Do.
	XXI	The Caste Disabilities Removal Act, 1850.	Do.
	XXXIV	The State Prisoners Act, 1850 ...	Do.
	XXXVII	The Public Servants (Inquiries) Act, 1850.	Do.
1851	VIII	Indian Tolls Act, 1851	Do
1852	XXX	The Indian Naturalization Act, 1852.	Do.
1853	II	The Landholders' Public Charges and Duties Act, 1853.	Do.
	XX	The Legal Practitioners Act, 1853.	Do.
1854	XXXI	The Conveyance of Land Act, 1854	Do.
1855	XI	The Mesne Profits and Improvements Act, 1855.	Do.
	XII	The Legal Representatives Suits Act, 1855.	Do.
	XIII	The Indian Fatal Accidents Act, 1855.	Do.
	XXIII	The Mortgaged Estates Administration Act, 1855.	Do.
	XXIV	The Penal Servitude Act, 1855 ...	Do.
	XXVIII	The Usury Laws Repeal Act, 1855	Do.
1856	XI	The European Deserters Act, 1856.	Do.
	XV	The Hindu Widows' Remarriage Act, 1856.	Do.
1857	XI	The State Offences Act, 1857 ...	Do.

CHAP. XIII.
APPENDIX.

Laws in force in the Agency—cont.

Year.	No.	Short title or subject.	Extent of application.
		(c) ACTS OF THE GOVERNOR-GENERAL IN COUNCIL—*cont.*	
1857	XXV	The Forfeiture Act, 1857 ...	The whole.
	XXVII	The Madras University Act, 1857.	Do.
1858	III	The State Prisoners Act, 1858 ..	Do.
	XXXV	The Lunacy (District Courts) Act, 1858.	Do.
	XXXVI	The Indian Lunatic Asylums Act, 1858.	Do.
1859	IX	The Forfeiture Act, 1859	Do.
	XIII	Workman's Breach of Contract Act, 1859.	Do.
	XXIV	Police, Madras	Do.
1860	XXI	The Societies Registration Act, 1860.	Do.
	XLV	The Indian Penal Code	Do.
	XLVII	The Indian Universities (Degrees) Act, 1860.	Do.
1861	V	The Police Act, 1861	Sections 15, 15-A, 16, 30, 30-A, 31 and 32.
	XVI	The Stage Carriages Act, 1861 ...	The whole.
1862	III	The Government Seal Act, 1862 ...	Do.
1863	XVI	The Excise (Spirits) Act, 1863 ...	Do.
	XX	The Religious Endowments Act, 1863.	Do.
	XXXI	The Official Gazettes Act, 1863 ...	Do.
1864	III	The Foreigners Act, 1864	Do.
	VI	The Whipping Act, 1864 ...	Do.
	XV	Indian Tolls Act, 1864	Do.
	XVII	The Official Trustees Act, 1864 ...	Do.
1865	III	The Carriers Act, 1865	Do.
	X	The Indian Succession Act, 1865.	Do.
	XV	The Parsi Marriage and Divorce Act, 1865.	Do.
	XXI	The Parsi Intestate Succession Act, 1865.	Do.
1866	V	The Policies of Insurance (Marine and Fire) Assignment Act, 1866.	Do.
	XXI	The Native Converts Marriage Dissolution Act, 1866.	Do.
	XXVII	The Indian Trustee Act, 1866 ...	Do.
	XXVIII	The Trustees' and Mortgagees' Powers Act, 1866.	Do.
1867	XXV	The Press and Registration of Books Act, 1867.	Do.
1869	IV	The Indian Divorce Act	Do.
	V	The Indian Articles of War ..	Do.
	XV	The Prisoners Testimony Act, 1869.	Do.
	XX	The Indian Volunteers Act, 1869.	Do.
1870	VII	The Court-fees Act, 1870	Do.
	XXIII	The Indian Coinage Act, 1870 ...	Do.
1871	I	Cattle Trespass Act, 1871 ...	Do.
	V	The Prisoners Act, 1871 ..	Do.
	XXIII	The Pensions Act, 1871	Do.
	XXXI	The Indian Weights and Measures of Capacity Act, 1871.	Do.

Laws in force in the Agency—cont.

Year.	No.	Short title or subject.	Extent of application.
		(c) ACTS OF THE GOVERNOR-GENERAL IN COUNCIL—*cont.*	
1872	I	Indian Evidence Act, 1872	The whole.
	III	The Special Marriage Act, 1872 ..	Do.
	IX	The Indian Contract Act, 1872	Do.
	XV	The Indian Christian Marriage Act, 1872.	Do.
1873	V	The Government Savings Banks Act, 1875.	Do.
	X	The Indian Oaths Act, 1873 ...	Do.
	XIV	The Lunatic Soldiers' Property Act, 1873.	Do.
1874	II	The Administrator-Generals Act, 1874.	Do.
	III	The Married Women's Property Act, 1874.	Do.
	IV	The Foreign Recruiting Act, 1874.	Do.
	IX	European Vagrancy Act, 1874 .	Do.
	XIV	The Scheduled Districts Act, 1874.	Do.
	XV	The Laws Local Extent Act, 1874.	Do.
1882	XIV	The Civil Procedure Code ...	Sections 223 to 229.
1888	VI	The Debtors Act, 1888	Section 10, sub-section (1).
1898	V	The Code of Criminal Procedure, 1898.	The whole.

CHAPTER XIV.

LOCAL SELF-GOVERNMENT.

THE LOCAL BOARDS—The Unions—Finances of the boards. THE FOUR MUNICIPALITIES—Anakápalle municipality—Bimlipatam municipality—Vizianagram municipality—Improvements effected by it—Water-supply and drainage—Vizagapatam municipality—Its many undertakings—The water-works.

CHAP. XIV.
THE LOCAL BOARDS.

THE district contains four municipalities; namely, those at Anakápalle, Bimlipatam, Vizagapatam and Vizianagram: and certain portions of the Agency (namely, the part of the Golgonda hills above the Gháts, the Pálkonda hills and the Savara and Kuttiya Khond country in the Gunupur and Bissamkatak taluks) are excluded from the operation of the Local Boards Act. Elsewhere, local affairs are managed by the District Boards of Vizagapatam and Koraput and the four taluk boards working under the former. The Koraput District Board has jurisdiction over all the Jeypore zamindari except the portions of it which lie in the taluks of Párvatípur, Ráyagada, Bissamkatak and Gunupur, and manages matters therein without the intervention of any taluk boards. It began work only on the 1st April 1905, but proposals to extend the Local Boards Act to parts at least of the Agency, so as to compel them to contribute something towards the large and increasing expenditure on local needs which is annually incurred within them, have been made at intervals ever since 1875. The Vizagapatam District Board controls affairs in the rest of the district except the municipalities and the excluded areas already mentioned. The charges of the four taluk boards under it—those of Narasapatam, Párvatípur, Vizagapatam and Vizianagram—correspond (excepting, again, these excluded areas) with the tracts comprised in the revenue divisions of these names already set out on p. 2.

The Unions.

The seventeen large villages noted in the margin have been constituted unions. As elsewhere, the chief item in their income is the house-tax, which is levied at half rates in Gunupur and Jeypore, but on the maximum scale elsewhere. The average

Narasapatam taluk board.
Chódavaram
Kasimkóta
Mádgole
Narasapatam
Yellamanchili

Párvatípur taluk board.
Bobbili
Gunupur
Párvatípur
Sálúr

Vizagapatam taluk board.
Srungavarapukóta
Jámi

Vizianagram taluk board.
Chípurupalle
Gajapatinagaram
Pálkonda
Pondúru
Rázám

Koraput district board.
Jeypore

assessment per house was $13\frac{1}{4}$ annas in 1903–04, or an anna less than the average for the Presidency in that year.

Finances of the boards.

The separate Appendix to this volume gives figures of the receipts and expenditure of the Vizagapatam District Board and the taluk boards subordinate thereto. As usual, the land-cess, which is collected at the rate of one anna in the rupee of the land assessment, is the chief source of income. It is followed by the receipts from tolls, which are collected at fourteen gates at half the maximum rates. The chief heads of expenditure, as usual, are the upkeep of the roads and of the medical and educational institutions. These have already been referred to in Chapters VII, IX and X, respectively.

THE FOUR MUNICIPALITIES.

Besides the four towns already mentioned, Pálkonda was also once constituted a municipality. This was effected in 1869, at the instance of the renters of the taluk, Messrs. Arbuthnot & Co. The next year a squabble occurred as to who should be vice-president, and the council resigned in a body. Three years later, the Collector reported that the secretary was incapable, that none of the inhabitants took the slightest interest in the municipality or desired its continuance, and that its funds were derived from an illegitimate source and were improperly spent. Government accordingly abolished the institution. Proposals to turn Bobbili and Párvatípur into municipalities have been twice (in 1884 and 1902) discussed and twice rejected.

Anakápalle municipality.

Anakápalle was constituted a municipal town in 1877 at the suggestion of the Collector. In December 1878 the same officer wrote to Government saying that a cyclone and flood had swept away three-quarters of the houses (and consequently, three parts of the council's income) and suggesting that the municipality should be abolished accordingly. Government, however, refused to do so, urging that times of calamity were just the occasions when councils could be of use. The council was given the power of electing its own chairman in 1885, but not until 1897 was it allowed the privilege of electing a proportion (four) of its thirteen councillors. The town is built in a cramped site among low-lying paddy-fields and is consequently difficult to keep clean, and the municipal income is small. The council has consequently effected little beyond the usual routine duties. It has constructed itself an office from borrowed money; started a small sewage farm; and established, with financial profit, a suburb to the north-west of the town (called Woodpéta after the then Divisional Officer) which affords some relief to the overcrowding which exists.

CHAP. XIV.
THE FOUR MUNICIPALITIES.

Bimlipatam municipality.

Bimlipatam has a much longer experience of local self-government, having established in 1861 a voluntary association, as it was termed, under Act XXVI of 1850, an enactment which permitted towns to voluntarily tax themselves for their own improvement and provided for the free grant by Government of a sum equal to the amount so raised. This association worked undisputed good. Its income amounted to about Rs. 4,000 and was mainly derived from a small tax on carts entering the town. The Government contribution brought the receipts to about Rs. 8,000.

In 1866 the association was replaced by a council established under the Towns Improvement Act of the preceding year, and this has since continued in existence under the successive municipal Acts which have since been passed. In the forty years since it originated, there have been but four changes among its chairmen; and this fact and the natural advantages of the place in the way of water-supply and drainage—it is situated on the side of a hill facing the sea and contains numerous good wells—have resulted in the town becoming clean and tidy beyond the normal. Four of the twelve councillors have been elected since 1900 and since 1885 the chairman has been chosen by the council.

Vizianagram municipality.

In Vizianagram a municipal association was founded at about the same time as in Bimlipatam. The average receipts (derived principally from a cart-tax) were about Rs. 450, and Government contributed an equal amount. In November 1866 a council was established under the Towns Improvement Act. In 1888 the rate-payers were permitted to elect twelve out of the sixteen councillors and the council chooses its own chairman. Matters in the cantonment, which has now recently ceased to exist, were separately managed by the military authorities.

Improvements effected by it.

Public improvements in Vizianagram have been due chiefly to the Rája and his predecessors and the members of their family, and the municipal council has effected little of note. The former have given the town the college, Sanskrit school, hospital and gosha hospital referred to in Chapters X and IX respectively, and also the large series of market stalls built in 1876 at a cost of half a lakh and known as the Prince of Wales' Market in commemoration of the present King-Emperor's visit to India in 1875.

Besides carrying on the usual routine duties, the municipality built, in 1885, the clock-tower in the bazaar-street, an octagonal building 68 feet high which cost, with its clock, Rs. 5,400;

erected its present office, at a cost of Rs. 7,500, in 1904; and maintains a dispensary in a rented building, a small sewage farm and a Victoria Jubilee Park. The last was brought into being chiefly by the enterprise of Rai Bahádur P. Jagannátha Rázu, Díwán to the then Mahárája and chairman of the council for some thirty years. In 1887 about 50 acres of land in the town (which were then part swamp, part paddy-fields and part general rubbish heap) were obtained from the Mahárája in exchange for other land elsewhere and converted into a garden under expert advice at a cost of Rs. 8,000. It lies in the centre of the town, is much resorted to, and is neatly kept up; and thus is in great contrast to the neglected wastes usually associated with the name Jubilee Park.

Water-supply and drainage.

The town has neither a regular water-supply nor any proper drainage. Water is obtained from wells and tanks, the principal of the latter being the Ayyakonéru and Buchanna's tank. The chief of such drains as there are discharge into the Pedda Cheruvu, the agricultural tank which (see p. 336) lies between the town and the cantonment. About 1888 the late Mahárája employed an engineer from England, Mr. Beckett, to draw up a water-supply scheme, but this gentleman went off with all the plans of the project he elaborated and no particulars of it survive except that it contemplated bringing water nearly 20 miles from the Mentáda river and was estimated to cost five lakhs. In 1897 two other suggestions were examined. Mr. Willock proposed to obtain a supply from the river at Nellimarla, while Dr. King favoured a scheme depending on a perennial stream called the Ottaigedda. The latter involved digging a trench 1,700 feet in length parallel to, and about 100 yards distant from, the gedda at a point about a mile and a half from the town; pumping the water so obtained to a reservoir on an adjoining hill and thence supplying the town by gravitation. The cost was put at Rs. 2·82 lakhs, and as the late Mahárája had expressed his willingness to contribute 1½ lakhs it was considered to be within the means of the town and ordered to lie over until the present Rája should attain his majority in August 1904. No further steps have yet been taken.

In 1888 a drainage scheme, estimated to cost Rs. 73,000, was drawn up by a Mr. Gauge of Calcutta; but it did not find acceptance locally, and in any case the water-supply will take precedence of it.

Vizagapatam municipality.

Vizagapatam began its career of self-government as early as 1858 by starting the most successful of the few municipal

CHAP. XIV. THE FOUR MUNICIPALITIES.

associations which were founded in this Presidency under the Act of 1850 already mentioned. This body derived its income chiefly from a tax on houses and carts and from ferry fees; and these eventually brought in as much as Rs. 10,500 a year, to which Government added a contribution of an equal amount. The association was nothing if not ambitious, and in its very first year of office it turned its attention to the widening and lighting of the streets, the establishment of markets, and even to schemes of drainage and water-supply. Its actual achievements included 'a commodious Municipal Hall' with which were connected 'a library, reading room and a young men's literary institution.' It continually emphasized the purely voluntary nature of the payments made to it, and the town obtained in consequence much credit for its public spirit; but the reports add naively that people who did not pay the house-tax were warned that they would be left to clean their own premises and the street in front thereof, and that they were liable to fine by the police if this duty was neglected. In 1866 a municipal council under the Act of 1865 was constituted. The council now chooses its own chairman, and three-fourths of its members are elected by the rate-payers. The incidence of taxation (excluding tolls) per head of the population is twice as heavy as in any other municipality in the district, and much above the average for the whole Presidency.

Its many undertakings.

The council has conferred many permanent benefits upon the town. It subscribed half the cost of the pontoon bridge which (see p. 135) for many years spanned the backwater; it now manages the Turner Chattram and the Bobbili Town Hall referred to on pp. 144 and 331; in 1899 it removed the fishermen's village which formerly occupied the site of this latter and the surrounding land, first across the backwater at a cost of Rs. 36,000, and then, when the fishermen began dying there with rapidity, to another part of the town; it has started two profitable sewage farms, one near Ross Hill and the other just west of the main bazaar street on land reclaimed gradually from the swamp there by operations begun as far back as 1872; it has made the beach road next the sea between Waltair and Vizagapatam, which was begun as long ago as 1864–65 and was carried on from Scandal Point to the Judge's bungalow at a cost of Rs 15,000 by the Mahárája of Vizianagram in 1896; with Rs. 10,000 contributed by Lady Gajapati Rao it has recently cleared of prickly-pear the old native infantry lines and driven a road from the Mahéránipéta so formed to the beach road; with Rs. 15,000 presented by the

Rája of Kurupám it has purchased a site for an 'Edward VII Coronation Market;' and lastly it has provided the town with a proper water-supply.

The water-works.

This supply depends upon the perennial stream known as the Hanumanta Vanka, which rises in the hills to the west of the town not far from the Simháchalam temple and flows down a deep valley about five miles long into Lawson's Bay. The stream has been dammed up to form a reservoir with a catchment area of six square miles and a capacity of 25 million cubic feet, and from this the water is led 5½ miles through a ten-inch iron main to a service reservoir near the jail, whence it is distributed in the usual way to stand-pipes. The scheme does not command Waltair, which gets its water from wells. The works cost 4½ lakhs, of which Government granted one half and lent the other on the terms then usual, were carried out by the Public Works department, and were handed over to the council in May 1903.

CHAPTER XV.

GAZETTEER.

ANAKÁPALLE TALUK—Anakápalle—Kasimkóta—Sankaram. BIMLIPATAM TALUK—Bimlipatam—Padmanábham—Potnúru—Santapilly. BISSAMKATAK TALUK—Bissamkatak. BOBBILI TALUK—Bobbili. CHÍPURUPALLE TALUK—Chípurupalle — Garugubilli— Gujarátipéta — Shérmuhammadpuram. GAJAPATINAGARAM TALUK—Andra—Gajapatinagaram — Jayati— Márupilli— Régulavalasa. GOLGONDA TALUK—Balighattam—Gúdem— Krishnadévipet—Lótugedda—Narasapatam—Uratla —Vajragada. GUNUPUR TALUK—Gudári—Gunupur — Jagamanda. JEYPORE TALUK — Guptésvara Cave—Jeypore—Kótapád. KORAPUT TALUK—Koraput. MALKANAGIRI TALUK—Kondakambéru—Malkanagiri—Mótu. NAURANGPUR TALUK—Naurangpur—Pappadahandi. PÁDWA TALUK—Borra Cave—Matsya gundam. PÁLKONDA TALUK—Pálkonda—Rázám—Siripuram—Víraghattam. PÁRVATÍPUR TALUK—Addápusila—Kurupám—Mérangi—Párvatípur—Sangamvalasa. POTTANGI TALUK—Nandapuram — Pottangi. RÁYAGADA TALUK—Páyakapád —Ráyagada—Singapur. SÁLÚR TALUK—Korravanivalasa—Páchipenta—Sálúr. SARVASIDDHI TALUK—Dimila — Gópálapatnam—Nakkapalli — Panchadhárala—Páyakaraopéta — Pentakóta — Púdimadaka — Ráyavaram — Sarvasiddhi—Uppalam—Vátáda—Yellamanchili. SRUNGAVARAPUKÓTA TALUK—Dharmávaram — Jámi — Kásipuram—Srungavarapukóta. VÍRAVILLI TALUK—Chódavaram—Mádgole. VIZAGAPATAM TALUK—Simháchalam—Vizagapatam. VIZIANAGRAM TALUK—Rámatírtham—Vizianagram.

ANAKÁPALLE TALUK.

CHAP. XV. ANAKÁPALLE.

ANAKÁPALLE taluk lies next south of Vizagapatam, on the coast of the Bay. Near the sea it includes low-lying and swampy ground; but a little further inland rises a disconnected line of the red hills characteristic of the plains of this district; then follows a plain of unusually rich land; while on the north a larger line of the red hills separates the taluk from Víravilli. Much of the tract of rich land is watered from the Sárada channels and grows excellent sugar-cane, other parts of it are dotted with wells and the patches of garden crop they irrigate, and the prevailing tree throughout the whole is the palmyra, which stands in rows along the boundaries of all the fields and grows in clumps in every hollow.

The whole of the taluk is zamindari land. It contains three places of interest, some account of which follows:—

Anakápalle: A municipality of 18,539 inhabitants lying on the trunk road and the Madras railway, 21 miles west of Vizagapatam in the midst of a level expanse of rich wet land watered by the Sárada, which river runs close by the town and is crossed by both the road and railway bridges. The place is badly-built and overcrowded, but is reputed to be extremely healthy and is a favourite place of residence with natives of the district. Its municipality is referred to in Chapter XIV. It contains a hospital, a school, a travellers' bungalow constructed on a highly original plan (opposite which is the much revered tomb of a woman who committed sati), a dharmasála and, to the south, the remains of a fort called after the famous Páyaka Rao mentioned in the account of Páyakaraopéta on p. 312 below. In this last are shrines to Bhógésvara and to the goddess Núkálamma, at the latter of which a largely-attended festival and buffalo sacrifice occur on each Telugu New Year's Day.

Anakápalle is known for its brass and iron vessels, made by Kancharis; for its cotton cloths and sheeting woven by Déván-gas, the latter of which are called *nágabandham* from their diamond patterns and are popular in the Gódávari district; for the sugar-cane growing conducted by those industrious and enterprising agriculturists, the Gavaras; for its large market on Sundays; and as being the head-quarters of the principal estate of the rich and influential family of landed proprietors known as the Godé family, who pay more peshkash to Government than any one in the district except the Rája of Vizianagram.

The founder of this family, whose members say that they are Perike or Puragiri Kshatriyas by caste, was Godé Jagga Rao, who was dubash (agent and interpreter) to Mr. Andrews, the Chief at Masulipatam, and came with him to Vizagapatam when (see p. 35) he became the first Chief of the latter district. He had two sons, Súrya Prakása Rao and Súrya Náráyana Rao. The former of these was a naturalist and botanist of repute (rare qualifications among men of his station in those days) and laid out the excellent garden at Anakápalle in which the Godé bun-galow now stands. Dr. Benza, in his notes of his journey through the Northern Circars with the then Governor, Sir Frederick Adam, in 1835, says of him that 'he speaks and writes the English language uncommonly well, and his pronunciation evinces hardly any foreign accent. He disregards the show and glitter, the suite of attendants, the umbrella-carriers, and other indispensable appendages of his countrymen of rank correspond-ing to his own; and wears none of their ornaments. He came

CHAP. XV. ANAKÁPALLE.

to visit the Governor on a superb Arabian horse, and was introduced without a single attendant. We accompanied him on his return to Anakápalle, and he conducted us to his garden, which was laid out in a most beautiful style, rich with indigenous and exotic plants and trees.' He also assisted in the capture of the notorious rebel Páyaka Rao (p. 313) in 1834. He had no son. His younger daughter married M.R.Ry. G. L. Narasinga Rao.

Jagga Rao's second son, Súrya Náráyana Rao, had two sons named respectively Venkata Jagga Rao and Náráyana Gajapati Rao. In those days there were few colleges at which a boy could be given an English education, and the alternative was a private tutor. Venkata Jagga Rao was accordingly sent all the way to Madras to be under the tuition of Mr. T. G. Taylor, F.R.S., then Government Astronomer. There he imbibed the keenest interest in astronomy (again a rare accomplishment in men of his position), writing, to the now defunct *Madras Journal of Literature and Science*, papers on points connected with that science and being on one occasion recommended to act for Mr. Taylor. On his return to Vizagapatam he built, in 1841, in the family residence there, Dábá Gardens, the well-equipped observatory which still goes by his name and is referred to in the account of Vizagapatam below (p. 332). He died in 1856 at the early age of 39 without male issue. His only daughter married M.R.Ry. Ankitam Venkata Narasinga Rao, a Deputy Collector (who continued and extended the meteorological observations which were being carried on at the observatory and became an F.R.A.S. and F.R.G.S.), and their son, M.R.Ry. A. V. Jagga Rao, who inherits a taste for science, is now in enjoyment of their share of the family property, including Dábá Gardens.

Súrya Náráyana Rao's second son, Náráyana Gajapati Rao, was born in December 1828; educated at the Hindu College, Calcutta; succeeded to his share of his father's property in 1853; took a prominent part in the founding of what is now the Mrs. A. V. Narasinga Rao College, in the erection of the civil hospital in Vizagapatam and in numerous other public benefactions; was a member of the Legislative Council for sixteen years from 1868; and was granted the title of Rája in 1881, a C.I.E. in 1892, the title of Mahárája in 1898, and a K.C.I.E. in 1903. He died in the same year and his widow, the Mahárání Lady Gajapati Rao (who was his cousin and the adoptive daughter of M.R.Ry. G. L. Narasinga Rao above referred to) survives him. He was the last of the family in the direct line. Of his two daughters one married into the Wadhwán family of the Bombay Presidency and now resides at Súrya Bágh, Vizagapatam, while the other (since deceased) married the Rája of Kurupám in this district. There thus now survive two chief representatives of the various branches of the family; namely, M.R.Ry. A. V. Jagga Rao and the Mahárání Gajapati Rao.

The property of the Godé family includes (besides land in the Gódávari and Ganjám districts) the nine estates of Anakápalle, Bharinikam and Munagapáka in Anakápalle taluk; Godicherla, Koruprólu, Nakkapalli and Srírámpuram in Sarvasiddhi; and Kuppili and Shérmuhammadpuram in Chípurupalle. Of these, all but Bharinikam and Koruprólu (which were subsequently carved out of other properties) were estates which were formed out of the havíli land and sold in auction at a fixed assessment in 1802. Except Shérmuhammadpuram, which was bought by Godé Jagga Rao himself, all the others were originally purchased by the Rája of Vizianagram. Anakápalle was sold by him to Godé Súrya Prakása Rao in 1810; Munagapáka was bought by the same Prakása Rao in 1830; Godicherla and Srírámpuram were purchased in 1818 by Súrya Náráyana Rao, but the latter resold Srírámpuram again and after changing hands several times it was eventually bought by Súrya Prakása Rao in 1835; Nakkapalli was sold for arrears of revenue in 1812 in three portions; namely, Nakkapalli, Koruprólu and Pedda Gummalúru, the first of which was eventually, in 1818, bought by Súrya Náráyana Rao; and Kuppili, after passing through several hands, was purchased by the same gentleman in 1836. Of the remaining two properties, Bharinikam consists of one village which originally belonged to the Chípurupalle estate but became separated from it in the course of sales for arrears and was bought by Súrya Prakása Rao in 1822; while Koruprólu, which (as has been seen) was a part of Nakkapalli, was purchased by the same gentleman in 1820. The third of the three subdivisions of Nakkapalli, the village of Pedda Gummalúru, changed hands, it may here be noted, several times until in 1863 the S. S. Prakása Rao and Mungamuri families, whose descendants still own it, acquired it jointly.

When Súrya Náráyana Rao died in 1853, his share of the property was divided between his two sons. Of the above nine estates, five (Anakápalle, Bharinikam, Munagapáka, Godicherla and Srírámpuram) are now in the possession of Mahárání Lady Gajapati Rao; two (Koruprólu and Nakkapalli) were bequeathed for life to her step-daughter, the Ráni Sáheb of Wadhwán, by the

CHAP. XV. ANAKÁPALLE.

will of Mahárája Sir Gajapati Rao executed in August 1896; one (Kuppili) was similarly bequeathed to the three children of his second daughter, wife of the Rája of Kurupám, named respectively V. Súrya Náráyana Rázu, V. N. Gajapati Rázu, and V. J. Ratnayamma, who now reside at Waltair; while the last of the estates (Shérmuhammadpuram) is the property of M.R.Ry. A. V. Jagga Rao.

The largest of these properties, as has been said, is Anakápalle. It comprises 22 villages, much of the land in which is watered by three channels from the Sárada which are supplied from two anicuts and equipped with head-sluices.

Kasimkóta: A crowded and untidy union of 7,450 inhabitants, lying amid level cultivation 3½ miles south-west of Anakápalle, just off the trunk road and on the bank of the Sárada river. Contains a railway-station. No traces survive of the fort after which it is named. During the Muhammadans' rule of the country it was 'ye chiefest Fort in the Country' and the head-quarters of a command in the Chicacole Circar (it still contains the descendants of the many Musalmans who received inam lands in those days); and it continued to be the chief town of a division for some time after the British acquired the district in 1768, and the doings of its Rája frequently figure in the old correspondence. Col. Forde's troops here joined those of Vizianagram previous to their march southwards against the French at Rajahmundry and Masulipatam in 1758 (p. 33). Glass bangles and coarse white cloths are made in the village.

The place is the residence of the Bráhman owner of the proprietary estates of Kasimkóta and Mélupáka, the latter of which lies in Sarvasiddhi taluk. These were two of the properties which were formed in 1802 out of the havíli lands and put up to auction at a permanent assessment. Mr. Carmichael says that they were then bought by the Rája of Vizianagram for Rs. 4,343 and Rs. 5,265, respectively; that two years later, the Rája sold them to Kárumanchi Venkatáchalam, at whose death in 1837 they passed to his maternal grandson, Mantripragada Venkata Rao; that on the latter's demise in 1845 his brother Chiranjívi Rao and his posthumous son Venkatáchalam jointly succeeded and, being minors, were put under the Court of Wards; and that the former died in 1851, while the latter attained his majority in 1863 and died in May 1865 leaving a minor widow, Rámayamma, and an infant daughter Mahálakshmamma. The former was made a ward of court until her majority in 1867, and died in

1883. The latter then succeeded to the estate; but she died in 1892 and the property passed to her minor son, the present proprietor, Márella Chinna Venkatáchalam. The estates were at first managed by the minor's father and uncle, but in 1896 were placed under the care of the Court of Wards until the minor attained his majority in October 1903.

The Rámayamma mentioned above purchased in 1883 (from her *stridhanam* property, she said) the proprietary estate of Mámidiváda in the Sarvasiddhi taluk, which consists (see p. 310) of one village subdivided off from the Chípurupalle estate. Her daughter Mahálakshmamma, the late proprietrix of Kasimkóta and Mélupáka, inherited this property and, at her wish, it was assigned to her two minor daughters, Nedunúri Ráma Lakshmamma and Vallúri Chinna Ammáyi. Their brother, the present proprietor of Kasimkóta and Mélupáka, has been appointed their guardian under section 59 of Act I of 1902.

Sankaram: A village of 441 inhabitants about 1½ miles north by east of the Anakápalle travellers' bungalow. In the fields belonging to it are two low, contiguous, rocky hills, running east and west, which are locally known as the Bojjanakonda and contain some of the most remarkable Buddhist remains in the Presidency. The more western of these hills is formed of a series of rock strata which have been thrust over into a vertical position, and along its crest these crop out in four or five low, parallel, walls of rock which have weathered into parallel rows of pinnacles. Each of these pinnacles, some scores in number and of all sizes, has been fashioned into a Buddhist stúpa of the usual pattern. The villagers, not recognizing what they are, call them the *Kótilingam*, or 'crore of lingams'. In three places the strata have compacted to form a solid mass of rock on the crest of the hill, and this has been cut, with immense labour, into three huge stúpas, the biggest of which is about 30 ft. in diameter and of corresponding height. On the southern side, these are weathered out of all shape, but on the north they are almost as sharp as the day they were cut. The villagers call them 'the heaps of grain.' To make these three great stúpas, cuttings have been driven right through the solid rock of the hill, and in the case of the largest of the three the excavation is some 6 feet wide and 20 deep. It contains, at the bottom, a porch about 27 feet long by 5 wide and 6 feet in height, also excavated in the solid rock, out of which opens a small, plain, shrine some 7 feet square.

CHAP. XV. ANAKÁPALLE.

But it is on the eastern of the two hills that the more remarkable of the remains are situated. Every rock pinnacle on this has similarly been carved into the semblance of a stúpa, and in a considerable outcrop of black, weather-beaten rock on its western face is a two-storeyed rock-cut temple, in and about which are numerous Buddhist sculptures. This outcrop stands perhaps 75 ft. above the surrounding fields and is reached by an irregular flight of broken steps. The face of it has been cut back to give a vertical façade to the shrine; and thus a small, level, rock-terrace has been formed. Out of the back of this opens the lower of the two chambers of which the temple consists. Above the entrance to it is sculptured a small figure sitting, with legs crossed, in the usual contemplative attitude, while on one side is a life-size, standing, nude Buddhist figure. The chamber itself is excavated out of the solid rock and is 30 ft. square and 8 ft. high. It was originally supported on 16 roughly cut pillars about 2 feet square, standing in four rows of four each, and each equidistant from the next. Five of them have disappeared, probably owing to fires having been lit round them, and the two nearest the entrance bear rudely sculptured figures about four feet in height. In the centre of the chamber stands a stúpa, about four feet high and almost shapeless from age.

Immediately above this chamber, excavated in the same outcrop of rock, is a smaller shrine. Over the entrance to this, in a large niche, is sculptured a seated Buddhist figure, cut in high relief. It is about five feet high and on either side of it is a standing figure, while two smaller ones hover about its head. On one side of the entrance is a second similar figure, and on the other is a third, rather smaller. All three of these have been whitewashed, and they are conspicuous for a great distance across the surrounding fields.

Passing through this entrance (immediately above, and on either side of, which are small seated figures) one reaches a rectangular chamber about 12 ft. by 4 ft. and 7 ft. high, on the walls of which are sculptured in relief two large seated images, two smaller ones, and a number of other figures. All of these are much dilapidated, the rock being of a soft variety and very coarse texture. Out of this chamber opens an inner shrine about 9 ft. by 5, on the back wall of which is carved a seated Buddhist figure 5 ft. in height and 18 inches in relief, behind which rises a cobra with hood expanded, while on the two side walls are two standing images of about the same size flanked by kneeling male or female figures in an attitude of adoration, and other lesser carvings—among them more stúpas. These figures are again much worn. They all exhibit the lengthened ear lobes and the closely curled hair which is characteristic of such images. Limits of space forbid any more detailed account of all these sculptures, and in any case no description would be very intelligible without the aid of drawings.

On the side of the hill a little above this upper chamber is a square pillar, 7 feet high, which is a conspicuous object from the fields below, and not far from it is a small detached cell about 18 ft. by 6 ft. and 7 ft. high, supported on four pillars ornamented with the conventional lotus and containing yet another seated Buddhist figure and certain other images.

Above all these, on the summit of the hill, are a large quantity of bricks, some in position and some scattered in every direction among the grass. It may perhaps be conjectured that these are the remains of a stúpa which was built above the rock-cut temples.

There appear to be no inscriptions on any part of these interesting remains.

At the Pongal feast a large gathering of some thousands of Hindus takes place at the foot of these two hills. Sundry religious ceremonies are performed and the village cattle are taken up to the lower of the two chambers above described and driven eight times round the stúpa in the centre of it. The crowd then disperses and the shrines are left to the bats and owls for another year. Similar rites are performed at other caves in this district.

At this feast, the curious stone image standing in the hollow between the two hills also comes in for some attention. This represents a woman surrounded by a border made up of tiny human figures and is locally declared to be the image of one Erinamma, who used to kidnap children and eat them. Every woman who comes to the Pongal feast hurls a stone at her, and she is now all but buried beneath the pile so formed.

BIMLIPATAM TALUK.

CHAP. XV. BIMLIPATAM.

BIMLIPATAM taluk lies on the coast next north of Vizagapatam. In appearance it resembles the rest of the low country of the district, the soil being red, palmyras the commonest trees, and low hills frequent. The chief places of interest in it are the following :—

Bimlipatam, the head-quarters of the deputy tahsildar and of an ámín of the Vizianagram zamindari, is a municipality of 10,212 inhabitants and the busiest sea-port in the district. The town is most picturesquely situated at the mouth of the Chittivalasa river, close under the big laterite-topped Narasimha hill, which is formed of deep-red soil scored with brown and purple streaks of rock and is well known to mariners from the prominent Narasimha temple half way up it.

Bimlipatam first came into notice as a settlement of the Dutch, who built a fort and factory here in the seventeenth century. The early records of the English factory at Vizagapatam are full of references to 'our neighbours the Dutch.'

The place played no prominent part in history. According to paragraphs 12 and 13 of Hodgson's *Short description of the Dutch Settlements* in the Madras records,[1] it was 'represented to be held under Fermans granted by the Nizam and confirmed by the Mogul or Emperor of Delhi, bearing various dates from A.D. 1628 to A.D. 1713, and by a Cowle granted by Hajee Housson in A.D. 1734 and A.D. 1752 by Jaffur Ally Khan. The two last mentioned persons were Naibs or deputies of the Nizam in the Circars. The Dutch are stated to have first occupied these factories about the year A.D. 1628.' In 1754, the factory was burnt by the Maráthas under Ragoji Bhonsla (see p. 31) and robbed of several chests of treasure. In the same year, say other old records, the then zamindar of Vizianagram granted pattas to the Dutch renewing permission formerly given to build a fort, possess a washing-green for bleaching cloth and establish a mint. Hodgson's report says that he is satisfied with the evidence

[1] See Mr. A. Rea's *Monumental Remains of the Dutch East India Co.*, Madras, 1897.

showing that the Dutch did actually coin copper there, but states that no territorial jurisdiction was attached to the factory (the only appendages to which were three washing-greens) and that it was 'merely a commercial factory or lodge with certain privileges.' On the outbreak in 1781 of the war between the English and the Dutch it (with the rest of the latter's possessions in India) was seized by the English East India Company and, under orders received from England, was destroyed. In accordance with the peace of 1784, it was restored in 1785. Ten years later war again broke out between the two powers and the place surrendered to the English. In 1819 it was restored by Mr. John Smith, the Collector, to the representative of the Netherlands Government in consequence of the convention of the allied powers in 1814; and was held by the Dutch until 1st June 1825, when, under the operation of the treaty of March 1824 between England and Holland, it was made over (with the other Dutch possessions in India) to the East India Company. The Collector, Mr. Robert Bayard, gave a receipt for 'the ruins of the Fort and Factory, with three bleaching grounds of Bimlipatam, with the Boundaries, according to the limits thereof.' Since then the place has been British territory and Government property. The three washing-greens (which are still known locally as *Valanda bhúmulu*, or 'the Hollanders' lands') have been rented since 1826 to the Rájas of Vizianagram, who pay Rs. 50 annually for them.

Little now remains of the fort except its flagstaff bastion, facing the sea, on which the existing flagstaff stands, and some massive brick-work (in the Mála quarter of the town, about 50 yards east of the clock-tower) which was perhaps once a magazine. The land between these is still known as *Kóta dibba*, or 'the fort mound.' An old plan of 1819 shows that the fort was then a rectangular construction, about 135 yards from east to west and 145 from north to south, containing a circular bastion at each corner and the ruins of certain 'ammunition godowns' and of the mint.

Some of the Dutch who manned this little outpost left their bones in the half-forgotten cemetery which lies hidden away among the plantain gardens and palm groves of Kummaripálem, near the 'Hollanders' lands' and about half a mile off the fort, in the angle formed by the two roads running to Vizianagram and Vizagapatam. This contains thirteen tombstones, made of the local garnetiferous gneiss, bearing Dutch inscriptions and coats-of-arms and ranging in date from 1661 (the oldest tomb in the Northern Circars) to 1720. In the other cemetery on the beach,

CHAP. XV. IMLIPATAM.

between the flagstaff and the sea, are several more Dutch tombs of later date.

After the Dutch finally relinquished the place it rapidly decayed, and up to 1846 it was 'a miserable fishing village.' About that time, Messrs. Arbuthnot & Co., having obtained (see p. 289) the lease of the Pálkonda estate, built a factory at Chittivalasa, about three miles to the north, for making jaggery from sugar-cane, the cultivation of which they set themselves to develop. This factory at one time turned out 6,000 tons of sugar annually. At about the same period the firm set on foot an export business in local produce, principally oil-seeds. The factory was afterwards (in 1867) converted into a mill for spinning and weaving by steam the local 'jute' referred to on p. 101. It is the only jute mill in the Presidency and is now a flourishing concern belonging to Arbuthnot's Industrials, Ltd., containing 98 looms (50 more are being added) and over 2,000 spindles, employing 800 hands, and turning out about 26 lakhs of gunny bags annually.

The export trade originated by Messrs. Arbuthnot & Co. quickly attracted other European firms, and the town took a fresh lease of life. The ruins of the residences erected by the merchants both during this period and at the end of the eighteenth century when the export of the hand-woven fabrics of the place was still a profitable business, stand along the road running to Chittivalasa, and are still known by their names. Dawson Méda, Lawson Méda and 'Malkan' (Malcolm) Méda are instances, and the last of these is now the property of the Vizianagram estate and is kept up as a halting-place. That estate also owns a large house (now much out of repair) near the clock-tower. The most favourite bungalows at present are those facing the sea, alongside the flagstaff bastion and the Club.

The European community thus established did much for the town. They supported the voluntary municipal association started in 1861 and referred to on p. 214 above and organized subscriptions for a hospital, school and church. This last was opened for worship in November 1863 and consecrated by the Bishop of Madras in the following March. The people of the place subscribed Rs. 3,011 towards the cost of the building and Government gave a similar sum on condition that it was handed over to them. The voluntary association is also responsible for the clock-tower already mentioned, a quaint erection with Gothic embellishments and buttresses, resembling the belfry of an English village church, which was put up to carry a clock presented to the community by one of its members, Mr. John Young.

By 1868 the total value of the imports and exports, including treasure, had risen to nearly 43 lakhs. But thirty-five years later, in 1902--03, the figure was still about the same, and the town cannot now be said to be in a flourishing condition. In the thirty years between the census of 1871 and that of 1901 its population only increased by 1,468 persons and the advance was relatively smaller than in any other town in the district except Rázám. The imports consist chiefly of cotton twist and piece-goods and the exports (to give them in order of value) of gingelly seed (sent mainly to Marseilles), other seeds, tanned hides and skins, raw and manufactured jute (sent to Dundee and Hamburg, chiefly), gingelly oil, and the produce of the neighbouring hill-tracts, such as myrabolams, horns, etc. The town owes its present importance to the fact that it is the nearest port to Vizianagram through which all the hill-produce comes, but when the railway runs from the hills to Vizagapatam it will probably dwindle rapidly. Seven European firms have export agencies in the place at present, and there are two steam, and two hand, presses for baling the raw jute of the district. The Clan Line steamers call regularly and the Bank of Madras has a branch in the town. The new port light erected in 1903 consists of a white dioptric light of the fourth order of 750 candle-power flashing four times a minute, and is visible eleven miles out at sea in clear weather.

The port consists of the mouth of the Chittivalasa river, which is almost silted up for much of the year but has been known to be scoured out to a depth of 16 ft., and a bight or bay protected on the south by a hill which runs a short distance out from the line of the coast and terminates seawards in a reef of rocks. The anchorage is in five fathoms about half a mile from the shore and cargo is landed and shipped by means of masúla boats.

Mr. W. Parkes, an expert sent by Government in 1882 to report on the capabilities of the port, gave it as his opinion that the existence of the river mouth so close to it was a great objection to the undertaking of any permanent works for the protection of the anchorage. He said [1]—

'The river is insignificant at ordinary times, but in floods it fills the eleven arches of a bridge, each 30 feet span and 15 feet high, with a torrent of silt-laden water. The solid matter thus carried to the sea is dispersed by the waves and currents over a large area, so that its effects are imperceptible upon the coast; but if those dispersing forces were interfered with, which it is the very object of a

[1] G.O., No. 1718 W., Public Works, dated 8th July 1882.

harbour to do, the movement of the solid matter would be arrested and it would remain as an accumulation possibly extensive enough to neutralize in a couple of days the effects of several years' work.'

Padmanábham: Village of 711 inhabitants ten miles north-west of Bimlipatam on the bank of the Chittivalasa river. Known in local history as the place where Viziaráma Rázu, Rája of Vizianagram, was slain in 1794 in the fight with the Company's troops referred to on p. 53. The spot where he fell is pointed out in a tope just north-north-east of the village and is marked by a small masonry erection which is cared for by the villagers. On the top of the hill which overlooks the place is a small Vishnu shrine reached by a flight of some 1,300 steps, and at the foot of it is another larger temple to the same deity. Tradition says that both were improved and endowed by Ananda Rázu, the predecessor of Viziaráma Rázu as Rája of Vizianagram, and that a Kápu who was previously in charge of the former was induced to relinquish his claims by the grant of a hamlet (which is still called Archakapálem or 'the priest's hamlet') and on the condition (still carried out by his descendants) that he should do worship every Saturday to the image on the slab which stands by the *dhvaja stambha* on the top of the hill.

Potnúru: Twelve miles from Bimlipatam, on the bank of the Chittivalasa river; population 2,834. At present insignificant enough, it was formerly of importance. Krishna Déva Ráya, the Vijayanagar king who conquered Orissa about 1515 (see p. 28), chose it as the place in which to plant the pillar of victory recounting his conquests. Allasáni Peddana, the then poet laureate of Vijayanagar, says in his poem *Manucharitra* (stanzas 36 and 38 of canto the first) that the 'fire-like prowess of Krishna Ráya destroyed Jámi, Kottam, Vaddádi and Pottunúru' and that the king planted in this last a pillar 'as high as a palm-tree' on which were inscribed stories of his victories over the Kalinga ruler which filled the eyes of the gods with tears when they read them. Another inscription recounting his successes is in the Simháchalam temple, see p. 29.

The tale is confirmed by a passage in the poem *Ámuktha mályada* (verse 290, canto the fourth), which is attributed to Krishna Déva himself, and by an inscription [1] of that king's at Séndamangalam in South Arcot. The pillar has now disappeared, but frequent discoveries in Potnúru of fragments of sculptured stones and gold coins bearing a bull upon them strengthen the traditions regarding its departed importance.

[1] No. 74 of 1903 in the Government Epigraphist's lists.

Santapilly (properly Chintapalle) is a small village 18 miles up the coast from Bimlipatam which gives its name to a dangerous ridge of rocks and the light erected to warn ships off them.

The rocks are about six miles from the shore, right in the track of coasting vessels; and as they give no indication of their presence in fine weather and are not visible until a ship is almost on them, they form one of the most dangerous reefs on the whole Madras seaboard. They are steep on all sides, surrounded with deep water. Between them and the land is a clear channel four miles in width and having a minimum depth of five fathoms, through which ships can pass safely.

The light was first erected in 1847, at the recommendation of Captain Biden, Master Attendant at Madras, who surveyed the Santapilly rock in September 1846, and it is a great boon to ships making Bimlipatam. In 1902 the old light was moved to Vizagapatam and a new light-house was erected in a position nearer the shore and the power of its light was increased. This now stands 140 feet above the sea and is a white light, flashing twice every ten seconds, of 45,000 candle-power. Three ships have grounded on the rocks since the light was first exhibited in 1847. Two of them floated off immediately, but the third, the *Jules Rose* (see p. 154) became a total wreck.

BISSAMKATAK TALUK.

CHAP. XV.
BISSAMKATAK.

THIS taluk was formed in 1884 out of Gunupur, and consists of the northernmost portion of the tongue of land which forces its way up between the Ganjám maliahs on the east and Kálahandi State on the west. The extreme north of it drops down into the valley of the Tél, but all the rest drains into the Vamsadhára. It is bounded on the west by the Nímgiri range, a remarkable and steep-sided mass of hills which rises in one place to 4,968 feet, and on the east by the hills of the Chandrapur and Bijápur muttas, inhabited by Kuttiya Khonds and covered with the sál forest referred to on p. 120 above. The southern portion contains a good deal of fine, open, dry cultivation resembling that of the adjoining Ráyagada taluk and consisting of valleys of fertile, light soil winding in and out among scattered low hills and dotted with tamarind, jack, mango and other trees, including some fine old banyans. In this land, wonderful tobacco is grown. It is exported in large quantities to Kálahandi and the Central Provinces, merchants coming even from Raipur and Sambalpur to buy it, but the people of this district pronounce it too full-flavoured. A great deal of paddy is also raised in the damper hollows and is exported to Gunupur. In the central and northern portions of the taluk the valleys are narrower and more shut in with jungle, but the soil is still rich, especially round about Ambadála. According to the census figures, 36 per cent. of the people speak Uriya and 43 per cent. talk Khond. The latter consist of the Désya Khonds, who are comparatively civilized and occupy the north-western corner, and the wild Kuttiya Khonds, who dwell on the hills between Dongasúrada and Karlaghati and the eastern frontier of the taluk, and are seldom found elsewhere in the district.

The only place of any note in the taluk is its head-quarters—

Bissamkatak, called by the natives Bissamkóta, a village of 2,026 inhabitants. It lies close to the beautiful Nímgiris at the point where the tracks running northwards from Ráyagada and Gunupur meet, and is 1,114 feet above the sea. The name means 'poisonous fort' and is usually supposed to have been earned by the virulence of the malaria there, which is a byword throughout the district.

The place is the residence of the Tát Rája, 'commander of the troops,' a feudatory of Jeypore who is required to pay an annual tribute of Rs. 15,000 and attend on the Mahárája at Dasara with a retinue of 500 paiks. The family are Shristi Karnams, a community who in the low country are usually accountants with a reputation for undue subtlety, but in the hills are a martial people. They have been here[1] for eight generations. The first of them, Krishna Tát Rája, came from Pedda Kimedi in Ganjám, cleared the jungle and received, it is said, a copper plate patta for Rs. 2,500 from the then Rája of Jeypore, Raghunátha Krishna Deo (1686–1708). His son, Pítámbara, built the mud fort in which the family still reside. He was succeeded by Sómanáth, and then by Rámachandra. The latter, when at Jeypore on one occasion, refused to make obeisance to the son of the Rája, Rámachandra Deo, and the latter shortly afterwards imprisoned him for fourteen months in Jeypore, where he died. His son Krishnachandra succeeded to the estate, but, hearing that the new Jeypore Rája, Vikrama Deo, was preparing hostilities, fled to one place after another and at last went to Kalyána Singapur (thirteen miles to the west of Bissamkatak), the Rája of which assisted him, and stayed there with his son four years until his death. He had been away from his estate for 17 years, and the Jeypore officials who had administered it during that time so mismanaged matters that the pátros rose against them, went to Kalyána Singapur, brought his son, Naréndra, to Bissamkatak and set him up as their Tát Rája. Four fights between the Bissamkatak and Jeypore troops occurred, the latter were defeated every time, and Vikrama Deo then left Naréndra Tát Rája in possession of the estate but gave him no patta.

Four years later (1855) disputes arose between Vikrama Deo and his son Rámachandra Deo and the latter went off and occupied Gunupur and other taluks. To secure to his cause the help of the Bissamkatak paiks, he sent for Naréndra to Gunupur, presented him with a turban and elephant, and made him Rája. Rámachandra succeeded to the Jeypore estate three years later, and on 8th January 1864 patta and muchilika were exchanged between him and Naréndra Tát Rája by which the latter agreed to pay the enhanced kattubadi of Rs. 5,000. Naréndra died on 9th May 1876. His son Rámachandra was asked to pay an additional Rs. 2,000 kattubadi, went to Jeypore to protest, and at length left the place without leave. This so angered the Jeypore Rája that he determined to attach the property. He was dissuaded by the then Agent, Mr. Goodrich, and eventually Rámachandra Tát

[1] Mr. H. G. Turner, in G.O., No. 3386, Judicial, dated 24th December 1883.

CHAP. XV. BISSAMKATAK.

Rája returned to Jeypore and agreed in 1877 to pay a kattubadi of Rs. 15,000 and to attend the Dasara with 500 paiks. He was given a patta allowing him to enjoy the estate in perpetuity on these terms, but for some years refused either to pay anything or go to the Dasara. He died in October 1889 and his heir, Naréndra, being a minor, the estate was administered by Government. The minor was educated at Párvatípur and Vizagapatam and married a daughter of the Belgám zamindar. He came of age on the 20th July 1903, but almost at once refused to attend the Dasara at Jeypore and has since declined to pay any tribute either. The Mahárája of Jeypore has now filed a suit to recover possession of the estate.

The Tát Rája's fief consists of eight muttas comprising some 500 Khond villages with a gross rental of about Rs. 40,000. Two of the muttas—Jagdalpur and Ambadála—are under pátros who pay an annual kattubadi (which the Rája claims to be entitled to raise if Jeypore raises *his* tribute) and in certain cases render feudal service. The relations between them and the Tát Rája have not always been satisfactory. The feudal tenure which once prevailed in these secluded areas is breaking down with the advance of new ideas, and the pátros have questioned the Tát Rája's authority to enhance their kattubadi because his own has been raised. The other muttas are managed directly by the Rája himself, nearly all the villages being rented out.

The Bissamkatak country was formerly one of the worst centres of Meriah sacrifice. In 1851, when a fight between the Jeypore and Bissamkatak troops was imminent, Col. Campbell found confined in the Tát Rája's residence a young boy who had been purchased to be offered up to propitiate Manaksuro (? Manikésvara), the god of war, as soon as hostilities began. In 1854, however, the Tát Rája prevented any of his people from going to get morsels of the flesh of a Meriah who had been sacrificed at Ráyabijji, by threatening to set his peons to shoot them down if they did; and the authorities gave him a double-barrelled rifle in appreciation of this achievement. At the Dasara four buffaloes, instead of human victims, are now sacrificed to the four goddesses Márkama, Tákuráni, Durgi and Nyámarázu. The Khonds come in great numbers for the event, and after the pújári has given the animals one blow they rush in and kill them with their tangis and each carry off a portion of the flesh. This is not buried in the earth to secure good crops, as is apparently done in Ganjám,[1] but is eaten in a convivial fashion and washed down with much strong drink.

[1] *Ganjám District Manual*, 86–7.

The *balli játra* (' sand feast ') is also a great day in Bissamkatak. It takes place in September-October. The people go in procession to the river, whence five men bring five baskets of sand to a building called the *balli ghoro,* or ' sand house.' In these are planted the nine kinds of grain. On the twelfth day, by which time the seeds have sprouted, a swing, the seat of which is covered with sharp nails, is set up before them, and on this a *bezzu* (medicine-man and exorcist) is swung, while goats and pigeons are sacrificed by those who have taken vows to do so. The *bezzu* then also performs a fire-walking of the ordinary kind. He spends most of the three nights before this day in dancing wildly and working himself up into a state of excitement, during which he prophesies both good and evil and pretends to grant boons (such as children to the childless and health to the sick) to those who ask them.

Similar feasts occur at Kutragada, Gudári, Gunupur and other places round, and buffaloes are often sacrificed at them instead of only goats and pigeons.

BOBBILI TALUK.

CHAP. XV. BOBBILI.

BOBBILI taluk lies inland, not far from the Jeypore hills and to the north-east of Vizianagram. In general appearance it resembles others of the plain taluks of the district. It is watered by the Suvarnamukhi and Végavati, which run in nearly parallel courses across it from west to east. The only place of note in the taluk is its head-quarters—

Bobbili, a town of 17,387 inhabitants. In this some weaving and work in brass and copper are done, but it is principally known as the chief town of the zamindari of the same name and the residence of its Mahárája. This estate pays a peshkash of Rs. 83,652 and land cess amounting to Rs. 32,090, or more than any other in the district except Vizianagram.

According to family papers,[1] the founder of the house was Pedda Ráyudu, fifteenth in descent of the Rájas of Venkatagiri and so a Velama by caste. In 1652 he entered the district in the train of Shér Muhammad Khán, Faujdar or Nawáb of Chicacole (see p. 30). Another retainer of the Faujdar's was Púsapáti Mádhava Varma, the ancestor of the Vizianagram family, and the rivalry between the two houses dates from this period. For services to the Faujdar, Pedda Ráyudu was eventually granted the Rázám hunda.

His son Lingappa succeeded him, selected Bobbili as his head-quarters, built a fort there, founded the town, and called it Pedda-puli (' great tiger ') out of compliment to the name (Shér, *i.e.*, ' tiger ') of the patron of the family. The word was corrupted into Pebbuli and Bebbuli, and at length became Bobbili. A son of his patron, say the family chronicles, was seized, when out shooting, by a rebel at Rangavaka near Palása in Ganjám, and Lingappa rescued him. For this service he was granted twelve villages and the hereditary title of Ranga Rao which all his descendants have since borne.

He was followed by his adopted son Vengal Ranga Rao, and the latter by Rangapati. Rangapati's son Ráyadappa succeeded, and then his adopted son Gópálakrishna. In the time of the

[1] See the Mahárája's *Account of the Bobbili Zamindari*. Addison & Co., Madras, 1900.

last-named, at the end of 1753, the Northern Circars were assigned to the French by the Nizam of Hyderabad (see p. 31) and Bussy, the French General, agreed to lease the Chicacole and Rajahmundry Circars to Pedda Viziaráma Rázu, the Rája of Vizianagram. A rupture between Bussy and the Nizam led to the weakening of the former's authority in the new acquisitions, but at the end of 1756 he arrived at Rajahmundry with a force designed to compel the payment of arrears of tribute and re-establish the position of the French. Viziaráma Rázu went to meet him accompanied by 10,000 troops of his own and other chiefs, and, while there, used all his influence to persuade him to remove his own powerful neighbour and rival, the Rája of Bobbili, between whom and himself much jealousy existed. Bussy proposed to Bobbili that he should leave his fort and receive instead other land of greater extent and value in another part of the province, but the suggestion was received as an insult. Soon afterwards one of Bussy's detachments was cut up in the woods of Bobbili and in his anger the General determined to expel that chief and all his family. The result was 'one of the most ghastly stories which even Indian history has to record.' Orme's description is as follows, and no apology is needed for inserting his explanatory account of the defences of Bobbili, since it applies to the scores of old mud forts with which this district is dotted and shows how formidable, when in repair, were the defences which now, in their ruined condition, seem so contemptible. Orme says :—

'The province of Chicacole has few extensive plains, and its hills increase in frequency and magnitude, as they approach the vast range of mountains that bound this, and the province of Rajahmundrum, to the north-west. The hills, and the narrower bottoms which separate them, are suffered to over-run with wood, as the best protection to the opener valleys allotted for cultivation. The Polygar [chieftain], besides his other towns and forts, has always one situated in the most difficult part of his country, which is intended as the last refuge for himself and all of his own blood. The singular construction of this fort is adequate to all the intentions of defence amongst a people unused to cannon, or other means of battery. Its outline is a regular square, which rarely exceeds 200 yards ; a large round tower is raised at each of the angles, and a square projection in the middle of each of the sides. The height of the wall is 22 feet, but of the rampart within only 12, which is likewise its breadth at top, although it is laid much broader at bottom ; the whole is of tempered clay, raised in distinct layers, of which each is left exposed to the sun, until thoroughly hardened, before the next is applied. The parapet rises 10 feet above the rampart, and is only three feet thick. It is indented five feet down from the top in interstices six inches wide,

CHAP. XV. BOBBILI.

which are three or four feet asunder. A foot above the bottom of these interstices and battlements, runs a line of round holes, another two feet lower, and a third within two feet of the rampart: These holes are, as usual, formed with pipes of baked clay: they serve for the employment of fire-arms, arrows, and lances; and the interstices for the freer use of all these arms, instead of loop-holes, which cannot be inserted or cut in the clay. The towers, and the square projections in the middle, have the same parapet as the rest of the wall; and in two of the projections, on opposite sides of the fort, are gateways, of which the entrance is not in the front, but on one side, from whence it continues through half the mass, and then turns by a right angle into the place; and, on any alarm, the whole passage is choked up with trees, and the outside surrounded to some distance with a thick bed of strong brambles. The rampart and parapet is covered by a shed of strong thatch, supported by posts; the eaves of this shed project over the battlements, but fall so near, that a man can scarcely squeeze his body between: this shed is shelter both to the rampart and guards against the sun and rain. An area of 500 yards, or more, in every direction round the fort, is preserved clear, of which the circumference joins the high wood, which is kept thick, three, four, or five miles in breadth around this centre. Few of these forts permit more than one path through the wood. The entrance of the path from without is defended by a wall, exactly similar in construction and strength to one of the sides of the fort; having its round towers at the ends, and the square projection with its gateway in the middle. From natural sagacity they never raise this redoubt on the edge of the wood; but at the bottom of a recess, cleared on purpose, and on each side of the recess, raise breast-works of earth or hedge, to gall the approach. The path admits only three men abreast, winds continually, is everywhere commanded by breast-works in the thicket, and has in its course several redoubts, similar to that of the entrance, and like that flanked by breast-works on each hand. Such were the defences of Bobbili; against which Mr. Bussy marched, with 750 Europeans, of whom 250 were horse, four field-pieces and 11,000 Peons and Sepoys, the army of Viziaráma Ráz u, who commanded them in person.

'Whilst the field-pieces plied the parapet of the first redoubt at the entrance of the wood, detachments entered into the side of the recess with fire and hatchet, and began to make a way, which tended to bring them in the rear of the redoubt; and the guard, as soon as convinced of their danger, abandoned their station, and joined those in the posts behind; the same operations continued through the whole path, which was five miles in length, and with the same success, although not without loss. When in sight of the fort, Mr. Bussy divided his troops into four divisions, allotting one, with the field-piece, to the attack of each of the towers. Ranga Rao was here, with all his parentage, 250 men bearing arms, and nearly twice this number of women and children.

'The attack commenced at daybreak, on the 24th January [1757], with the field-pieces against the four towers; and the defenders, lest fire might catch the thatch of the rampart, had pulled it down. By nine o'clock, several of the battlements were broken, when all the leading parties of the four divisions advanced at the same time with scaling ladders; but, after much endeavour for an hour, not a man had been able to get over the parapet; and many had fallen wounded; other parties followed with as little success, until all were so fatigued, that a cessation was ordered, during which the field-pieces, having beaten down more of the parapet, gave the second attack more advantage; but the ardour of the defence increased with the danger. The garrison fought with the indignant ferocity of wild beasts defending their dens and families: several of them stood, as in defiance, on the top of the battlements, and endeavoured to grapple with the first ascendants, hoping with them to twist the ladders down; and this failing, stabbed with their lances, but being wholly exposed themselves, were easily shot by aim from the rear of the escalade. The assailants admired, for no Europeans had ever seen such excess of courage in the natives of Indostan, and continually offered quarter, which was always answered by the menace and intention of death: not a man had gained the rampart at two o'clock in the afternoon, when another cessation of the attack ensued; on which Ranga Rao assembled the principal men, told them that there was no hopes of maintaining the fort, and that it was immediately necessary to preserve their wives and children from the violation of Europeans, and the more ignominious authority of Viziaráma Rázu. A number called without distinction were allotted to the work; they proceeded, every man with a torch, his lance, and poignard, to the habitations in the middle of the fort to which they set fire indiscriminately, plying the flame with straw prepared with pitch and brimstone, and every man stabbed without remorse, the woman or child, whichsoever attempted to escape the flame and suffocation. Not the helpless infant, clinging to the bosom of its mother, saved the life of either from the hand of the husband and father. The utmost excesses whether of revenge or rage, were exceeded by the atrocious prejudices which dictated and performed this horrible sacrifice. The massacre being finished, those who accomplished it returned, like men agitated by the furies, to die themselves on the walls. Mr. Law, who commanded one of the divisions, observed, whilst looking at the conflagration, that the number of the defenders was considerably diminished, and advanced again to the attack: after several ladders had failed, a few grenadiers got over the parapet, and maintained their footing in the tower until more secured the possession. Ranga Rao hastening to the defence of the tower, was in this instant killed by a musket-ball. His fall increased, if possible, the desperation of his friends; who, crowding to revenge his death, left the other parts of the ramparts bare; and the other divisions of the French troops, having advanced likewise to their

CHAP. XV. Bobbili.

respective attacks, numbers on all sides got over the parapet without opposition: nevertheless, none of the defenders quitted the rampart, or would accept quarter; but each fell advancing against, or struggling with, an antagonist; and even when fallen and in the last agony, would resign his poignard only to death. The slaughter of the conflict being completed, another much more dreadful, presented itself in the area below: the transport of victory lost all its joy: all gazed on one another with silent astonishment and remorse, and the fiercest could not refuse a tear to the deplorable destruction spread before them. Whilst contemplating it, an old man, leading a boy, was perceived advancing from a distant recess: he was welcomed with much attention and respect, and conducted by the crowd to Mr. Law, to whom he presented the child with these words: "This is the son of Ranga Rao, whom I have preserved against his father's will." Another emotion now succeeded, and the preservation of this infant was felt by all as some alleviation to the horrible catastrophe, of which they had been the unfortunate authors. The tutor and the child were immediately sent to Mr. Bussy, who, having heard of the condition of the fort, would not go into it, but remained in his tent, where he received the sacred captives with the humanity of a guardian appointed by the strongest claims of nature, and immediately commanded patents to be prepared, appointing the son lord of the territory which he had offered the father in exchange for the districts of Bobbili; and ordered them to be strictly guarded in the camp from the malevolence of enemies.

'The ensuing night and the two succeeding days passed in the usual attentions, especially the care of the wounded, who were many; but in the middle of the third night, the camp was alarmed by tumult in the quarter of Viziaráma Rázu. Four of the soldiers of Ranga Rao, on seeing him fall, concealed themselves in an unfrequented part of the fort until the night was far advanced, when they dropped down the walls and speaking the same language, passed unsuspected through the quarters of Viziaráma Rázu, and gained the neighbouring thickets; where they remained the two succeeding days, watching until the bustle of the camp had subsided; when two of them quitted their retreat, and having by their language again deceived those by whom they were questioned, got near the tent of Viziaráma Rázu; then creeping on the ground they passed under the back part, and entering the tent found him lying on his bed, alone and asleep. Viziaráma Rázu was extremely corpulent, insomuch that he could scarcely raise himself from his seat without assistance: the two men, restraining their very breath, struck in the same instant with their poignards at his heart; the first groan brought in a centinel, who fired, but missed; more immediately thronged in, but the murderers, heedless of themselves, cried out, pointing to the body, "Look here! We are satisfied." They were instantly shot by the crowd, and mangled after they had fallen; but had stabbed Viziaráma Rázu in thirty-two places. Had they failed, the other two remaining in the forest were bound by the same oath to perform the deed or perish in the attempt.'

The situation of this historic fort can still be traced on the west side of the town, its site being a little higher than the ground about it, and here the present Mahárája of Bobbili erected in 1891 an obelisk bearing inscriptions on stone commemorating the tragedy. In these, and also in the *Ranga Rao Charitram*, the popular ballad on the subject which is still sung all over the district, the slaying of Viziaráma Rázu is attributed, not to two men as in Orme's account, but to a single individual named Tándra Pápayya, a sirdar of the fort at Rázám. To keep his memory green, the Velamas of Bobbili town erected there in 1900 a chávadi which bears his name.

Two members of the Bobbili family escaped from the massacre of the 24th January 1757; namely, the zamindar's brother, Vengal Ranga Rao, and his infant son Venkata Ranga Rao referred to by Orme, who was usually known as Chinna Ranga Rao. Mr. Carmichael says that 'they fled to Bhadráchalam, but two years afterwards (1759) when Ananda Rázu of Vizianagram was at Masulipatam with Colonel Forde, they returned, and assembling their old retainers, got possession of the fort at Rázám. The Púsapátis at last were glad to compromise with them, giving them a lease of the Kavite and Rázám *hundas* for Rs. 20,000 a year. Vengal Rao lived three years after this, and was succeeded by Chinna Ranga Rao for four years, when in 1766, Sítaráma Rázu, growing apprehensive of his influence, managed to seize him and, imprisoning him in the fort at Vizianagram, resumed the taluks. Chinna Ranga Rao was in confinement till the year 1790, when he found means to make his escape. He fled into the Nizam's country, whence he was invited back by the Collector of the Northern Division in 1794, on the dismemberment of the Vizianagram zamindari. His old taluks were restored to him, and shortly afterwards he adopted a distant kinsman, Ráyadappa, for his son. He died in 1801, when great efforts were made by the Púsapátis to get his country incorporated with Vizianagram, but their prayer was rejected, the permanent settlement being made with the deceased's adopted son.

Chinna Ranga Rao was the builder of the oldest part of the present palace at Bobbili, the Saracenic arches on which its first floor is supported being perhaps due to ideas of architecture imbibed at Hyderabad. Ráyadappa, and after him his son Svétáchalapati (who succeeded in 1830 and lived till 1862), were excellent managers of their property. The latter made large

CHAP. XV. BOBBILI.

additions by purchase to the estate, and loans from Bobbili saved half the estates in the district from confiscation and ruin. He also rendered assistance in arresting the fitúridars who disturbed the peace of the district in the thirties, and was thanked by Government. He finished the temple to Vénugópálasvámi at Bobbili—to which the present Mahárája is building a *gópuram* (the only one of its kind in the district) similar to those so common in the Tamil country—and made the Púl Bágh garden in 1851.

His adopted son Sítarámakrishna, who belonged to the family of the zamindars of Pithápuram in Gódávari, lived till 1868, when his wife Lakshmi Chellayamma (afterwards granted by Government the title of Ráni for her many charitable acts) took over the management of the estate. In 1871 she adopted the present Mahárája, Sir Venkata Svétáchalapati Ranga Rao, K.C.I.E., the third son of the Rája of Venkatagiri, and she died in 1887.

The present Mahárája took over charge in 1881, and has done a great deal for the property and the town. In 1882 he raised the local middle school to high school standard and built the existing poor-house in which about 70 people are fed daily; in 1886 he built the new wing of the palace; in 1887 the Victoria market; and in 1888 the Ráj Mahál, a most pleasantly situated house to the south-west of the town. In 1890 his title of Rája was formally recognized as hereditary by the Government of India. He went to Europe in 1893, was presented to the Queen-Empress, and on his return began the Victoria Town Hall, opposite to the main entrance of the palace, in commemoration of the event. In 1894 he started the gosha hospital, which he eventually handed over to the District Board with an endowment of Rs. 20,000. He was created a K.C.I.E. in 1895, a member of the Madras Legislative Council in 1896, and a Mahárája in 1900, and he went a second time to Europe as one of the two Madras representatives at the coronation of the King-Emperor. He also constructed the house and graceful mantapam in the Púl Bágh already mentioned, maintains a caste girls' school, is putting up a new building for the high school and has endowed several beds at the Victoria Caste and Gosha Hospital at Madras. He has also added largely to the estate, which has now been declared impartible and inalienable by Act II of 1904, has lent large sums to brother zamindars in difficulties, has offered such substantial inducements to the people of Bobbili to build tiled and terraced houses that the town is now one of the smartest and neatest in the district, and has terminated the ancient feud between his family and the Rájas of Vizianagram. He has two sons, Venkata Kumára Krishna, born in 1880, and Ráma Krishna, born in 1892.

CHÍPURUPALLE TALUK.

Is the most northern of the coast taluks of the district and is divided from Ganjám by the Lángulya river. It is perhaps the least picturesque part of the whole district. The coast, which further south is relieved by bold hills and headlands, is here flat and uninteresting, and the centre of the taluk is an undulating plain, sparsely dotted with small, bare hills. It is, however, carefully cultivated, and in the dry weather, when elsewhere there is little crop on the ground, the patches of ragi, tobacco and chillies under its numerous wells give it a flourishing appearance.

Among the few places of interest in it are the following :—

Chípurupalle: A union of 2,916 inhabitants, the head-quarters of the taluk and a railway-station. Though now unimportant, it seems to have been of some note in days gone by, as it contains the remains of what was once a considerable fort, bricks of ancient pattern are often dug up round this, and in 1867 three sets of copper sásanams were found in the village, one of which records a grant by Vishnuvardhana I of the Eastern Chálukya dynasty, who flourished from 615 to 633 A.D.[1]

Garugubilli: Five miles north of Chípurupalle. About two miles west of it is a hill with three peaks, in the northernmost of which, Dévudukonda, is an odd natural cave which is reached by a passage through the hill some 30 feet long, and is about 10 feet in diameter. Out of it lead two other chambers accessible with the help of a ladder. In this cave is a stone which is supposed to be a lingam and in the month of Kártigam people flock to do púјá to it.

Gujarátipéta: A village of 1,272 inhabitants on the bank of the Lángulya facing Chicacole, with which it is connected by a masonry road bridge of 24 spans which was built in 1854, partly washed away in the cyclone of 1876 (see p. 154) and repaired in 1886. Being outside the municipal limits of Chicacole, it is a favourite haunt of gamblers of that town who wish to avoid the attentions of the police. The village is said to get its name from the circumstance that it was founded many years ago by a number of Gujaráti Bráhmans who traded in precious

[1] For further particulars, see G.O., No. 28, Public, dated 3rd August 1869, and *Ind. Ant.*, xviii, 143–230.

CHAP. XV. CHIPURU-PALLE.

stones. Some of their descendants still live there, carry on the same business, and keep up relations with their castemen in Benares. The pillars of the Lakshésvara temple here are said to have been found in the river-bed, and one of them bears Uriya inscriptions.

Near the river is a brick and stone octagonal column 20 feet high, surmounted by a small dome, which is called the *burrala kóta* or 'skull fort.' The story goes that it was made from the skulls of Hindus slain by Musalmans in a battle here. Near by are a number of neglected Muhammadan tombs, and these are said to cover the remains of the slain of the other side.

Shérmuhammadpuram: Four miles west of Chicacole; population 2,582. Is named after Shér Muhammad, Faujdar or Nawáb of Chicacole under the Nizam, and the man who built the Chicacole mosque between 1641 and 1645. Tradition says he erected a summer palace for himself about a mile to the west of this village and brought a channel to it from the Lángulya. The ruins of the building are still to be seen and the ground is called Shér Mahál Tótam. Not far off is a great irrigation tank, which is worth a visit.

The village is the chief place of the proprietary estate of the same name. This is referred to in the account of Anakápalle on p. 221 above.

GAJAPATINAGARAM TALUK.

CHAP. XV. GAJAPATINAGARAM.

This lies next north of Vizianagram, and on the west runs up to the Jeypore hills. Except in this western corner, where the scenery is picturesque and even wild, the taluk resembles in appearance the rest of the plain country of the district, consisting of a wide expanse of red soil dotted with low, red hills.

The places of interest in it include the following :—

Ándra: Lies ten miles north-west of Gajapatinagaram near the mouth of a valley at the foot of the hills ; population 2,724. The hills behind it are sometimes called 'the Ándra hills.' On Tuesdays a big market is held, whereat quantities of hill produce are exchanged for the commodities of the plains.

The village is the chief place in the impartible ancient zamindari of the same name. This is said to have been granted, along with the title of Pratápa Rao, by Visvambara Deo, Rája of Jeypore from 1713 to 1752, to Pedda Ráman Dora of the Konda Dora caste. The permanent settlement was made in 1803 with this man's grandson, Gárayya Dora. These Doras had allied themselves to the Vizianagram family and paid them tribute. Mr. Alexander reported that the inaccessibility of their estate and their active and enterprising spirit rendered them much more desirable as allies than enemies, and so the tribute had always been light. On the death of Viziaráma Rázu at the battle of Padmanábham in 1794, the Ándra property was left in their possession at the same peshkash (Rs. 1,500) ; and this sum (less the value of land-customs resumed) was again continued at the permanent settlement. The present holder is Sanyási Dora *alias* Gárayya Dora, who is the adopted son of the son of the Gárayya Dora above mentioned.

He also owns the small impartible estate of Sarapalli-Bhímavaram. In the days when the Púsapátis were in power this, says Mr. Carmichael, was a separate zamindari with a tribute of Rs. 600. The owner, Jógi Rázu, in 1796 joined the notorious outlaw Mukki Rájabhúpála Rázu (see p. 54), and was turned out by Mr. Webb, who gave the property to the then holder of Ándra.

Gajapatinagaram is the head-quarters of the taluk and a union of 2,724 inhabitants, but is otherwise uninteresting. It

CHAP. XV. GAJAPATI-NAGARAM.

stands on the north bank of the Champávati, and, being a place of halt between Vizianagram and Sálúr, contains an excellent chattram and (south of the river) an indifferent travellers' bungalow. Before Sálúr grew so prominent, the place was a great mart for hill produce, but its importance has now departed.

Jayati: A small village eight miles north-west of Gajapatinagaram in which there are two odd little deserted shrines, each consisting of a single cell about 12 feet square surmounted by a pyramidal roof running up about 16 feet from the ground. They are built without mortar and contain a number of unusual little sculptures. The villagers say they are Jain shrines, but a description of the carvings in them which has been furnished shows that this is doubtful. Another tradition says that Jains once lived in the village and that they were great astrologers. A Hindu overheard one of them calculating in deeply learned fashion the exact hour and minute at which it would be propitious to sow his corn and slipped out and sowed his own at the moment in question. The field produced a crop of solid golden grain. The local king was so impressed with the miracle that he forbore to take an ounce more than his usual share of the crop, and the lucky husbandman spent some of his windfall in building these two shrines.

Márupilli: Three miles north of Gajapatinagaram; population 1,809. Is widely known for its hook-swinging festival in March, which is conducted by certain Mettu Jangálu, in whose families the privilege is hereditary, in honour of the local Ellamma. The feast is a favourite occasion for the fulfilment of vows and many of the upper castes participate in it.

Régulavalasa: Eleven miles north-north-east of Gajapatinagaram. East of it is a jungle the game in which was preserved by the late Mahárája of Vizianagram. The place is sometimes called Shikárganj in consequence. South of the village are the ruins of the Mahárája's shooting-box.

GOLGONDA TALUK.

CHAP. XV. GOLGONDA.

This is one of the three Government taluks in the district. It consists of two widely differing portions—the low country and the hills.

The former resembles generally the rest of the coastal plain of the district, sloping towards the sea and being covered with undulating red land broken up by low hills. The southern boundary of the taluk runs along a fairly continuous line of the latter, the highest point in which is the striking Sanjívikonda, 2,145 feet, so named because it is supposed to produce medicinal herbs good for many ailments. Near Kottakóta is the Komaravólu áva, one of the few natural lakes in the Presidency.

The hill portion of the taluk is all within the Agency and forms the southernmost corner of the '3,000 feet plateau' already several times referred to. It drains northwards, mainly through the Gureprau or Páléru river, which is full of fish, into the Siléru. It consists of a jumble of steep and broken hills which average about 2,500 feet, contain some fair plateaus at about that level, run up in many places to 4,000 feet and over, and produce the heaviest jungle of any part of the plateau. Some of this (round Gúdem, for instance) is moist evergreen growth and includes (see p. 114) tree-ferns, orchids, and many varieties of the smaller ferns. The *maddi* (*Terminalia tomentosa*) and gall-nut (*T. chebula*) trees are especially numerous. The tops of the higher hills are usually bare, their sides and the lower hills carrying most of the forest, while the more level country is often covered with large stretches of grass land dotted with scattered trees gnarled and twisted by the annual jungle fires. The outer southern slopes are clothed with good forest which is seldom burnt, and at the foot of them, especially round Kondasanta, are masses of splendid bamboos.

The principal ghát is from Kondasanta to Lammasingi, nine miles, part of which is just practicable for carts. Rougher tracks lead up from Krishnadévipet and Koyyúr to Peddavalasa. From Lammasingi two jungle paths lead northwards across the hills to Kondakambéru in Malkanagiri taluk, one *viâ* Lótugedda and Kórukonda and thence alongside the Gureprau river down a bad ghát to Kondakambéru; and the other through Chintapalle,

CHAP. XV. GOLGONDA.

Peddavalasa, Gúdem and Dárakonda, and thence down an even worse ghát. There is not a cart-road in the whole of the hills, and even horses are almost useless in such rough country. Officers do most of their marches on foot.

The people, who all speak Telugu, consist chiefly of Bagatas (immigrants from the plains and the aristocracy to which belong the muttadars referred to below), Konda Doras, and Konda Málas or 'hill Paraiyans.' The last are a pushing set of traders who are rapidly acquiring wealth and exalted notions. In 1901 certain envious Bagatas looted one of their villages on the ground that they were becoming unduly arrogant. The immediate cause of the trouble was the fact that at a cockfight the Málas' birds had defeated the Bagatas'. The Konda Doras, and to a less extent the Bagatas, are the cultivators. Ragi is their favourite crop. Their methods are very casual. The soil is undoubtedly rich (the luxuriance of the grasses proves it) but the people go in for *pódu* cultivation (mainly on the southern side of the plateau, less further inland, and not at all on the southern slopes) or till the ground carelessly, making scant use of the irrigation possible from the numerous hill streams. Rather than toil at cultivation, they prefer to live by the sale of the natural products of the hills. These are very numerous and include limes, particularly sweet oranges, guavas, mangoes (the kernels and stones of which are pounded and made into porridge), tamarinds, jack-fruit, gall-nuts, turmeric, long pepper, mustard, wax, horns, honey and so on. At Peddavalasa are some coffee trees, grown from seed sent up by the Captain Owen referred to below, which have flourished immensely and are surrounded with self-sown seedlings.

The people seem happy and contented as a class and in the ten years ending 1901 increased by nearly 10 per cent. They still, however, number only 46 to the square mile; and in the plateaus inland the only cultivation to be seen is small scattered patches hidden away among the almost continuous sheet of jungle. In days gone by, tigers, fever and rebellion did much to thin their numbers. Almost every one eats opium.

The taluk has a romantic history. An early Rája of Jeypore, says Mr. Carmichael, had two of his cousins for umbrella-bearers and was pleased to promote them to the dignity of feudatories, placing one at Golgonda and the other at Mádgole and honouring both with the title of Bhúpati or 'lord of the earth.' This Golgonda is a village ten miles west of Narasapatam. The name is supposed to be a corruption of *Golla konda*, 'the hill of the Gollas,' a race of shepherd-kings of whom (see p. 28) misty traditions survive in this corner of the district.

The Golgonda chieftains afterwards became tributary to the Rájas of Vizianagram, but when the English were established at Vizagapatam they required the Rájas to resign this supremacy. In 1776, however, Bhairava Bhúpati sheltered two refractory subjects of the Company (the zamindars of Parlákimedi and Mádgole) and he was again subordinated to the Púsapátis, who raised his tribute from Rs. 5,000 to Rs. 23,000 and also made him keep up a large body of paiks. After the death of Viziaráma Rázu at the battle of Padmanábham in 1794, the Golgonda zamindar paid the Company a peshkash of Rs. 10,000 and this was the figure entered in his sanad at the permanent settlement in 1802. In 1836 the incapacity of the then zamindar, Ananta Bhúpati, brought the estate to the verge of ruin; and he was persuaded by the district officers to resign in favour of Jamma Dévamma, the widow of a predecessor. The hill sirdars or muttadars, however, objected that they had not been consulted and that no woman had ever ruled them before; and they carried off the unfortunate lady and murdered her. Mr. Freese, the Collector, moved up troops and confiscated the estate. Ananta Bhúpati was convicted of complicity in the murder and was confined in the fort at Gooty in Anantapur, where he subsequently died. In 1837 the zamindari was sold in auction for arrears and bought in by Government for Rs. 100.

The hill sirdars were not disturbed in their tenures, and were given pattas for their muttas *dum se bene gesserint*; but they found their status seriously lowered by their being subordinated to an ordinary ámín, and they grew discontented and finally united to restore the Bhúpati family by force. They withheld their rents, barricaded the hills, and made constant excursions with fire and sword against the villages in the plains. They set up one Chinna Bhúpati, a lad of nineteen, as their 'Rája,' and for three years, from 1845 to 1848, they successfully held their jungles against the troops employed against them, only abandoning their enterprise at last on the promise of an amnesty to all concerned. Chinna Bhúpati gave himself up and was granted villages worth Rs. 4,000 annually as maintenance for himself and his three brothers, the representatives of the ancient zamindars of Golgonda.

In 1857–58, during the excitement of the Mutiny, another insurrection, having a similar object to the last, broke out under the leadership of Chinna Bhúpati's nephew Sanyási Bhúpati. The Sibbandi corps under its Commandant, Captain Owen, assisted by some of the leading hill sirdars, promptly put it

CHAP. XV. GOLGONDA.

down; and Sanyási Bhúpati and his uncle were tried by the Agent, convicted, and sentenced to transportation for life. Subsequently, however, Government directed that they should merely be kept as State *detenus* under surveillance, and that their share in the maintenance villages should be continued to them. At his death in 1886 Sanyási Bhúpati was drawing no less than Rs. 913 per annum.[1]

In 1864–65 police-stations were posted in the hill muttas and for a time the country was quiet. The unrest caused by the Rampa rebellion in the neighbouring Gódávari Agency in 1879–80 spread, however, to this tract and Captain Blaxland, who had come down from Jeypore with 50 police and some of the Rája's paiks, was attacked by a party of insurgents on 3rd June 1879 in a densely-wooded valley and driven back. The next year the sirdar (muttadar) of Gúdem Pátavídi, Tagi Vírayya Dora, joined another party of rebels. The leaders of this bound themselves by an oath, solemnly taken at the sacrifice of five human victims, to attack the police-station at Kondakambéru. The enterprise, however, was never undertaken: chased by sepoys and constabulary in every direction, the band was broken up into insignificant parties; and on the 7th October Vírayya Dora was shot. His last message to his pursuers was that he would never surrender unless his Rája, Chinna Bhúpati, bade him do so.[2]

It was in consequence of this rebellion that the Dutsarti and Guditéru muttas of Golgonda were transferred in 1881 to Gódávari, from which they were more accessible. The other Golgonda muttadars were given sanads stating that they held their muttas (which were declared inalienable by sale, gift or otherwise) on service tenure, subject to the payment of an annual kattubadi and to the conditions that the grantee was to capture and hand over to the authorities offenders who were in the mutta or came into it, and was to give immediate information of fitúris or other offences. As long as these conditions were fulfilled the grantee, and such of his heirs as Government might appoint, was to enjoy the mutta under the protection of Government. The penalty for non-fulfilment was the forfeiture of the mutta, Government reserving the right to do as seemed proper with the muttadar. These terms, which were re-affirmed and added to in

[1] Note in G.O., No. 30, Political, dated 17th January 1891, which gives an account of the complicated history of the many Golgonda pensions.

[2] For further details, see Minute by Mr. Carmichael, Special Commissioner, in connection with these outbreaks, dated 1st November 1881.

1888,[1] are of much importance, and deserve to be borne in mind in all dealings with these men.

In 1886, excited by the preachings of several Konda Dora priests who had been travelling round the hills for months declaring that the hill gods had directed a fitúri, a gang of about 30 men got together, went to Gúdem, burnt and looted the police-station (the police all fled) and the rest-house there, came to Chintapalle next day and burnt the rest-house there, and were moving on Lammasingi when they were dispersed by the police and eventually all captured. The muttadar of Lammasingi Pátavídi had shown sympathy with the outbreak and his mutta was forfeited. The police were shortly afterwards all concentrated at Chintapalle, where is now stationed one of the four reserves of the district.

The last Golgonda fitúri occurred in 1891. Santa Bhúpati, son of the Chinna Bhúpati already mentioned, discontented with the allowance granted him by Government, encouraged no doubt by the extreme leniency with which his father had twice been treated, and aided by a man who had taken part in the Rampa rising and been too gently dealt with, got together a party of some 200 men. On 23rd May these looted the house of the constable who had shot Tagi Vírayya Dora eleven years before, and rushed the Krishnadévipet police-station at night, killing five constables, carrying off all the arms and ammunition, and setting fire to the building. They then made for the hills and eluded pursuit for a month. On the 24th June their leader Santa Bhúpati died of fever and dysentery and they dispersed. Thirty-three of them were eventually arrested. Santa Bhúpati left a mother, widow and daughter, and a compassionate allowance was granted them.

Not one of the muttadars gave any information or assistance to the authorities either before or during this fitúri, and as a consequence Koyyúr and Chittampád Bandavalasa were resumed; the muttadars of Lammasingi Kottavídi and Lótugedda were deposed and their heirs appointed in their places; and Sobilan Dora, muttadar of Gúdem Kottavídi, was arrested under an agency warrant and deported, and his mutta eventually taken under management on behalf of his minor son. He now resides in Vizagapatam under surveillance and the mutta has been restored to his son.

Including the two thus resumed, the Golgonda hills now comprise ten muttas. It has already been mentioned that

[1] G.O., No. 744, Judicial, dated 26th March 1888.

CHAP. XV. GOLGONDA.

Lammasingi Pátavídi was resumed after the 1886 fitúri. Lótugedda was also attached in 1895, the muttadar resigning his position.[1] Antáda mutta has just been resumed for mismanagement and violations of the sanad.[2] The remaining five (Lammasingi-Kottavídi, Mákáram, Gúdem Pátavídi, Gúdem Kottavídi and Dárakonda) are still held by their muttadars. Parts of the resumed muttas are managed on the ryotwari system by village establishments under a revenue inspector. In the rest of them and in the unresumed muttas, joint-renting is in vogue, each village paying to Government or the muttadar a lump sum assessed on the number of houses (or of ploughs) within it, which is collected by the village head at customary rates and seldom varies.

The chief places of interest in the taluk—plains as well as hills—are the following :—

Balighattam : A small village two miles south-west of Narasapatam on the bank of the Varáhanadi. It is known throughout the district for its temple to Brahmalingésvara, which stands at the foot of a small hill on the other side of the river and at which there is a large festival at Sivarátri. The shrine, like that of Visvésvara at Benares, faces west, instead of east as usual, and this peculiarity and the fact that the river for a short distance here flows north and south have led to the spot being considered peculiarly sacred. The local pandits quote with unction the slóka which says 'where a lingam faces west and a river runs north, that place is equal to Kási (Benares), and there one will surely obtain celestial bliss.'

The shrine is almost all quite modern and is not interesting architecturally. It is supposed to have been built by Brahma ; the river is declared to have been made by Vishnu, during his incarnation as a boar (*varáha*)—whence its name ; and some deposits of white clay in the river bank are supposed to be the ashes of a sacrifice performed here by Bali, the demon-king from whom the village takes its name.

Gúdem : A village of 501 inhabitants 43 miles by the hill paths north-west of Narasapatam among the Golgonda hills. It was once one of the chief places of the Golgonda Bhúpatis and the Golgonda hills are often called 'the Gúdem hills.' It stands 2,580 feet above the sea on one side of an open valley and is divided into Kottavídi and Pátavídi (new and old streets) between which lie the remains of a rude fort. One of the hills above it,

[1] G.O., No. 1685, Judicial, dated 10th August 1895.
[2] G.O., No. 1747, Judicial, dated 4th November 1905.

Bodakonda, rises to about 4,000 feet. No native will go up this. A goddess named Sambari lives there and animal sacrifices are made to her. One day, says the story, a man went to her temple just after the sacrifice to fetch a brass pot which he had forgotten, and came upon the goddess drinking the blood of the offerings. She was furious at being seen, and flung his pot two miles away, where it made a deep hole (still shown) in a piece of rock. Since then no native has ventured up the hill. A survey party of Europeans, it is locally declared, laughed at the superstition and set out one fine day to take bearings from the top of the hill. But they had hardly got half way up when they were surrounded by a forest fire which burnt up much of their kit and so frightened a horse they had with them that it bolted over a precipice and was killed.

Krishnadévipet: Sixteen miles west of Narasapatam and close under the hills. A thriving little place of 493 inhabitants which, like Kondasanta at the foot of the Lammasingi ghát, does a busy trade in the produce of the hills, such as tamarind, saffron, gall-nuts, long pepper, honey, bees' wax, soap-nut, horns, mustard and *kamela* dye. It is full of money-lenders, who have obtained possession on mortgage of much land in the Antáda mutta. Water is difficult to get, as the village is perched high above a river-bed.

Lótugedda ('deep stream') stands about 26 miles in a direct line north-north-west of Narasapatam among the Golgonda hills. It contains the ruins of three or four old granite temples dedicated to Siva, in the largest of which the sculpture is elaborate. One odd group depicts [1] four men with long pointed beards and long pigtails, carrying pickaxes on their shoulders, holding out their hands to receive a reward which a king, sitting on a throne with three ladies behind him, is in the act of bestowing. The villagers say the men are the builders of the temple, and are content to account for the long beards by the conjecture that barbers were probably rare on the hills in those days. On three sides of a pillar here are Telugu inscriptions.

Narasapatam: Head-quarters of the Divisional Officer, Assistant Superintendent of Police and tahsildar, and a union of 10,589 inhabitants. It is 19 miles north-west of the railway-station called Narasapatam Road and in wet weather the journey thence is unpleasant, as the road crosses several unbridged streams and in one place shares a narrow gorge with the Varáha river. An estimate for diverting the road awaits allotment of

[1] G.O., No. 1941, Judicial, dated 23rd November 1882.

funds. The town stands amid the palmyra-dotted red land usual to this corner of Vizagapatam, in a wide valley bounded on one side by the Golgonda hills and on the other by rising ground and smaller elevations which are just high enough to cut off the sea breeze. It is consequently one of quite the hottest spots in the district.

The Divisional Officer's bungalow and office and the new taluk cutcherry (the latter of which is surrounded by a high wall provided with loop-holed bastions at the corners, intended to render it secure from attack by fitúridars) stand in a row beside the road east of the town. The house of the Assistant Superintendent, however, is built off the road to Kondasanta, at the other end of the place. Nearly opposite this last are the old parade-ground and magazine of the former Sibbandi corps which was stationed here to check fitúris in the Golgonda hills and was amalgamated with the ordinary police force in 1861. An old race-course may be traced not far off on the same side of the road. The cemetery next the Divisional Officer's bungalow contains the grave of Captain Gibson of the 26th N.I. who died in 1849 and was apparently an officer employed in the outbreak of that date referred to above. The name of Captain W. G. Owen, 11th N.I., who commanded the Sibbandi force from 1851 until it was reconstituted, was thanked for his services in the 1857–58 fitúri (see p. 249) and in 1859 was made Assistant Agent at Narasapatam, is still remembered. He was a great tiger-slayer and he built the Divisional Officer's house (and also, it is said, the bungalows at Kondakarla áva and on the shore at Pólavaram) and handed it on to his successor, C. T. Longley, who in 1865 sold it to its present owner, the Rája of Vizianagram.

Narasapatam contains the remains of an old mud fort which is said to have been built by one of the Golgonda Bhúpatis above referred to. Enough of the walls remains to screen the public latrine which has now been established within it.

The town boasts no noteworthy products unless it be the mango pickle its Kómatis make.

Uratla: A dirty village of 3,196 inhabitants, nine miles south-east of Narasapatam, off the road to the railway-station. Is only noteworthy as the chief place of the estate of the same name, which was one of those formed out of the havíli land and sold by auction at a fixed peshkash in 1802. It was then bought by the Rája of Vizianagram, who sold it in 1810 to one Sági Rámachandra Rázu. In 1832 it was sold for arrears and bought by a lady named Dantalúri Achayya, who in 1843 gave it to her daughter Sági Subhadrayya. She died in 1867 and the property descended to her adopted son, S. Venkata Súrya Náráyana Jagannátha Rázu, the present nominal owner. He mismanaged the estate, the peshkash fell into arrears, and the property was attached and taken under Government management for a time. Subsequently the owner alienated seven different portions of it, and these have been separately registered.

In 1875 he alienated Chouduváda, for services received, to one of his uncles, Kákarlapúdi Narasa Rázu, who had it registered in the name of his minor son, K. Rámachandra Rázu, the present proprietor.

In the same year he also granted Pondúru and Mallavaram to another uncle, K. Chinna Narasa Rázu. This man died in 1876, leaving a minor son, and the estate was taken under the Court of Wards. The present holder is Kákarlapúdi Venkata Rámayya.

In 1877 the village of Bayyavaram was sold to Dátla Rámachandra Rázu, who disposed of it to J. Rangáchári, who ten years later sold it to a dancing-girl named K. Simháchalam. She died in 1896 and the estate devolved on her adopted daughters, K. Kannamma and B. Rámayamma, the present holders.

In the same year 1877,[1] Tangédu and Gotiváda were transferred by a rázináma decree to Sági Sítaráma Rázu, whose brother, S. Buchchi Rájagópála Rázu, and his three nephews now hold them.

In 1879 Kondala agraháram was disposed of to Púsapáti Súrya Náráyana, whose daughter-in-law, P. B. Bangárayya, and granddaughter, Chitti Ammanna *alias* Venkata Narasayya, are now the proprietors.

In 1884 Jaggampéta, Tadaparti and Timmapuram were sold to Lolla Sanyási Rázu, who in 1888 transferred them to the present proprietrix, a dancing-girl named Pilla Gangu *alias* Chamanti.

This lady had already obtained the seventh of the subdivisions, Peddapálem, in 1884.

In 1898 the zamindar of Tuni, in the Gódávari district, obtained possession of what was left of the estate under a mortgage and through process of the civil courts.[2] It is now registered in his name.

Vajragada ('diamond fort') is a small place of 1,247 inhabitants, lying six miles from Narasapatam off the road to Anakápalle.

[1] B.P., No. 201, dated 24th January 1878.

[2] O.S. No. 9 of 1894 on the file of the Vizagapatam District Court.

CHAP. XV. GOLGONDA.

The ruins of a very large fortress, built at the base of two hills and now all cultivated, are still to be seen in it, and local tradition gives the names of seven forts with which it was once defended. These are said to have been constructed by the Golla kings already referred to. A tale is told of their having kidnapped a daughter of the ruler of Mádgole and held out here against his attacks for months until they were betrayed by a woman of their own caste who showed the enemy how to cut off their water-supply. They then slew their womenkind, says the story, dashed out against the besiegers, and fell to a man, fighting to the last. Small gold coins of two kinds, neither of which have yet been satisfactorily identified, are found round about the fort after heavy rain, and a small square stone with old Telugu inscriptions on all four sides is to be seen near the middle of its eastern wall.

GUNUPUR TALUK.

CHAP. XV. GUNUPUR.

GUNUPUR is the most easterly taluk in the district and the richest in the Jeypore zamindari. It consists of a portion of the valley of the Vamsadhára and of the hills which enclose this. The valley is quite level (the western side of it most monotonously so) and in it is grown paddy which is the best in the district and is favourably known even in distant Calcutta. The outlet for this and other products is at present through the Parlákimedi zamindari of Ganjám to Chicacole, but when the line is opened to Párvatípur it will doubtless travel thither *viâ* Kurupám.

The hills on the west are called the Kailásakóta hills and consist of a range averaging 2,500 feet high which divides the watersheds of the Vamsadhára and Lángulya and near the top of which is an undulating plateau. They once contained quantities of sál, but little is left now. The hills on the eastern frontier are mainly inhabited by the Savaras (38 per cent. of the people of the taluk speak that language) and in them dwell the only remnants of the real hill Savaras who survive in this district.

These people have been referred to on p. 95 above. They are known for the industry with which they cultivate. They terrace the steep hill-sides with great revetments of stone, often fifteen feet deep; grow splendid cholam twelve or fourteen feet high on the slopes; preserve every pound of fodder by cutting the crops close to the ground and storing the straw on platforms or up trees to save it from damp; and utilize for irrigation every rill in the country. Their well-kept fields, with the numerous *ippa* trees scattered about them, have been likened to Italian homesteads surrounded with their dark olives.

At the end of the eighteenth century the taluk was taken by force [1] from Jeypore by Náráyana Deo of Kimedi. He gave it to his brother, Pratápa Deo, but the latter was eventually driven out by Sítaráma Rázu, díwán of Vizianagram, with the help of the Company's troops. Finding himself unable to manage it, Sítaráma Rázu gave it back to Jeypore after he had held it three years. In 1803 Mr. Alexander reported that it was a kind of hereditary farm belonging to the family of a former pátro or díwán, then represented by one Náráyana Pátro, who paid a rent

[1] See Proceedings of the Committee of Circuit, dated 12th September 1784.

of Rs. 15,000 for it. The attachments of this and the neighbouring tánas of Jeypore which were necessitated by the disturbances of 1849–50 and 1855–56 are referred to on pp. 268–9 below.

In July 1864 trouble occurred with the Savaras. One of their headmen having been improperly arrested by the police of Pottasingi, they effected a rescue, killed the Inspector and four constables, and burnt down the station-house. The Rája of Jeypore was requested to use his influence to procure the arrest of the offenders, and eventually twenty-four were captured, of whom nine were transported for life and five were sentenced to death and hanged at Jaltéru, at the foot of the ghát to Pottasingi. Government presented the Rája with a rifle and other gifts in acknowledgement of his assistance. The country did not immediately calm down, however, and in 1865 a body of police who were sent to establish a post in the hills were attacked and forced to beat a retreat down the ghát. A large force was then assembled, and after a brief but harassing campaign the post was firmly occupied in January 1866. Three of the ringleaders of this rising were transported for life. The hill Savaras remained timid and suspicious for some years afterwards, and as late as 1874 the reports mention it as a notable fact that they were beginning to frequent markets on the plains and that the low country people no longer feared to trust themselves above the gháts.

The only places of interest in Gunupur taluk are the following :—

Gudári : Eighteen miles north of Gunupur, on the bank of the Vamsadhára ; the second largest village in the taluk (population 2,250) and the head-quarters of an ámín of the Jeypore zamindari. The Gudári tána forms part of the estate of Naurangpur referred to in the account of the latter village below. Colonel Campbell, of the Meriah agency, was the first European to visit the place (in 1851) and he built a guard-house and small bungalow in it and left a guard of sibbandis there.

The town is healthy and is a centre for the trade in the produce of the country, especially sál wood. Its inhabitants are largely immigrants from the plains.

Gunupur, the head-quarters of the deputy tahsildar and of an ámín of Jeypore estate, contains (including its suburb Kápugúda) 5,187 inhabitants. The public buildings stand in Kápugúda and include the deputy tahsildar's cutcherry, built in 1900, a hospital (1890), school (1893) and travellers' bungalow. The place is picturesquely situated on the bank of the Vamsadhára and, though irregularly built, has a bright and busy appearance. It originally stood on the right (western) bank of the Vamsadhára, but one fine day the river turned to the south-west and flowed on the other side of it, and the village is now perched on a sort of island on the left (eastern) bank, with the old bed of the river to the east of it. In flood time this fact and the presence of several big channels on its southern side make the place almost inaccessible.

The Báláji *math* here contains a granite temple which is designed on generous lines and contains some excellent carving, but is only partly finished. It was begun by Balaráma Dás, the late mahant of the *math*, but before he could complete it he was turned out of his post in virtue of a decree of the courts obtained against him by the present Jeypore Mahárája, who himself claimed the position of dharmakarta. North of this temple are the remains of an extensive mud fort which is supposed to have been built by the Rájas of Kimedi. Within it, near a tamarind, is pointed out the spot where the wives of the renter Náráyana Pátro mentioned above committed sati on his death.

Jagamanda: Lies about thirteen miles north-east of Gunupur. On a small hillock near it is a little shrine to Mallikésvarasvámi which is known throughout the taluk. It is built in an uncommon fashion of big blocks of stone without the use of mortar; and the people believe that individuals afflicted with leprosy and similar diseases will be cured if they live in it for a fortnight or so and offer small pieces of their person as sacrifices to the deity.

JEYPORE TALUK.

CHAP. XV. JEYPORE.

THIS, the head-quarter taluk of the zamindari of the same name, lies on the '2,000 feet plateau,' which is made up of this taluk and Naurangpur. It is bounded on the north by the Indrávati, west by the Koláb river and Bastar State, east by the '3,000 feet plateau,' and south by the drop down into Malkanagiri taluk. Along this descent, and also in the west round about Rámagiri, is much excellent sál forest, but the greater part of the taluk consists of a flat plain dotted with a few small hills and chiefly cultivated with paddy watered by the ample rainfall, which averages 75 inches and is the heaviest in the district. The people, over nine-tenths of whom speak Uriya, are more numerous to the square mile here than in any other part of the Agency.

The more interesting places in the taluk are the following :—

Guptésvara Cave : On the bank of the Koláb, about nine miles west of Rámagiri by a path which leads through wild sál jungle, is a cave near the top of a limestone hill about 500 feet higher than the surrounding country. It is approached by a modern flight of steps flanked with lines of trees and the entrance is about nine feet wide and eight high. Facing this, near the centre of a roughly circular chamber about ten feet high and forty feet square, is a natural boulder somewhat resembling a lingam, which is held very holy and is called Guptésvara, 'the hidden Siva,' because it was there for generations before any man knew of it. It is said to have been first discovered in the time of Víra Vikrama Deo, Rája of Jeypore from 1637 to 1669, who established the great feast in its honour which is still held every Sivarátri and is under the special patronage of his descendants. The place is now popularly declared to have been the scene of several of the episodes in the Rámáyana. Behind the lingam, the cave slopes downwards into the hill, and becomes very dark. Here are several stalactites, two of which form natural pillars while another is supposed to resemble the sacred cow Kámadhénu. From the udders of this latter water drips at long intervals, and pilgrims sit with their hands spread out beneath, waiting intently to catch a drop when it falls. There are several other caves in the limestone through which the Koláb winds its way at this point, but none so famous.

Jeypore, 'the city of victory,' the capital of the taluk and the zamindari and the place of residence of the Mahárája, is a union of 6,689 inhabitants and is most picturesquely situated close under the western slopes of the 3,000 feet plateau, at the bottom of an irregular amphitheatre formed of its wooded spurs. The place consists of one wide street—some 25 yards broad and running north and south, along which stand all the public offices and some good private residences—and a few lanes on the western side of this. At the northern end of the street are the bungalows of Dr. J. Marsh, tutor to the Mahárája's son, of the Forest Officer of the estate, and of the members of the Schleswig-Holstein Lutheran Mission; while at the southern end stand the Mahárája's palace, a large temple to Rámachandrasvámi facing it, and, beyond, in an extensive rose-garden, the new palace which was built about 1895 while the estate was under management during the present Mahárája's minority, but is now considered an unlucky residence and is used only as a guest-house.

Immediately west of the town is a great tank a mile long and half a mile wide, which never dries up and is kept as a sanctuary for wildfowl, large flocks of which swim fearlessly about it. West of this again are extensive groves of ancient mangoes and from the circular road through these is obtained the fairest view of Jeypore—in the foreground the tank, reflecting every tint of the sky above it; behind, the steep wooded line of the higher plateau; and in the middle distance the town itself, almost hidden amid its numerous trees, with the white tops of the main gate of the palace rising above the mass of foliage.

Both the town and the palace have been immensely improved in late years. In 1855 the former was described as being 'a most wretched place, there being scarcely half a dozen tiled houses, and those of the most inferior description. . . . There is not an artisan in the place, save one carpenter, and he a Telugu man and not a native of the country.' The palace was then 'a paltry collection of tiled buildings in bad repair in a court-yard surrounded by a mud wall.'

Since the opening of the Pottangi ghat road and the roads to Naurangpur and to Bastar through Borigumma and Kótapád (see pp. 139 and 141), the town has risen in importance, as nearly all the produce of the 2,000 feet plateau passes through it on the way to the coast. In the busy part of the export season hundreds of carts enter and leave it every day. A Musalman has opened a tannery in it and others of the same faith have started shops where all sorts of commodities can be obtained. The daily market under

CHAP. XV. JEYPORE.

the palace walls is thronged with a collection of hill people from the surrounding villages selling fish, vegetables, bamboos and the like and wearing quaint dresses and ornaments which are in startling contrast to those of the Telugu immigrants from the low country who may be seen purchasing from them. The palace is surrounded no longer by a mud wall, but by a high masonry erection put up by the present Mahárája, which is entered by an imposing three-storeyed gateway known (like all other front entrances in the Jeypore country) as 'the Lion Gate.' Within, one block of masonry buildings has already been completed and an even larger one is in course of construction. But though it is advancing with the times, Jeypore still suffers from its remoteness from the outer world, and is a sleepy hollow where leisurely ways are the fashion.

It is malarious (partly, perhaps, because the only water-supply is from tainted tanks and wells) but in this respect also it has greatly improved. When British officers were first appointed in the Jeypore estate in 1863, this place was made their head-quarters; but so greatly did they all suffer from malaria that it was reported in 1869 that 'no officer in the northern division will come up unless compelled to do so. Neither the Assistant Agent nor Superintendents of Police ever stay a day longer than they are absolutely obliged to do, and the consequence is that work is carried on anyhow, and the only wonder is that it has been possible to keep matters going at all.' The native staff suffered every wit as much, and it was said that 'no decently qualified person will accept the post of sub-magistrate, which entails a broken constitution and enforced retirement at the end of six months.' In 1870, accordingly, the head-quarters of the European officers were transferred to Koraput and the sub-magistrate was stationed at Kótapád, where he remained until about 1882.

The great event of the year in Jeypore is the Dasara feast, which lasts for sixteen days and includes several ceremonies in honour of the goddess Kanaka ('golden') Durga whose temple is within the palace walls. The image of this goddess (other names for whom are Káli and Tákuráni) is said in the Jeypore family chronicles to have been originally captured at the end of the fifteenth century from the great Purushóttama Déva of Orissa (see p. 28) when he was returning through the Jeypore country after his conquest of Conjeeveram. Human sacrifices used to be made to the goddess. The reports of the Meriah Agents say that in 1861 a kidnapped girl of about twelve years of age was offered up to her in the hope of staying an epidemic of cholera in the town. Nowadays sheep and goats take the place of human victims, but the flowers with which they are decked beforehand, which are brought specially from Nandapuram in Pottangi taluk, the old capital of the estate, are still known as *meriah pushpa*.

Sheep and goats are sacrificed on each of the first thirteen days of the Dasara and on the fourteenth some buffaloes as well. On that day, which is known in consequence as the *Bodo Uppano* ('great offerings') day, the Mahárája, dressed in white, himself visits the goddess' shrine and then holds, from a white throne, a darbar which is attended by the bollo loko (courtiers) and lampatas (servants) and others, while the senior Mahárání (called the Patta Mahádévi) does the same after him, receiving bhét (presents) from the ladies who attend. On the sixteenth, or *Sanno Uppano* ('little offerings'), day the Mahárája, who this time is dressed in scarlet, worships the goddess in the Darbar hall of the palace and holds, from a scarlet throne, a darbar at which bhéts are offered. Neither of these thrones are used except at the Dasara. It is customary for the Mahárája's feudal retainers to come into Jeypore with their followers to pay their respects at this second darbar, and many of the inams and mokhásas in the estate (see, for example, the account of Bissamkatak above) have been granted on the express condition that the grantees do this annual service.

On the eighteenth day, preceded by the goddess Kanaka Durga and a white flag which was captured long ago from the troops of Bastar in one of the many skirmishes which took place with that State, the Mahárája and his son, seated in ambáris on elephants and followed by the European and other officials of the place in howdahs on other elephants, go in procession to the *Dasara poda* in a mango grove to the north of the town. There worship is paid to the goddess by the Mahárája and afterwards the crowd proceed to shoot a brinjal off the top of a long bamboo. This custom is followed at Dasara all over the Northern Circars and the country west of them, and is supposed to symbolise the general rejoicings which took place when Durga succeeded in overcoming the buffalo-headed demon Mahishásura.

The family chronicles, a résumé of which has been kindly furnished by the Mahárája, ascribe a very ancient origin to the line of the Jeypore zamindars. Beginning with Kanakaséna of the solar race, a general and feudatory of the king of Kashmir, they trace the pedigree through thirty-two generations down to Vináyaka Deo, a younger son who left Kashmir rather than

CHAP. XV. JEYPORE.

hold a subordinate position, went to Benares, did penance to Kási Visvésvarasvámi there, and was told by the god in a dream to go to the kingdom of Nandapuram belonging to the Silavamsam line, of which he would become king. Vináyaka Deo, continue the legends, proceeded thither, married the king's daughter, succeeded in 1443 A.D. to the famous throne of 32 steps there, and founded the family of Jeypore.[1] His dates and those of his descendants (all of whom bore the title of Deo) may be quoted here at once for reference:—

Vináyaka Deo	1443–76
His son Vijaya Chandrakhya	1476–1510
His son Bhairava	1510–27
His son Visvanádha	1527–71
His son Balaráma I	1571–97
His son Yesvanta	1597–1637
His son Víra Vikrama	1637–69
His son Krishna	1669–72
His son Visvambara I	1672–76
His brother Mallakimardhana Krishna	1676–81
His brother Hari	1681–84
His brother Balaráma II	1684–86
His adopted son Raghunátha Krishna	1686–1708
His son Rámachandra I	1708–11
His brother Balaráma III	1711–13
His brother Visvambara II	1713–52
His step-brother Lála Krishna	1752–58
His brother Vikrama I	1758–81
His son Rámachandra II	1781–1825
His son Vikrama II	1825–60
His son Rámachandra III	1860–89
His son Vikrama III	1889

Not long after his accession, some of his subjects rose against him, but he recovered his position with the help of a leader of Brinjáris; and ever since then, in grateful recognition, his descendants have appended to their signatures a wavy line (called *valatradu*) which represents the rope with which Brinjáris tether their cattle.

Vináyaka Deo and his six successors, say the family papers, had each only one son; and the sixth of them, Víra Vikrama (1637–69) accordingly resolved to remove his residence elsewhere. The astrologers and wise men reported that the present Jeypore

[1] Mr. Oram's report of 1784 on the estate says that the family is descended from a Rája who was a favourite of an ancient king of Jagannáth and sovereign of the Northern Circars, and was given his daughter in marriage and this tributary principality as her dower.

was 'a place of the Kshatriya class' and it was accordingly made the capital and named after the famous Jeypore of the north. Víra Vikrama's possessions at this time included not only the country now comprised in the Jeypore zamindari but also the strip of land which lies at the base of the Gháts, and even, it is averred, places as far east of them as Potnúru and Bhógapuram. He paid a tribute of Rs. 24,000 to the king of Golconda. In 1664 one of that king's family invaded the Jeypore hills on some pretext, but the affair ended happily, Víra Vikrama being given by the king in the following year a sword, ensigns and standards, and likewise a copper grant (which is still preserved in the Jeypore palace) conferring upon him certain titles, among them that of Mahárája.

Visvambara Deo I (1672–76) was the originator of the feudal system of which traces still survive in Jeypore. He divided his possessions into a series of estates in charge of each of which he placed some faithful retainer (often conferring on him at the same time some high-sounding title) who was made responsible for its peace and order and required to acknowledge his suzerain's authority by appearing, when called upon, with a certain armed force. Several of the existing zamindars, as will be seen later on in this chapter, trace their origin to the feudal lordlings then appointed, but the only one of them from whom any similar service is still required by Jeypore is the Tát Rája of Bissamkatak.

In the time of Mallakimardhana Krishna Deo (1676–81), the chronicles relate, the French attacked Jeypore but were beaten off with the loss of a number of cannon. Fourteen cannon, said to be those captured on this occasion, are still in the palace at Jeypore, but they contain no marks by which they can be identified as French.

Rámachandra Deo I (1708–11) quarrelled with his younger brother, the Balaráma Deo III who eventually succeeded him, and the latter established an independent principality with its capital at Náráyanapatnam, to the west of Párvatípur, and continued to reside in that village when he came into the estate. Some of the outlying portions of his possessions passed to the Rájas of Vizianagram, who were fast rising to great power in the low country. His brother Visvambara Deo II, who succeeded him in 1713, was also a weak ruler. He likewise lived at Náráyanapatnam and is said to have dug tanks and wells there, dammed the Janjhávati to supply them with water, and made a big seraglio for his numerous wives and mistresses. The spot

CHAP. XV. JEYPORE.

where the latter committed sati at his death is still pointed out and is known as *sati garbha*. It lies within the ruins of the old fort, and not far off is a curious old cannon, of great length and made by shrinking successive rings of iron on to a central iron core.

In 1752 Lála Krishna Deo came into the estate, but the succession was soon afterwards claimed by his brother Vikrama Deo. Viziaráma Rázu, Rája of Vizianagram, sided with the latter; drove out Lála Krishna, who retired to Kalyána Singapur;[1] but obtained as the price of his assistance the fiefs of Mádgole, Kásipuram, Andra, Sálúr, Páchipenta, Chemudu, Belgám, Sangamvalasa, Kurupám and Mérangi, all of which were then held by vassals of Jeypore.

In 1768, three years after the English had obtained the Northern Circars, Viziaráma Rázu wrote[2] to the Government of Madras stating that in 1752 Salábat Jang, Subadar of the Deccan, had granted him the Jeypore country as a jaghir on an annual payment of Rs. 24,000, and asking that the grant might be renewed. He produced an English translation of the sanad, and this set out that 'the villages of Casseypatnam (Kásipuram), Nandapore (Nandapuram), Maulgal (Mádgole), etc., amounting to 24,000 Rupees' were 'assigned by way of Jaggeer to Rajah Viziaramraz Manna Sultan.' Manna Sultan may mean 'Lord of the hills,' but Mr. Grant (in his *Political Survey of the Northern Circars* appended to the *Fifth Report on the affairs of the E. I. Co.*) translates it 'King of the Jungles' and says it was conferred on Viziaráma, in derision, but at the request of Bussy, by Salábat Jang. In September 1768[3] the Madras Government, in consideration of the past services of the Rája to them, decided to 'confirm him in the possession of the Jagueer he has requested, so long as he continues obedient to the Company's Authority and exerts himself in promoting their influence in the Circar,' but the cowle issued accordingly in March 1769 merely granted and confirmed to him and his heirs 'the said revenue of Rs. 24,000 issuing out of the said Districts of Casseypatnam, Nandaporam and Maulgal.'

In 1775,[4] while disturbances were occurring in Kimedi, Vikrama Deo of Jeypore assembled a force in the Ráyagada valley and threatened to support the malcontents, so Captain Richard

[1] Family papers. Mr. Oram's report of 1784 says he fled to the Marathas.
[2] Madras records, Military, Country Correspondence, Vol. XVI, 228.
[3] Minutes of Consultation of 30th September 1768.
[4] Extract from Military Consultations for that year.

Mathews, commanding the Northern Circars, accompanied by some of the sibbandis of the Vizianagram Rája, marched to Jeypore. His report states that Vikrama Deo 'came and agreed to surrender the Fort and quit all pretensions to the several passes leading into the Circar, requesting that he might be suffered to keep the Country to the Westward of them ; I took possession of the Fort on the 11th March. It is a square of about one Thousand yards built of Mud. The wall 20 feet high, the Bastions very good, the Rampart tolerable, and a ditch 20 feet wide and as many deep ; I have ordered it to be destroyed.' The ruins of it may still be seen to the east of Jeypore village in what is known as 'old Jeypore.' The demolition was carried out by the sibbandis from Vizianagram, who were afterwards put in charge of all the passes.

Mr. Oram's report of 1784 and the report of the same year of the Committee of Circuit, of which he was one of the members, state that the frequent revolts and disturbances of the Jeyporeans soon afterwards decided the Vizianagram Rája to hand back the whole country to Vikrama Deo for an annual sum of Rs. 40,000, of which no more than three-fourths was ever paid. This restoration was apparently effected before 1777, as in that year (see p. 274) we find the Jeypore Rája assisting the Bastar chief to regain his throne.

The Committee said that the Rája of Vizianagram none the less claimed before them that the Jeypore country was his jaghir, producing as evidence of his assertion the cowle of 1769 above mentioned. 'After an attentive perusal and investigation of his pretensions,' they wrote, 'we observe that the cowle, which is to be regarded as the only substantial authority, does not assign to him the whole District in possession, but only admits the payment of Rs. 24,000 therefrom, as an inheritance during the Zamindar's good conduct and obedience to the Company.' The Committee accordingly proposed to constitute Jeypore into a separate zamindari with a peshkash of Rs. 35,000, arguing 'that these lands being so entirely dependent on Vizianagram is not only in appearance derogatory and detrimental to the Company's interest and authority, but actually dangerous from the retreat it affords the guilty in cases of insurrection, from the command of troops and the only accessible passes that it leaves in the hands of that Zamindar.'

The suggestion was not adopted, and the position remained unchanged until Viziaráma Rázu was killed by the Company's troops at Padmanábham (see p. 53) in 1794. To reward the Jeypore family for holding aloof from the Vizianagram party in the

CHAP. XV. JEYPORE.

disturbances which followed, Lord Hobart gave the then Rája, Rámachandra Deo II, a permanent sanad of the usual kind granting the estate to him and his heirs in perpetuity on payment of a peshkash of Rs. 25,000. When the permanent settlement was introduced in 1803, this sum was reduced to Rs. 16,000.[1] In addition, Rs. 3,000 is paid for the pargana of Kótapád referred to below.

From 1803 to 1848 Jeypore remained an almost unknown country to the officers of the district. Once, when the Rája was behindhand with his peshkash and a military expedition seemed to be the only way of making him pay up, 'the Government proposed to transfer the zamindari to the Nagpur State, but the offer was declined.'[2] In 1848 great complaints reached Vizagapatam of the feebleness of the Rája, Vikrama Deo II, and the tyranny and misrule of his managers. Large bodies of ryots found their way to the coast and represented the country to be the scene of plunder, murder and rapine. At last the Rája's officials were driven out of the Gunupur taluk and disturbances of some importance immediately arose. The faction opposed to Vikrama Deo (whose avowed object was to remove him) was headed by his eldest son (a youth of thirteen who was afterwards Rámachandra Deo III) and the latter's mother, the Patta Mahádévi; and their following comprised the most influential muttadars of the country.

Both parties agreed to abide by the decision of the Agent regarding the dispute, and in April 1849 Mr. Smollett accordingly set out for Párvatípur. He was met there by the son, who travelled with great pomp of elephants, palanquins and horses and a guard of 1,000 matchlock men, while the Rája was represented by some of his officers. A compromise suggested by the Agent was accepted by neither party, and, to prevent further anarchy, Mr. Smollett attached the four tánas of Gunupur, Ráyagada, Náráyanapatnam and Álamanda.

Not long afterwards he arranged to meet both father and son together; and after wearisome and protracted negotiations a reconciliation was effected and the attachment withdrawn. A breach, however, soon ensued, and on the 16th September 1849 the son seized his father and the latter's chief servants and confined them all in the fort at Ráyagada. They were released by a company of sibbandis under Captain Haly, but the old man's authority was completely gone and the villagers would not even bring him any food. A second reconciliation was afterwards effected and it was

[1] Government's letter to the Board, dated 22nd October 1803, para. 20.
[2] Mr. Russell's report of 18th November 1834, para. 70.

agreed that Gunupur should be attached and that the revenues thereof should be devoted to paying off the Rája's debts and liquidating the arrears of peshkash. The Rája appears to have lost all self-control at this point, and to have sunk into the deepest abasement. He did not return to his capital, but allowed his son to proceed thither and administer all his affairs. He himself remained on at Náráyanapatnam, deserted by his servants, given up to the most besotted sensuality, and subsisting on the charity of the villagers, 'who were heartily tired of his residence among them.'

In 1855 Jeypore affairs again attracted attention, the existence in the zamindari of the practice of sati being brought to notice. Mr. Smollett reported that cases were frequent; that moreover, owing to Vikrama Deo's incapacity, the country was in a state of complete anarchy; that the Rája's younger son had seized Gunupur; and that the only means of ensuring security to life and property was to post a European officer to Jeypore. Vikrama Deo was sounded regarding this suggestion and in reply wrote a long letter promising to stop all crime in the country, asserting his competence to rule, and earnestly deprecating the interference of Government. Meanwhile, however, the retainers of his two sons had come to blows over the seizure of Gunupur and a severe fight had occurred. In July 1855 Government authorized the Agent to assume 'the control, both police and revenue, of the tracts above the gháts, the taluks below being managed by the agency direct.' Lord Dalhousie, however, was then at Ootacamund and objected, considering that the step was likely to 'involve the British Government in a protracted jungle and hill war, such as that of Gúmsur.' Mr. Smollett protested that the two cases were in no way parallel, but no further action was taken until Vikrama Deo's death in 1860.

The Agent, Mr. Fane, then revived Mr. Smollett's proposal; this was ultimately sanctioned; and in January 1863 Lieutenant Smith was located at Jeypore as Assistant Agent and Captain Galbraith as Assistant Superintendent of Police. Some hostility was evinced at first to the arrangement, and it was necessary to deport, under agency warrants, two leading malcontents, both ex-díwáns of the estate. Nor was this astonishing. 'Truth to say,' as Mr. Carmichael, then Agent, wrote in 1864, 'we are working out in Jeypore an experiment which has never been tried before. Eighty years of independent native misrule have been succeeded at once, without compromise and without any exhibition of military or semi-military force, by an administration which aims at the same completeness as prevails in our oldest provinces.'

Vikrama Deo's son Rámachandra Deo III held the estate until his death on 27th August 1889. 'He was a man of much character and considerable ability, and though his property was incredibly mismanaged in some respects, in others he showed prudence and foresight. Had his education and training been such as to allow of his going into details, he would probably have administered his estate admirably. He was immensely popular with his people, with whom he mixed very freely and to whom his great liberality justly endeared him.' His son, the present Mahárája, Vikrama Deo III, was born in 1875 and so was a minor at the time of his father's death, and the estate was taken under the management of Government under the agency rules. The taluks above the gháts were put in charge of Mr. H. D. Taylor, I.C.S. (who held the post until the property was eventually handed back) and the others were managed by a Deputy Collector. The minor was educated under the care of Dr. J. Marsh, who had already been his tutor for some time, and in February 1893 married the eldest daughter of the Rája of Udaipur, a native state in Chota Nagpur. A son, Rámachandra, was born to him on the last day of the same year and is now being educated at Jeypore by Dr. Marsh.

The estate was handed back on the 27th November 1895 with a balance of some 7½ lakhs in Government paper and another lakh in cash, besides Rs. 1,05,000 which had been lent to the Sálúr estate and Rs. 3,53,500 secured by the mortgage of half of Mádgole. The accounts had been systematized, the forest revenue increased, saw mills put up at Mattupáda near Rámagiri, granaries built to receive the large amount of rent which is paid in kind, nearly a lakh spent on improving communications, the 'new Mahál' in the palace completed, the other palace above referred to practically finished, the tána establishments reorganized, and the former guards replaced by a small body of well-drilled and well-armed men. The minor's mother's eyesight was also restored by a successful operation on the cataract from which she was suffering. The title of Mahárája was conferred on the Rája as a personal distinction in 1896.

The Jeypore zamindari is scheduled as impartible and inalienable in Act II of 1904 and is divided for purposes of administration into the upper (or Jeypore) and the lower (or Gunupur) divisions, which are each administered by a manager (stationed at Jeypore and Párvatípur respectively) subordinate to the díwán. The upper division consists of the tánas of Jeypore, Koraput, Nandapuram, Rámagiri, Malkanagiri, Kótapád, Umarkót, Bhairava Singapur and Naurangpur; and the lower of those of Gunupur, Gudári, Ráyagada, Kalyána Singapur and Náráyanapatnam. In addition there are certain scattered villages in other parts of the district, and half of the Mádgole estate (68 villages) has been mortgaged (see p. 322) to Jeypore. The net income from all sources is some seven lakhs per annum. The land revenue is highest in Gunupur, Kótapád and Ráyagada, and lowest in Rámagiri and Malkanagiri. Each tána is divided into vaguely defined muttas and is in charge of an ámín (also styled a nigamán) under whom are revenue inspectors, sometimes called samutdars. The village establishments consist of the headman, or naik, and certain menials called bárikes, chelláns or gondas, and they are remunerated by the profits of cultivating certain land set aside in each village for them, and called 'the naik's land,' or by grain fees from the villagers. In Khond villages the headman is called the majji or sámanto and in Savara villages the gomángo. These people also have a kind of spokesman called the péshini, who arranges matters with officials. Round about Naurangpur, headmen of big villages are sometimes called báranaiks, which literally means head of twelve villages.

The land revenue is administered on methods which are without a parallel in other Madras districts and are interesting from the survival of the ancient feudal spirit which they exhibit. No survey or settlement has ever been carried out; and though in the lower division a good deal of the land is held on ryotwari tenure most of that above the Gháts is administered under a village-rent system called mustájari. The mustájars, or renters of the villages, are very usually the naiks. They are yearly tenants and receive pattas (locally known as cowles) from, and give muchilikas (kadapás) to, the Mahárája; but the amounts they pay vary but little from year to year and often the same mustájar holds his village for a long term. They send in no accounts. In theory they are merely agents for the collection of the revenue, being remunerated by being allowed to cultivate, rent free, a certain definite piece of land ear-marked for the purpose, by immemorial custom. They are supposed to have no power to eject ryots or enhance their sists, though they may profit by the sist of any land newly brought under cultivation during their lease. In practice, however, it is admittedly difficult to prevent them from oppressing their ryots and levying forced labour for the cultivation of their own lands; while the fact that the villagers have no occupancy right in their fields renders the latter unwilling to sink money in permanent improvements. The uncertainty of their tenure, however, confers the advantage that they lose little by emigrating elsewhere, and emigration is the time-honoured remedy for over-assessment In this sparsely-peopled country the land-owner wants every ryot he can get, and is careful not to provoke any of them into betaking themselves to a rival estate.

The sist is paid either in cash or kind, cash rents being commoner on the 3,000 feet plateau (where the crops are mostly dry) and in the lower division than on the 2,000 feet plateau of Jeypore itself, where so much paddy is raised. The grain received as rent is stored in huge granaries at Jeypore, Kótapád, Naurangpur and other places and held up until prices are high and then sold to traders from the plains. It would fetch better prices if the sample were not so mixed. The assessment is generally a certain sum on each plough and hoe used. This usually varies from Rs. 6 to Rs. 2 per plough and from as. 4 to as. 8 per hoe, according to the quality of the soil and the accessibility of the village. There is a vague understanding as to the amount of wet land covered by the assessment for a plough, but on dry land a ryot may cultivate as much as he likes when he has paid his assessment for his implement. The ámins have power to vary the rates and they also fix the amounts to be paid for the hill-cultivation called *kondapódu* (see p. 111). In the old days the assessments used to include a number of miscellaneous items, such as stated quantities of oil, ghee, skins, arrowroot and so on; but when the estate was under Government management these were very generally commuted into money payments. The only important item of this kind which survives is the grass sist in certain tánas of the upper division. The ryots there are required to pay part of their assessments in thatching-grass, which is difficult to get and is necessary for the annual repair of the estate buildings.

The Jeypore ryots are undoubtedly far more lightly assessed than their brethren in the zamindaris on the plains, but they are casual in their methods of cultivation Except in the Singapur tána and the Wondragedda mutta, there is no irrigation; and the latter is the only place in the upper division where two crops are raised. In the Koraput and Nandapuram taluks the ryots are often, also, deeply in debt to the Sondi liquor-sellers and bound down to them under the góti system referred to on p. 109 above.

Besides the ordinary, or jeráyati, land, the estate includes certain dévadáyam, or temple, property which is managed by the Mahárája direct. There are likewise numerous inams and mokhásas held on favourable rates, in which the grantees deal directly and independently with their ryots. These are apparently of three main kinds; namely, gift (dáno) or agraháram, mokhása and service; but the last two terms are often used as interchangeable. The local customs regarding their devolution and liability to resumption are said to be unusual, but have never been authoritatively set out. Dáno grants are made to one man only, agrahárams to a set of people in fixed shares. Both usually pass to the next heir, whether direct or not. The payment due to the Mahárája is called tonki. Mokhásas were usually granted in favour of the Rájas' relations or other persons of rank and generally lapse on failure of direct heirs. The payment due on them is called kattubadi but on 'sarva mokhásas' nothing is due. Service inams are mostly hereditary and can only, except as a matter of grace, be held by direct male descendants in the eldest line of the original grantee. The payments made for them are known as kattubadi or talapu díwáni and the services required are very various. Besides the common condition already mentioned, requiring the grantee to appear with a certain number of retainers at the Dasara darbar, they sometimes include such minor duties as doing worship to certain deities, supplying the Mahárája with household necessaries and performing domestic service in the palace. The Uriya pátros (pátro is a title conferred by former Rájas) were service inamdars, and some of them (such as he of Sirdarpur) pay their dues to the Mahárája direct, while others (like the pátros of Jagdalpur and Ambadála under the Tát Rája of Bissamkatak) pay it to their immediate feudal superior.

None of these inams were dealt with at the time of the Inam Settlement. While the estate was under management title-deeds were called for and checked, but in the majority of cases the inamdars were unable to produce any deeds at all. It was decided that in the case of inams granted subsequent to the permanent settlement the desirability of resumption was a matter which, except in very clear cases, was best left to the decision of the Mahárája when he came of age.

Besides his income from land and forests and the tribute from Bissamkatak (see p. 233) the Mahárája receives a certain revenue from bhéts. These were originally Dasara offerings, and now include sums paid on the formal grant of titles (such as Visvása Rai, Bakshi Bahádur and many others) and the bestowal of special privileges such as the right to travel in a palanquin, ride on a horse, or wear a sacred thread.]

CHAP. XV. JEYPORE.

Kótapád: Twenty-five miles in a straight line north-west of Jeypore; population 3,154. Is the residence of an ámín of the Jeypore estate and a station of the Schleswig-Holstein Lutheran Mission, and was formerly the head-quarters of the sub-magistrate of Jeypore taluk. It lies on the important main road (through Borigumma) from Jeypore to Jagdalpur, the capital of Bastar, in a wonderful level expanse of rich rain-fed paddy-fields, diversified by topes and bounded on the east by a low line of scattered hills, which extend for miles and form the most important granary in all Jeypore. The village itself is well drained and stands in open ground on laterite soil, and so is a healthy spot. To the west of it is the great Damayanti tank, a picturesque sheet of water.

The place gives its name to the Kótapád pargana, a portion of the Jeypore zamindari which was long held on different terms from the rest of the estate and has an interesting history. It consists of the five garhs or forts of Kótapád, Churuchúnda, Poragarh, Umarkót and Raigarh, the country subject to which runs along the Bastar frontier from about ten miles north of Jeypore town for 80 miles northwards, and has an average breadth of 30 miles and an area of some 2,500 square miles.

In 1777[1] the Chief of Bastar was driven out of his dominions by his brother and took refuge in Jeypore. The Rája of that place assisted him to recover his territories and in return, on 6th April 1778, the Bastar Chief ceded to Jeypore these five garhs, free of rent and on certain conditions, among which was the stipulation that Bastar should be entitled to collect in the pargana a tax, called mahádán, of Rs. 25 on every 100 bullock-loads of merchandise imported or exported. In 1782 hostilities broke out between Bastar and Jeypore in consequence of the latter having neglected to fulfil certain of these conditions, and the Bastar forces recaptured three of the garhs. The Bastar Chief, however, was in arrear with his tribute to his suzerains, the Maráthas, and their troops came and sequestered all five of the garhs. It is alleged that in 1811 the Marátha deputy, Rámchanda Wágh, granted all five to the Rája of Jeypore under a new sanad, on certain conditions. However this may be, they have since remained in the possession of his descendants. Bastar was by no means pleased, and the quarrels and mutual raids and reprisals between the two chiefs kept that part of the country in a perpetual state of anarchy for years, and obliged Jeypore to

[1] Government of India's letter in G.O., No. 2075, Judicial, dated 20th December 1862, which contains a history of the case up to then.

maintain garrisons of Uriya paiks at each of the five forts. Correspondence regarding the right to the pargana also occurred at intervals throughout the first half of the last century between the Madras Government and the authorities at Nagpur, and the question was not finally set at rest until in 1862 the Government of India ruled that it should be left to the management of Jeypore in the same manner as the rest of that zamindari, and ordered (in 1863 [1]) that the Jeypore Rája should pay Rs. 3,000 per annum for it, being compensation to Bastar for the cessation of the right to collect mahádán. 'After this adjudication everything promised fair: the rabble of spearmen kept up by Jeypore at Kótapád and other frontier villages was dispersed; the ryot ploughed the land and got in his harvests without molestation; in short, the land had peace for the first time, perhaps since 1777.' But this fair promise was belied on several subsequent occasions.

The Rs. 3,000 was for many years paid with the rest of the Jeypore peshkash and remitted by the Vizagapatam officers to the Government of the Central Provinces, and the latter paid Rs. 2,000 of it to the Bastar Chief and kept the other Rs. 1,000 because in 1819 a remission of Bastar tribute to this amount had been made in consideration of the alienation of the pargana.

The pargana was not included in the sanad granted to the Rája of Jeypore at the permanent settlement in 1803 and the Rs. 3,000 was not in any sense peshkash. Jeypore thus held the Kótapád pargana free of any peshkash at all.

This fact was brought to notice in 1888; the Rs. 3,000 was ordered to be credited to Madras, and not Central Provinces' revenues; and the question as to the amount of peshkash which should be levied was raised. After considerable correspondence a provisional sanad was granted to the Mahárája in 1897 which treated the pargana as an estate held in perpetuity upon a quit-rent liable to revision from time to time, and provided for his paying for twenty years an annual quit-rent, liable to subsequent revision and in addition to the Rs. 3,000 already being paid, of Rs. 13,666, or one-fifth of the total revenue demand, gradually decreasing deductions being provided for in the first ten years on account of the cost of certain semi-military paiks which had been maintained in the pargana and were to be gradually done away with.

The Mahárája appealed against this decision on the grounds that the pargana was a feudatory state, and not part of British

[1] Government of India's letter in G.O., No. 1597, Judicial, dated 5th October 1863.

CHAP. XV. JEYPORE.

India, and so could not be assessed to quit-rent; and that the arrangement of 1863 was permanent. In 1899 the Government of India overruled both pleas but directed that the quit-rent should be inclusive of, and not in addition to, the Rs. 3,000. A revised sanad was accordingly granted in 1900. The Mahárája, however, appealed to the Secretary of State, who, while holding that Kótapád was part of British India, ordered that the arrangement of 1863 should be adhered to. Thus only Rs. 3,000 is now paid for the pargana.

KORAPUT TALUK.

KORAPUT taluk forms the portion of the 3,000 feet plateau just above, and east of, the town of Jeypore. It is perhaps the barest of vegetation of any part of that plateau, there being no forest anywhere in it except along the edge of the ghát to Jeypore. The landscape consists of an undulating expanse of red and brown earth, with laterite cropping out here and there and coarse grass growing in the hollows, thickly dotted with small red hills covered to their very tops with permanent dry cultivation, between which meander small rivulets the beds of which have been levelled and planted with paddy. Three-quarters of the people speak Uriya and a fifth talk Khond. After Vizagapatam, the taluk contains more Christians than any other. The head-quarters is—

Koraput, the residence of the Divisional Officer, the Superintendent of Police, and his Assistant (who live together in one large bungalow begun in 1873) and of the deputy tahsildar. The place contains the lines and hospital of a body of reserve police and a large sub-jail capable of holding 87 persons, and is a station of the Schleswig-Holstein Lutheran Mission. It is a neatly-kept village with a population of 1,560 persons, and lies on the main road which runs from Jeypore to the plains by the Pottangi ghát (see p. 139). The head-quarters of the officers in charge of Jeypore was transferred hither from Jeypore town in 1870, as it was fondly hoped that a place standing so high and so clear of jungle would be free from the malaria which infested Jeypore. Curiously enough, these expectations have by no means been fulfilled and the station is not healthy, the south-west monsoon driving through it with great violence and malaria (even the black-water variety) attacking residents. The latter is usually ascribed to the breeding ground for mosquitoes which is afforded by a nullah fed from springs which runs through the place, and in 1904–05, in the hope of removing this superfluous moisture, eucalyptus trees were planted round about the nullah and the latter was revetted throughout with stone. The trees all died, and so far no noticeable improvement has resulted from the revetment.

MALKANAGIRI TALUK.

CHAP. XV. MALKANAGIRI.

MALKANAGIRI (the largest, and at the same time the most sparsely-populated, taluk in the Presidency) occupies the southern third of the part of the district which lies immediately west of the main line of the Ghâts; and forms a plateau which is from 1,000 to 1,500 feet lower than the rest of this. Its northern boundary is the crest of a sál-clad line of heights which run along the southern edge of the 2,000 feet plateau formed by Jeypore and Naurangpur taluks; but southwards from this it drops sharply down to the south-west, Malkanagiri village being only 641 feet above the sea and Mótu, at the southernmost corner, considerably less. On the west, Bastar State and the Saveri river form the boundary; to the south, the beautiful Siléru divides the taluk from the Gódávari Agency and joins the Saveri at Mótu; while on the east the frontier follows an ill-defined line running along the head of the ghâts which uphold the 3,000 feet plateau and lying nearly parallel to the Machéru, as the upper waters of the Siléru are there called.

Malkanagiri differs widely from any other part of the Jeypore zamindari or the Vizagapatam district. Almost the whole of it is one vast jungle. As has already been mentioned (p. 121), there is little good timber in this; but in places (between Balaméla and Kondakambéru and on to the Golgonda boundary, for example) the growth is exceedingly thick and contains much bamboo. Further south, beyond Venkatapálaiyam, are many square miles covered with coarse grass, ten feet high, among which are scattered saplings. As one approaches the extreme southern corner at Mótu, whence there is an outlet by the river to the Gódávari district, the country becomes visibly more civilized, grass and jungle giving way to paddy-fields, dry crops and palmyras, the last of which are rare in other parts of Jeypore.

The south-west monsoon is heavier in this taluk than in any other in the district except Jeypore, and in the rains the country is impassably swampy. The north-east monsoon, on the other hand, is fended off by the hills and is very light. Consequently for half the year much of the taluk is under water and for the other half it is parched in the extreme. The hills similarly keep off the sea breeze, and the heat is sometimes terrific. Malaria, too, is probably worse here than in any other part of the district.

Malkanagiri also differs from the rest of Vizagapatam in its inhabitants. In the north and north-west the people are largely Mattiyas; on the hills to the east, on either side of the Machéru, live the Banda (or 'naked') Porojas, whose women wear the irreducible minimum of clothing; round Malkanagiri and Kórukonda are colonies of Ronas, who came here as paiks; while south of Malkanagiri village the prevailing caste are the easy-going Kōyas, who have pushed their way up from the Gódávari district and speak a language of their own. These various communities have already been referred to in Chapter III. They are even more nomadic in their ways than the rest of the agency population, and a Malkanagiri village is here to-day and gone to-morrow.

The dry crops are much the same as elsewhere. A little paddy is raised in the lower hollows, along the banks of the Siléru is a good deal of tobacco, and particularly sweet oranges are grown in places. Exceptional facilities for irrigation exist in the many streams which run from the hills on the east into the Saveri, but they are quite neglected.

Not much is known of the taluk's early history. Local tradition carries it back to the times of one 'Orjon Malik', who was set upon by a confederacy which included the Jeypore Rája and was slain in a fort near Kórukonda. Jeypore obtained the taluk, and granted it on service tenure to the Uriya paik who had shot Orjon Malik in the fight, whose family held it hereditarily until comparatively recently. They were called Tát Rájas and apparently did much for the country, old tamarind groves, deserted tanks and forgotten forts testifying to their efforts. About 1835[1] the last of the line, Paramánando, died; and his widow's díwán, Erramma Rázu, being overthrown by a faction, procured the aid of some Rohillas from Hyderabad, regained the upper hand, and cut off the noses of four of his chief opponents. These gentlemen went and complained to Mr. Reade, the Agent (who happened to be at Narasapatam), and he sent up a party of sibbandis who captured Erramma Rázu. The latter was sentenced to transportation for life, but died suddenly in the Vizagapatam jail in 1859.

Soon afterwards Paramánando's widow died, and her daughter Bangára Dévi succeeded. But all authority vested in one Sanyási Pátro, a very turbulent character, who gave trouble by refusing to pay any kattubadi to Jeypore and by insisting on collecting moturpha and sayar in spite of the Agent's orders to the contrary. He was eventually imprisoned in 1865, and about 1869

[1] See Mr. Carmichael's *Manual*, 17.

Bangára Dévi obtained a lease of the taluk for Rs. 3,500, though the usual figure had been only Rs. 750.

In 1870 it was realised that Malkanagiri required a sub-magistrate of its own, but as the Government of India said this must be arranged without making additions to the existing establishment, the deputy tahsildar of Nandapuram was moved thither and his charge was added to Koraput. The country at that time was divided into four dwáros or gates (each of which was supposed to lie under one of the gates of Malkanagiri village), was sub-divided into muttas, and was in charge of a nigamán. Round Malkanagiri and Kórukonda, land was held rent free by the paiks on the plea that they performed military service.

Bangára Dévi's exactions led to much discontent and emigration to the Golgonda hills; and in 1872 she was deposed and granted a village for maintenance, the Rája appointing a new manager. In the same year Mr. H. G. Turner and the Rája's díwán conducted a rough three-years' settlement (by villages in the north and by muttas in the south) abolishing the former plough and hoe taxes and making the paiks pay for their fields. The demand under this was some Rs. 6,400. In 1877, and again in 1878, this figure was raised by the Rája's officers and the plough and hoe taxes were reintroduced, and in 1879 the discontent in Rampa not unnaturally spread to this taluk. It was fanned by the scandalous conduct of the local police. The Inspector had 'worried and insulted all the respectable people in the country by his violence, extortion, drunkenness and lechery. The constables of course followed suit.' Roads near the stations were deserted in consequence, and markets were closed. In April 1880 Tamma Dora, the great Kóya leader, entered the taluk and captured the Podeh police-station after a fight. Colonel Macquoid of the Hyderabad Contingent marched with 100 men to protect Mótu, but was attacked on 6th May and retreated. This set the country in a blaze, and Tamma Dora was hailed as the Rája of Southern Malkanagiri. Later on, however, he was driven back to the Rampa jungles and in July 1880, refusing to surrender, was attacked and shot by the police.

This outbreak resulted in the abandonment of many villages and set the taluk back for years. The Rája reintroduced the old settlement by muttas and reduced the demand to Rs. 6,300; but six months afterwards he appointed a new ámín who at once began arbitrarily raising assessments and reviving discontent. The Agent intervened and had the man removed. In 1885 more trouble occurred, a corrupt ámín again harassing the ryots. He was similarly removed on the motion of the Agent, who introduced a new three-years' settlement. Of late years matters have gone on quietly, and in the decade 1891–1901 the increase of population in Malkanagiri (26·8 per cent.) was proportionately higher than in any other taluk in the district.

Three places in it deserve a note:—

Kondakambéru, a village of 122 souls containing a police-station and a travellers' bungalow, is most picturesquely placed among heavy bamboo jungle on a spit of land between the Machéru and the Páléru, which here unite. Through it runs the track from Malkanagiri (25 miles to the north-west) to the Golgonda hills. It is the chief place in the mutta of the same name, the muttadar of which was hanged for joining the 1880 fitúri. About a mile to the north-east, amid the jungle, is a dilapidated stone shrine to Siva with an inscription in it, where worship is still maintained and into which every passer by tosses a flower. Tradition says it was once the centre of a flourishing village. Stone temples and inscriptions are rare things in this taluk.

Malkanagiri, the deputy tahsildar's and ámín's station, contains a dispensary and a bungalow and 1,025 inhabitants, most of whom live in thatched huts. Déva Dóngar, the hill about two miles to the east, contains remains of old ramparts; and other heights to the north-east are supposed to resemble an old man, his bundle of fried mohwa flower, his dog, and a hare the latter is chasing, and bear appropriate names.

Fifty years ago the village was described as 'a hot-bed of Meriah sacrifices'. Four victims were annually offered up at the four gates of the fort; six were killed triennially in the four dwáros; and other sacrifices were made on special occasions—the ráni, for example, slaying a girl of ten in May 1854, in fulfilment of a vow, on her recovery from illness. As many as one hundred meriahs were surrendered on one occasion to the authorities.

Mótu, which lies at the junction of the Saveri and Siléru in the southern corner of the taluk, contains only 163 inhabitants. Facing it, across the river, is Kunta, the head-quarters of a tahsildar of Bastar. The place has the advantage of being in communication, by the Saveri and the Gódávari, with Rajahmundry. Timber used to be exported by this route, but all that goes down now is a certain amount of minor forest produce. About 1890 a colony of Patháns settled in this village and began bullying the people round. In 1898 their leader, Róza Khán (since dead), was put in jail for six weeks under an agency warrant, and since then they have given no trouble.

NAURANGPUR TALUK.

CHAP. XV. NAURANG-PUR.

This comprises the north-westernmost corner of the district, and its southern boundary is the Indrávati river. After Malkanagiri, it is the largest taluk in the Presidency. It consists of a level plain, without hills of note, which lies about 2,000 feet above the sea and in the north falls gradually away to the valley of the Tél. The southern portion of it, round about the Indrávati, contains some of the most fertile land in all the district—wide expanses of paddy, fed by the heavy rainfall and dotted with patches of sugar-cane, wheat and Bengal gram, extending in every direction. The Mális, who are noted for their skill in cultivation, hold much of the best land. Further north the country is equally rich, but is very sparsely populated, hundreds of square miles crying aloud for exploitation. It consists of miles and miles of beautiful jungle, mostly sál, hidden among which are many little swampy glades in which paddy is grown. The road northwards alternately emerges into one of these glades and then buries itself again in the jungle.

About 1880 a number of people immigrated to this country from Kálahandi, because the umbrella-tax and other vexatious imposts had been laid upon them there; but in the decade 1891-1901 the population declined again considerably. Four-fifths of the inhabitants speak Uriya, but in the Tél valley the people resemble those of Kálahandi, being Gónds or Central Provinces traders with their attendant Brinjáris. These Brinjáris are found in this part in great numbers, and many villages are almost entirely occupied by them. From here come the gangs which trade with Sálúr. Two places of interest in the taluk are the following:—

Naurangpur is the station of the deputy tahsildar and of an ámín of the Jeypore estate. Population 3,203; height above the sea, 1,918 feet. It consists of one broad street, in which are the public offices and the residence of the ráni referred to below, with a few lanes on either side. The place is a great centre for the export of grain, and is known for the lac toys (see p. 129) which are made in it and for its splendid avenues and topes, one of which consists of a quadruple row of trees two miles long. It was once a centre for the reeling and weaving of tassar silk.

The tána of Naurangpur (with that of Gudári in the Gunupur taluk) was granted by Rámachandra Deo II of Jeypore in 1820 to his nephew Krishna Deo and his brother Narasimha Deo jointly. The line of the former soon afterwards died out and the property descended to Chaitono Deo, the son of the latter. He was a loyal old gentleman and managed his property excellently. Most of the avenues and topes in Naurangpur were planted by him, and it was said that he insisted on there being a tank, a well and a tope in every one of his villages.

On his death in 1876 his three widows, usually known as the Naurangpur Ránis, retained possession of the estate, but in 1896 the present Mahárája resumed it. In 1900 two of the Ránis (the third had died) brought a suit in the Agent's Court for the recovery of the property and won their case. The Mahárája appealed to the High Court, but eventually (in 1904) a compromise was effected by which the estate (exclusive of its forests) was handed over for her life to the then surviving ráni, Sulóchana Patta Mahádévi, who now administers it, with the help of a díwán, independently of the Mahárája.

Pappadahandi: Eight miles north of Naurangpur at the point where the road to Maidalpur and Bhavánipatnam branches off from the main track to the Central Provinces; population 432; height above the sea, 1,922 feet. Contains a fine tope and good water, the remains of an old fort overgrown with jungle, and some magnificent banyan trees. The Déva Saras, or 'holy tank,' in it is well known. According to current tradition, whenever the wooden posts which represent the deity in the temples to Bhairavasvámi in this village and at Naurangpur become rotten, a new one miraculously appears in this tank. If it leans north it is assigned to the Pappadahandi shrine; if south, to that at Naurangpur. In either case it is taken from the tank with much ceremony. A new cloth is tied round it; silver eyes, nose, mouth, ears, etc., are affixed to the upper end of it to cause it to resemble the deity; it is smeared with saffron; sacrifices are made to it; and it is taken in procession through eager crowds to the shrine for which it is destined, where yet more sacrifices accompany its formal installation.

PÁDWA TALUK.

CHAP. XV.
PÁDWA.

PÁDWA lies on the 3,000 feet plateau next north of Golgonda and is made up of parts of the estates of Mádgole (in the south) and Jeypore and Páchipenta (in the north and north-east). It is drained by the Machéru, which runs nearly north and south across it. In places (as between Wondragedda and Hukumpet, and from Páderu to Gangaráz Mádgole) the jungle is thick; but most of the country consists of exceedingly bare red hills, covered with dry cultivation, coarse grass or dwarf dates, and boasting hardly a tree. The taluk contains two notable valleys, those of Aruku and Pádwa, and in these the cultivation is careful and the crops, owing to the excellent rainfall, most flourishing. Ragi four feet high is no uncommon sight; cattle are plentiful, and manure is carefully conserved. But the taluk as a whole is more sparsely-peopled than any other in the district except Malkanagiri. The history of the attempts to give it an outlet to the coast through Anantagiri has been sketched on pp. 137–9 above.

The taluk was constituted in 1893, on the motion of Mr. Willock, by taking the Aruku and Pádwa country from the Pottangi taluk and adding it to the old Páderu taluk, and then transferring the head-quarters from malarious Páderu to Pádwa. Mr. H. G. Turner wished this country to be placed under the Narasapatam Divisional Officer, but Government did not approve.

The people somewhat resemble those of the Golgonda hills, half of them speaking Telugu and the Bagatas being numerous and influential. In the interior of the Mádgole part of the taluk 'nearly every village has its rival claimants for headship, and every village in a mutta disputes about its superiority. These disputes are often very absurd, as about the right to have the hind legs of game killed, to be carried in a palanquin, to wear anklets, etc. The people are also extremely litigious. They are not adverse to education except at Sujanakóta, where, notwithstanding frequent warnings, the Dombus have put devils into two consecutive school-masters [1]

The only two places of interest in the taluk are the Borra Cave and the pool called Matsya gundam.

[1] Mr. G. F. Paddison's annual report for 1899–1900.

Borra Cave: Borra village lies about six miles north of Anantagiri, from which it is best reached, near the eastern edge of the hills upholding the 3,000 feet plateau. A stream there (which eventually falls into the Peddagunda, an affluent of the Chittivalasa river) disappears suddenly into a low limestone hill, works its way through it along a chain of most interesting limestone caves, full of excellent specimens of stalagmites and stalactites, and eventually reappears again 300 feet lower down in a deep gorge. Like the somewhat similar Guptésvara cave above referred to, the place is accounted holy and a festival is held there at Sivarátri. At one spot on the hill an opening leads abruptly downwards into the top of the largest of the chain of caves below, and one looks down into dim depths from which issues the murmur of running water, as in the place where—

> 'Alph the sacred river ran
> Through caverns measureless to man
> Down to a sunless sea.'

About fifty feet below the northern brow of the hill[1] a wide but low entrance leads into this cave. The roof of it, in which is the orifice above mentioned, is crossed or irregularly ribbed with thick, short, curtain-like masses of stalactitic deposit, beautifully fluted and wrinkled, one or two of which, at the sides of the cavern, are connected with the thickly-grouped mounds of stalagmite forming on the floor. The whole interior is covered with dull cream-white travertine, the surface of which sparkles a little owing to minute sparry facets. The stream descends from a series of cavernous recesses above, passes along the eastern side of the cave through a deep rift, and runs down through other caverns to the gorge of the Peddagunda.

This latter stream, further up its course, itself encounters this same limestone; and in one place has cut two channels for itself through a wall of the rock, 20 or 30 yards wide, which bars its passage. These two channels run through the wall one above the other, the upper one having apparently been the outlet before the river wore its way down and made the lower.

Matsya gundam ('fish pool') is a curious pool on the Machéru ('fish river') near the village of Matam, six miles north-north-west of Páderu and close under the great Yendrika hill, 5,188 feet above the sea. A barrier of rocks runs right across the river there, and the stream plunges into a great hole and vanishes beneath this, reappearing again about a hundred yards lower

[1] See Dr. King's description in *Records of the Geol. Surv. of India*, xix, 154.

CHAP. XV. PÁDWA.

down. Just where it emerges from under the barrier it forms a pool which is crowded with mahseer of all sizes. These are wonderfully tame, the bigger ones feeding fearlessly from one's hand and even allowing their backs to be stroked.[1] They are protected by the Mádgole zamindars—who (see p. 320) on several grounds venerate all fish—and by superstitious fears. Once, goes the story, a Brinjári caught one and turned it into curry, whereon the king of the fish solemnly cursed him and he and all his pack-bullocks were turned into rocks which may be seen there till this day. At Sivarátri a festival occurs at the little thatched shrine near by (the pújári at which is a Bagata) and part of the ritual consists in feeding the sacred fish.

[1] Description given by Mr. J. A. Sandell, Superintendent of Police, Jeypore.

PÁLKONDA TALUK.

CHAP. XV. PÁLKONDA.

PÁLKONDA ('the pot of milk,' so called from its fertility) lies on the north-east of the district, adjoining Ganjám, and is drained and irrigated by the perennial Nágávali or Lángulya and its tributary the Suvarnamukhi. It is one of the three Government taluks of Vizagapatam, is the richest portion of the district, and contains a greater and a denser population than any other taluk therein. Statistics regarding it will be found in the separate Appendix to this volume. It consists of two widely differing parts; namely, the ordinary tracts, which form a level plain, nearly one half of which is paddy-fields, inhabited by Telugus; and the Agency in the group of low hills on the north, which run up to 3,000 feet and are 160 square miles in extent, where three-quarters of the people are backward Játapus or Savaras and cultivation has hardly emerged from the *kondapódu* stage. The forests on these hills have been referred to on p. 113 and the Sítámpéta pass through them on p. 142.

The taluk has had an eventful history. Visvambara Deo I, Rája of Jeypore from 1672 to 1676, is said to have granted it to a Játapu on whom, 'seeing his wisdom and his skill in archery,' he also conferred the title of Naréndra Rao. In 1779 the country was reduced by the Rája of Vizianagram with the help of the Company's troops (internal disturbances affording a pretext for interference) and the Pálkonda fort was captured. The taluk was soon afterwards restored, and the Committee of Circuit's report of 1784 says that Viziaráma Rázu, the then representative of the Játapu family, paid the Rájas of Vizianagram a tribute of Rs. 52,000 besides rendering service with his paiks, 'who are esteemed the best troops in the country.' From 1793 to 1796[1] he was in open revolt against the Company, but Víraghattam and others of his strongholds having been seized, he surrendered and was deposed. His son Sítaráma (who had taken no part in the rebellion) succeeded, but died in 1798 and was followed by his minor brother Venkatapati Rázu, with whom the permanent settlement was made in 1803 on a peshkash of Rs. 55,000. In 1811 Viziaráma, his deposed father, assembled a body

[1] Mr. Russell's report of 18th November 1834, published in 1856 as No. XXIV of the *Selections from the Madras Records*, paras. 10 to 61 of which give a detailed narrative from which the following account has been greatly abridged.

of followers near Víraghattam, and began collecting the revenue and plundering. A brigade and two guns were sent after him and he escaped across the hills to the Nagpur country.[1]

In 1828 Venkatapati Rázu quarrelled with his díwán and had him and his brother murdered at Pálkonda. The police there consisted of only five men and did nothing, and the District Magistrate reported that as there was no clear proof of guilt he 'did not consider it advisable to attempt the seizure of a powerful zamindar in possession of an extensive hill country, almost inaccessible to the inhabitants of the plains, fatally noted for the insalubrity of its air and inhabited by a turbulent race of the zamindar's own dependents.' He contented himself with sending a clerk of his office 'to discover, if possible, some clue to the mysterious circumstances with which the murder was attended.' Nothing, of course, came of this. and in October 1828 Venkatapati died.

He was succeeded by his eldest son Kúrma Rázu, who, though illegitimate, was recognized by the late zamindar's widows—he had left no less than eight—as the rightful heir. The lad being a minor, the estate was managed by one of the widows. Each of these ladies (the ablest of whom was Pedda Jagayya, a dancing-girl) had however a factious following of her own among the mokhásadárs and leaders of the hill men, and a party had also formed to oust Kúrma Rázu in favour of his younger brother, Viziaráma Rázu. The rivalries of these factions resulted in endless disturbances and even in the plundering and burning of villages within three or four miles of Pálkonda itself. At the expiration of the minority in 1831 the arrears of peshkash were Rs. 93,000 and the Collector reported that the turbulence of the zamindari was of so serious a nature as to render it necessary for him to continue the management. Among other outrages, a party of sibbandis at Búrja had been attacked in broad daylight, two of them being killed and seven wounded, ten muskets being captured and the village plundered. The young zamindar was by this time entirely under the influence of Pedda Jagayya the dancing-girl.

In January 1833—or only a few weeks after Mr. Russell, the Special Commissioner (see p. 57), had arrived in the district—the insurgents had the audacity to make an attack on the ámín's office in Pálkonda to rescue a notorious offender kept in custody there. It failed, and to procure the release of the prisoners taken by the Government's men on that occasion, a very extensive plan of operations was organized. The rebels

[1] Wilson's *History of the Madras Army*, iii, 322.

collected in the fort of Atsapavalasa, near Pálkonda, and on the 9th March Lieutenant Curre, commanding at Pálkonda, resolved to forestall them by attacking them there. He was beaten off at the first assault and narrowly escaped being shot himself, but eventually the rebels evacuated the place and fled.[1] Within the fort were found by chance a number of letters, some from Pedda Jagayya to the insurgents supplying them with information, money and ammunition, suggesting plans for 'taking care of' (murdering) the ámín and the Government manager of the estate and proposing methods of combating the troops; and others in like terms from the zamindar himself and several members of his family. On reaching Pálkonda, Mr. Russell in consequence marched a detachment of sepoys into the fort there, before resistance could be made, and captured ten of the zamindar's household, including Pedda Jagayya. The zamindar himself was arrested later. Six of these people were tried by court martial (Mr. Russell had already proclaimed martial law), and two were executed. Pedda Jagayya and the zamindar were condemned to death, but eventually they and all the latter's family were detained as State prisoners. The zamindari was forfeited (1833) and became Government property. The zamindar died in Gooty fort in 1834. Forty-five years later his younger brother, the Viziaráma Rázu mentioned above, who was confined at the time in the fort at Vellore, brought a suit against the Government for the possession of the estate with mesne profits, but this was dismissed by the High Court in 1882 and an appeal to the Privy Council was also rejected. One of the family is still resident in Madras, and that they are not forgotten in the district is shown by the fact that in 1900 one of the Korravanivalasa fitúridars (see p. 304) wrote and asked this man to join that luckless enterprise.

After its forfeiture in 1833, the estate was managed by the Collector until July 1846, when it was leased, with the zamindari of Honzarám, to Messrs. Arbuthnot & Co. for five years at an annual rental of Rs. 1,10,908. This lease was renewed on the same or enhanced terms for periods of five and ten years until 1892, when the taluk was again taken under the management of Government.

Honzarám was one of the estates formed in 1802 out of the havíli land. It was purchased by the Rája of Vizianagram in that year. He sold it in 1810, and in 1811 it was bought in by

[1] A detailed account of the affair appears in the *Asiatic Journal* xiii, 24.

CHAP. XV. PÁLKONDA.

the Collector at a sale for arrears of revenue and became Government land.

During their lease Messrs. Arbuthnot greatly encouraged the growth of sugar-cane, from which sugar was manufactured at their factory at Chittivalasa, made unsuccessful experiments with Mexican cotton and foreign paddy and, from 1848, stimulated the cultivation of indigo. This last venture was a great success, and the taluk is still dotted with the ruins of the factories which were put up to deal with the crop. When the taluk was taken under Government management the mustájari system in the three muttas (Kondà, Kottam and Ráma) in the Agency, which had led to serious abuses, was abolished and the ryotwari tenure introduced.[1] A new settlement was carried out shortly afterwards (see p. 173) in the ordinary tracts.

The places of interest in the taluk include the following:—

Pálkonda: The head-quarters of the taluk and a union of 10,615 inhabitants. It lies about four miles south of the hills on low ground amid wet fields and contains the remains of the zamindar's fort above mentioned, in which a market is now held, and a half-finished Roman Catholic chapel. To the east, on higher ground commanding a beautiful view of the hills, are a picturesque drinking-water tank covered with lotuses, the taluk and other public offices,[2] the travellers' bungalow, the house used by the gentlemen who from time to time managed the taluk during Messrs. Arbuthnot's lease, and that firm's office and indigo warehouse.

Rázám: About fourteen miles from Pálkonda and eleven from Chípurupalle railway-station; a union of 5,096 inhabitants and the head-quarters of a district munsif. The latter's court is within the old fort, which once (see p. 241) was commanded by the famous Bobbili sirdar, Tándra Pápayya, and was afterwards captured by Vengal Ranga Rao on behalf of the son of the Bobbili Rája who was slain in 1757 by Bussy's forces. The weaving and silver-work of Rázám have been referred to on pp. 123 and 126.

Siripuram: Four miles west of the Lángulya river and the same distance north-east of Pondúru railway-station; population

[1] See the report of Deputy Collector V. Jagannátha Rao in G.O., No. 2731, Judicial, dated 1st December 1887, which contains a quantity of information about the Agency.

[2] Lest antiquarians should hereafter be puzzled by the two apparently aimless arches which flank the taluk office, it may be explained that they were erected to test the stability of the soil and the depth of the foundations required for buildings constructed upon it.

2,988. Is known for its great tank, the embankment of which is two miles long. This, says local tradition, was made by two sisters, dancing-girls named Chinna Kanchamma and Pedda Kanchamma, to expiate an offence against religious precepts; and after breaching several times, was at last rendered safe by the sisters burying themselves alive in the embankment. On this latter are still standing some stone images of the two girls, and numerous legends cluster about their names. Formerly, it is declared, poor people who could not afford the jewels and so on indispensable for their weddings used to pray to the sisters and next day find these requisites lying on the embankment. Custom required them to be eventually returned, but one day an avaricious potter kept them. He and his wheel and all that was his were turned into stone in consequence; since when no potter has dared sleep in Siripuram.

The village is the chief place in the proprietary estate of the same name, which is one of those carved out of the havíli land and sold by auction in 1802. It was bought then, says Mr. Carmichael, by the Rája of Vizianagram, who in 1811 sold it to Rája Rao Venkataráyudu, who transferred it shortly afterwards to Bobbili Venkatakrishnama. In the same year 1811 it was sold for arrears and passed to Yellumahanti Parasuráma Pátro, who sold it to the Inuganti family, relations of the Rájas of Bobbili. In 1868 it belonged to Inuganti Sítarámasvámi, díwán of Bobbili, and it is now the property of Inuganti Rájagópál Rao.

This same gentleman is also the proprietor of the three estates of Mantena and Ungaráda in this taluk and Kintali in Chípurupalle. At the sale of estates in 1802 Kintali was bought by Kálabariga Chinna Lakshanna. It was subsequently divided into the two properties of Kintali and Mantena under orders of the Northern Provincial Court conveyed by a precept of the Zilla Court at Chicacole dated 16th July 1832, and these were held respectively by the above Lakshanna and one Venkanna. These two sold the estates in August 1837 to the Rája of Bobbili, who resold them to Inuganti Ráma Rao, husband of his half sister Inuganti Sítáyamma, in 1841. This Ráma Rao had already, in April 1825, purchased from Bobbili the estate of Ungaráda in the Pálkonda taluk. On Ráma Rao's death the three estates—Kintali, Mantena and Ungaráda—fell to his son Ráyadappa, who died childless and unmarried in 1861. His mother Sítáyamma succeeded, and on her death in 1886 left the estates to her daughter, Ravu Lakshmi Kantayammi. The present holder

CHAP. XV. PÁLKONDA.

Inuganti Rájagópál Rao, however, brought a suit for them, claiming to be the reversionary heir of Ráyadappa, and won his case.[1]

Víraghattam: Stands nearly midway between Pálkonda and Párvatípur; population 5,738. Contains the remains of a considerable mud fort, in which are now located the dispensary and the police lines. This was strongly held by Viziaráma Rázu, zamindar of Pálkonda, in the disturbances of 1793–96 above referred to. In February 1795 the Company's troops, which had no guns big enough to effect a breach, were twice repulsed in attacks upon it by escalade. The village does a great trade in leaf-platters, which are sent as far afield as Madras.

[1] I.L.R., Madras XXI, 344–46 and 349–51.

PÁRVATÍPUR TALUK.

THIS lies east of the north end of the 3,000 feet plateau, and includes the tangle of foot-hills which there hedge in that table-land. These latter belong to the Agency, and are chiefly inhabited by the more civilized kinds of Khonds, with a sprinkling of Konda Doras, Paidis, Ghásis and Gadabas. The rest of the taluk resembles in its appearance and people the adjoining parts of the plain country. The perennial Ṅágávali bisects it east and west, and for months in every year greatly impedes communication.

The more interesting places are the following :—

Addápusila : Three miles south-east of Párvatípur ; population 748. Above the village stands a conspicuous hill which differs from the many others in the neighbourhood in being covered with bamboo and crowned with a row of naked black and yellow tors and pinnacles. Several of these latter have crashed down its sides to the bottom, and under the overhanging side of the most enormous of them are built four shrines which are cared for by a bairági and have a great local reputation. In front of these stand two small brick and plaster temples of the usual pattern, and the place is picturesquely surrounded by trees planted by the faithful. The stone from this hill is being used for the new dam across the Ṅágávali (p. 106).

Kurupám : Twelve miles north-east of Párvatípur, on the road to Gunupur ; population 2,364 ; the head-quarters of the ancient zamindari of the same name. The newer part of the place (founded by and called after the present Rája's father Súrya Náráyana Rázu) contains a guest-house, choultry and dispensary maintained by the estate ; while in the older quarter are the remains of the former fort, in honour of whose guardian goddess, Paidi Máramma, a festival is held in Vaisákha each year, the chief rites in which are the taking in procession of nine pots, the wearing of disguises (*véshamulu*) and the sacrifice of a buffalo.

Tradition says that the estate was originally given on the usual feudal tenure by Rája Visvambara Deo I of Jeypore (1672–76) to an Uriyá named Sanyási Dora, with the title of Vairicherla ('a spear against the enemy') which is still borne by its owners.

CHAP. XV. PÁRVATÍPUR.

In 1775, when the lesser zamindars rose in revolt against Sítaráma Rázu, brother and díwán of the Rája of Vizianagram (see p. 46), the head of the Kurupám family, Sivaráma Rázu (who had usurped the estate and imprisoned his elder brother), attacked the rear-guard of Captain Mathews' and Sítaráma's force as it was marching to reduce Jeypore (see p. 267) and cut off its supplies. In the next year, Sítaráma accordingly proceeded to Kurupám and treacherously seized Sivaráma and all his family at an entertainment at which he was a guest.[1] They were kept for some time in confinement in the fort of Dévapalli, near Gajapatinagaram. Sivaráma was afterwards released at the intercession of Viziaráma Rázu, Rája of Vizianagram, and in 1778 [2] bribed the subadar of the 1st Circar battalion who was in charge of the Kurupám fort to deliver it over to him, garrisoned it with a force of his own, and began fomenting disturbances in the adjoining Pálkonda estate. In 1779 a detachment composed of the Company's and the Vizianagram troops accordingly marched against him. It retook Kurupám fort without resistance,[3] the estate was added to the Vizianagram possessions, and Sivaráma was brought to Vizagapatam, kept under surveillance, and granted a subsistence allowance. He seems to have died there in 1794.

When the Rája of Vizianagram was killed at Padmanábham in that year (p. 53) and the lesser zamindars rose in revolt against the Company, Kurupám fort was occupied by Venkata Rázu, zamindar of Mérangi (whose estate had been forcibly seized by Sivaráma) who garrisoned it with 1,000 men and defied the Company. Captain Cox marched against the place, it was evacuated, and the fort was occupied in April 1795 and destroyed.[4]

Captain Cox said that Sanyási Rázu, Sivaráma's young son, 'conducted himself with much zeal for the service' on this occasion, and Mr. Webb, the Collector, reported that his family 'by their influence over the inhabitants helped greatly to accelerate the bringing the country under obedience.' The estate was accordingly handed over to Sanyási Rázu, Mérangi being first separated from it and restored to its original owners. In 1803 the permanent settlement was concluded with this lad.

[1] Mackenzie MSS., Local Records, iv, 251–60 and Progs. of the Circuit Committee of 12th September 1784.

[2] Vizag. Cons. dated 21st September 1778.

[3] Captain Lane's letter of 17th February 1779 to the Vizagapatam Chief and Council.

[4] Captain Cox's letter of 25th April 1795 to Mr. Webb at Vizagapatam.

He died in 1820 and was succeeded by Sítaráma Rázu, a cousin's son whom he had adopted. This man died in 1830 and was followed by his widow Subbadramma; who, dying in 1841, was followed by her maternal grandson Súrya Náráyana Rázu. He was then an infant, and the estate was managed by the Court of Wards until 1857. Súrya Náráyana was a careful administrator, doubled the income of his property, lent his neighbours $3\frac{1}{2}$ lakhs and invested a like sum in buying land.

Among his purchases was the small estate of Chemudu, a fief of Jeypore which had been seized by Vizianagram but restored to its ancient proprietors in 1794, had been constantly in financial difficulties and was sold in 1889. The Kottaparuvu subdivision of this (four villages) had already been granted to a Konda Dora named Sarike Bhíman Dora, for services rendered, and separately registered in 1883. It is now held by the Rája of Vizianagram, who acquired it by purchase.

Súrya Náráyana successfully defended a suit brought by his brothers for partition of the property [1] and the estate is now scheduled in Act II of 1904 as inalienable and impartible. He died on 5th January 1891 and was succeeded by his son Vírabhadra Rázu, the present Rája. The latter was only thirteen years of age at the time and the estate was managed by the Court of Wards until 1898. The minor was educated under an English tutor and in 1895 married Lakshmi Narasayamma, second daughter of Mahárája Sir Gajapati Rao (see p. 221) who bore him two sons and a daughter and died in child-birth in 1901. In 1906 he was granted the personal title of Rája.

Mérangi (or Chinna Mérangi, Pedda Mérangi lies just west of it) is twelve miles north-east of Párvatípur and contains 3,987 inhabitants. It was formerly the capital of the zamindari of the same name which has now, see below, been split into four subdivisions.

This zamindari, according to tradition, was granted, like Kurupám, on the usual feudal tenure by Visvambara Deo of Jeypore to an Uriya named Jagannátha Dora, with the title (still borne by his descendants) of Satrucherla, or 'destroyer of the enemy.' As has been stated just above, the estate was afterwards seized by Sivaráma Rázu of Kurupám, but in 1796 it was separated from that property and given by Government [2] to one Ganga Rázu of the original Mérangi family. Another member of the family, Jagannátha Rázu, son of the Venkata Rázu who had

[1] I.L.R., XVII Madras, 287.

[2] Mr. G. E. Russell's report of 18th November 1834 already several times cited. This is also the authority for much of what follows.

CHAP. XV. PÁRVATÍPUR.

seized Kurupám in 1794, claimed the estate on the ground that his father had been last in possession, but his claim was rejected because of his father's rebellion. It was afterwards in part conceded in order to keep him quiet, but he was still dissatisfied, and when Ganga Rázu died and the permanent settlement was made in 1803 with the latter's son Chandrasékhara, Jagannátha sued for the whole estate. He died soon after, but his son Vírabhadra continued the suit, was cast in costs, and in his indignation, broke out into open rebellion, seized the zamindar, robbed him and his manager of all they possessed, collected the revenues on his own account, was twice engaged with the Company's troops and was only at last pacified by the grant of a small pension in 1809. The grant, however, was conditional on his living in Vizagapatam and this he steadfastly refused to do. In 1816 he went on the warpath again, devastated villages, murdered the zamindar's grandfather, and at last, having been unceasingly pursued and hunted out of his lurking-places, was captured in Jeypore. He was detained under surveillance at Vizagapatam, but continued to foment disturbances and in 1821 was removed to Chingleput, where he eventually died.

Meanwhile the young zamindar Chandrasékhara, whom Mr. Russell describes as 'a perfect idiot,' ran heavily into debt. His estate was eventually attached by the courts and put up for sale, and, no one being bold enough to purchase it, was bought by Government in 1833 for Rs. 500. At that time the Pálkonda rebellion (see p. 288) had not been completely crushed, three principal insurgents, known as 'the Atsapavalasa brothers,' lurking with their retainers in the Mérangi jungles. The manager of the estate assembled a body of hill peons, and, after a desperate fight near 'Górai' in the hills to the south-east of Mérangi, slew all three of them. He and his peons begged that their reward for this service might be the restoration of Mérangi to Chandrasékhara's young son Jagannátha Rázu, 'a remarkably fine boy,' and in 1835 this was done. The estate was managed by the Court of Wards until the lad attained his majority in 1843. He died in 1864 and was followed by his son Chandrasékhara, who died on 7th September 1869 leaving an infant son named Jagannátha and three brothers called Rámabhadra, Sómasékhara and Jógirázu. The Court of Wards took charge of the estate. In 1884 the three brothers sued for the partition of the estate and won their case in all the courts up to the Privy Council.[1] The estate was accordingly divided in 1894 into

[1] I.L.R., XI Madras, 380–93 and XIV, 244–7.

four parts, of which Chinna Mérangi went to the then minor zamindar Jagannátha, Lakhanapuram to Rámabhadra, Pedda Boddedi to Sómasékhara, and Pedda Mérangi to Vírabhadra Súryanáráyana and Jagannátha, the two minor sons of Jógirázu, who had died in 1890.[1] The whole of it was taken under the Court of Wards. Meanwhile in 1893 the late Mahárája of Vizianagram had bought Chinna Mérangi, which still belongs to his family. Pedda Mérangi is now held by Súrya Náráyana, his brother Jagannátha having been shot dead by one of his own servants in 1904.

Párvatípur, the head-quarters of the taluk and division, and the residence of the Divisional Officer, Assistant Superintendent of Police, deputy tahsildar, and district munsif, lies in a low situation among wet land, only 395 feet above the sea and surrounded by small hills which shut out the breeze and make the place very hot in the summer months. It consists of Párvatípur proper, the commercial quarter, an overcrowded and dirty spot containing little of interest except the ruined gateway of a former fort, and, about a mile to the south, the pleasanter suburb of Belgám, where the officials live and have their offices, which was much improved in 1882–83 by convict labour. The two together make up a union of 17,308 inhabitants, and the place is the fifth largest town in the district and one the people of which, owing to the growing trade with the Agency, have increased at a faster rate (102 per cent.) in the last thirty years than those of any other in the district. In Belgám, besides the offices already mentioned, are the abandoned jail referred to on p. 207 (which occupies the site of the old fort), the lines of the police reserve alluded to on p. 206 and a station of the Schleswig-Holstein Lutheran Mission.

Belgám was once the head-quarters of the estate of the same name. The Circuit Committee's proceedings of 12th September 1784 show that this was originally a fief of Jeypore which was seized by Vizianagram.

Mr. Carmichael says that in 1796 fourteen villages (apparently part of the original estate) were granted by Lord Hobart for life to Sómasundara Náráyana Pátro, an Uriya, in acknowledgment of the services of his father to the State. This father, Jagannátha Pátro, was díwán to Rámachandra Deo II, Rája of Jeypore from 1781 to 1825, had been largely instrumental in preventing the Jeypore people from joining in the disturbances which (see p. 54) followed the death of the Rája of Vizianagram in 1794, and was afterwards confidentially employed by Mr. Webb,

[1] G.O., No. 896, Revenue, dated 22nd December 1894.

CHAP. XV. PÁRVATÍPUR.

the Collector, in settling the north of the district when it was then taken from Vizianagram and re-apportioned among its former proprietors. At the permanent settlement of 1803 this property .was granted to Sómasundara Náráyana Pátro as a permanent zamindari under the name of the Belgám estate.[1] The family use the title Tát Rája. Sómasundara Náráyana died in 1814; his son and successor Dhananjaya in 1849; his brother Visvambara, the third zamindar, in 1865; his son and successor, Náráyana Rámachandra in 1871; his nephew and adopted son[2] Sivanáráyana, the fifth zamindar, in 1882; and the last-named's son and successor, Dhananjaya, died in 1888, without issue, leaving a widow to whom he had given power to adopt. The widow was not competent to manage the estate and it was accordingly taken over by the Court of Wards. In 1891 the widow adopted a son who was taken under the charge of the Court. Meanwhile, however, Súrya Náráyana and Sundaranáráyana, two cousins of her late husband's (descendants, with him, of the Visvambara who died in 1865) had brought suits for the partition of the estate. They won their cases both in the District and High Courts and before the Privy Council,[3] and the property was recovered from the Court of Wards and divided into the two portions (or 'hundas') of Párvatípur and Belgám, of which Súrya Náráyana took the former and Sundaranáráyana the latter.

Súrya Náráyana Tát Rája died on 8th December 1900, leaving a minor son, Chandrasékhara, born on 6th June 1894; and his brother Sundaranáráyana died on the 9th February following, leaving two sons of whom the elder, Janárdana, was born on 9th March 1888. Both estates were taken again under the Court of Wards. The two brothers had jointly borrowed 5½ lakhs from the Mahárája of Jeypore on a mortgage of the two hundas. To liquidate this and other debts the Court sold Narisipuram and eight other villages in the two properties in 1902 to the Mahárája of Jeypore. These are sometimes called the Narisipuram tána of Jeypore estate.

Sangamvalasa: Lies four miles west of Párvatípur; population 1,335. It is the chief village in the ancient zamindari of the same name, which has been scheduled as inalienable and impartible in Act II of 1904.

Tradition says that this estate was originally granted by Rámachandra Deo I of Jeypore (1708–11) to a favourite retainer,

[1] Mr. Alexander's report of 26th April 1803.

[2] A suit (O.S. 18 of 1870 on the file of the District Court) questioning this adoption was eventually compromised.

[3] *Madras Law Journal* (1893) iii, 100 and I.L.R., XX Madras, 256.

an Uriya, who at the same time was given the title Nissanku, meaning 'the fearless.' His family, like the other lesser zamindars, was dispossessed by Vizianagram about 1769. In 1796, after the death of the Vizianagram Rája, the property was restored by Government to the representative of the eldest branch, Venkanna Nissanku, and with him the permanent settlement of 1803 was made. Mr. Carmichael says that Venkanna was succeeded by his son Peddanna, whose mental incapacity led to the Court of Wards assuming the management of the estate, who died in 1829, and who was succeeded by his posthumous son Mrityunjaya. The latter came of age in 1847 and built the house in the pettah east of Sangamvalasa called Mrityunjaya-nagaram. He was known for his literary tastes and held the estate for no less than 58 years until his death in 1904. The second of his three sons brought a suit[1] against him for the partition of the estate, but it was dismissed. He was followed by his eldest son's son Visvésvara. The estate suffers at present from financial embarrassment.

[1] O.S. No. 21 of 1899 on the file of the Vizagapatam Distr ct Court.

POTTANGI TALUK.

CHAP. XV. POTTANGI.

POTTANGI taluk stands in the centre of the 3,000 feet plateau. In general appearance it much resembles its next neighbour Koraput, already referred to above, consisting (except along the edge of the plateau, which is fairly wooded and comprises a line of fine hills running up to 5,000 feet) of an almost totally bare, red soil, table-land dotted with small, bare, red hills, both of which are cultivated with dry crops and a little paddy in their damper hollows. It is traversed from east to west by the important road which runs from Sálúr on the plains, up the 'Pottangi ghát' (see p. 139), past Pottangi, the taluk head-quarters, to Koraput, and thence down to Jeypore. Two places in it may be mentioned :—

Nandapuram, once (see p. 280) the head-quarters of a taluk, about 15 miles west of Pottangi as the crow flies and is reached by a track taking off at Sembliguda from the Pottangi-Koraput road. As has been stated above (p. 264), this village, which now contains only 1,051 inhabitants, was formerly the capital of the Jeypore estate. In old records the property is always called the Nandapuram zamindari. It still contains relics of its former importance. Remains may be seen of a mud fort which apparently surrounded the whole place; in the northern part of the village are two boulders on one of which are sculptured two figures in relief while the other has been fashioned into an elephant; near the cutcherry of the ámín of the Jeypore estate is a stone bearing an inscription; about a mile to the south-east is a stone Ganapati some six feet high; the same distance to the north is the shrine of Sarvésvara, in which are more inscriptions (inscriptions are rarities in the hills); and in the village itself are the ruins of the famous 'throne of thirty-two steps'—a flight of this number of stone steps which leads to a roughly circular granite slab on which, it is said, the early chiefs of Jeypore were always installed. About three miles along the track to Sembliguda is a still more ancient and curious relic, namely, a small shrine in which are three stone images of nude individuals sitting cross-legged, which appear to belong either to Buddhist or Jain times.

Pottangi, the head-quarters of the taluk, is a small village of 726 inhabitants built at the foot of the great Damuku hill and containing the deputy tahsildar's office and a pleasant travellers' bungalow surrounded with good trees. It gives its name to the ghát road from Sálúr at the head of which it stands, and the Tádivalasa (or Turner's) ghát from the plains also ends there.

RÁYAGADA TALUK.

RÁYAGADA lies next north of Párvatípur and is in the Agency. It consists of the upper valley of the Nágávali and is a charming country. Along either side of it runs a line of hills, now advancing, now receding, sometimes rocky and bold, but oftener rounded and wooded. Between these, stretches an undulating plain, part woodland, part green fields. Among the latter, tamarind, jack, mango and other shady trees stand up singly or in groups and give the country almost the appearance of some gigantic park, and through them shows now and again the glint of some broad reach of the perennial river. The population, which is denser than in any taluk in the Agency except Jeypore, consists mainly of Khonds of the more civilized kinds, is industrious and frugal, and has an excellent outlet for its produce in the road between the Kálahandi State and Párvatípur, which traverses the taluk from north to south. Three places in Ráyagada may be referred to :—

Páyakapád : An agraháram of 431 people on the bank of the Nágávali which contains the uppermost of the five shrines (see p. 10) built along that river and is the chief place in a mokhása granted by a former Mahárája of Jeypore to Bhuvanésvara Praharázu, an Uriya Bráhman. On the grantee dying and leaving a minor son named Gangádhara Praharázu, the estate was taken under management by the Agent in 1869. Gangádhara was put in possession in 1875, but died in 1881 leaving a childless widow who was incapacitated by age, weak health and deficient intelligence; and the estate was again taken under management. The widow eventually adopted a son, to whom the estate was handed over on 25th March 1901.

Ráyagada ('king's fort') is the head-quarters of the taluk and a thriving trading village of 1,999 inhabitants. It stands 687 feet above the sea on the high red bank of the Kumbikótagedda (near its junction with the Nágávali) about 150 feet above the bed of that stream. Consequently, wells are useless and all water has to be carried up from the gedda. The latter flows along a fairly wide valley with steep banks which suddenly contract to form a gorge about 120 feet deep and 70 feet wide with sheer rock sides. The approach to Ráyagada used to be exceedingly difficult for carts, as they had to descend to the bottom of the wider part of this valley and then climb a severe ascent on the other side. Mr. Willock (see p. 142) threw a girder bridge across the gorge and took the road over this, almost on the level. The new road from the bridge to the town was cut through the large and substantial old mud fort which gives Ráyagada its name. This is supposed to have been built by one of the Rájas of Jeypore, who made it his residence. Within it, near the tumble-down temple to its guardian deity Majji Giriya, is pointed out the spot where his wives committed sati on his death. Alongside the road is a black slab called the Janni pothoro, or 'priest's stone,' on which human sacrifices are said to have been offered formerly. The hill people still regard it with awe and decline on any account to touch it. In the police-station compound lies an old iron cannon which was taken from the fort. It is an exceedingly primitive weapon consisting of a core made of straight bars on to which successive rings of iron have been shrunk. It is some six feet long and is provided with four iron rings for lifting it. The imprisonment of Rája Vikrama Deo in this fort by his son in 1849 is referred to on p. 268 above and the neighbouring falls of the Nágávali are mentioned on p. 9.

Singapur, usually known as Kalyána Singapur to distinguish it from Bhairava Singapur in Jeypore taluk, stands 30 miles north by west of Ráyagada on the main track to Kálahandi 997 feet above the sea in a narrow valley immediately west of the Nímgiris. The population is 1,996. It contains the remains of an old fort, is surrounded on three sides by the Nágávali river, and is almost buried in a jungle of bamboo. Just south-west of it rises sacred Dévagiri, a steep rocky hill in which there is a cave containing a lingam where a feast is held at Sivarátri, and on which are several pools of water and an inscription which seems undecipherable.

Singapur is the chief village of a subdivision of Jeypore, consisting of Khond villages, which was granted by Rája Vikrama Deo II (1825–60) to a kinsman on service tenure. In 1864[1] the then Rája sued the grantee's son, Krishna Deo, for the possession of the property or an annual payment of Rs. 5,000 for it. It was decreed that the Rs. 5,000 should be paid and the decision was upheld on appeal by the High Court[2] and the Privy Council. Krishna Deo, who was always known as the Rája of Singapur, died in 1884 leaving a young widow named Níla Dévi, to whom he had given authority to adopt, and an illegitimate son named Gópinátha Deo, twelve years of age. The

[1] O.S. No. 22 of 1864 on the Agent's file.

[2] Madras High Court Reports (1866), 154–7.

Jeypore Maháraja claimed that on the death of any holder he was entitled to resume the estate and allow the heirs maintenance; and he sent men to take over the management of the property. The widowed Ráni disputed his right; and the Khonds of the place all wanted to have Gópinátha for their Rája saying that, whether legitimate or not, he had often been pointed out to them by his father as their future chief and that Srípati Dolapati, the Ráni's manager and right hand man, bullied them unbearably.

Exciting events followed in this triangular duel.[1] At the next Dasara the thousands of Khonds assembled at Singapur demanded that Gópinátha should play the part usually allotted to the Rája at that feast. The Ráni refused to allow this, so the Khonds broke into the fort, carried off the boy (who joined in their views with much spirit) and took him to Jeypore, with an escort 300 strong, to represent matters to the Mahárája. There they were persuaded to take him down to Párvatípur, that the Divisional Officer might enquire into the case, and from that place the boy was induced to go to Vizianagram, where he was given an allowance and sent to the local college.

For a time the threatened trouble seemed to have blown over. But the Ráni's manager continued to oppress the Khonds and in the beginning of 1885 a party of 70 of these people marched all the way to Vizianagram, intending to seize Gópinátha, carry him to Singapur and make him Rája. The Agent then sent a nominee of his own to manage the estate, removing the Ráni's man, and the hill men were once more pacified. The Ráni, however, proceeded to adopt an heir, and once more care was required to check trouble with the Khonds.

Meanwhile the Jeypore Mahárája brought a suit for the possession of the property or the enhancement of the quit-rent paid upon it, and the Ráni, a most determined lady, fought the case, waving aside the Agent's repeated suggestions that she should compromise. She was defeated, the Agent holding that her family were only tenants-at-will and directing the enhancement of the rent from Rs. 5,000 to Rs. 20,000. An appeal preferred to Government was transmitted to the High Court for decision and decided against the Ráni. The property was handed over to the Mahárája in 1892 and the Ráni was given an allowance of Rs. 500 a month and the produce of certain land yielding about 30 garces of paddy. The Khonds' desire to have Gópinátha Deo as their chief died a natural death, and he retired to Jeypore.

[1] G.Os., Nos. 2220, Judicial, dated 25th August 1885 and 1326, Judicial, dated 19th May 1886.

SÂLÚR TALUK.

CHAP. XV. SÁLÚR.

Lies next west of Bobbili, under the 3,000 feet plateau, the slopes of which, up to the main crest, belong to it but are included in the Agency. In the plains, four-fifths of the people are Telugus, but in the Agency nearly two-thirds of them are Játapus, Konda Doras and the more civilized classes of Khonds, amongst whom are a considerable sprinkling of Gadabas, who often occupy whole hamlets by themselves.

Korravanivalasa, an insignificant hamlet under the hills near Páchipenta, was the scene, in May 1900, of a riot attended with unusual and interesting circumstances. A Konda Dora of this place named Korra Mallayya pretended that he was inspired; and gradually gathered round him a camp of four or five thousand people, mostly hill men, from various parts of the Agency.

At first his proceedings were harmless enough, but in April he gave out that he was a re-incarnation of one of the five Pándava brothers; that his infant son was the god Krishna; that he would drive out the English and rule the country himself; and that to effect this he would arm his followers with bamboos which should be turned by magic into guns and would change the weapons of the authorities into water. Bamboos were cut and rudely fashioned to resemble guns, and armed with these the camp was drilled by 'the svámi,' as Mallayya had come to be called. The assembly next sent word that they were going to loot Páchipenta, and when, on the 1st May, two constables came to see how matters stood, the fanatics fell upon them and beat them to death. The local police endeavoured to recover the bodies, but owing to the threatening attitude of the svámi's followers had to abandon the attempt.

The District Magistrate then went to the place in person, collected reserve police from Vizagapatam, Párvatípur and Jeypore, and at dawn on the 7th May rushed the camp to arrest the svámi and the other leaders of the movement. The police were resisted by the mob and obliged to fire. Eleven of the rioters were killed, others wounded or arrested and the rest dispersed. Sixty of them were tried for rioting (of whom 57 were convicted) and three, including the svámi, for murdering the constables. Of the latter, the svámi died in jail and the other two were convicted and hanged. The svámi's infant son, the god Krishna, also died and all trouble ended at once and completely. Its odd mixture of religious enthusiasm, desire for loot and political aspiration differentiate this fitúri from most of its predecessors.

Páchipenta: Seven miles west by south of Sálúr, picturesquely situated on a slight eminence close under the hills; population 5,381. It is the chief village of the ancient zamindari of the same name which is scheduled in Act II of 1904 as inalienable and impartible and includes a considerable area on the hills which is often called 'Hill Páchipenta.'

Tradition says that Tamanna Dora, the first of the zamindar's family, was a naik of peons under Jeypore who held the fort of Téda (or Tyáda) on the plateau, and that he was appointed by Visvambara Deo I of Jeypore (1672–76) to guard the track which in days gone by led up from Páchipenta to the 3,000 feet plateau and the Jeypore country, and was given the title of Dakshina Kaváta Yuvarázu or 'lord of the southern portal.' Mr. Carmichael states that in 1754 when (see p. 31) Jafar Ali, Faujdar of Chicacole, called in the Maráthas to aid him against the Rája of Vizianagram and the French, the then Páchipenta zamindar Vírappa Rázu (who, according to Orme, had been dispossessed by Vizianagram) showed the Maráthas the way across the hills and down the Páchipenta track and was afterwards in consequence imprisoned for life in the Vizianagram fort. At his death in 1789 a small maintenance was allowed his son Mallappa Rázu, and this man was restored to the estate after the death of the Rája of Vizianagram (p. 53) in 1794.

He died in 1797 and the permanent settlement was made with his only son Annam Rázu, who was followed by a son Mallappa, who was succeeded in his turn by his son Annam Rázu in 1846. Owing largely to numerous alienations made by Mallappa Rázu, the estate was then heavily involved and it has ever since continued to be one of the most bankrupt and mismanaged properties in the district. In 1855, Mr. Smollett, the Agent, borrowed Rs. 11,500 from Vizianagram to clear off the estate's debts, and took the property under management for five years on his own authority until the money was repaid. It was then found that while the demand of the estate was only Rs. 6,000, land assessed at more than Rs. 10,000 had been granted away to relations and other mokhásadárs. For arrears of peshkash in 1866 and 1867 Karrivalasa and Tótavalasa (now separate estates) were sold and bought by the zamindar's brother-in-law Basava Manga Rázu. The former was sold by him, it may here be noted, in 1874 to Kákarlapudi Nílayamma, who afterwards

CHAP. XV. SÁLÚR.

disposed of it to its present owners, the Vizianagram family. The latter was given by him to his daughter, the mother of the present zamindar, as her dowry, and is still in her enjoyment.

In the next two years further arrears accrued, but the Collector found that they were being purposely permitted so that the property might be bought up in small bits by the relations of the zamindar's second (and favourite) wife to the detriment of his heir Jagannátha Mallappa Rázu, a son by the first wife whom he bitterly disliked. In 1869, therefore, the estate was again taken under management for five years. In 1875 Kotikapenta, which had been sold by the courts [1] and bought by Kákarlapudi Nílayamma, was registered as a separate estate. It also was afterwards purchased by the Mahárája of Vizianagram. In 1879 Dattivalasa and Márlavalasa were similarly sold [2] to the same lady and eventually bought from her by the Mahárája.

In 1880 the zamindar Annam Rázu died and was succeeded by Pedda Mallappa, the elder son of his second wife, who died in June 1906 and was followed by his eldest son Lakshmi Narasimha Rúpa. The property was again in arrears and was again attached. The new incumbent was urged to enquire into the extravagant alienations made by his predecessors and to put the estate on a sound footing by resuming as many as possible, but instead of doing so he took to raising money by alienating afresh a number of villages which had already been parted with, and thus leaving the ryots at the mercy of two or more claimants to their assessments. The lawless oppression of these mokhásadars has necessitated on more than one occasion the intervention of the authorities; vetti, or forced labour, is still commonly exacted; and recently the zamindar attempted arbitrarily to double his assessments, with the result that a number of the ryots emigrated to the Nandapuram country of the Jeypore estate.

In 1905 the zamindar asked Government to treat him as an incapacitated proprietor and take the estate under their management, but the insolvent state of the property rendered this step inadvisable. The Mahárája of Bobbili holds a decree for some $3\frac{1}{4}$ lakhs against the property and the civil courts have ordered its sale. Four villages, including the head-quarters Páchipenta, have already been sold and bought by the zamindar of Tuni, and others must also be brought to the hammer at an early date.

Sálúr, the head-quarters of the taluk, is a union of 16,239 inhabitants situated 570 feet above the sea on the bank of the Végavati, five miles from the foot of the Pottangi ghát. It

[1] O.S. No. 39 of 1865 on the District Court's file.

[2] O.S. No. 23 of 1874.

contains a station of the Schleswig-Holstein Lutheran Mission and its travellers' bungalow is picturesquely placed on high ground overlooking a winding reach of the river. Before the Pottangi ghát was begun, Sálúr was a small place, but, as soon as traffic began to come down from the hills by that route, its situation raised it into importance as a trade mart, and when, in 1884, the ghát was improved into a cart-road the place very rapidly expanded from a village to a busy town. Unluckily, the site is cramped and shut in by the river, a big tank and wet fields; the soil is soft and dries slowly; no one supervised the sudden growth of the place; the new houses were run up anyhow and anywhere on no plan and with narrow, crooked lanes between them; and Sálúr is now so notorious for its dirt and general unloveliness that men say its name must surely be derived from the French *sale*.

The importance of its trade, however, is undeniable. It has a very big weekly market; is the timber-yard of the Agency adjoining, the Pottangi ghát being the only outlet for that commodity; and also deals largely in all kinds of produce from the hills (such as niger and gingelly seed, mustard, myrabolams, rice and ragi); exports thither salt, tobacco, kerosine, beads and other jewellery, and cloths; and collects, for transmission to Bimlipatam, the jute and castor crop of the adjoining villages of the low country. The merchants of the place keep up, at an annual cost of Rs. 800, a flourishing Véda school maintained from the proceeds of self-imposed fees levied on all their purchases.

The town is the head-quarters of the inalienable and impartible ancient zamindari of the same name, the proprietor of which resides in a house built within an old mud fort which is as little dilapidated as any in the district. According to tradition, the estate was originally granted by the Visvambara Deo of Jeypore already several times mentioned to a chief on whom he conferred the lofty title of Boliyaro Simho, or 'mighty lion.' Like its fellows, it was eventually absorbed by Vizianagram. Mr. Carmichael says that when the English first obtained the country, the then zamindar, Sanyási Rázu, headed a revolt against Vizianagram and in consequence lost the hunda of Makkuva. On his death in 1774 the Vizianagram Rája confiscated the whole of his estate, imprisoned his three sons in the fort of Dévapalli near Gajapatinagaram, but released them on a small allowance in 1793.

After the fight at Padmanábham (p. 53) the estate was handed over by the Collector to Rámachandra Rázu, Sanyási

CHAP. XV. SÁLÚR.

Rázu's eldest son, who died in 1801, and with whose son, another Sanyási Rázu, the permanent settlement was effected in 1803. This man died in 1830, and was succeeded in turn by his son Náráyana Rámachandra Rázu; by the latter's minor son, Sanyási Rázu (who was a ward of court until 1855) in 1846; and by this man's son (another Náráyana Rámachandra) in 1869.

Náráyana Rámachandra was a minor, and the Court of Wards managed the estate until he came of age in 1879. He was a weak individual who was totally incapable of restraining the extravagance and mismanagement of his mother, and at the end of three years he was 2½ lakhs in debt and earnestly begged Government to take over the management of the estate and get it and him out of their embarrassments. Government accordingly assumed charge at the end of 1882, but by April 1883 the zamindar had changed his mind and wanted his estate back again. It was restored accordingly. He died of leprosy on the 8th September 1894, and as his heir Sanyási Rázu, the present proprietor, was a minor, the estate once more came under the Court of Wards. It was over seven lakhs in debt, of which 5½ lakhs were due to the Mahárája of Bobbili, who had a mortgage on almost half the property. To help clear off this, Peddapenki and nine other villages were sold to Bobbili in 1897 and now form a separately-registered estate. Other subsequent alienations included the sale by public auction in the same year of Mukavalasa; the subdivision of Bhúdévipéta in 1899; the grant of Kásidhoravalasa in 1900; and the registry of Gangachollapenta and three other villages in the name of the zamindar's grandmother. These four also now form separate estates. The zamindari was handed back to its owner on 22nd May 1906 on his attaining his majority, and by that time all but Rs. 25,000 of the debt had been cleared off.

SARVASIDDHI TALUK.

THIS lies along the Bay in the southernmost corner of the district. In general aspect its interior resembles the other coastal areas, but along the shore are several saltish swamps and the coast line itself is diversified with picturesque headlands. It is one of the three Government taluks and comprises a large extent of rich wet land under the Varáha and Sárada rivers. Its rainfall, however, is the lowest in the district. Statistics regarding Sarvasiddhi will be found in the separate Appendix. The following are the more interesting places in it :—

Dimila : A village of 2,944 inhabitants $2\frac{1}{2}$ miles south by east of Yellamanchili. It was once of much more importance than now, and seems, from a copper plate grant found at Chípurupalle in 1867 (see J.A.S.B., xxxix, 153–8) to have been the chief town of a district. The village temple, an unpretentious building, is dedicated to Siva in the uncommon form Nagnésvara, or 'the naked.' The story goes that the rishi Agastya was unable, to his great grief, to be present at the marriage of Siva with Párvati, and that the former accordingly promised to appear before him with his bride whenever he wished it. Agastya expressed the wish at a moment when neither of them had any clothes on, but they appeared none the less just as they were, and the temple was erected to commemorate the event.

Gópálapatnam : A village of 781 souls in the south of the taluk, two miles from the coast and close under the block of hills known as Sudikonda. On the top of these hills is a spring called the *Kási bugga*, in which the devout bathe at Sivarátri and the water of which is believed to be very efficacious in curing blighted crops. Near another pool close by is a little shrine in which are two slabs bearing Telugu inscriptions and scattered round about which are a number of fragments of sculptures, among them a spirited representation of Káli slaying the buffalo-demon Mahishásura. Not far off is a tiny circular shrine cut out of the rock. The place thus seems once to have been of religious importance, and several legends still cluster about it.

Nakkapalli : Fourteen miles south-west of Yellamanchili, on the trunk road ; population, 2,459. In pre-railway days it was an important halting-place, as its neglected encamping-ground for troops and its large chattram show. The old travellers' bungalow has been turned into a dispensary. The industries of

CHAP. XV.
SARVASIDDHI.

the place are the weaving of coarse white cloths by a number of Padma Sáles and the making, by one family of Kamsális, of lacquered toys (unusually well finished and prettily coloured) on a lathe in the ordinary manner.

The proprietary estate which is named after the village has already been referred to on p. 221 above.

A quarter of a mile to the south of the village is the agrahéram of Upmáka, on a hill near which is a well-known shrine to Venkatésvara, the famous god of Tirupati in North Arcot. This is approached by 295 steps and consists of a kind of grotto, partly formed by two enormous overhanging masses of rock, on the wall of which is rudely chased a representation of the deity. Another temple to the same god stands at the foot of the hill. At the celebration of the god's marriage, in March, huge crowds assemble from all over the Northern Circars.

Panchadhárala : Seven miles in a direct line north-east of Sarvasiddhi and about fifteen by road from Anakápalle ; population, 2,284. The name means 'five fountains' and is derived from five jets of water fed by a perennial natural spring which are to be found in a paved enclosure to the south of the Siva temple. Close by these is a lingam on which are carved 1,020 other lingams in 12 rows of 85 each, and which is inconsequently known as the *kótilingam,* or 'crore of lingams.' The temple itself is not wonderful architecturally, but on the pillars of the mandapams within it are several inscriptions of historical interest, two of them (dated in years corresponding to A.D. 1407 and 1428, respectively) giving a genealogy of a branch of the Eastern Chálukya kings. Further particulars appear in paragraph 41 of the Government Epigraphist's report for 1899–1900.

Panchadhárala once gave its name to one of the estates which were formed out of the havíli lands and put up to auction at a fixed assessment in 1802. But subsequently, on the discovery being made that it and some of the villages adjoining were really within the ancient limits of the Vizianagram zamindari, they were transferred thereto and the estate was named Chípurupalle, after the most central of the villages remaining. This property, which comprised 24 villages, was bought at the auction by the Rája of Vizianagram. Subdivision after subdivision followed ; fifteen of the villages were bought in by Government at sales for arrears ; and the remaining nine now form no less than eight proprietary estates, namely, Bharinikam, Chípurupalle, Idulapáka-Bónangi and Rávåda in Anakápalle taluk, Mámidiváda in Sarvasiddhi, and Appikonda, Kúráda-Kondayyavalasa and Siddhésvaram in Vizagapatam. The history of Bharinikam has been referred to on p. 221 above.

Except Mámidiváda (the story of which is given on p. 223) the other seven were bought in 1812 by Gangabattulu Sámayya. Chípurupalle itself (which should not be confused with the place which is the head-quarters of the Chípurupalle taluk) consists of the village of that name and was bought by Garuda Sanyási Chetti in 1825. It was sold by him in 1844 to Jagga Rao of the Godé family, on whose death it passed to his son Venkata Náráyana Rao. The latter died without male issue in 1882 and the estate came under the Court of Wards. In 1895 the widow adopted her daughter's son, Venkata Náráyana Rao, who is now the minor proprietor and comes of age in 1908.

Idulapáka-Bónangi, which consists of two villages, was sold by the above-mentioned Gangabattulu Sámayya in 1820 to Vasanta Rao Lakshminaráyana Rao, a Bráhman, whose son Bayanna transferred it to his brother Achyuta Narasinga Rao in 1863 in accordance with a rázináma in a suit. On the death of the latter in 1891, his five sons became the proprietors.

Ráváda was sold by Sámayya's family in 1820 to Dátla Venkatapati Rázu, who sold it in 1821 to Vasanta Rao Ananta Rao. He disposed of it to the Bobbili estate in 1832, but the above Bayanna bought it back in 1847. He died in 1869 and the property was under the Court of Wards during the minority of his son, the present proprietor, Lakshminaráyana Rao.

Appikonda was transferred as a gift by Gangabattulu Sámayya to Gangabattulu Rájanna in 1821. The latter was succeeded in 1856 by his minor son G. Sattayya, who died in 1870 and was followed by his widow Sattaiyamma. The property was subsequently sold to a Bráhman, Mindi Vásudéva Rao, who had made a fortune out of abkári contracts. He died in 1886 and his three sons (Rámayógi, Rámachendrudu and Subrahmanyam) are now the joint proprietors.

Kúráda-Kondayyavalasa was sold by Sámayya in 1820 to N. Venkanna and D. Venkanna, the latter of whom transferred it in the year following to Dátla Venkatapati Rázu, who sold it again the same year to Vasanta Rao Ananta Rao. Like Ráváda, it was sold in 1832 to the Rája of Bobbili and bought back in 1847 by Bayanna, who in 1850 sold it to C. V. Narasinga Rao, Perike Kshatriya by caste. The latter's son, Rájagópál Rao, and afterwards this son's daughter, Atti Chellayyamma the present proprietrix, followed as owners of the property.

The last of the eight estates, Siddhésvaram, was sold, with Idulapáka-Bónangi, in 1820 to V. R. Lakshminaráyana Rao, whose son Bayanna followed him. In 1864 his brother, Achyuta Narasinga Rao, bought it in public auction, and in the following

CHAP. XV. SARVASIDDHI.

year he sold it to Erramilli Mallikárjuna Rao, another Bráhman. The latter died in 1881 and his maternal grandson, Chatrázu Mallikárjuna Rao, whom he had adopted, is now the proprietor.

Páyakaraopéta : Contains 2,688 inhabitants and stands on the trunk road just where it leaves the district and on the bank of the Tándava stream opposite Tuni village in Gódávari. It contains a fine, but neglected, encamping ground for troops and is known (see p. 123) for its weaving.

Tradition has it that the man from whom the place is named was one Kákarlapudi Appala Rázu of Chandanádu in this taluk, who was granted, for services at Hyderabad, the title of Páyaka Rao, or 'foremost in battle,' and the estates of Anakápalle and Satyavaram in this taluk. The fort and its two temples at the former place (see p. 219) are said to have been built by him. Mr. G. E. Russell says[1] that a descendant of his of the same name, who was still in possession of these properties when the English acquired the district, died in 1776 without lineal descendants but leaving a widow and a widowed mother. The estates were consequently made over to the then Rája of Vizianagram on condition of his paying Rs. 90,000 more peshkash and Rs. 10,000 annually for the maintenance of the widows.

One of these ladies died in 1804 and the other in 1814. The friends of the latter declared that she had adopted a son, but Government had evidence of her mental incapacity to do any such thing and discontinued the maintenance. In January 1832, Jagannátha Rázu, a cousin of the boy who was supposed to have been adopted, appeared at the head of a large body of armed followers, assumed the title of Páyaka Rao, and began committing depredations. His ostensible grievance was the discontinuance of the maintenance, but in reality he was merely the puppet of Náganna Dora, díwán to the zamindar of Golgonda, a double-faced scamp who had long fomented risings against the Government while vehemently protesting all the time his unswerving loyalty. This rascal eventually, it may here be noted, met with a dramatic end.[2] He had betrayed to Government a companion of Páyaka Rao's called Venkatapati Rázu, and the man was tried and duly hanged. Two of his friends, however, broke into Náganna's house one night soon afterwards, woke him by shouts of 'Venkatapati Rázu has come back!', smote off his head and affixed it to the very gibbet from which Venkatapati's body was still swinging.

[1] Paragraph 6 of his report of 18th November 1834 printed in Vol. I of No. XXIV of the *Selections from the Madras Records* (Madras, 1856).

[2] See the *Asiatic Journal*, 1833, xii, 172 ff.

Soon after Mr. Russell appeared upon the scene in 1833 (see p. 57), Páyaka Rao disappeared, going, it was supposed, into the Nizam's country. But in 1834 he returned [1] at the head of a party of adventurers. Troops were sent after him; he fled to Rampa in Gódávari; the chief there gave him up; he was hanged in Páyakaraopéta on the river-bank; and his body, after the fashion of those times, was suspended in an iron cage on a gibbet there and left to moulder away. Forty years later [2] his skull and a bone or two still remained, but the masonry foundation is all that is now left of the gibbet. Among the villagers the spot goes by the suggestive name of 'Páyaka Rao's slip-knot post.'

Pentakóta: Lies at the mouth of the Tándava stream near the southern extremity of the taluk and district; population 1,646. Contains the remains of the fort after which it is named and a considerable mosque. Was once a salt-factory and port. The latter, though unsafe in the south-west rains, was sheltered during the north-east monsoon and formerly did a considerable export trade at that season. It (and also Púdimadaka) was closed to regular trade in 1881 for the curious reason that it was too far from Vizagapatam and Cocanada for the European merchants to be able personally to supervise exportation, which resulted in the native contractors so adulterating the exports that the shippers incurred heavy losses.

Púdimadaka: Fourteen miles south of Anakápalle by a metalled road; population 1,816. Was formerly a port, but was closed at the same time, and for the same reason, as Pentakóta (*q.v.*). It has been described as 'one of the safest ports on the coast of Orissa'—a ledge of rocks, terminating in the conspicuous landmark called the Pillar Rock, running out seawards to the south of it into five fathoms of water and efficiently protecting shipping during the south-west monsoon.

Ráyavaram: Eight miles south-west of Yellamanchili, population 2,625. Was formerly the station of the district munsif who now sits at Yellamanchili. Is said to be named after king Krishna Déva of Vijayanagar, who is supposed to have halted here during his expedition against Orissa about 1515 and to have recorded his victories on the big slab known as the *ráchabanda*, or 'king's slab,' which still lies in the market place.

The village formerly gave its name to one of the hundas or properties which were formed in 1802 (see p. 170) out of the havíli land and put up to auction as permanently-settled estates. This was then bought by the Rája of Vizianagram, who in 1810, says Mr. Carmichael, sold it to Sági Rámachandra Rázu, his

1 Mr. Russell's report cited, paragraph 78.
2 General Burton's *An Indian Olio*, 323.

maternal aunt's husband. In 1815 it was attached for arrears and was purchased by Godé Súrya Náráyana Rao (see p. 219) for Rs. 40,500. The constant irrigation disputes between the ryots of Ráyavaram and those of the lapsed hunda of Sarvasiddhi rendered this gentleman's position extremely unpleasant, and in 1844 he resold the property to Government, who still own it, for Rs. 30,000.

Sarvasiddhi: Lies 5½ miles south-south-west of Yellamanchili and now contains only 1,015 people. It was, however, the head-quarters of the taluk up to 1861, and in days gone by was apparently of considerable importance, tradition declaring that it was one of the seats of the Golla kings (see p. 28) who ruled in these parts. Bricks of the large kind used in ancient buildings are constantly dug up in its fields.

The place was the chief village of another of the hundas just referred to which were formed in 1802. Like Ráyavaram, this was purchased in that year by the Rája and sold in 1810 to S. Rámachandra Rázu. His son fell into arrears, and in 1831 the property was bought in by Government at auction. It has since remained Government land.

Uppálam (or Pedda Uppalam): Nine miles south-west of Yellamanchili, population 2,649. Planted in the ground near the Mála quarter here is a most curious stone, roughly cylindrical, about 3 feet in diameter and 6 feet high. It does not appear to be a piece of rock *in situ*, but the villagers on one occasion failed to reach the bottom of it though they dug with energy throughout a whole day. It is called 'Bhíma's club', and there is a local tale to account for it. Near here, says this story, lived once upon a time a demon named Bakásura, who had to be propitiated by a daily meal of human flesh. One day it fell to the lot of a youth who was the only son of his mother, and she was a widow, to furnish the monster's breakfast. Bhíma the Terrible chanced to hear of this and volunteered to go instead. He was late, and the demon angrily demanded the reason and called for a twig wherewith to clean his teeth. Bhíma in reply pulled up a palmyra tree and tossed it over to him, whereon the amazed monster took to his heels. Bhíma pursued him, flung his club at him (this stuck in the ground where it still rests) and at last ran him to ground in the cave still to be seen in the 'Quoin rock' at Pólavaram (a hamlet of Uppalam) which juts out into the sea and is washed by the waves. Dragging him out by the nose, Bhíma there slew him.

Pólavaram contains a salt-factory (see p. 183) and was once a port. This latter was closed in 1863 as its trade was insignificant.

Vátáda (*alias* Révu vátáda): Now a hamlet of Vákapádu, but better known formerly. It lies on the coast at the point where the Sárada and Varáha rivers unite and enter the sea. It used to be a port, but this was closed at the same time, and for the same reasons, as Pólavaram.

Yellamanchili: Head-quarters of the taluk and a union of 6,536 inhabitants; contains a railway-station, a district munsif's court, a station of the Canadian Baptist Mission and a travellers' bungalow. Dominating the whole place rises a hill on the top of which are many broken stones and bricks of the ancient pattern, and—a landmark for miles round—the two stone posts and lintel of a doorway. These are locally declared to be the remains of a palace and fort of the Golla kings and the hill is called Núki Pápa's hillock after, it is said, the sister of one of these rulers. On this hill two lots of ancient coins have been found. Mr. Sewell[1] says the first find was made in 1863 and consisted of cast copper coins bearing the device of a bull couchant and the legend Srí Chanda Dé (va). The second find was in 1895 and comprised a number of copper coins identified by Dr. Hultzsch as being those of the Eastern Chálukya king Vishnuvardhana (A.D. 663–72).[2] That the place was anciently of much importance is shown by the fact that whenever any considerable excavations are made the ruins of old temples and buildings are unearthed.

Close under the south face of Núki Pápa's hillock is the shrine to the village goddess, Rámachandramma. She is declared to appear to her worshippers at her annual festival (when a buffalo is sacrificed to her) in the form of flashes of lightning in the sky. Paiditalli of Mámidiváda does the same.

Yellamanchili lies on the trunk road and the spacious military encamping-ground (still called by the natives 'the cantonment') shows that it was once an important halting-station. On one side of this stand the taluk office and the bomb-proof hospital, formerly a travellers' bungalow. Near one corner of it is the shrine of Achayamma Pérantálu, which affords a good instance of the genesis of local deities and their shrines. Achayamma, a Kápu woman, committed sati on this spot some 60 years ago (her sister is still alive) and the reverence which would in any case have been paid to the place in consequence was increased a hundred-fold by the eventual appearance of an ant-hill over it. The hill was duly protected by a small thatched building; and now an annual festival is held, vows are paid to the lady, and her resting-place is covered with *ex voto* offerings.

[1] *Lists of Antiquities*, i, 18.

[2] G.O., 454, Educational, dated 1st August 1896.

SRUNGAVARAPUKÓTA TALUK.

LIES west of Vizianagram and includes a considerable area in the Agency from the foot of the lower slopes of the 3,000 feet plateau up to its main crest round about the great Gálikonda hill (p. 6). This part of it is reached by the Anantagiri ghát (p. 137) and drains southwards into the Sárada river, while the low country is included in the basin of the Chittivalasa river. The appearance and inhabitants of the latter area resemble those of the rest of the plains.

The undermentioned places deserve a note :—

Dharmávaram: A thriving trading village of 3,317 inhabitants lying three miles east by north of Srungavarapukóta. In its hamlet Sanyásipálem is a shrine to a sanyási which is known all over the low country and resorted to by people of all castes. This ascetic, say the legends, came to the village centuries ago at a time when the local goddess, Paiditalli, insisted on having a meal of human flesh every day. At the earnest prayer of the people, he pronounced powerful spells which bound her down to her temple and prevented her from getting out to seize her victims. She complained bitterly of the pangs of hunger she suffered in consequence, but he told her she must do the best she could on the offerings which were voluntarily brought to her. When the sanyási eventually died, the greatful villagers put up a shrine to him and under his image therein they buried some magical emblems he had made. These are now declared to make the cattle give milk in plenty, to cure those possessed of devils and to grant offspring to the childless. Children born after vows to the shrine are called Sanyási, and the name is astonishingly common round about this village. When any worshipper supplicates for a boon, the pújári puts a bilva leaf on the head of the sanyási's image, and if it shortly falls off this is taken as a favourable sign.

Jámi, on the south bank of the Chittivalasa river, is the most populous village in the taluk, possessing 5,967 inhabitants. It is a union, and contains many Bráhmans. Drinking-water is obtained from the river and the cremation ground is up-stream. The shrine of the local goddess, a deification of a Bráhman woman who committed sati, is held in much local repute for the benefits it is supposed to grant to the devout, and a large annual festival is celebrated at it. Near it stand three slabs bearing ancient sculptures of goddesses. The cotton carpets made in the village are referred to on p. 123.

Kásipuram, population 280, lies eight miles nearly north of Srungavarapukóta in a valley among the foot-hills. Its Wednesday market is well known as a mart for hill produce.

It is the chief village of the inalienable and impartible estate of the same name, which comprises all the agency portion of the taluk. This, says Mr. Carmichael, formed part of the ancient barony of Srungavarapukóta, belonging to the Mukki family. Like other petty chiefs, the Mukkis were evicted by Vizianagram, but in the general confusion consequent on the sequestration of that zamindari in 1793 (p. 50), one of the old family, Mukki Rájabhúpála Rázu, took forcible possession of Kásipuram.

In 1794, however, burying the old animosities, he was one of the most active protectors of Náráyana Rázu, the young son of the Rája of Vizianagram who had been slain in that year (p. 53) at Padmanábham. When the Vizianagram zamindari was restored in 1796, the Collector, unwilling to give its chiefs any footing in the hills, kept the Kásipuram estate under his own management and leased it first to the zamindar of Ándra and afterwards to one Sági Tirupati Rázu. The latter was avowedly a servant or dependent of Vizianagram, and seeing this and that the property was too small to be made into a separate zamindari estate, the Collector eventually assigned it, on a separate sanad, to the Vizianagram family, whose property it still remains. At Anantagiri on the hills here, the Rája of Vizianagram possesses a coffee estate under European management.

After his restoration to his estate in 1796, Rája Náráyana Rázu mentioned above took Vírabhadra Rázu, the son of his old protector Rájabhúpála Rázu, under his care, making him one of his principal retainers and giving him an allowance of Rs. 200 a month. When, however, he went to Benares in 1827 (p. 339) and handed over his estate to the Collector, he by some mischance omitted to include this allowance in the list of stipends due to retainers. The omission was subsequently rectified, but Vírabhadra Rázu cherished a grievance against the authorities, and set himself to create disturbances with such energy that in 1832, when Mr. Russell arrived in the district on his special commission, there was a reward of Rs. 5,000 on his head and the residents in Waltair thought it necessary to post guards at their houses. The troops sent after him by Mr. Russell burnt Kásipuram and chased Vírabhadra Rázu so relentlessly about the hills that time after time he only escaped by his superior knowledge of the country and was often reduced to living on jungle fruits. He was at last betrayed in January 1833 by one of his own gang, tried by court martial and sentenced to death as a rebel. Government, however, reduced the sentence to one of imprisonment for life, and sent him to the fort of Gooty in the Anantapur district,[1] where so many of the rebels of the Northern Circars ended their days.

Srungavarapukóta, the taluk head-quarters, is a union of 5,862 inhabitants, most of whom live in indifferent huts. It was once the residence of the Mukki family referred to just above and the remains of their old fort are still visible.

The local goddess, Yerakamma, is another deification of a woman who committed sati. Ballads are sung about her which say that she was the child of Dásari parents and that her birth was foretold by a Yerukala woman (whence her name) who prophesied that she would have the gift of second sight. She eventually married, and one day she begged her husband not to go to his field, as she was sure he would be killed by a tiger if he did. Her husband went notwithstanding, and was slain as she had foreseen. She committed sati on the spot where her shrine still stands, and at this there is a festival at Sivarátri.

Two miles west of the town, at the foot of an outlying spur of the hills called Punyagiri, is a garden belonging to the Vizianagram estate. A flight of steps said to have been built by one of the Rájas leads up the hill to a wooded gully in which is a quaint shrine to Dhára Gangamma consisting of a boulder poised on two others between which trickles a small stream. A festival takes place here at Sivarátri and the people then crowd to bathe in this. Further up, the stream tumbles over a little fall which is held sacred and under which the bones of the dead are placed.

[1] *Asiatic Journal* (1833), xii, 172–3.

VIRAVILLI TALUK

ADJOINS Srungavarapukóta on the south-west and, like it, lies close under the 3,000 feet plateau and includes the slopes of this up to the main crest. The Minamalúr ghát (p 136) leads up to the plateau from Mádgole. The area on the hills is inhabited almost exclusively by Telugus and contains scarcely any of the real hill tribes. The low country resembles the adjoining tracts and includes only two places of interest :—

Chódavaram is the head-quarters of the taluk, the station of a district munsif, and a union of 5,705 inhabitants. It contains an old fort where little gold coins are sometimes found and in which lies an ancient cannon, seven feet long.

In the small temple of Késavasvámi are six inscriptions of which five (one of which is dated in Saka 1389, or A.D. 1467) mention[1] Sríman Mahámandalésvara Pratápa Vallabha Rája, who, from his title Mahámandalésvara, must have been some local chief and not a ruling king Perhaps he built the fort.

Hanging from a tree in the deputy tahsildar's compound is one of the old iron cages in which (*cf.* p. 313) the bodies of notorious criminals used to be gibbeted after execution. It was formerly suspended from a gallows, but this rotted to pieces and it was then brought to its present situation. It was made for the body of one Ási Dora, mokhásadár of Pedda Madina, who was hanged in March 1840 for the murder, on the night of 6th March 1837, of Kastúri Appayya Pantulu, the Collector's sheristadar, as he was returning from office in a palanquin. It appears that after the Vizianagram estate was placed under the management of the Collector in 1827 (p. 339), endeavours, in which the sheristadar was very active, were made (see p. 176) to assess to kattubadi the numerous mokhásas and inams which up to then had escaped rent-free. The murder was a result of the unpopularity which the sheristadar incurred in consequence, and the Government gave his widow a life pension of Rs. 105 a month, being half the salary her husband was drawing at the time of his death.

Mádgole (Mádugula): A union of 8,952 inhabitants lying eleven miles north-west of Chódavaram, close under the hills near the foot of the Minamalúr ghát. Its position makes it an important mart for the produce of the hills.

[1] See Sewell's *Lists of Antiquities*, i, 15.

CHAP. XV. VÍRAVILLI.

It is the head-quarters of the inalienable and impartible ancient zamindari of the same name. This comprises the agency portion of the taluk, which in consequence is often called 'Hill Mádgole.' The Mádgole zamindars claim to be descended from the rulers of Matsya Désa ('the fish country', *cf*. p. 28). They are installed at Pádéru on a stone throne shaped like a fish, display a fish on their banners, use a figure of a fish as their signature, and zealously protect from harm the mahseer in the Matsya gundam ('fish pool') referred to on p. 285 above. Some of their dependents wear earrings shaped like a fish. Other accounts say that they came to this country with the founder of the Jeypore family, whose cousins they were, who gave them the Mádgole country as a fief, and the title of Bhúpati ('lord of the earth') which they still bear.

No details of their history survive until 1770, when, says Mr. Carmichael, Linga Bhúpati, the then zamindar, joined in the general revolt against the power of Vizianagram (p. 46), was dispossessed by Sítaráma Rázu with the aid of the Company's troops, and fled with his family to Jeypore, where he eventually died. Sítaráma is said to have made the oblong brick fort with five bastions at Mádgole within which is the present residence of the zamindars. The Circuit Committee (p. 167) said in 1784 that it had been constructed after the European model by bricklayers from Madras and was then garrisoned with a battalion, about 1,000 strong, dressed and armed in the European manner.

After the Rája of Vizianagram was slain at Padmanábham in 1794 (p. 53), the Collector recalled the Mádgole family from their exile at Jeypore and gave the estate to Jagannátha, the paternal nephew of the Linga Bhúpati mentioned above. His title was contested by Appála Bhúpati, an illegitimate son of his uncle; the claim was rejected; but the pretender managed to collect the revenue of the hill villages and to give a great deal of trouble. In 1803 the permanent settlement was made with Jagannátha Bhúpati.

In 1813 the estate was sold for arrears and bought for Rs. 5,000 by one Chintalapati Rázu, who transferred it in the next year to Chinchiláda Venkata Rázu. In 1814 this man sold the Chídikáda subdivision (which however returned to the estate in 1821) and in 1817 he transferred the rest of the property to Linga Bhúpati, eldest son of Jagannátha. Linga Bhúpati was succeeded in 1831 by his eldest wife, Rámayya, who in the following year transferred the estate to her husband's half brother, Harihara, who died the same year and was followed by his brother Krishna Bhúpati. In 1833 the zamindari was again sold for arrears; was bought by Government for Rs. 1,000; but in 1834 was handed back to Krishna Bhúpati on his tendering the amount outstanding.

In 1833 the latter had again alienated the Chídikáda subdivision, selling it to one Mandapáka Jagannáyakulu. This man transferred it in 1835 to the Rája of Bobbili, who in 1836 also bought the Jagannáthapuram subdivision. These two estates are still separate properties. In 1848 the then Rája of Bobbili gave them to his sister's husband Inuganti Rájagópál Rao, whose widow retransferred them to him in 1856. In 1862 he conveyed them to Sítarámasvámi, the son of another sister. The present Mahárája of Bobbili, who is the adoptive grandson of the above Rájagópál Rao, afterwards brought a suit to recover the property, which was carried as far as the Privy Council[1] but was unsuccessful, and the two estates now belong to Inuganti Chinna Sítarámasvámi, who succeeded to them in 1898 as the heir of Sítarámasvámi's widow.

Krishna Bhúpati held Mádgole from 1834 until 1870, when he mortgaged the whole estate to the Mahárája of Jeypore for sixteen years in consideration of a loan of five lakhs. He died on Christmas Day 1875, and left two widows (sisters) named respectively Síta and Nílamani, a daughter called Ammi Dévi who was married to the Jeypore Rája's brother, but no son.

The two widowed Ránis were registered as his joint successors, but they quarrelled, serious affrays occurred between their retainers, a vakil named Lingam Lakshmaji who had sub-leased the estate from Jeypore was stated to be defrauding them, and eventually in 1877 the estate was taken under the management of the Court of Wards. In 1880, however, the junior Ráni was removed from the protection of the Court by an order of the High Court.

Meanwhile the senior Ráni, in virtue of authority given her by the will of the late zamindar, had adopted as a son a boy belonging to the Jeypore family. The junior Ráni disputed the legality of the step, but the High Court upheld the adoption and in 1885 the boy was consequently made a ward of court and the estate treated as his property. The Privy Council, however, set aside the adoption[2] and in 1888 the Collector was instructed to hand the estate over to the senior Ráni (the junior Ráni had died in 1886 leaving a granddaughter named Rájéndramani Dévi), who held it until her death in May 1901. She was succeeded by

[1] I.L.R., XXIII Madras, 49–55.

[2] I.L.R., XI Madras, 486.

CHAP. XV. VÍRAVILLI.

Rájéndramani Dévi and Mukunda Deo (adopted son of Krishna Deo, son of the daughter of Linga Bhúpati mentioned above), who divided the property. Their succession is now disputed in a civil suit brought by one Linga Bhúpati, who says he is the grandson (through an adopted son) of the Rámayya above mentioned. Mukunda Deo died in February 1905, and his widow Chandramani holds his share of the estate.

Meanwhile, in 1882, the account running between the zamindar and the Mahárája of Jeypore had been balanced by a committee appointed by the Collector, and showed that the former owed the latter some Rs. 5,07,000. In 1890 it was agreed that the Mahárája should accept Rs. 3,53,000 in settlement of all his claims and that the repayment of this sum with interest at 4½ per cent. should be secured by the mortgage with possession to the Mahárája of 68 villages of the estate. This mortgage is still running, and the estate is thus divided into two parts, of which one is administered by the Mahárája of Jeypore and the other, which includes the hill villages, by the Mádgole family.

All this litigation, mortgaging and changing of management naturally had the worst possible effect on the administration of the estate, which became a byword for inefficiency. The hold over the hill muttadars maintained by the senior Ráni (Síta) who died in 1901 was most ineffectual; and they quarrelled among one another, bullied their tenants and defied their suzerain until the District Officers were forced to interfere and remove some and punish others. Matters have improved but little since, and it has been necessary to warn the present holders of the estate that they will be held responsible for any trouble that may arise in the hills owing to their unsuitable methods of managing that country.

VIZAGAPATAM TALUK.

CHAP. XV. VIZAGAPATAM.

VIZAGAPATAM is the smallest taluk in the district and, next to the ordinary tracts in Pálkonda, the most densely populated. Its inhabitants increased at a relatively higher rate than those of any other taluk both in the decade 1891–1901 and in the thirty years ending with 1901. It contains more Musalmans and Christians than any other taluk, and its people are also better educated than those of any other. It is a picturesque tract. The coast line is broken by the bold headland called the Dolphin's Nose (1,174 feet above the sea), the hills which run down to the shore by Lawson's Bay, just north of Waltair, and the Sugar-loaf hill which separates this from the bay just beyond it; and inland stands the Simháchalam range of rounded red hills and its continuation northward towards Bimlipatam. The Simháchalam temple and the head-quarters are the chief places of interest within the taluk.

Simháchalam ('the lion hill'), which rises to about 800 feet above the sea, stands just north of Vizagapatam. Near the top of the north side of it, in a wooded hollow surrounded by a wide circle of higher ground, is the temple to Narasimha, the man-lion incarnation of Vishnu, which gives the hill its name. This is the most famous, richest, and best sculptured shrine in Vizagapatam, and in its honour numbers of the people of the district are named Simháchalam, Simhádri, Narasimha and so on. From the hollow in which it stands, a deep glen, watered by a rivulet and clothed with many trees in striking contrast to the bare flanks of the rest of the hill, runs down to the foot of the northern slope, where, about ten miles by road from Vizagapatam, is a rose-garden which is traditionally declared [1] to have been planted by the well-known Sítaráma Rázu of Vizianagram and is watered from the rivulet. The Rájas of Vizianagram have been wardens of the shrine for over two centuries and have endowed it with land worth some Rs. 30,000 per annum.

The way up to the temple runs along the glen from near the rose-garden, through terraced fields of pine-apples dotted with mango, jack and other trees. It passes up a broad flight of well-kept stone steps, over a thousand in number, on either side of which trees have been planted to give shade and a rill runs in a

[1] Mackenzie MSS., Local Records, iv, 265–9.

stone channel to refresh weary pilgrims. At frequent intervals are images of the various Hindu gods in little niches, and on festival days the steps are lighted from top to bottom. The steps eventually reach the narrow mouth of the glen, and here the path is barred by a bold portal called Hanumán's gate, by the side of which the rivulet which passes down the glen is led into two pools where pilgrims bathe before they continue the ascent. This gate was apparently part of the fortifications which in former days guarded the temple and other remains of which may be traced on the high ground surrounding it. Tradition says that these included as many as 24 bastions.

Passing through Hanumán's gate, the pilgrim traverses a narrow part of the glen where the rivulet is led through pipes and channels over several artificial cascades surrounded by more sculptures of the gods, and at length reaches the amphitheatre in which, on a terrace partly cut out of the hill-side, stands the temple itself.

The local *sthala purána* contains a mythical account of the foundation of the building which relates the well-known story of how the demon Hiranya-Kasyapa, furious with his son Prahláda's devotion to his pet aversion Vishnu, had the boy thrown into the sea and Simháchalam hill placed on top of him; how Vishnu in his man-lion incarnation went to the youth's rescue, stood on one side of the hill and tipped it up so that the boy could crawl out on the other; and how Prahláda in his gratitude founded this shrine.

The exact age of the temple is not known, but it contains an inscription, dated as far back as 1098–99 A.D., of the Chóla king Kulóttunga I who conquered the Kalinga territories (see p. 27), and it must thus have been a place of importance even then. Another inscription shows that a queen of the Velanándu chief Gonka III (1137–56) covered the image with gold; a third says that the Eastern Ganga king Narasimha I built the central shrine, the mukhamandapam, the nátyamandapam, and the enclosing verandah in black stone in 1267–68; and the many other grants inscribed on its walls (the Government Epigraphist's lists for 1899 give no less than 125 of these) make it a regular repository of the history of the district. The records left here by the victorious Krishna Déva of Vijayanagar have been referred to on p. 28 above.

Architecturally the temple apparently deserves high praise. Europeans are not admitted within the central enclosure, but this is said to contain a square shrine surmounted by a high tower, a portico in front with a smaller tower above it, a square sixteen-

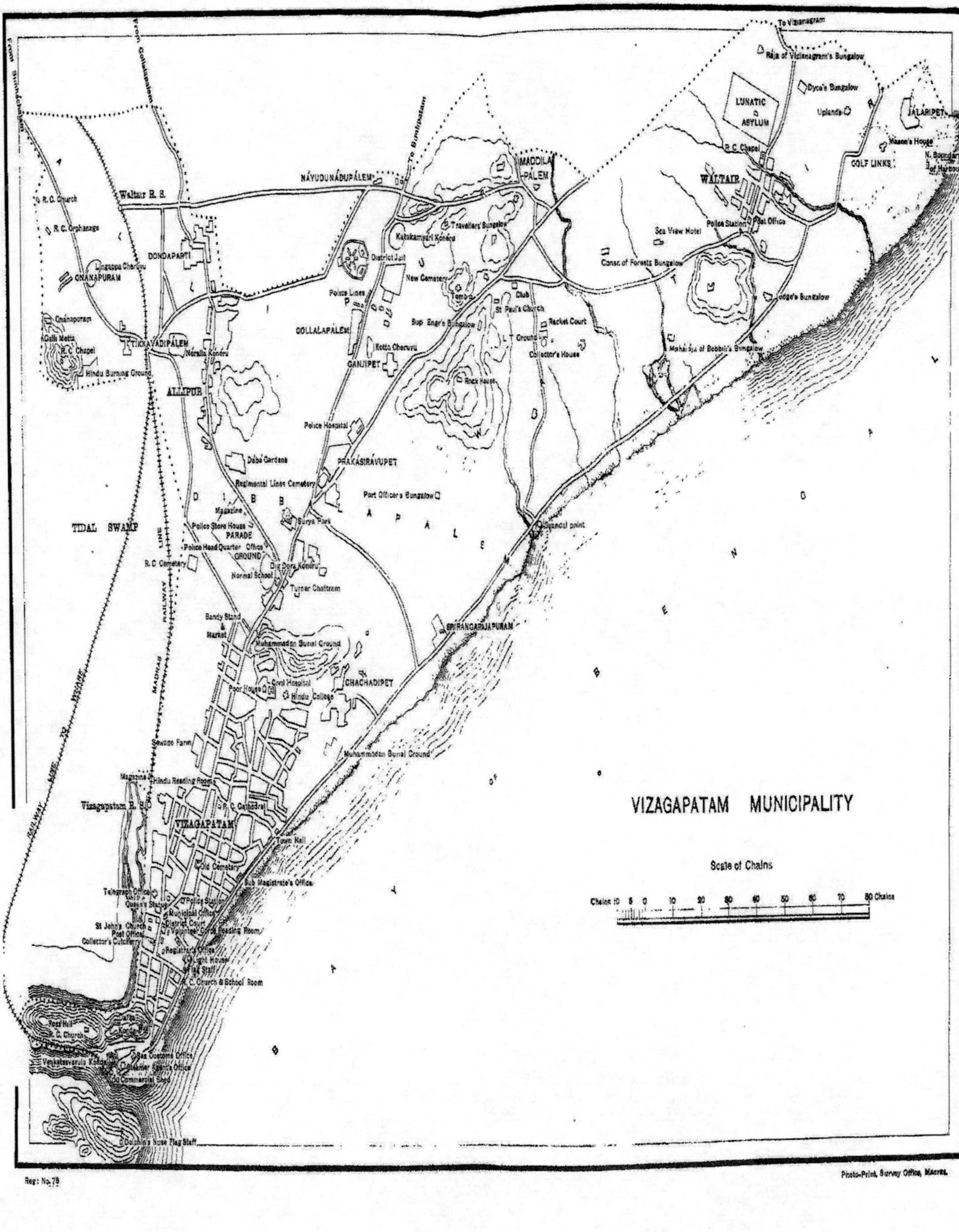

Reg: No. 78

Photo-Print, Survey Office, Madras.

pillared mandapam (called the mukhamandapam) facing this, and an enclosing verandah, all made of dark granite richly and delicately carved with conventional and floral ornament and scenes from the Vaishnavite purános. These are doubtless the work of the Narasimha I referred to above. Much of the carving is mutilated (by Muhammadan conquerors, it is said) and much more has been covered over with a thick coat of plaster at the order, it is locally declared, of a Rája of Vizianagram, whose wife was disgusted at its indecencies. One of the pillars is called the *kappam stambham* or 'tribute pillar.' It is credited with great powers of curing cattle-disease and granting children, and the right to collect the numerous tributes paid to it in consequence is annually sold by auction. In the verandah is a stone car with stone wheels and prancing stone horses. The image of the god is small and is kept covered with an unctuous preparation of sandal paste. Once a year, in May, this is removed with much ceremony at the festival called Chandanayátra.

Outside this inner enclosure there is little worthy of note except the excellent nátyamandapam on the north side of the temple, where the god's marriage is performed and which is also the work of Narasimha I. This is supported by 96 pillars of black stone, arranged in sixteen rows of six each, which are more delicately carved than any others in the temple, are all different in the details of their design, and yet avoid incongruity of effect by adhering to one general type—especially in their capitals, which are usually of the inverted-lotus shape.

Vizagapatam: The head-quarters of the taluk and district and a municipality of 40,892 inhabitants. The municipal limits (see the map attached) include the suburb of Waltair, where the European officials reside and several of the zamindars of the district have bungalows. The history and achievements of the municipal council have already been referred to on p. 215 above; the medical and educational institutions in the town are mentioned in Chapters IX and X respectively; its arts and industries in Chapter VI; and its jail in Chapter XIII. Besides the officers usually found at a district head-quarters, the place is the station of a Superintending Engineer, Conservator of Forests, Deputy Commissioner of Salt, Abkári and Customs, Deputy Inspector-General of Police, Inspector of Schools, Inspectress of Girls' Schools and Port Officer, and is the head-quarters of the Bishop of the Roman Catholic diocese of Vizagapatam and of sections of both the Madras and Bengal-Nagpur railways.

The town is built along the shore of a wide bay, five miles across, which is bounded on the south by the Dolphin's Nose headland already mentioned and on the north by a small point which separates it from the picturesque little cove called Lawson's Bay after the Patrick Lawson, Commander of the *Lord Hobart* Indiaman, who lies buried (1820) in the old cemetery. Vizagapatam proper lies at the southern end of this bay and Waltair at the northern, and between them, along the shore, runs a fine road which opens up a whole series of splendid (but so far greatly neglected) building sites.

Immediately north of the Dolphin's Nose is a small river called the Upputéru ('salt river') which drains a land-locked tidal swamp four square miles in extent and the land behind it, and flows to the sea over a sandy bar of the usual kind. This swamp, which (see the map) is crossed by the railway line leading to the port, runs along the west side of Vizagapatam town and crowds it into a narrow triangle at the apex of which is a small eminence called Ross' Hill and at its base a higher and larger height formed of rock but covered with blown sand. Close under the west side of this latter runs the main bazaar-street leading north-eastwards to Waltair, a clean, bright, well-built line of houses wearing a prosperous air.

Waltair, which includes not only the native village of that name, but all the area between 'Rock House' on the map and the northern extremity of the municipality, is built on a stretch of very broken ground which runs up to about 250 feet above the sea and is partly barren, rocky soil dotted with black boulders and stunted scrub and partly a curious vivid red earth. Towards the sea, the latter has been worn by the streams which cross it (see the map) into a series of impassable crevasses and gullies separated from one another by hummocks and pinnacles of fantastic shapes. The scene from this high ground is probably the most beautiful on the east coast of India. The sombre purples of the Dolphin's Nose on the south, the vivid chrome-yellow of the blown sand on the hill above Vizagapatam, the olive-coloured slopes of the scrub-covered heights scattered with glossy apple-green palmyras, the bright red soil running down to the sea and the dark trees at the northern end of the bay, backed as they all are by the brilliant turquoise of the Bay with its white edge of breakers, make up an unrivalled blaze of colour. The climate and temperature of this part of the place have already been referred to (p. 14). Among natives its air is reputed to be beneficial in lung troubles; and it is threatened in consequence with an invasion of Bengalis, who have already occupied several of its better houses.

The Dolphin's Nose is known to the natives as 'Blackmore's hill.' In 1801 Captain Thomas Blackmore, of the Artillery stationed at Vizagapatam, obtained a grant from the Company for 44 acres of land on the hill (on which, 'some years before,' he had built a house) and also permission to 'occupy, enclose and embellish the declivity of the hill next the sea.' This house was perhaps the building of which the ruins still stand on the very top of the hill near the banyan tree. The remains of foundations by the neighbouring flagstaff seem to show that there was also once a battery there, and from this were perhaps taken the ten old cannon which have been used to anchor the guy-ropes of the flagstaff and ornament the doorway of the enclosure round it. It is stated[1] that there was once a light-house here, and that it was blown down in the cyclone of 1876 referred to on p. 154. Lower down the hill, on the side facing the town, are the ruins of a bungalow built, on land granted him by the Collector in 1856, by Mr. J. W. McMurray, Treasury Deputy Collector, who died in Vizagapatam in 1883 and is buried in the Regimental Lines cemetery. Below this is the so-called 'Dutch Battery' mentioned on p. 44. Near it, washed by the surf, is a cave which is fabulously supposed to run inland for miles. The sea is declared to have made great encroachments on the point of the Dolphin's Nose, and tradition says that the people of Yerráda, the village at its southern foot, used to be able to walk round the headland to Vizagapatam. They now come over its crest by the paved path which leads up there. The sea has undoubtedly encroached near the 'Dutch Battery' and it also threatened to eat away the sand in front of the sea-customs office, but was checked by the series of loose stone groins (still visible) which Sir Arthur (then Major) Cotton put down in 1844. The river between the Dolphin's Nose and the town is crossed by a passenger ferry at its mouth and also by a pontoon ferry higher up, on the road to Anakápalle. The latter replaces the Turner pontoon bridge referred to on p. 135.

The tidal swamp or backwater drained by the river is completely sheltered on the south by the Dolphin's Nose and the hills behind it, and on the other sides is also protected by lesser and more distant heights. Proposals to turn it into a harbour have consequently been long debated. Borings show that a deep navigable channel 100 yards wide could be cut through it without difficulty, and the chief problem is the removal of the sand bar at the mouth of the river, which, though periodically scoured out by floods, carries only from two to three feet of water at low tide at certain seasons of the year.

[1] *Manual of Administration*, iii, 280.

CHAP. XV. VIZAGAPATAM.

The authoritative account of the difficulties involved and the remedies for them is the report on *Vizagapatam Harbour Investigations* written by Mr. A. T. Mackenzie of the Public Works department in 1899 at the close of a year's special work on the subject. He considers that the bar and the sea-bottom outside it change but little from year to year; that the currents outside the bar are so variable and of so low a velocity as to affect the position but slightly; that the range of tide is small (generally under five feet and much less on an average) so that the scour from the backwater cannot be expected to do much to keep the bar open; that this scour has been diminished by the reclamations made and attempted in the backwater; and that the sand on the bar is brought by the south-west, and partly denuded by the north-east, monsoon—so that the bar shallows during the former and deepens during the latter. The conclusion he comes to is that a groin from the end of the Dolphin's Nose, running first eastwards and then north-eastwards, would stop the formation of the bar, which is produced by waves acting on sand from the south. The cost of the groin he estimates roughly at Rs. 1,000 per foot run, or 30 lakhs for 3,000 feet. The probability of the completion in the near future of the line from Viziánagram to Raipur has brought the proposals for a harbour into the field of practical politics, and the question of the action which should be taken is now under consideration.

The chief of the attempted reclamations in the swamp above referred to was undertaken by a Roman Catholic Bishop of Vizagapatam who obtained [illegible],000 acres of the swamp on certain conditions regarding the extent to be periodically reclaimed. Beyond the building of an embankment (now dilapidated) round this, nothing has been done in the way of reclamation; but the embankment restricts the area of the tidal gathering-ground and so lessens the daily scour across the bar. The railway line has a similar effect. The land which is now the municipal sewage farm was partly reclaimed by convict-labour between 1872 and 1875. Ships used to be built there in former days. Loading and unloading at the port is now done by masúla boats from the north side of the river. A stone jetty and two cranes assist. Steamers anchor comparatively close to the shore in 6½ to 8 fathoms. In 1891 a landing and shipping fees committee was started under Act III of 1885. The trade of the port is referred to on p. 129. Native schooners, which used to be numerous, have been ousted by the steamers and the railway. The port office occupies the site of the old ice-house. Five European firms are represented at the place.

Just behind the jetties and the port office are Ross' Hill and two other knolls occupied respectively by a Roman Catholic church, a Hindu temple, and a Musalman mosque, all in close proximity. Mr. Ross was a Sub-Judge who (notwithstanding some opposition from the Musalmans) built a bungalow, about 1848, on the hill which bears his name. The Roman Catholic Mission bought the property in 1867 and erected a church on the site. This was afterwards enlarged and opened in 1877. The darga to which the mosque is attached is widely known. It is the tomb of Saiyad Ali Medína *alias* Ishák Medína, and Hindus make vows at it as often as Musalmans. The saint is considered to be all potent over the elements in the Bay of Bengal. Mr. Carmichael says that when he wrote (1869) every vessel passing the harbour inwards or outwards used to salute the saint by hoisting and lowering its flag three times, that many a silver dhóni was presented to him by Hindu ship-owners after a successful voyage, and that in a suit between a Kómati owner of a vessel and his Muhammadan skipper about a settlement of accounts, the latter charged for a purse of rupees vowed to the darga during a hurricane and the former disputed the item solely on the ground that the vow had never been discharged; and never questioned the propriety of conciliating the old fakír in dirty weather.

The actual history of the darga and mosque is forgotten. The inscriptions in and about them might afford information if deciphered. The inamdars in charge of them, who hold the Yerráda and Déváda villages for their upkeep, stated in a recent suit[1] that the date of the grant of the inam was prior to 1706. The early records of the English settlement at Vizagapatam speak of the frequent visits paid to the place by the Faujdars of Chicacole.

The southernmost part of Vizagapatam, in the apex of the triangle already referred to, is still known as 'the Fort.' Its former defences have been mentioned on p. 44 above and the map there given shows what immense changes a century and a half have effected in the place. The old fort itself evidently occupied much of the open green which now lies between the Collector's office, the District Court and the light-house. Pharoah's *Gazetteer* (1855) speaks as if it was still in existence then and says 'within the fort are the barracks for the European invalid soldiers, the arsenal, the officers' quarters and various public buildings. Immediately outside the fort gate, and in an open space, near which the pettah commences, is the garrison and European Veteran Company hospital, an upstair building.' Not

[1] O.S. No. 16 of 1902 on the District Court's file.

a vestige of the fortifications survives, but the garrison hospital is the building now occupied by Messrs. Simpson & Co. the 'open space' is doubtless that in which stands the bronze statue of the late Queen-Empress, given to the town by M.R.Ry. A. V. Jagga Rao in 1904; the invalid barrack (after being in turn a medical store, the Collector's treasury and the quarters of two medical warrant officers) has now become the Volunteer armoury and reading-room; and the arsenal is the Collector's office.

The history of the District Court building is alluded to on p. 207. The Collector's office was at one time in the building (now the property of M.R.Ry. Dharma Rao Náyudu) which was afterwards occupied by the Waltair Orphan Asylum; was removed to the house now used as Messrs. Arbuthnot's office; and at the end of 1873 was transferred to its present quarters. These are most inconvenient, and a new building is to be put up on the sand-hill on one of the fine sites already mentioned overlooking the sea.

The Waltair Orphan Asylum (*alias* the Vizagapatam Male and Female Orphan Asylum) was founded in 1817 by the Rev. C. Church, Chaplain. It was remodelled in 1831 and was subsequently described as being intended 'to afford a shelter and home to destitute children, orphans and foundlings of the Northern Circars, and to provide for the maintenance of the offspring and descendants of the men of the Carnatic Veteran Battalion who were disbanded in 1842 and who left their children and grandchildren in a state of destitution.' In the sixties of the last century it contained some 50 inmates and in 1863 the new orphanage above mentioned was built for it. It afterwards declined in prosperity and eventually, in 1894, was abolished, the few orphans remaining in it being sent to other asylums and the building being sold.

Facing the Collector's office is the light-house, the light on which (formerly at Santapilly) was removed hither in 1902 and is a white dioptric light of the fourth order, flashing every twenty seconds and visible twelve miles at sea in clear weather. Near it is the Roman Catholic church of the Sacred Heart of Jesus, built in 1887. The cathedral of St. Anne's, a brick building in Gothic style erected in 1854, stands (see the map) on higher ground to the north.

Adjoining the Collector's office is St. John's, the Church of England place of worship. It was built in 1844 by Sir Arthur Cotton and consecrated in 1846. St. Paul's church in Waltair, it may here be mentioned, was built in 1838 by Captain J. H. Bell. The belfry was blown down in the cyclone of 1870 (p. 153) and rebuilt by Government.

North of the fort, in a lane off the bazaar-street, chocked up by houses, is the old cemetery, often wrongly called 'the Dutch Cemetery.' There are no Dutch tombs in it, but it is the last resting-place of many of those who made Vizagapatam history and the burials date from 1699 to 1823. Among the graves are those of four Chiefs of the settlement, Simon Holcombe (1705), Sandys Davis (1734), Charles Simpson (1741) and Alexander Davidson (1791); of Kingsford Venner, a cadet of 19 who was killed in the sepoy mutiny of 1780 (p. 47); of John Dykes, a young seaman of H.M.S. *Centurion*, 50 guns, who was killed in a stirring fight in the Vizagapatam roads on the 18th September 1804, between his ship and a French man-of-war of 80 guns aided by two frigates, which resulted in the enemy being beaten off; [1] and of Benjamin Roebuck (1809), builder of the Mint at Madras and the docks at Coringa, who was sent to Vizagapatam as a punishment for supposed complicity in the scandals connected with the debts of the Nawáb of the Carnatic.[2]

North-east of the fort, on excellent sites facing the sea, are the new office of the deputy tahsildar and the Town Hall presented to the place by the Mahárája of Bobbili to commemorate the late Queen-Empress' diamond jubilee. They stand on land which used to be occupied by a very dirty fishermen's hamlet called Jáláripéta. In 1896–99 the houses in this were bought up at a cost of Rs. 27,000 and the fishermen transferred to a site across the river purchased and improved at a cost of Rs. 9,000. The fisher people, however, died at such a rate in their new quarters that in 1900 they were brought back and settled on a new site on the sand-hill.

On this hill are the civil hospital (see p. 157), the Mrs. A. V. Narasinga Rao college (p. 161), the site destined for the medical school and the Gajapati Rao poor-house. This last was started in 1863 by the then voluntary municipal association, was managed by a committee from 1866 till 1871, when it was taken over by the municipality; fell to a committee again between 1878 and 1886, when the council once more assumed charge; and in 1899 was taken over by Mahárája Sir Gajapati Rao.

The Turner Chattram and the new market, both in the bazaar-street, have been referred to elsewhere. Dábá Gardens,

[1] See Col. Campbell's letter describing the fight in *Asiatic Annual Register* for 1805, 32.

[2] More particulars of the various graves will be found in Mr. J. J. Cotton's *List of Inscriptions on Madras Tombs*.

the residence of M.R.Ry. A. V. Jagga Rao (see p. 220), contains the Godé Venkata Jagga Rao observatory. This was established in 1841 by the gentleman whose name it bears who (p. 220) had imbibed a taste for astronomy from his tutor, the then Government Astronomer. He erected the existing flagstaff on the Dolphin's Nose, the flag on which used to be hauled down precisely at 9 A.M. to set the time for the station. After his death his daughter, Mrs. A. V. Narasinga Rao, and her husband added largely to the equipment of the observatory and the institution began the contribution to the Bengal and Government of India Meteorological departments of the series of observations which is still continued. In 1884 Mrs. Narasinga Rao proposed to endow the institution with a fund of three lakhs and hand it over to trustees under the control of the Madras Government. Government did not find themselves able to accept the position, but eventually, in 1895, the Government of India[1] vested the observatory, the Dolphin's Nose flagstaff and the three lakhs in the Madras Treasurer of Charitable Endowments and the immediate management of the institution in a committee comprising the Collector for the time being, the Meteorological Reporters to the Governments of Madras and Bengal, the Government Astronomer and others. Subsequently M.R.Ry. A. V. Jagga Rao regained control of the observatory and its endowment. The instruments there include a 6-inch equatorial, a 3-inch transit instrument, a sidereal clock and a photographic telescope.

Facing Dábá Gardens is the old parade-ground, now used by the police. The lines of the two infantry regiments which used to be stationed in Vizagapatam were near this, on the other side of the road to Waltair. With Rs. 10,000 presented by the late Mahárája Sir Gajapati Rao and after his death by his widow, the site of these has recently been cleared and levelled, and the hamlet growing up on it is called Mahháránipéta. A road leads from it across the slopes of the sand-hill to the road along the shore.

Near this hamlet is Súrya Bágh, the residence of the Ráni of Wadhwán (p. 221), just north of which, at the junction of the roads to Waltair and to Bimlipatam stands the cemetery usually called 'the Regimental Lines cemetery,' or, from the inscription over its gateway, the *Mors janua vitæ* cemetery. This was consecrated by Bishop Spencer in 1847. The tombs in it date from 1819 to 1883, and include those of two Collectors of the

[1] See the fuller account of the matter in the Report on the observatory for 1895.

district (John Smith, 1824, and William Mason, 1834, the name-father of 'Mason's House' in Waltair) and of many military officers belonging to the troops formerly stationed in Vizagapatam. The Protestant cemetery now in use is near the District Jail and was consecrated by Bishop Gell in 1864. The oldest European tomb in Waltair is that by the side of the road a little below the Club. The natives call it *Ghanudu goli* or 'great man's tomb' and say it is haunted, but no one knows who is buried under it. One story says it covers the body of a Frenchman killed at Bussy's capture of Vizagapatam in 1757, but, as has been seen (p. 45), the place was taken then without a shot being fired.

Of the origins of the various bungalows in Waltair no records are traceable, mainly because the land is zamindari property. The Waltair estate was one of those carved out of the old havili land and sold by auction in 1802 (p. 170). It was bought, says Mr. Carmichael, by Mosalakanti Venkóji, a high official in the Collector's cutcherry, who died in 1821, leaving two minor sons. The Court of Wards managed the property until 1833, when it was handed over to the elder son, Venkata Náráyana Rao, who was followed in 1859 by Venkata Jagannátha Rao. On his death in 1873 the estate was divided into the three properties of Allipuram, Maddilapálem and Waltair, and in 1888 the Guntubóyinapálem village of the latter was sold and made into yet another separate property.

It has already (p. 42) been seen that the first move to Waltair was made by the Company in 1727 for the reason that the water there was excellent for bleaching the cloths made by their weavers. The golf links are still called by the natives *Chalavalu*, which means 'bleaching.' Round about them are the ruins of several bungalows occupied in the old days by the officers of the Northern Division of the Madras Command, and down by the sea are the ruins of their swimming-bath and of the well from which it was filled. Vizagapatam was the head-quarters of the Northern Division until its abolition in June 1878, and the troops stationed there included the General (who lived in what is now the Judge's bungalow) and his staff, two Native Infantry regiments and their officers and the officers commanding the European Veteran Company.

West of Waltair rises a bare, whale-backed spur of the Simháchalam hills, about 1,600 feet above the sea, which goes by the names of Kailása and 'Thomas' Folly.' In 1871 Mr. E. C. G. Thomas, Judge of Vizagapatam, built himself quarters on the top of this and used to go down every morning

CHAP. XV. VIZAGAPATAM.

to the foot of it in a tonjon, be driven thence to his court, and ride up again at night. When Government were looking about for a sanitarium for Calcutta in 1872, he wrote to them bringing the place to notice and stating that it was quite free from fever, possessed of good soil, covered with interesting plants, contained space for 100 houses, was from ten to fourteen degrees cooler than Vizagapatam, and had a most invigorating climate. He had by then laid out Rs. 6,000 in roads, reservoirs (there was no spring higher than half way up the hill) and temporary buildings, and the Mahárája of Vizianagram (owner of the hill) had erected, at a similar cost, a permanent house which Mr. Thomas rented. The remains of this last are still visible from Waltair.

Government called for the opinion of the Collector, Superintending Engineer and Zilla Surgeon on the place. They reported that the water difficulty was serious, the place cramped, the difference of temperature only four degrees, the building sites exposed, the evening mists unpleasant and the absence of any shade a drawback. Government accordingly decided in 1873 to spend no money on the hill.

VIZIANAGRAM TALUK.

CHAP. XV. VIZIANAGRAM.

RESEMBLES in general appearance the rest of the low country of the district, consisting of a plain of red soil scattered with red hills. The most prominent of the latter stand just north and west of Vizianagram town.

Next to those of Vizagapatam, the people of the taluk are better educated than any others in the district and increased at a relatively faster rate both in the decade 1891–1901 and in the thirty years ending with 1901.

There are two places of interest in the taluk :—

Rámatírtham lies about eight miles north-east of Vizianagram and contains 986 inhabitants. North of it stand two hills which are in striking contrast to the rounded red heights so common in this district, and consist of bare, solid rock, dotted with tors and worn into sheer precipices like the hills of the Deccan. The nearer of these is called Bódikonda, or 'bald hill.' On the top of the western end of it is a ruined brick shrine in which stand three images of Jain tirthankaras, some 1½ to 3 feet high, neatly carved out of the local garnetiferous gneiss. They are of the ordinary nude, seated, cross-legged, contemplative type, have the usual long ear-lobes, triple crowns and chámaras, and rest one foot on a figure of the animal which is their cognizance. Higher up this hill, under an immense overhanging rock, is another much mutilated Jain image.

On the hill next to the north, known as Gurubhaktudukonda, are three more slabs (one broken) bearing other sculptures of the same class.

At the western foot of Durgikonda, the second of the bare hills above referred to, under a great overhanging rock weathered into smooth rounded curves which look almost as if they were due to the action of running water, are yet other Jain remains. On the rock is carved a small, standing, nude image, beside which is a much defaced inscription which the Government Epigraphist says is a record of an Eastern Chálukya king who is probably identical with the Vimaláditya who reigned from 1011 to 1022 A.D. Near it lie two slabs, on one of which is sculptured another standing Jain image, behind whom curls a cobra with expanded hood playing above the head of the figure, and on the other a greatly mutilated sculpture of the same class. Above

CHAP. XV. VIZIANAGRAM.

these, in a rounded alcove formed by the weathering of the rock, is a third and smaller slab on which is cut a seated Jain figure.

These sculptures form the only Jain relics which have so far been brought to notice in the plains of this district. No local legends connect the Jains with the place, and the village is chiefly known nowadays for its modern temple to Ráma and the sacred Rámatírtham, fed by a spring, which lies close by this.

Vizianagram, the second largest town in the district, is a rapidly growing municipality of 37,270 inhabitants, the head-quarters of the deputy tahsildar, the Divisional Officer and the Rája of Vizianagram, and a station on the Bengal-Nagpur railway which will probably be the point at which the railway from Raipur will join the coast system. A Native Infantry regiment used to be stationed there, but the cantonment was abolished at the end of 1905. The town does much trade with the hill tracts to the west and with the port of Bimlipatam, and between 1871 and 1901 its population increased by no less than 84 per cent. The improvements in the place effected by the municipal council and the Vizianagram zamindars have been mentioned in Chapter XIV, the principal medical and educational institutions in Chapters IX and X respectively, and the climate in Chapter I.

Vizianagram consists of two parts—the native town surrounding the fort on the east and the former cantonment and civil station on the west. These are separated from one another by the Pedda Cheruvu ('large tank') which never dries up, irrigates a considerable area of wet land, supplies numerous wells sunk on its shores and is a famous sanctuary for wildfowl.

The civil station and deserted cantonment are neatly and regularly laid out with shady roads running at right angles to one another leading past numerous (often empty) bungalows in pleasant compounds. On high ground to the west of them stands the old parade-ground, bounded on one side by ancient trees and a line of bungalows, and faced by the buildings formerly used for the unmarried lines (the married lines were to the east, near the railway) and the military hospital. The last regiment to occupy the cantonment before its abolition was the 63rd Palamcottah Light Infantry, formerly the 3rd M.L.I. Just before it left, its mess-house was burnt to the ground and most of the regimental plate destroyed.

An avenue of fine trees running parallel to one side of the parade-ground leads past the Roman Catholic church of St. Maurice, built in 1882–83, and the small Church of England place of worship, erected in 1902 at a cost of Rs. 5,000. The latter replaced St. Mary's church, which stood just south of the parade-ground. This was originally called Holy Trinity and was built in 1850 at a cost of Rs. 2,600 on land granted the year before by the Mahárája of Vizianagram, and was consecrated by Bishop Dealtry in 1852. The building was badly injured by the cyclone of 1867 (p. 153), afterwards cracked badly, and was abandoned as dangerous in 1899. The Protestant cemetery is not far from its site. The graves in this date from 1811 to 1876. The earliest are those of three subalterns of the 10th Regiment of Native Infantry and a cenotaph to the Colonel and a Major of the same regiment. Other tombs are those of three officers who succumbed during the operations of 1834–36 in this district and Ganjám, and of several other members of the various regiments which have been cantoned here.

Along the road to Bimlipatam are the deserted race-course and grand stand, and a dilapidated racquet-court built about 1855. Ichabod is indeed writ large all about the cantonment. Nowadays it leads only a subdued existence, but forty years ago things were very different. In 1862 the Collector strenuously opposed a suggestion that Vizianagram should be made the head-quarters of the district, on the ground that it would be impossible for the Collector to do any work in so frivolous a spot. He said it was 'a scene of endless pastime: a race-course, a pack of hounds, cheetah-hunting, ram-fights, balls, nautches, joustings, junketings of every kind.'

The native part of the town offers a marked contrast to the cantonment, and is a bustling place. One wide street, called Santapéta, leads through it, and in this are many excellent two-storeyed houses belonging to wealthy Kómatis, their wide verandahs supported on Moorish arches; a conspicuous white temple to the well-known Kómati goddess Kanyaká Paramésvari, ornamented with little domes of the Rájputana pattern; and the clock-tower and market mentioned on p. 214.

The Rája's fort lies south of this street, on the shore of the Pedda Cheruvu. It is a great square erection of brick and stone, measuring about 250 yards each way, surrounded by the remains of a ditch, and having a big bastion at each corner. Two main entrances lead into it, one from the south by the tank, and the other (the elaborate gateway over which was constructed about 30 years ago) from the north. In front of the former are now being erected, under canopies of carved Puri stone, bronze statues of the late Mahárája and his father and a fountain to perpetuate their memory. Within the fort are the apartments of the Rája and his family and a building, called the Móti Mahál,

CHAP. XV. VIZIANAGRAM.

which is furnished in European style and contains portraits of several former Mahárájas. Tradition says that five 'Vijayas,' or signs of victory, were present at the inception of this fortress. It was named Vijaya-nagaram ('place of victory') after its founder, Rája Vijaya-ráma (Viziaráma) Rázu; and the foundations were laid on Tuesday (Jaya-váram), the tenth day (Vijaya Dasami) of the Dasara festival, in the year Vijaya (1713–14 A.D.) of the Hindu cycle. It is stated that the present building is a reconstruction of the original edifice carried out by one of Bussy's officers in or about 1757.

The Rája has two other residences outside the town; namely, the Púl Bágh bungalow situated in an extensive garden about two miles along the road leading north-eastwards out of the town, and a bungalow on the top of the bare, rocky hill which is so prominent to the north of the place and is locally known as Chóta Himálaya.

The ancient zamindari of Vizianagram, which has been scheduled in Act II of 1904 as inalienable and impartible, pays peshkash and road-cess amounting to some Rs. 5,82,000, or much more than any other in the Presidency. The early history of the family is obscure. Mr. Carmichael's account of it is apparently based on a narrative furnished him by the then Mahárája. The only other chronicle available is one of the Mackenzie MSS.,[1] which is incorrect in several matters admitting of check and cannot therefore be trusted. The whole subject is a material issue in the big suit about the right to the property which is now being fought out in the District Court, but no pronouncement regarding it is likely to be made for some time. Mr. Carmichael's account may therefore be followed meanwhile [2].

This says that the founder of the family was Púsapáti Mádhava Varma, who took his title from the village of Púsapádu, near Kondapalli in the Kistna district, where he resided. In 1652 he moved to Vizagapatam and obtained from Shér Muhammad Khán, the then Faujdar of Chicacole, a lease of the country

[1] Local Records, iv, 1–441. Mr. Grant's 'Political Survey of the Northern Circars' appended to the *Fifth Report on the affairs of the E. I. Co., 1812*, also contains a few particulars.

[2] A statement on the matter compiled (mainly from official records) for the purposes of the suit by Mr. H. W. F. Gillman, I.C.S., has since become available. This differs from Mr. Carmichael's version in saying that Mádhava Varma died in 1685 and that Sítarámachandra was followed in turn by his son Annama Rázu (killed without issue near Rajahmundry in 1696), the latter's brother Tammi Rázu (died without issue in 1698 or 1699), Tammi's adopted son Ananda Rázu (who founded Vizianagram in 1713 and died about 1731), the latter's first cousin Sítaráma Rázu (poisoned in 1740) and then by Viziaráma Rázu I (Ananda Rázu's son) who was assassinated at Bobbili in 1757.

of Kumili and Bhógapuram. He was succeeded in 1690 by his son Sítarámachandra, who secured the lease of ten additional taluks and established himself at Potnúru. Five zamindars followed, each of whom added something to the rapidly growing power of the family, and then came Viziaráma Rázu I, who in 1713–14 built the fort at Vizianagram and transferred his residence thither. He and his successors all bore the title of Gajapati, or 'lord of elephants.' The assistance he gave to Bussy in 1756–57, when that officer came to quiet the Northern Circars, has already (p. 32) been referred to, as have also the attack upon the Bobbili fort which Viziaráma instigated (p. 237) and his assassination in consequence. The latter was succeeded in 1757 by Ananda Rázu, son of his first cousin. The story of this man's quarrel with Bussy, seizure of Vizagapatam from the French, co-operation with Colonel Forde's expedition in driving that nation out of the Circars, and death at Rajahmundry in 1759, has also been recounted (pp. 33–4). He was succeeded by a boy of twelve, the second son of the late Viziaráma Rázu's cousin Rámabhadra Rázu, who had been adopted by Viziaráma's widow Chandrayya and was afterwards known as Viziaráma Rázu II.

The fortunes of the house of Púsapáti under the administration of this chief and his brother Sítaráma Rázu have been sketched on pp. 46–53, where it is shown that from the date of the expulsion of the French they rapidly became more and more powerful until they controlled almost all the district, so abused the authority they had acquired that the Company was compelled to intervene, and so defied that body's authority that Sítaráma Rázu was eventually deported to Madras and his brother was slain at the fight at Padmanábham in 1794. The latter's son, Náráyana Rázu, succeeded in the circumstances related on pp. 54–5.

In 1817 he was twelve lakhs in debt and agreed to mortgage his property to Government until this was cleared off. Government paid off the debts so as to make themselves the sole creditors, gave Náráyana Rázu an allowance of Rs. 80,000 a year, and in 1822 returned the estate to him free of arrears. In 1827 he again made over his zamindari to the Collector and went to Benares on an allowance of a lakh a year. He died there in 1845 and his debts then amounted to eleven lakhs, a considerable portion of which had been contracted in the sacred city.

He was succeeded by his son Viziaráma Rázu III, a boy of nineteen, who at first showed no alacrity to return to the district but, when Government insisted, came back at last in 1848. His estate was managed at first by a Special Agent, Mr. Crozier, who handed it over to him in July 1852 clear of debt and with a surplus in hand of over two lakhs. His subsequent management of the property was excellent and his public liberality most marked, and he became a Member of the Viceroy's Council, was granted in 1864 the personal title of Mahárája, and was created a K.C.S.I. in 1876. He died in 1879 and was followed by his only surviving son Ananda Rázu. The latter was also granted the personal title of Mahárája, was a Member of the Madras Legislative Council for many years, and was created a G.C.I.E. in 1892. He died without issue on the 23rd May 1897 and by a will made in July 1896 appointed the present Rája, Viziaráma Rázu IV, his mother's brother's son, as his successor. His mother adopted this lad in December 1897, and as he was a minor the estate was managed by an Indian Civilian appointed under the Guardians and Wards Act until he attained his majority in August 1904, and has since been administered by a Civilian whose services have been lent for a limited period. The zamindari (including the tracts belonging to it in the Ganjám and Gódávari districts) comprises thirteen tánas, the area under cultivation in which aggregates some 289,000 acres assessed (including land-cess) at about 18½ lakhs, while the receipts from inam and dévastánam land, forests, house property, the estate in Benares (157 villages) and other items bring the total income to about 22¼ lakhs. While the zamindari has been under management, a survey and partial settlement have been carried out and the irrigation works have been greatly improved.

In 1903 four dáyádis of the late Mahárája brought a suit in the Vizagapatam District Court against the present Rája, questioning the validity of his adoption, and claiming that he had only a life interest in the estate, which on his death should revert to them. This suit is now being heard.

INDEX.

Note.—The italic letters in brackets printed immediately after the names of places, etc., refer to the squares of the map in the pocket within which the places, etc., will be found.

A

B

C

E

F

G

L

N

O

S

T

U

V

W

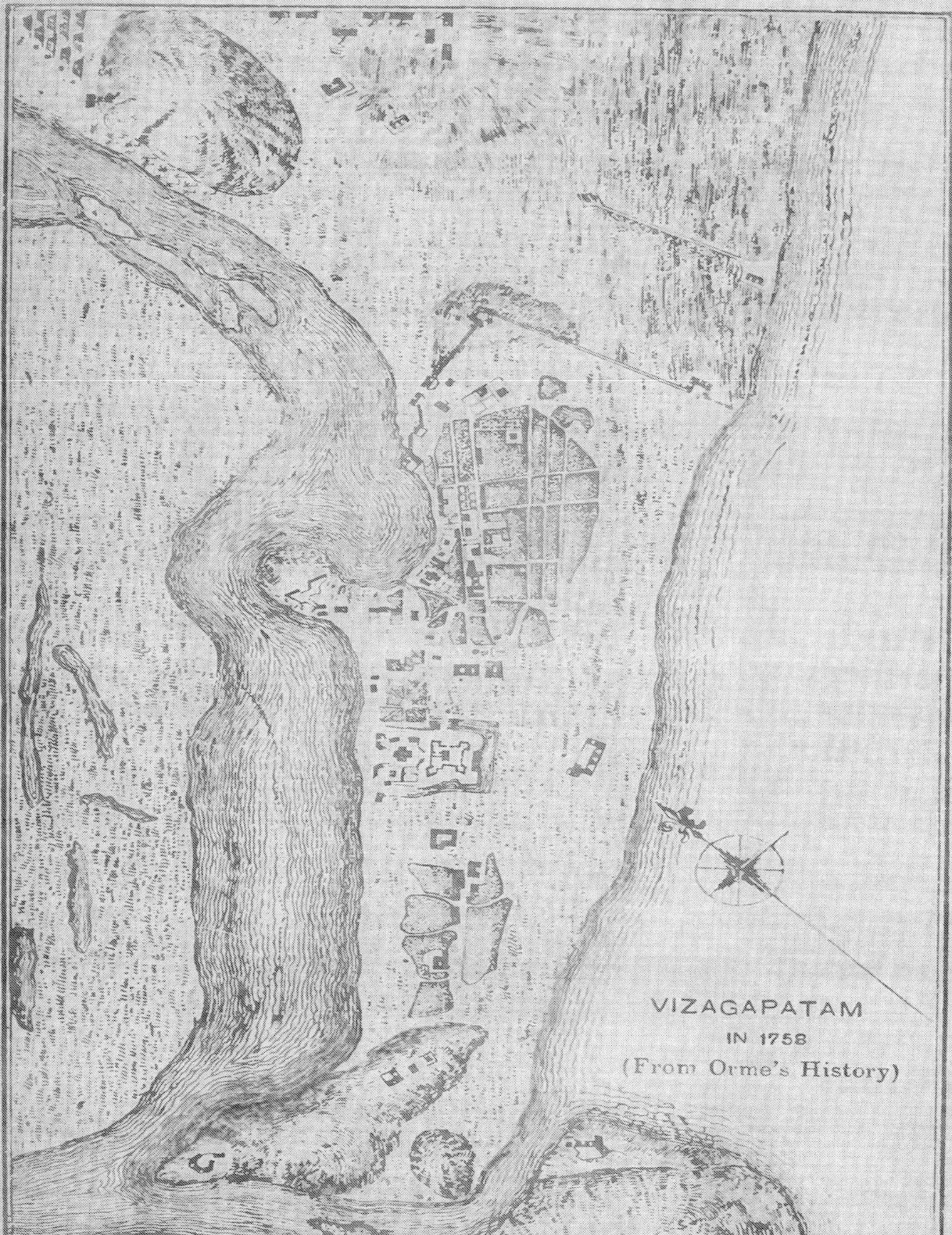

VIZAGAPATAM
IN 1758
(From Orme's History)

Reg No. 123
Copies 500